# Cultural Governance and Resistance in Pacific Asia

What do Miss Thailand, the brochure of the US Army's chemical demilitarization project, and Mao's portrait on the hundred yuan bank note all have in common? They are all involved in the dynamic of cultural governance and resistance in Pacific Asia. Using a diverse set of artifacts from both official and popular culture this book looks at the interplay between culture and politics, examining how the state seeks to match territorial and cultural boundaries not just through military coercion and fiscal regulation, but also through a management of identity practices. Callahan applies poststructuralist theory to analyze the powerful dynamic between culture and politics that generates East–West discourse and national identities. Drawing on original ethnographic research and primary source materials, the book sets out a critical methodology with which to study the cultural governance of capitalist modernity from a social, economic and cultural perspective.

In taking both a theoretical and empirical approach to the subject, *Cultural Governance and Resistance in Pacific Asia* provides a multidisciplinary study of Pacific Asia that will appeal to students and scholars of Asian studies, cultural studies, comparative politics, sociology and anthropology alike.

**William A. Callahan** is Professor of International Politics at the University of Manchester, and has taught in Thailand, China, South Korea and the United States. His most recent book is *Contingent States: Greater China and Transnational Relations* (University of Minnesota Press, 2004).

# Cultural Governance and Resistance in Pacific Asia

William A. Callahan

LONDON AND NEW YORK

First published 2006
by Routledge
2 Park Square, Milton Park, Abingdon, Oxon OX14 4RN

Simultaneously published in the USA and Canada
by Routledge
270 Madison Ave, New York, NY 10016

*Routledge is an imprint of the Taylor & Francis Group, an informa business*

© 2006 William A. Callahan

Typeset in Times New Roman by
Florence Production Ltd, Stoodleigh, Devon
Printed and bound in Great Britain by
TJ International Ltd, Padstow, Cornwall

All rights reserved. No part of this book may be reprinted or
reproduced or utilized in any form or by any electronic, mechanical,
or other means, now known or hereafter invented, including
photocopying and recording, or in any information storage or
retrieval system, without permission in writing from the publishers.

*British Library Cataloguing in Publication Data*
A catalogue record for this book is available from the British Library

*Library of Congress Cataloging in Publication Data*
Callahan, William A.
    Cultural governance and resistance in Pacific Asia/William A. Callahan.
        p. cm.
    Includes bibliographical references and index.
    1. Pacific Area – Politics and government.   2. Politics and culture.
    I. Title.
    JQ750.A58C35 2006
    306.2095–dc22                                                       2005029115

ISBN10: 0–415–36899–5 (hbk)
ISBN10: 0–415–36900–2 (pbk)
ISBN10: 0–203–02925–9 (ebk)

ISBN13: 978–0–415–36899–5 (hbk)
ISBN13: 978–0–415–36900–8 (pbk)
ISBN13: 978–0–203–02925–1 (ebk)

**To Mike Shapiro**

# Contents

*List of figures* viii
*Acknowledgments* ix

Introduction 1

1 Culture, the military and the "South Pacific" 21

2 Beauty queens, national identity and transnational politics 43

3 Gender, democracy and revolutionary photo albums 71

4 Popular politics, civil society and social movements 99

5 Corruption, political reform and the deferral of democracy 124

6 Cosmopolitanism, nationalism and diasporic politics 146

Conclusion 174

*Notes* 192
*Bibliography* 225
*Index* 243

# Figures

| | | |
|---|---|---|
| 1.1 | JACADS chemical weapons cake, 2004 | 28 |
| 1.2 | Cover of chemical weapons disposal brochure, 1990 | 31 |
| 2.1 | Miss Thailand in basic training, 1998 | 44 |
| 2.2 | Miss Thailand the professional housewife, 1994 | 52 |
| 2.3 | Miss Siam crowned, 1934 | 54 |
| 3.1 | The cover of *Burma's Revolution of the Spirit* | 82 |
| 3.2 | At a Marcos rally | 83 |
| 3.3 | Constructions of male violence | 85 |
| 3.4 | Revolutionary heroes at Tian'anmen | 90 |
| 3.5 | Chairmen Mao #3 (1989), by Zhang Hongtu | 96 |
| 4.1 | Confucian temple at Songgyun'gwan, 1997 | 111 |
| 5.1 | Campaigning under the mango tree | 133 |
| 5.2 | A "godmother" describes how to buy votes in rural Thailand | 138 |
| 6.1 | Sun Yat-sen memorial statue in downtown Honolulu | 156 |
| 7.1 | Reconstructing the Mao statue in Shenyang, 2005 | 178 |
| 7.2 | Mao talismans in Shaoshan, 1999 | 183 |
| 7.3 | Mao mausoleum tea towel, Beijing, 1985 | 183 |
| 7.4 | Shrine in Mao Family Restaurant, Beijing, 1999 | 184 |
| 7.5 | PLA dancing for Mao, Shaoshan, 1999 | 186 |
| 7.6 | New Mao currency, 1999 | 187 |

# Acknowledgments

This book is the result of many years of research, starting in Hawai'i, continuing in Thailand, China and South Korea, and finishing in England. Since I was an outsider in these places, many people provided both intellectual stimulation and friendship. For their aid in research, helpful comments on draft chapters and generous hospitality, I would like to thank David Armstrong, Mark Aspinwall, Scot Barmé, Poka Laenui, Chaiwat Satha-Anand, Michael Kelly Connors, Arif Dirlik, Kathy Ferguson, Gothom Arya, Han Sang-Jin, Kevin Hewison, Jia Qingguo, Richard Kraus, Laddawan Tantiwittayaphitak, Liao Shaolian, Margot Light, Liu Hong, Duncan McCargo, Craig Mulling, Naruemon Thabchumpon, Steve Olive, Frederic Schaffer, Andreas Schedler, Michael J. Shapiro, Somchai Phatharathananund, Song Xinning, Gayatri Chakravorty Spivak, Sukunya Bumroongsook, Sumalee Bumroongsook, Suparat Lertphanichkul, Suwanna Satha-Anand, Teera Vorrakitpokatorn, Thavesilp Subwattana, Thongchai Winichakul, Marie Thorsten, Viengrat Netipho, Wang Gungwu, Geoff White, Endymion Wilkinson, Rob Wilson, Carl Young, Zha Daojiong and Zhang Xiaojin. I would especially like to thank Sumalee Bumroongsook for interpreting Thai texts and interviews, Steve Olive for allowing me to republish our jointly authored article as Chapter 1, and Zhang Hongtu for generously providing access to his paintings.

This research was funded by grants from the East–West Center (Honolulu), the Institute for Southeast Asian Studies (Singapore), the Korea Foundation Research Fellowship Program, the British Academy (South-East Asia Committee), the Universities' China Committee in London, the University of Durham's Centre for Contemporary China Studies, the British Academy, and the European Commission's Asia Link programme.

Chapter 1 is based on William A. Callahan and Steve Olive, "Chemical Weapons Disposal in the *South Pacific*," *boundary* 2, 22: 1, 263–85. Copyright, 1995, Duke University Press. All rights reserved. Used by permission of the publisher.

Chapter 2 is based on William A. Callahan, "The Ideology of Miss Thailand in National, Consumerist and Transnational Space," *Alternatives*

23: 1 (Jan.–Mar. 1998), 29–62. Copyright © by Lynne Rienner Publishers. Used with permission.

Chapter 3 is based on William A. Callahan, "Visions of Gender and Democracy: Revolutionary Photo Albums in Asia," *Millennium: Journal of International Studies* 27: 4 (1998), 1031–60. It is reproduced with the permission of the publisher.

Chapter 4 is based on William A. Callahan, "Comparing the Discourse of Popular Politics in Korea and China: from Civil Society to Social Movements," *Korea Journal* 39: 1 (Spring 1998), 277–322.

Chapter 6 is based on "Beyond Cosmopolitanism and Nationalism: Diasporic Chinese and Neo-nationalism in Thailand and China," *International Organization* 57: 3 (Summer 2003), 481–517. © Cambridge University Press. Reprinted with permission.

Every effort has been made to contact all copyright holders. However, if anyone has not been contacted they should contact the publisher in the first instance.

# Introduction

In 2002 Zhuo Ling was crowned Miss China in a fairy tale whose drama went far beyond the usual struggles with rival contestants over talent, poise and figure. Just as Zhuo pranced on stage to open the bathing suit competition, the Miss China pageant was raided by the police and closed down; the contest was declared illegal because it lacked the permit required for all cultural events in China. Yet after night had fallen, contestants and judges crept back into the auditorium to finish the Miss China pageant.[1] This tragicomic story actually has close parallels with official narrative of the founding of the Chinese Communist Party (CCP) in 1921: after its first meeting in downtown Shanghai was interrupted by a police spy, the meeting was reconvened on a hired boat floating on a lake in a neighboring province.[2] Eventually, Ms Zhuo was crowned Miss China—but much like the founding of the CCP—with little fanfare. But would the Miss China pageant eventually rock the Chinese world in the twenty-first century as much as the CCP had in the twentieth century?

Zhuo was the first Miss China since the communist revolution in 1949. Until recently, beauty pageants were seen by officials and the general public in China as evidence of bourgeois decadence and Western corruption.[3] The pageant organizer, a businessman from Beijing, had been petitioning the Ministry of Culture for a permit for years. He had little success until 2002 when the officials told him that, although they would not issue a permit, they would not criticize him if he kept the event low key. In the end, another group of less sympathetic officials raided his Miss China pageant. But after Zhuo's reasonable success in the Miss Universe 2002 pageant—she came in third—the Chinese people caught the beauty pageant bug, with contests proliferating throughout the country.[4] Some Chinese women saw the pageants as a new measure of their skills: "I believe that while I win in university entrance examinations, I can also win in beauty contests," said an elite student at Beijing University.[5] After the Miss China pageant received official blessing in 2003, the new enthusiasm did not stop with the national contest: China aggressively (and successfully) lobbied to host the Miss World pageant in December 2003. For the first time, an international beauty pageant was broadcast nationwide on state-controlled television. The contest was so successful (Miss China again came in third) that the Miss World pageant returned to China in 2005. Still, the contest's unstable beginning demonstrates how Chinese officials are still deeply ambivalent about the Miss China beauty pageant.

There are many ways to understand this odd convergence of culture and power. The first would be to recall that Maoist China was officially friendly to feminism; the All China Women's Federation is one of the People's Republic of China's (PRC) major mass organizations. Fighting against the feudal thinking that justified binding Chinese women's feet, Mao Zedong declared that "women hold up half the sky." The first major United Nations (UN) conference held in China was the Fourth World Conference on Women (1995), which discussed the theme "Action for Equality, Development and Peace." Hence, it is not strange that influential voices in China would criticize beauty pageants for exploiting women and exacerbating gender inequality.

Indeed, the pageant commodifies women as an example of the down side of the economic reforms that introduced the market and capitalism to China in 1978. While many have become rich in the new political economy of reform and opening, many others have become poorer—especially women. The beauty contests themselves are business ventures that hawk luxury items to the urban elite: the organizers, promoters and sponsors of the contest are businessmen, while the contestants generally are models who sell health and beauty products in a gendered political economy. As activists who criticized the Miss World 1996 pageant in India reasoned, "Are beauty pageants the type of social progress and economic development that [economic reformers] had in mind?"[6] Indeed, beauty pageants seem to be clear examples of cultural imperialism; Miss China's main task is not to reign in the PRC, but to participate in the pageants of Miss Universe, Inc. (an American corporation) and Miss World, Ltd. (a British corporation). Zhuo's seemingly innocent trip to the Miss Universe pageant in Puerto Rico risked precipitating a rapid opening up of the lucrative Chinese market to transnational beauty corporate conglomerates.[7]

But the way that the Miss China pageant was approved, banned and then approved again suggests a less radical interpretation of this odd event. There are few, if any, independent organizations in China; even nongovernmental organizations (NGOs) are required to have close relations with the state and are better described as GONGOs (government-oriented NGOs). Businesses are allowed more leeway, so long as they do not directly dabble in politics or challenge the state. But where does "Miss China" fall in this cultural–political–economic matrix? The pageant certainly is a business venture, but since the title of the winner is also the title of the state this causes complications. The Chinese state closely guards how it is represented to the Chinese people. Since the pageant was sponsored by a non-state organization, the party-state sees this rival representation of China as a challenge to its sovereign authority: "Chinese officials apparently could not fathom yielding power over the choice of such a representative to a private group."[8] Thus, the pageant was raided by more orthodox representatives of the party-state as a way of asserting official governance over the image of China.

A third explanation for the party-state's ambivalence emerges from the state control of the representation of China on the international stage, where it exercises even more control over its image than it does over domestic representations of China. Miss Universe, Inc. is not just a corporation; it is an international organization that closely models the UN General Assembly in form, if not in content: beauty queens are seen as ambassadors who represent nation-states. If Zhuo went to participate in the 2002 pageant in Puerto Rico, it would be a matter of national concern since Zhuo would not only represent China on the international stage, but would carry the title of Miss China. Indeed, the US government recognized Zhuo as "Miss China, going to Miss Universe Contest" on her US visa.[9]

But once Zhuo arrived in San Juan, she was surprised to see two rival groups of Chinese officials trying to convince Miss Universe, Inc. to choose China to host a future pageant. Indeed, once the Chinese state decided that the pageant was kosher, they not only organized the Miss China beauty pageant in 2003, but hosted the Miss World pageant later that year. This reversal seems odd, but it makes sense in terms of China's recent mad rush to join high-profile international organizations and host prominent international events: after entering the United Nations in 1971, it has joined international organizations (IOs) at a feverish pace, by 2000 surpassing the world average to participate in fifty IOs.[10] This world-embracing achievement was capped in 2001 when China joined the World Trade Organization and was chosen to host the 2008 Olympics. Like hosting the UN's Fourth World Conference on Women in 1995, hosting Miss World 2003 (and again in 2005) is another feather in the PRC's internationalist cap, for it demonstrates how China is a productive citizen in international society.

Indeed, the Chinese state is not a passive participant in international beauty pageants. It actively uses them as a new diplomatic tool for pursuing its broad foreign policy strategy. One of the main objectives of China's public diplomacy is to exclude Taiwan and Tibet from international society by making sure that no other state or IO recognizes them as independent bodies. Immediately after officially entering the world of beauty pageants in 2003, the Chinese Foreign Ministry successfully lobbied Miss Universe, Inc. and Miss World, Ltd. to not allow Taiwan to be represented as "Miss Taiwan" in their pageants; following the formula used in the Olympics, Miss Taiwan was forced to change her sash to one that read "Miss China, Taipei."[11]

Although Tibet is more known for its meditating monks than bathing beauties, a Miss Tibet pageant has been held in Dharmasala since the late 1990s—although it is not sanctioned by the Tibetan government-in-exile.

While the main objective of the pageant is to liven up the annual "Tibetan Free Spirit Festival," the beauty contest also has geopolitical implications. As the conference promoter reasons, "When one reads the words Miss Tibet, Tibet is thought of as a separate entity and not part of China."[12] Although the geo-beauty map of Miss Universe and Miss World does not include the Himalayan country—Miss Tibet is not invited—the Chinese state takes Miss Tibet very seriously. China's diplomatic corps pressured the organizers of the Miss International Tourism pageant to exclude her from their contest—just as they forced Miss Taiwan to change her sash to "Miss China, Taipei" at the same event in 2005.[13]

This curious mixture of state policy and popular culture is not limited to China: indeed, the official debates over the status of national beauty queens also were held in Vietnam; the state decided to recognize and certify "Miss Vietnam" one year earlier than in China, in 2002.[14] But what does this culture–power dynamic mean? Where is power and where is resistance? Is the Miss China beauty pageant an opportunity for resistance because it challenges the state's tight hold on cultural activities? Or is the pageant an exercise in state power, an arena whereby the state distracts its citizens from the problems of their daily life, while it bullies weaker nations, or is it a sign of the power of a transnational regime of capitalist modernity, where identity is commodified and culture is marketed? The meaning of "Miss China" shifts according to context, from fulfilling one young woman's dream, to resisting an authoritarian state, to financial gain in domestic and international markets, to the high diplomacy of geopolitics, to the spread of capitalist modernity, and so on.

I will explore these complicated questions in this book through an examination of cultural artifacts such as Miss Thailand, the Johnston Atoll Chemical Agent Disposal System brochure, the commemorative photo album *Bayan Ko! Images of the People Power Revolt*, and Mao's portrait on the 100 yuan Chinese bank note. Like Miss China, this odd assortment of artifacts is involved in the dynamic of cultural governance and resistance in Pacific Asia. In this sense, the region is not unique; it is participating in the process of capitalist modernity where the state seeks to match territorial and cultural boundaries not just through military coercion and fiscal regulation, but also through a management of identity practices. Since the state can never exhaust cultural production, resistance to these centralizing efforts takes the form of alternative cultural productions. Indeed, as we will see, the Miss Thailand beauty pageant is both an important site of the state's cultural governance of gendered identity, and a site of resistance to official views of masculinity and femininity in Thailand—in ways very different from Miss China. Likewise, in the twenty-first century, Mao is less a historical figure than an image that is mobilized in debates about China's past and future as a global power. Mao's symbolic capital legitimates not just the geopolitical power of world revolution. The image of Mao now also aids marketing products both at home and abroad.¹⁵ In the 1990s the Mao Family restaurant chain, which originated in his hometown in rural China, spread to have branches in Pacific Asia. While many discussions of cultural politics assume the conceptual integrity of East and West, and the stable identity of nation-states, *Cultural Governance and Resistance in Pacific Asia* will use poststructuralist theory and semiotic methods to analyze the powerful dynamic of cultural politics that produces East/West discourse, national identities—and resistance to them.

## Why Pacific Asia?

In the past decade much has been said about the relation between cultural tradition, economic growth and political power in Pacific Asia. The spectacular success of the Asian Tiger economies in the 1980s and 1990s provided an alternative cultural model of capitalism, an Asian way that questioned Anglo-American neoliberal capitalism. Yet Pacific Asia has provided more than just an alternative economic model. Some have promoted "Confucian capitalism" as an alternative social and political model that stresses communal authority and duty over individual equality and rights: Confucian democracy and Asian democracy.

Since the financial crisis hit Pacific Asia in 1997, the understanding of the political-economy of the region has reversed: Confucian capitalism became crony capitalism, Asian values are now seen as the thin veil that hid corrupt political-economic regimes.¹⁶ Yet the crisis hit different countries in the region in different ways. Despite the economic problems of its neighbors, China continues to rise economically and politically. This is leading to a new discussion of the Asian way to the good life for the twenty-first century: for example, in 2004 some proposed a "Beijing Consensus" of economic development and political order to replace the Washington Consensus. Hence both promoters and critics of the Asian way rely on cultural arguments to explain political-economic success and failure. According to this argument, the Asian alternative is no longer Mao's socialism or Tagore's Pan-Asianism, but a different form of capitalist modernity.

Unfortunately, this civilizational approach to politics and culture in Pacific Asia tends to reproduce stereotypical views of East and West that do not lead us to a better understanding of the region. Indeed, both the promoters and critics of the Asian way commonly limit their consideration to elite cultures of national/regional identity, and thus tend to reproduce Orientalist discourse that equates culture with idealized tradition. But one of the main developments in Pacific Asia has been a growing sophistication of popular culture as part of the emerging cultural-economy. Although popular culture is commonly condemned as the foreign invasion of globalization (through McDonalds, Hollywood films or Miss Universe), or dismissed as politically irrelevant "entertainment," popular culture is an important site of both power and resistance in Pacific Asia.

Indeed, cultural governance is not new in Pacific Asia. The "soft power" of Confucian ideology, which ordered society through cultural governance more than coercive force, was one of the main sources of legitimacy in the Chinese empire and the surrounding kingdoms of Korea, Vietnam and Japan. In the Qing dynasty, China's equivalent of a ministry of foreign affairs was called the Board of Rites. This traditional mode of cultural governance has been modernized in Pacific Asia through state control of the media, arts and literature, not just in extreme cases like Maoist China, but also in the relatively open society of Thailand.[17] Ien Ang thus argues that postcolonial states in the region

> developed ultramodernist media policies, based on a strict imagined (and imposed) equivalence of territorial state, media, culture and nation. The control of the media messages circulating within the nation, for example, through censorship, or more positively, through the promotion of national television industries which it can regulate and oversee, is part and parcel of this desire for the state to vindicate the cultural solidity of its national boundaries.[18]

On the other hand, both popular and elite cultural artifacts have been an important part of social movements for political change throughout Pacific Asia. As the chapters will show, these social movements involve networks that go beyond the boundaries of the nation-state and traditional "area studies" regions of East Asia and Southeast Asia. While many studies of culture and politics look to Japan's role in the region,[19] since the early 1990s after the Japanese economy faltered, China has become a dominant player in regional issues.[20] But, rather than taking a Sinological "middle kingdom" approach that names the object of inquiry according to stable continental markers that are backed by institutional forces, I use the term "Pacific Asia" to chart the transnational flows of governance and resistance that traverse Asia, the Pacific and North America.[21]

Pacific Asia thus is interesting not just as a site of field work where empirical data can confirm Euro-American theory, but as a provocation for theoretical debate itself. A century ago, Max Weber's path-breaking study of the Protestant ethic and the spirit of capitalism grew out of his comparative research on China and India. More recently, Rey Chow has argued that the tactics and discourses of poststructuralism, feminism and subaltern studies have grown out of the revolutionary experience in China as Euro-American intellectuals looked East for alternatives.[22] The list of Pacific Asian connections of key political and social theorists is long, with contributions that have shaped debates over popular resistance,[23] feminist IR,[24] poststructuralist IR,[25] nationalism[26] and postcolonialism.[27]

## Orientalism, postcolonialism and occidentalism

In *Orientalism,* Edward Said underlines the importance of considering the relation of culture and power.[28] Indeed, the Euro-American imperial project was not just for material gain; one of Christopher Columbus's main missions was to convert the Chinese emperor to Christianity.[29] Euro-American powers did not just send soldiers and bureaucrats to their colonies; they also sent anthropologists, philosophers, artists and writers. The British Empire was not just about taking control of the territory and administration of places like India and Hong Kong, it was about colonizing the mind and the imagination of the Indians and the Chinese. Indeed, imperialism as ideological domination actually succeeds best without physical coercion. Rather than simply deploying the restrictive power of violence and economic extraction, Euro-American imperialism deployed the distinction of Oriental/Occidental, East/West in a productive sense of power that generated knowledge and identity as tools for imperial governance:

> A very large mass of writers, among whom are poets, novelists, philosophers, political theorists, economists, and imperial administrators, have accepted the basic distinction between East and West as the starting point of their elaborate theories, epics, novels, social descriptions, and political accounts concerning an Orient, its people, customs, "mind," destiny, and so on.[30]

Moreover, the East/West division was not a distinction of equals, but a hierarchy of governance that turns the difference of multiple cultures and political-economies into a general Oriental Otherness: the strong, mature, wise, progressive, male Occident over an Orient that is constructed as weak, needy, ignorant, backward and female. Orientalism, thus, is not simply an idea or a description, but

> the corporate institution for dealing with the Orient—dealing with it by making statements about it, authorizing views of it, describing it, by teaching it, settling it, ruling over it; in short, Orientalism as a Western style for dominating, restructuring, and having authority over the Orient.[31]

Framing imperialism as a cultural practice thus graphically demonstrates how the links between knowledge and power support the grossly hierarchical power relations of the Occident and its Orient.

Said's critique of Orientalism is part of a broader movement of postcolonial criticism that emerged as a strategy to contest the enduring knowledge-power dynamic that survived the formal decolonization of the second half of the twentieth century. Since the Euro-American representations of the Oriental are seen to silence non-Western voices, the former empire has been fighting back through cultural politics. Postcolonial theory is a broad and controversial area of activity;[32] here, I would like to rehearse some of its themes as a way of framing the analysis of cultural governance and resistance in Pacific Asia. One of the debates in postcolonial theory is whether "postcolonial" refers to a place, "the postcolonial world," or whether it is a discourse for understanding power relations in an imaginative geography. In his influential introductions to postcolonialism, Robert J.C. Young argues that postcolonial names a place, the place that we used to call the Third World. Indeed, Young further glosses these territorial terms to employ the neologism "tricontinental"—Asia, Africa and South America—to clarify the meaning of the postcolonial world.[33] Designating the tricontinental world as postcolonial underlines how, even though the former colonies achieved political sovereignty with the decolonization process, they still are trapped in a neocolonial economic and cultural system that is dominated by Euro-America. To fight this economic and cultural imperialism, Young argues that the tricontinental world needs to unite and assert its agency through a "postcolonial critique from victims not perpetrators" that would "turn the world upside down."[34]

Hence, to "decolonize the mind," postcolonial theory argues that "the intellectual and cultural traditions developed outside the west constitute a body of knowledge that can be deployed to great effect against the political and cultural hegemony of the west."[35] In this way, "postcolonialism has marked the beginning of the west's undoing ... [because] Postcolonial criticism forms part of a critique of European civilization and culture from the perspective of the cultures of the tricontinental world."[36] The postcolonial goal is to incite political, economic, social and cultural change from the bottom up, not just in terms of class warfare in domestic politics, but by having the world underclass of tricontinental nations challenge Euro-America. Postcolonialism thus serves as a rallying cry to deal with enduring injustice on the global stage. Unfortunately, Young's territorialized figuration of tricontinentalism, where the Global South is separate from the Euro-American North, risks reproducing a colonial imaginary that does not appreciate the transnational nature of the global political economy.

Although most postcolonial criticism addresses such issues in terms of the cultural politics of South Asia, the Middle East, Africa and Euro-America,[37] it has provoked interesting reactions in Pacific Asia where postcolonialism is framed more as a discourse than a territory.[38] In *Occidentalism*, Chen Xiaomei thinks that Pacific Asians can have agency of their own not just in opposition to Orientalism, but using its categories for their own purposes. She argues that Chinese intellectuals have been constructing Occidentalism as a liberating discourse:

> Orientalism has been accompanied by instances of what might be termed *Occidentalism*, a discursive practice that by constructing its Western Other, has allowed the Orient to participate actively and with

indigenous creativity in the process of self-appropriation, even after being appropriated and constructed by Western Others.[39]

Although Occidentalism and Orientalism use similar tactics, Chen argues that they have very different strategies: while the objective of Orientalism was Euro-American world domination, Occidentalism is deployed in Chinese society for domestic politics. As Dai Jinhua argues more generally, in the Third World "the appropriation of western discourse can have a politically and ideologically liberating effect on contemporary non-Western culture."[40] Hence, in China Occidentalism is not essentially bad or good: it can be a force for either oppression or liberation. Certainly, the Chinese state demonizes the West to buttress its official nationalism, in what Chen calls "official Occidentalism." But she insists that even official Occidentalism does not aim to dominate the West as Other. Rather, Occidentalism serves "to discipline, and ultimately dominate, the Chinese Self at home" by telling citizens who they can (and cannot) be.[41] Dai argues that this official Occidentalism creates an official self-Orientalization: "The establishment of China's socialist ideology has always more or less relied upon a type of self-Orientalism, emphasizing the 'uniqueness' of China's history and current state to pronounce and establish a powerful, unyielding national order."[42]

Chen's main contribution to the cultural politics debate, however, comes from her discussion of how "anti-official Occidentalism" is deployed in China by opponents of the party-state. Instead of essentializing Euro-America as the Occident to argue for Chinese superiority as Mao did with official Occidentalism, critics of the party-state use "the Western Other as a metaphor for a political liberation against ideological oppression within a totalitarian society." Chen argues that, while Said's analysis of Orientalism does not allow much scope for the emergence of counter-discourses, "Occidentalism can be used by marginals to oppose internal dominant power" in China.[43] Resistance, here, emerges in a different site from that described in most postcolonial critique. Rather than focusing on broad struggles between Euro-America and the tricontinental world, Chen focuses on how Chinese dissidents employ transnational images in their struggle with the state at home.

Even though postcolonialism as territory and as discourse frame power relations in very different ways, they share a conceptual problem: both often reassert the territorial and conceptual boundaries that they are questioning. Young's shift from postcolonialism to tricontinentalism reasserts the binary oppositions of north/south, while Chen's Occidentalism restricts our imagination to the political division of East/West. Although most postcolonial critics insist that they are trying to evade or transcend the binaries of East and West, the arguments in the following chapters will show how these binary divisions have staying power; as they are redeployed, these essentialized distinctions tend to reproduce power as dominance.

Rather than separate the Orient from the Occident in order to assert a purer form of pan-Asianism or tricontinentalism, Arif Dirlik argues that the Orient and the Occident have always been interlinked:

> Rather than view Orientalism as the autochthonous product of a European modernity, therefore, it makes some sense to view it as a product of those "contact zones" in which Europeans encountered non-Europeans, where a European modernity produced and was also challenged by alternative modernities as the Others in their turn entered into the discourse on modernity.[44]

Hence, neither imperialist center nor colonial periphery is pure or coherent by itself. Modernity was not foisted upon an unsuspecting traditional Pacific Asia by Euro-American imperialism so much as it is the product of these interactions. This new understanding of the relations between East and West changes the way we frame key historical events. In China (and to a large extent in Euro-America) the Opium War (1839–42) where Britain pried open the Chinese empire is canonically understood as a geopolitical turning point not just of one country invading another, but of one system invading another. This has important conceptual implications: the modern period begins in 1842 for Chinese historiography. As David E. Apter and Tony Saich explain, "Everything before the Opium Wars (1839–1842) is prehistory. In Mao's storytelling the Opium Wars are to China what capitalism was to Marx, history with a capital H."[45] Rather than seeing it as a clash of civilizations, Carl A. Trocki argues that the Opium War was part of the production of capitalist modernity, whose new institutions and technologies (from international finance to agro-industry to mass consumer markets) emerged through the interactions of the transnational opium trade in the nineteenth century.[46] Rather than dividing East and West, opium provided a contact zone that blurred the territorial and cultural boundaries of empires and nation-states as it constructed and institutionalized capitalist modernity.

Hence, Dirlik argues against any postcolonial discourse that reduces the critique of hegemony to a critique of Eurocentrism: "It is the irony of contemporary anti-Eurocentric movements that they themselves are entrapped in the history and geography of Orientalism. In other words, the very effort to counteract Eurocentrism is bound by the categories of Eurocentric Orientalism."[47] Moreover:

> Merely to claim a cultural identity against the "West" is no longer sufficient, not only because the "West" is already an inextricable part of East Asia, but also because such claims may only serve to perpetuate social injustices and oppressions in a new cultural guise. A radical vision of East Asia needs to recognize that the modernity to be transcended is no longer just a "Western" but an East Asian modernity.[48]

Here, Dirlik is addressing the problems of self-Orientalization raised when postcolonial theory shifts to value nativist national identities.[49] Some Pacific Asian states use the idea of Asian Democracy, for example, to denounce liberal democracy and human rights as Western spiritual pollution in order to buttress their regimes (see Chapter 3), while accepting other important aspects of Euro-American statecraft. Anti-official Occidentalism likewise perpetuates existing systems of power; it is complicit in oppression because its focus on Chinese identity as "national" erases regional class, gender, and ethnic differences within the country.[50] Dirlik thus concludes that the problem is not cultural representations themselves, but Orientalism/Occidentalism's guiding logic of cultural essentialism, which serves to reify culture and naturalize the hegemony of capitalist modernity.[51]

Although postcolonialism takes the Euro-American empire since the nineteenth century as its reference point, the cultural politics of essential distinctions such as Occidental/Oriental is neither new, nor limited to Europe's interaction with its East. The East/West distinction first was deployed in European discourse to distinguish democratic Athens from despotic Asia in the war between Greece and Persia in 480 BC.[52] Indeed, Herodotus's *Histories* traces the cause of the Persian War to gender politics: the Greek and the Asian armies' abduction of each other's women. While the Asians did not put much stock in protecting their womenfolk, *Histories* tells us that the Greeks mobilized an army to save theirs.[53] Moreover, China and Japan have used their own versions of Orientalism to support their own imperial projects in pre-modern and modern Pacific Asia.[54] Orientalism/Occidentalism thus is an example of a more general knowledge-power strategy that relies on a civilization/barbarism distinction in Pacific Asia as well as Euro-America. Dirlik concludes that the way to criticize this system of knowledge-power hegemony is to historicize capitalist modernity not just as Euro-American neoliberalism but also as Confucian capitalism in Pacific Asia. By deconstructing and denaturalizing the permutations of capitalist modernity, we can identify alternative modernities "not in terms of reified cultures, but in terms of alternative historical trajectories."[55] The goal for Dirlik is to question identities that are imposed from above by the state and transnational capital, and create communities from the bottom up.

While Dirlik concludes that postcolonial criticism creates more problems than it solves,[56] I think that the issues it raises are still pertinent to the study of culture and power in Pacific Asia. Jan Nederveen Pieterse and Bhikhu Parekh's formulation of the knowledge-power dynamic allows us to critically employ postcolonial studies in a way that tries to avoid reproducing hegemonic power. They argue that, while colonization imposes boundaries of self/Other, West/East, civilized/barbaric, traditional/modern, empire/nation and male/female, anti-colonization movements and the resulting decolonization typically accept these boundaries. Decolonization projects thus organize resistance around the reversal of these binary oppositions in an "emancipation through mirroring" that entails a "mix of defiance and mimesis."[57] The "binary, dichotomizing approach" of decolonization movements "contrasts colonial culture to national culture, cultural imperialism to cultural resistance, Pan-Europeanism to Pan-Arabism, Pan-Africanism," and now Asian values.[58] Hence, rather than Orientalism where Euro-American imperialists construct submissive identities for Pacific Asians, decolonization often includes Occidentalism that demonizes Euro-America. As Chen's analysis and Dirlik's critique both show, Occidentalism takes the Orientalist categories for granted, and mirrors them in self-Orientalization: although it often is presented as "the latest example of American foolishness,"[59] the cultural enclave logic of the clash of civilizations is very popular among Pacific Asian elites, especially since it recognizes Confucianism as a world-class civilization.[60] Such a combination of Occidentalism, self-Orientalization and decolonization, then, risks reproducing the power of domination; it homogenizes identity and political life at the national level, thus denying other practices of regional, gender, class or ethnic identity.

According to Pieterse and Parekh, the postcolonial approach avoids reproducing power as dominance because it questions the colonial and decolonial essences of East/West, woman/man, domestic/foreign and self/Other. Rather than reasserting these conceptual boundaries, "it is an open-ended field of discursive practices characterized by boundary and border crossings."[61] Postcolonialism's knowledge-power dynamic has a more fluid relation to boundaries than the confrontation and reconquest characteristic of both the colonial and the decolonial: "to those who have experience crossing them, boundaries become a matter of play rather than an obsession. The element of play opens possibilities for innovation beyond the logic of opposition-through-imitation."[62] Although most postcolonial critics agree with this broad outline of colonial/decolonial/postcolonial relations, as we saw above it is common for their analyses to reassert the essential binaries of Orient and Occident.[63] This problem underlines how we have to be vigilant in maintaining a self-reflexive approach to understanding cultural politics in Pacific Asia, and view power relations not just in terms of the West constructing the East, but also consider how power reproduces itself in the discursive arena of Pacific Asia. Rather than focus on directional markers such as Orient/Occident or territorial bodies such as the tricontinental, the key is to frame our analysis in terms of self/Other relations.

Rather than seeking to define stable continental identities of East Asia, this book will examine the transnational flows of people, capital and ideas that produce Pacific Asia. Instead of following Arjun Appadurai to celebrate the loosening of the hyphen that links the nation and the state,[64] I will consider how cultural governance's "hyphenoplasty" reasserts the link between East and West as a way of stabilizing the link between nation and state. The point is not to erase borders as part of the ideology of a globalized, tricontinental or cosmopolitan world, but to examine how borders are constructed and resisted by both state and non-state actors. Rather than fetishize the East and the West by asserting a Pacific Asian alternative,[65] this book examines how such categories have come into being as part of a broader capitalist modernity. As we will see, Confucianism is not a source of liberation through an alternative modernity, so much as a different cultural-economic logic that asserts a new set of distinctions, which entails a different power dynamic that institutes new borders, and thus new sites of resistance. The resistance then is not (just?) to Euro-American cultural imperialism or the cultural governance of the state in Pacific Asia, but often to the workings of modernity itself. Rather than employing the binary political geometry of top down versus bottom up, I seek to examine power and resistance through an analysis of the complex interplay of forces that constitute social relationships. Michel Foucault's notion of governmentality and Michael J. Shapiro's discussion of cultural governance provide the broad outlines of a method for studying the dynamic of culture and power in Pacific Asia.

## Governmentality and resistance

Foucault's concepts of "governmentality" and "pastoral politics" expand the notion of politics from juridical concepts of power that restrict action, to productive understandings of power that are generated by social relationships.[66] Foucault argues that, while canonical writers such as Machiavelli concentrated on the prince and state sovereignty, the "art of government" that developed in response to such state-centric approaches locates power in the many relationships that constitute social life:

> the practices of government are, on the one hand, multifarious and concern many kinds of people: the head of a family, the superior of a convent, the teacher or tutor of a child or pupil; so that there are several forms of government among which the prince's relation to his state is only one particular mode; while on the other hand, all these other kinds of government are internal to the state or society. . . . Thus we find at once a plurality of forms of government and their immanence to the state; the multiplicity and immanence of these activities distinguishes them radically from the transcendent singularity of Machiavelli's prince.[67]

Foucault underlines how this new practice of power is not part of the heroic narrative of the rise of the secular state; it emerges from the Church,[68] where pastoral politics is

> no longer a question of leading people to their salvation in the next world, but rather ensuring it in this world. In this context, the word

*salvation* takes on different meanings: health, well-being (that is, sufficient wealth, standard of living), security, protection against accidents. A series of "worldly" aims took the place of the religious aims of the traditional pastorate.[69]

Hence, while the pastoral politics of governmentality grew out of the Catholic Church in early modern France, Foucault argues that "the function of pastoral power has spread far beyond the church to inform the state's modes of managing society."[70]

Even though Foucault characteristically understands China in an Orientalist fashion as the "exotic East" that is the opposite of the modern West,[71] there are interesting parallels between Confucianism and the pastoral politics of governmentality. One of the *Four Books* of the Neo-Confucian orthodoxy—*The Great Learning* [*Daxue*]—that governed China for the millennium preceding the twentieth century also seeks order through a "plurality of forms of government." *The Great Learning*'s governance transgresses the binary distinctions of state and civil society to make individual, civil society and state coterminous and mutually entailing. This practice of governmentality joins the personal, familial, communal, political and cosmic in a Chinese articulation of pastoral politics:

> Those in ancient times who wanted their pure and excellent character to shine in the world would first bring proper government to the empire; desiring to bring proper government to the empire, they would first bring proper order to their families; desiring to bring proper order to their families, they would first cultivate their persons; desiring to cultivate their persons, they would first attune their hearts-and-minds; desiring to attune their hearts-and-minds, they would first make their purposes sincere; desiring to make their purposes sincere, they would first extend their understanding to the utmost; and desiring to extend their understanding to the utmost, they would first investigate things and events.[72]

The passage continues in the opposite direction, taking us from investigation and understanding back through the person, family, state to pacifying the empire "suggesting that each of these dimensions in the human experience is necessary for the success of the rest" in the governance of social and political life.[73]

Both *The Great Learning* and Foucault's governmentality show how framing power and resistance solely in reference to the state misses the multiple and ironic practices of governance. In an eerie similarity to *The Great Learning*, Foucault tells us that:

> Upwards continuity means that a person who wishes to govern the state must first learn how to govern himself, his goods and his

patrimony, after which he will be successful in governing the state. ... On the other hand, we also have a downward continuity in the sense that, when a state is well run, the head of the family will know how to look after his family, his goods and his patrimony, which means that individuals will, in turn, behave as they should.[74]

Whereas juridical sovereignty is discontinuous in that it tries to draw a line between the power of the prince and any other form of power, *The Great Learning* illustrates Foucault's point that the task of the art of government is to establish continuity between different spaces of activity, in both an upwards and a downwards direction, linking the global and the local.

This different geometry of power produces a different geometry of resistance: "the strictly relational character of power relationships ... depends on a multiplicity of points of resistance."[75] Foucault thus states that:

> Where there is power, there is resistance, and yet, or rather consequently, this resistance is never in a position of exteriority in relation to power. ... Hence there is no single locus of great Refusal, no soul of revolt, source of all rebellions, or pure law of the revolutionary. Instead there is a plurality of resistances, each of them a special case.[76]

Rather than focusing solely on the state, it is important to see resistance in terms of its relations with the multiple forms of governmentality that are much more complex than top down or bottom up.

Shapiro's application of this complex notion of governance and resistance is useful for understanding cultural politics in Pacific Asia. His analysis shows how cultural politics emerges not just in Orientalism or Occidentalism, but as the national self produces Others both at home and abroad. In *Methods and Nations*, Shapiro examines how states have asserted their sovereignty by constructing nations where culture, race and territory are coterminous. Rather than simply charting the process of nation-building, as the subfield of comparative politics teaches us, Shapiro maps out the costs of the nation-destroying of indigenous peoples and ethnic minorities that nation-building continues to entail. Like many critical approaches to nationalism, Shapiro treats the nation not as a primordial or natural "thing," but as a narrative performance that is contradictory, incomplete, and thus contains within itself sites of resistance. The nation therefore is not the political solution, but a theoretical problem: "The nation-state is scripted—in official documents, histories, and journalistic commentaries, among other texts—in ways that impose coherence on what is instead a series of fragmentary and arbitrary conditions of historical assemblage."[77]

Shapiro thus examines how identity takes on coherence through cultural governance that expends large amounts of financial and symbolic capital. While state sovereignty initially relied on "military and fiscal initiatives," Shapiro argues that by the nineteenth century these "coercive and economic aspects of control have been supplemented by a progressively intense cultural governance, a management of the dispositions and meanings of citizen bodies, aimed at making territorial and national/cultural boundaries coextensive."[78]

Yet, since the state can never attain complete dominance over cultural production, resistance to these centralizing and homogenizing efforts takes the form of alternative cultural productions:

> At the same time, other modalities of writing—e.g., journals, diaries, novels and counter-historical narratives—challenge the state's coherence-producing writing performances. ... I treat governance not as the management of a people who belong by dint of character or other distinguishing attributes within a discrete territory, but rather as a historical process in which boundaries are imposed, and peoples are accorded varying degrees of cultural coherence and political intelligibility—not on the basis of natural divisions, but as a result of the exercise of power.[79]

Shapiro's semiotic approach to politics both deconstructs the power of international regimes and nation-states, and then looks to indigenous and minority writers, artists and scholars to recover different ways of thinking, feeling and being. Drawing on a wide range of sources, Shapiro charts examples of critical resistance to the knowledge-power dynamic of capitalist modernity. The purpose is not to find and define the proper nation or identity that is more inclusive, but to engage in "critique [that] is aimed at resisting closure, at challenging the assumption that there is a political vocabulary which, once achieved, can be adequate to a common political experience."[80] In this way, *Methods and Nations* resists the pitfall of much postcolonial literature that romanticizes the non-West as the answer to modernity's contradictions; like Dirlik's research, it encourages us to speak truth to power whenever and wherever we encounter it.

## Contents

This book will develop the theme of cultural governance and resistance through an examination of case studies in the North Pacific, China, Taiwan, South Korea, Thailand and Southeast Asia that highlight both "the politics of culture" and the "culture of politics." Although the cultural and historical context of each chapter is quite different, the book explores the following general themes: the relation of culture and technology; the relation of the state, civil society and social movements; the relation of gender, identity and democracy; and the relation of national and transnational identity. While most comparative politics texts begin with an elaboration of social science theory and methodology, the first three chapters of this book stress the interpretive process enabled by cultural theory. Rather than seek a single correct answer to the questions of governance and resistance, I develop semiotic approaches that seek to interpret the political meanings of cultural artifacts. With this interpretive method in mind, the last three chapters of the book more directly address the social science categories of civil society, elections and citizenship. Rather than take for granted the utility of these concepts, the chapters take a critical approach that, for example, argues that "civil society" is often deployed in Pacific Asia by conservative groups as a method of containing voices of popular resistance. In this way, the second group of chapters uses cultural theory to interpret political events and social movements.

Because it deploys hardware that kills people and destroys social and natural environments, the military is the prime example of destructive power. Since the military is the most extreme force for a negative politics of coercion, it thus is the most obvious place to start an analysis of the productive politics of identity. Chapter 1 examines the cultural politics of the US Army's chemical weapons disposal program at the uninhabited Johnston Atoll in the North Pacific. It will show both how the state uses cultural governance to promote its policies in a semi-foreign land, and how resistance to this project questions not just the army's public policy, but the "continental" imaginative geography that frames it. While the Army's arguments for weapons disposal rely on the language of technology, its sovereignty performances to the "general public" in the project's brochure and at public hearings rely on a cultural logic that would be familiar to Orientalists. The chapter thus uses the feature film *South Pacific*, which is about the US Navy's wartime experience in an exotic land, to deconstruct the political and geographical imagination that informs current military practices. Chapter 1 semiotically analyzes a conflict between geopolitical discourse and local resistance that is not just political, but conceptual. Using Euro-American continental geography that represents the Pacific as an empty space, the army constructs the image of the South Pacific that is devoid of local voices. This continental geography is contrasted with a maritime geography that constructs the Pacific as a dynamic living space traversed by wind, waves, peoples—and sites of resistance.

While Chapter 1 argues that Hollywood has misrepresented the Pacific to the Euro-American public, Chapter 2 uses the Miss Thailand beauty pageant to examine how Thailand represents itself to a national and a global audience—but in a very different way from Miss China. The chapter historicizes the beauty pageant to show that it is not simply an artifact of American "cultural imperialism"—indeed, the contest emerged at roughly the same time as the Miss America pageant in the late 1920s and early 1930s. The long history of Miss Thailand shows that this institution has been part of the key political-economic transitions in the kingdom: from absolute to constitutional monarchy (1930s), from mercantilism to an export-oriented economy (1960s), and from a nativist national identity to

Thailand as part of a transnational cultural economy (1980s to the present). The chapter further develops semiotic analysis to show how the beauty pageant was an important site of the state's cultural governance of gendered identity. Indeed, Chapter 2 here is linked with Chapter 1 since Miss Thailand is characteristically framed as the ideal mate of the model of Thai masculinity: the heroic soldier. Yet, Miss Thailand is also a site of resistance to the iconic narrative of the nation as family. Moreover, rather than simply promoting essential (and exotic) Thai identity, the pageant has been part of constructing national identity in an explicitly transnational way: as we will see, Miss Thailand is often the product of the international linkages of mating and education.

Chapter 3 continues to explore the gender and cultural governance theme by examining the curiously gendered sites of explicitly political resistance in a series of democratic rebellions in Pacific Asia: the Philippines (1986, 1998), Taiwan (1987), South Korea (1987), Burma (1988), China (1989), Thailand (1992) and Indonesia (1998). To gain purchase on this diverse set of events, Chapter 3 examines how the memory of these resistance movements is constructed through a strange set of "commemorative revolutionary photo albums." A close reading of albums from the Philippines, Burma, China and Thailand shows that patriarchal politics is very active in Pacific Asia's democratic struggles, and highlights how transnational resistance forces struggled for domestic power in a very gendered space. Thus, the struggle is not just a matter of men exploiting women; the photographic discourse of these albums shows how the memory of these democratic events is constructed to reverse the patriarchal stereotype: virtuous women opposing corrupt men, and patriotic youth opposing a tyrannical "gerontocracy." The chapter concludes that this celebration of democratic revolution is problematic. The simple reversal of images and roles does not contest the political logic of the patriarchal regime that relies on a set of essential Oriental/Occidental images. For a more radical resistance, the chapter looks to another de-essentialized set of gendered images that make a more thorough ironic critique of patriarchal authoritarian states.

After the first three chapters have used semiotic approaches to shift the mode of analysis from a social science search for truth to an interpretation of the play of differences, the last three chapters return to reconsider the traditional vocabulary of power and resistance. While Chapter 3's democratic revolutions are struggling for state power, Chapter 4 uses the debate over civil society in China and South Korea to question how we conceptualize resistance to state power. Since the failure of China's democratic movement in 1989, there has been a vigorous debate over the existence and authenticity of civil society in China; a similar debate emerged in South Korea in the late 1990s. The chapter first deconstructs these debates to suggest that they are asking the wrong question: these civil society debates are limited because they frame the issues in terms of an East/West logic of the idealized ideologies of Confucianism, communism and liberalism. Rather than asking the idealized question of whether Confucian culture can accommodate civil society (or not), I explore how the civil society debate is part of state-led cultural governance; conservative groups construct "civil society" as a way of preserving state power. Then I use cultural events and popular texts to show how social movements in South Korea and China have been resisting the conceptual governmentality of the state/civil society dynamic. In this way, Chapter 4 further develops the theoretical arguments rehearsed in this Introduction; it shifts the locus of resistance from the essential East/West dynamic to problematize the new forms of capitalist modernity that are developing in Pacific Asia.

Chapter 5 continues the interrogation of the conservative politics of civil society through an examination of Thailand's "political reform movement." This powerful group of activists emerged after Thailand's 1992 democratic uprising. It was able to change not just political leaders, but the rules of the political game, writing a new constitution that came into effect in 1997. Rather than assessing this democratization project through a Schumpeterian checklist of democratic characteristics (free and fair elections, civil society, rule of law, free press), this chapter argues that democracy in Thailand takes shape against its negative opposite: vote buying. In the 1990s vote buying turned from being one of many campaign tactics into the guiding metaphor of the "political disease" not simply of elections, but of Thai society in general. To understand the power of this image, I deconstruct Thailand's key political discourses to show how the concepts of law, "good and able leaders," gangsters, the middle class, civil society and village life are central in defining vote buying and democracy as complementary opposites. The chapter will show how vote buying (and democracy) is produced through specific relations of political and economic power, urban and rural power, and official and unofficial power; to resist vote buying (and conservative constructions of civil society) we need to challenge the cultural governance of these relations. Like Chapters 3 and 4, this chapter deconstructs democracy through an examination of the tension between elite civil society and grassroots social movements.

While Chapters 3, 4 and 5 shift analytic focus from civil society to social movements, Chapter 6 examines how social movements often entail "moving societies" such as the Chinese diaspora. I first deconstruct the image of diasporic Chinese as transnational yuppies whose Confucian capitalism effaces national boundaries along the Pacific Rim. Then I show how overseas Chinese in Thailand have been crucial in defining boundaries in national, regional and global space. Diaspora thus both construct and deconstruct the seemingly opposing forces of nationalism and cosmopolitanism. The chapter uses an ethnographic approach to question research on national identity that searches for norms and formal institutions; it highlights how the struggle of cultural governance and resistance takes place in the context-sensitive relations between identity and difference, self and Other. The national, cosmopolitan and the transnational are not rival concepts or communities: the Chinese diaspora shows how each is necessary to produce the other.

The Conclusion will examine how contact zones are not just between cultural systems, but between "the politics of issues" and "the politics of rhetoric." To consider import of cultural politics in Pacific Asia, I will explore how Mao has been institutionalized as an image that is exchanged in revolutionary, moral and financial economies. It considers how the themes of market, state, nation, gender, democracy and identity take shape in Pacific Asia, and will discuss the strengths and weaknesses of explaining politics in terms of cultural governance. The book concludes that rather than focus on East/West relations or the Orientalizing/Occidentalizing process, it is necessary to deconstruct self/Other relations in order to focus our critical gaze on the power of global capitalist modernity—wherever we find it.

# 1 Culture, the military and the "South Pacific"[1]

While we characteristically understand the military in terms of the power of its destructive force, and study hardware that kills people and destroys environments, this chapter will reframe military power into a productive force that generates civilian identity in the context of problems and solutions that perpetuate the militarization of political life. Traditionally, the military has been the main beneficiary of the state's deployment of technologies of power, either in the form of centralized military hardware or centralized television networks. But cultural production can also be a source of empowerment in resistance to the state. Since the 1980s new information technologies have provided many channels for resistance to the state's cultural governance: cassette tapes of Ayatollah Khomeini's sermons were key in mobilizing resistance to the Shah in Iran (1979), faxes were instrumental in spreading the word about the People Power revolution in the Philippines (1986) and the Tian'anmen democracy movement in China (1989), mobile phones were crucial for the Thai democracy movement (1992), and now text messages and the internet are key technologies of resistance around the world.[2]

In addition to examining how technology produces and distributes artifacts of power and resistance, this chapter will consider the broader politics of the dynamic relationship between technology and culture. It will deconstruct how technology itself is a cultural artifact that is produced and circulated through symbolic politics. Using the concept of cultural governance, the chapter will shift from examining how the state uses technologies to restrict the flow of information, to consider how cultural technologies produce a range of hegemonic images and thus produce discursive power. For example, although the Chinese party-state is notorious for censoring independent voices, the People's Liberation Army (PLA) is one of the largest employers of artists in China, if not the world. The PLA's cultural activities go far beyond military bands that perform at solemn ceremonies, or picture books that justify the crackdown on the 1989 Tian'anmen demonstrations.[3] The PLA also runs a fine arts academy in Beijing, and regularly sponsors national television programs that headline uniformed officers belting out patriotic songs as show tunes.[4]

This chapter will explore the politics of the culture/technology dynamic through an examination of how the US Army exerts its power not just with guns on the battlefield, but also through the productive use of symbolic power. This symbolic power is not just for entertainment or for the success of specific missions—such as the Iraq War and its aftermath. The army's cultural governance works more generally to reproduce the context of a set of problems and solutions that justify the necessity of maintaining a strong military regardless of any particular threat. The army's discursive arsenal produces meaning to make sure that the army's mission is accomplished, and also to suppress, control and manage resistant voices and political alternatives. Through a close analysis of the US Army's cultural representations, this chapter will show how the army frames policy statements to guide the discourse to questions that will legitimate its actions, and, perhaps more importantly, guide the discourse away from questions that might serve to problematize its policies.

To illustrate the intimate relation of knowledge/power and culture/technology in the policy process, the chapter analyzes the plan the US Army developed in 1990 to transport chemical weapons from Europe to Johnston Island for incineration and disposal at the Johnston Atoll Chemical Agent Disposal System (JACADS) facility despite protests from a number of local, national and international groups. JACADS is an important example because it shows how cultural theory and public policy analysis can aid each other: to understand the public policy of "chemical demilitarization," it is important to understand the discourse of the "South Pacific."

Although JACADS is certainly an example of the secretive nature of militaries around the world, it should be clear that this chapter is not concerned with conspiracy theories, secret information, or the private motives of individual leaders and officers. Rather, it aims to show how the army manages resistance to its policies through the discourse of public representations to civil society. In other words, I did not have to dig through documents released through the Freedom of Information Act; I am on the army's mailing list.[5]

However, just because I use the army's public information materials does not mean that the research is limited by military propaganda. There are many meanings contesting each other in these seemingly straightforward public information documents. In shaping this discursive event the army concentrated on the "Why" questions, arguing that chemical weapons disposal is part of a noble narrative of disarmament, and on certain "How" questions, assuring the public through a narrative of technical expertise that the process is safe. In this way, the army is deploying what Kathy Ferguson and Phyllis Turnbull call the double-narrative of naturalization and reassurance, whose "interbreeding" frames military policy with "a tone of inevitability; what is, is good and in any case cannot be changed."[6]

This tactic was demonstrated most clearly at a public meeting when the commander of the JACADS facility slipped into "Why" questions when the "How" questions of public safety were asked too loudly. His response was, "Wouldn't the world be a better place without these chemical weapons?" In this chapter, I follow Hawaiian activist Poka Laenui's response to this question: "Yes, but why are you destroying weapons made in America and deployed in Europe in the Pacific?" Indeed, we cannot let the thrill of disarmament blind us from seeing how it is carried out, and who bears the costs—especially when this "disarmament" was actually an upgrading for a "new generation" of chemical weapons.[7]

The narrative of reassurance and safety can be politicized by shifting the military's line of inquiry from "What (JACADS is)" and "Why (it needs to be done)" to the questions "Who (is making the decisions)," "Where," and "When (these decisions are carried out)." While "What" and "Why" questions are more metaphysical and tend to naturalize the discourse, the "Who," "Where," and "When" queries provide discursive openings where environmental and human rights questions can be raised. All of these political questions are wrapped up in the issue of "How" the discourse was produced. In short, while the army directs our gaze to the technology of the JACADS incinerators, this chapter focuses on the technology of the "chemical weapons disposal" discourse. In this way, technology is reframed from being about material mechanisms into technology as "a positing, ordering, and placing of all beings."[8] Although poststructuralist analysis is often criticized for depoliticizing issues, this chapter will end with a set of policy proposals that appeal to a broader notion of civil society that includes peoples beyond the boundaries of any particular nation-state.

## Geography and representations

Geography is central in both the positioning of JACADS in the "empty" Pacific and Pacific Islanders' resistance to it. Yet, is this a physical geography or a symbolic geography? The answer to this question is "yes," and to see how symbolic and physical geographies are intertwined, we need to go to *South Pacific*, if not to the South Pacific itself.

The film *South Pacific* is an entertaining example of the production, circulation and management of signs that directs our understanding of the region.[9] This film, which was produced in Hollywood and is one of the few links connecting the mainland American audience with the "Pacific Islands," is thus both a product and a producer of the myth of the "South Pacific." The film is also helpful in explaining how the US Army and recent presidents have formed their policies: considering his World War II military service as a pilot in the Pacific War, George H.W. Bush could very well have been a character in *South Pacific*. Jimmy Carter, himself a former submarine captain, blurred the material and symbolic even more when he sent James A. Michener, author of *Tales of the South Pacific* on which the film is based, to be the US representative at Vanuatu's independence declaration in 1980. Although Michener is well known for his adventure novels, in 1942 he was the navy's historical officer for the South Pacific Command where his mission was to "to start compiling a history of the Navy . . . in these waters."[10]

How is the "South Pacific" produced in this film? Though the title of the film tells us it is about "the Pacific," the story is more about Americans and Europeans—like the most recent Pacific narrative about chemical weapons formerly stored in Germany. The Pacific setting appeals mostly to its exotic, scenic environmental background. When the "natives" do appear in this film, they are not (clearly) Pacific Islanders. In both the film and Michener's book the sacred island of Bali-h'ai has Tonganese/Tonkinese living on it, reproducing a blurring of race and place in Pacific Asia that follows imperial history: the French brought laborers from their other colonies in Indochina (Tonkin) to work on Pacific plantations. Bloody Mary is Tongan, yet her daughter Liat is clearly Tonkinese. The actress playing Liat is herself a blurring of Asia and Europe in both parentage and naming: France Nuyen. Moreover, the film's scenes contain a scattered mixture of romanticized representations from all over the Pacific and Asia: although Vanuatu is in Melanesia, the film credits list a group of actors under the heading "the Polynesians." In short, the film is a pastiche of various exotic cultures that serve to build the myth of "South Pacific Paradise"—even though the film was shot in the North Pacific space of the Hawaiian island of Kaua'i, not to mention the Hollywood sets in California.

George H.W. Bush reproduced this romanticized representation of the Pacific in the closing remarks of the "United States–Pacific Island Nations Summit," which was held in October 1990 to address the Pacific Island leaders' concerns about JACADS:

> The Pacific Islands have a special place in the minds and hearts of the American people. And on my own visits, starting almost fifty years ago, I've witnessed the natural charm of the Island peoples and the natural beauty of the Islands. Their reputation is well deserved.[11]

These natural charms and beauties are technically constructed in *South Pacific* through an obvious manipulation of colors as signs. Film producer Buddy Adler states in the film's promotional brochure that: "We hope we have captured the magic of the 'South Pacific'." Just after this natural description, however, Adler recounts the technical marvels of this magic: "Cinematographer Leon Shamroy introduced revolutionary ideas to create the imaginative mood lighting which subtly accentuates the romance of a moment or a melody's enchantment."[12] Apparently, the South Pacific itself is neither charming nor romantic enough; red and blue filters are used not so "subtly" to manage colors to evoke the passion of the paradise of Bali-h'ai. Yellow, orange and pink are deployed for the toast of two lovers on "Some Enchanted Evening." The whole sequence of scenes on Bali-h'ai is shrouded in a soft colorized focus. This management of color is hard to read at first; with the signifying power of music and song, it sweeps you away like a breeze through mists of dried ice. The technical power of signification is manifest once the coloration is removed and the characters are back to "normal."

Indeed, there are so many shifts in color that it is difficult to gauge what is real—are the nights really so royally blue in the South Pacific? Although Michener underlines the truth claims of this story as "a report of what life was actually like on a Pacific backwater,"[13] a semiotic analysis questions this reality effect. The story is a complex of representations; it is a multi-layered myth far removed from any nameable time or place. Indeed, the film itself is hard to pin down since it comes at the end of a chain of representations: it is based on a Broadway play, originally produced by Richard Rogers, Oscar Hammerstein II, Leland Hayward and Joshua Logan, which in turn is based on James A. Michener's war stories in *Tales of the South Pacific*.

Moreover, no one can locate the elusive Bali-h'ai on a map. Many have speculated about Bali-h'ai's location and origin.[14] Michener was stationed in Vanuatu (then the New Hebrides) on Espiritu Santo and said that Bali-ha'i was a neighboring island. Yet, there is no island in the location that he charts for us. Indeed, Bali-ha'i might have some relation to the Indonesian island of Bali; because of its beaches, coral and surf, Bali was an elite tourist destination in the Pacific before World War II.[15] Yet, now the symbolic/physical geography has shifted. During World War II, a new geographical entity, "Southeast Asia," was created as a war theater to include islands such as Bali.[16] The Pacific now starts in the snowcapped mountains that divide Indonesia from Papua New Guinea. Thus, "Bali-h'ai" and the "South Pacific" are both unstable concepts. Michener later revealed that the name Bali-ha'i is taken from "one of the most miserable Melanesian villages" located on Mono Island in the Solomon Islands.[17] Although this instability adds to the power of the mystery and the magic, the image still needs to be managed: "Bali-ha'i" is an empty sign that needs to be filled up to produce meaning. In short, *South Pacific* is not a simple reflection of a pre-existing place; the film was directed to produce a new space.

To a large extent, this representation is directed by the powerful relationship between the military and the "South Pacific": recall that in 1942 Michener was writing not a history of the Pacific, but a "history of the [US] Navy ... in these waters."[18] In the opening sequence of the film, the following statement is superimposed on a "tropical beach scene" with swaying palms at sunset: "The Producers thank the Department of Defense, the Navy Department, the United States Pacific Fleet, and the Fleet Marine of the Pacific for their assistance in bringing this motion picture to the screen." "South Pacific," then, is an example of the construction of meaning through a management of signs that is guided by military policy as well as aesthetic values.[19] It is not a place in relation to the physical geography of the equator (i.e. South) and a large body of water (i.e. the Pacific), so much as a production in the symbolic geography of power relations. The following sections will examine the army's more sophisticated telling of the narratives of naturalization and reassurance through the topics of technology and disarmament. This narrative constructs the JACADS project as part of its latest cultural production of the "South Pacific"—even though Johnston Island and Hawai'i are both in the North Pacific. Like Bali-ha'i, the Pacific is constructed in the popular and military imagination as an empty place, a sign that not only needs to be filled with exotic meaning, but often filled with toxic waste as well.

## Chemical weapons settings

During World Wars I and II, lethal and highly toxic chemical weapons were manufactured in the US by the army. Most of these weapons were stored at military bases in the US, while the rest were shipped to Europe and Okinawa as part of Cold War strategy. In 1970, as the result of an accidental leak of the deadly nerve agent VX that injured twenty-three US servicemen and one civilian, the Okinawans and the Japanese demanded that the weapons be removed from Okinawa. In 1971 they were shipped to Johnston Island. Because these rockets were obsolete and had begun to leak, the US Congress mandated that all nerve gas rockets stored within the US be destroyed by 1995. An Environmental Impact Statement (EIS) was written by the army, which argued that the best method for disposing of the nerve gas rockets was to incinerate them on-site at Johnston Island and at the other eight army bases in the continental US where the rockets are stored, because transporting these weapons would be "too risky." Despite a great deal of public protest, the EIS was adopted by the US Environmental Protection Agency (EPA) in 1988, and incinerators were scheduled to be built at Johnston Island and the eight storage sites on the continental US. The JACADS facility was built first to serve as a model for the other incinerators; it was completed and started chemical weapons disposal on June 30, 1990. It was then tested for eighteen months to ensure the safety of its technology before the construction of other incinerators on the mainland US could begin.

By 2000, JACADS completed its mission of destroying over 400,000 chemical weapons on Johnston Island. The decommissioning, dismantling and clean-up of JACADS was finished in 2003. JACADS needed to apply to the EPA for an extension and modification of its EIS in 1997, and for a closure plan in 2000. These two applications generated numerous public documents and public hearings. After negotiations with the EPA, JACADS was eventually granted an extension of its EIS in 1998, a closure plan in 2002, and final certification of Johnston Atoll as a safe environment is expected in 2006. JACADS has been presented as a complete success, "the world's first full-scale facility built to destroy chemical weapons"; it thus serves as a model not just for the chemical weapons incinerators in the continental US, but around the world.[20]

In February 1990, however, there was a development that challenged this reassuring narrative of disarmament. European chemical weapons were added to the list of Pacific-based rockets to be destroyed at JACADS. The army thus submitted a draft supplemental to the 1988 EIS that would allow it to meet President George H.W. Bush and German Chancellor Helmut Kohl's commitment to transport nerve gas weapons out of Germany to Johnston Island by the end of 1990. This shift in plans—from destroying chemical weapons on-site to shipping them halfway around the world to Johnston Island—aroused much public opposition. The EIS process mandates a public hearing and a period of time for the public to submit comments before it is approved. Therefore, a public hearing was held on March 20, 1990, and the deadline for public comments was set for March 26, 1990.

The 1990 public hearing could easily be seen an example of the military using its power to censor resistance and restrict meaning production. It attempted to limit the impact of this public hearing by (1) releasing the draft copy of the EIS only a short time before the public hearing, (2) limiting the distribution of the EIS, and (3) allowing only six days for the public to submit written comments after the public hearing. Clearly, the army was trying to exclude opposition by limiting opportunities for the public to review and criticize this intensely technical document.

Yet it is also important to focus on how the army deploys productive power to generate meaning; it uses the discursive technologies of naturalization and reassurance to frame JACADS. As Ferguson and Turnbull explain for the Hawaiian case:

> The narratives of naturalization imbricate military institutions and discourses into daily life so that they become "just the way things are." The narratives of reassurance kick in with a more prescriptive tone, marking the military presence in Hawai'i as necessary, productive, heroic, desirable, good.

This chapter's analysis of JACADS discourse follows Ferguson and Turnbull in addressing "not the military per se, but militarization as a dynamic, contested process of constituting a particular kind of order, naturalizing and legitimating that order, while simultaneously undermining competing possibilities of order."[21] A close reading of the public policy process through the military's use of public hearings, glossy brochures and EIS documents will demonstrate how "public opinion" is produced through the "South Pacific," and show how the military's symbolic activities have a very material impact on the North Pacific.

## Naturalization and reassurance

Safety is the main topic of the cultural productions of "chemical demilitarization," strategically linking together the narratives of naturalization and reassurance. Indeed, at a ceremony in 2004, JACADS workers celebrated the closing of the plant with a cake that was decorated with images of chemical weapons, suggesting that the project was not just safe, but good enough to eat (see Figure 1.1). The army utilizes a complex network of signs to trumpet the strong points of its plan to incinerate the weapons, while at the same time distracting attention away from the weak points of the plan. These diverse sets of representations are unified through the narrative of naturalization: they serve to naturalize the army's statements, shifting them from arguments for possible options to reports of the "facts" of their policies. "Naturalize" here refers to the process whereby a discourse hides its own process of production, and thus limits space for critique.

In its public representations, the army appeals to the naturalizing power of photographs and the discourse of science. Although both seem beyond manipulation, photographs are orchestrated productions of light, and the practice of natural science contains value decisions, such as which questions should be asked and which ones should not. Following Roland Barthes's analysis, I argue that the army utilizes these naturalizing signs to represent the myth of disarmament and safety: "Myth consists in turning

*Figure 1.1* JACADS chemical weapons cake, 2004. Courtesy of the US Army Chemical Materials Agency

culture into nature or, at least, the social, the cultural, the ideological, the historical into the 'natural'."[22] Indeed, myth is depoliticized speech that entails a loss of history in the sense that "things lose the memory that they once were made." Hence myth is "a conjuring trick: it has turned reality inside out, it has emptied it of history and has filled it with nature."[23] Photography and science thus both efface questions of how, where and when their discourses are produced, guiding us to focus on what the picture is and why science studies chemical weapons. The army's management of public opinion then makes Umberto Eco's definition of semiotics seem frighteningly appropriate: "Semiotics is in principle the discipline studying everything which can be used in order to lie."[24]

One of the key artifacts in the army's semiotic arsenal is an informational brochure, "The United States Chemical Stockpile Disposal Program," which was distributed at the public hearing on March 20, 1990.[25] The informational brochure, which was produced by the military to promote its public policy, provides an intriguing entrance into the analysis of the US Army's discourse of chemical weapons disposal that utilizes technical reports, public performances, popular culture and advertising. Indeed, there was a gift shop on Johnston Island that sold postcards and commemorative calendars to celebrate the military in the Pacific and the history of JACADS.[26]

The US Army's promotional brochure serves as an exemplary case of the management of signs for legitimization through the rhetoric of "the natural." It functions much like the advertising in the promotional brochure for *South Pacific*, since both promote technical marvels that produce natural charms. The army's ten-page, full-color glossy publication is packed with signs: a written text laid out around figures, maps and photographs, with a patriotic eagle always in the upper right-hand corner. The information xeroxes of the Committee for a Sane Nuclear Policy (SANE) and Greenpeace that were available on a different table at the hearing paled in comparison to the army's slick brochure. Yet, as in other military representations, important things are missing from this sophisticated cultural/technical production. Indeed, there are no page numbers, thus making it unac-count-able and difficult to cite.

This complex brochure tells many stories, and it is useful to temporarily divide the narrative of chemical weapons disposal into visual and written texts before examining how they interrelate. In many ways, the two texts are separate and free-floating: there are few captions to tie the written and visual texts together. More to the point, the two sets of texts often work against each other. While the written text is committed to—as one subheading tells us—RAISING THE LEVEL OF KNOWLEDGE, the visual discourse's pretty pictures serve to raise the level of distraction in our increasingly post-literate society.

It is very easy to just flip through this attractive brochure looking only at pictures and pausing on the boldfaced all-cap headings: HISTORY OF

OUR COMMITMENT, FOCUS ON SAFETY and PROTECTING THE PUBLIC AND THE ENVIRONMENT. The visual signs draw our attention away from the factual "information." For example, the RAISING THE LEVEL OF KNOWLEDGE section, which claims to "provide information on the characteristics and effects of the two primary categories of chemical agents designated for destruction," has three visuals: (1) a photograph of a white man instructing a white woman in a parklike setting, (2) a photograph of a pristine lake, and (3) a figure representing molecular structures. Yet rather than "keeping the public informed," these visuals actually have little to do with the "characteristics and effects" of chemical weapons. They certainly do not show the effect that chemical weapons have on people and the environment. Rather, they deploy the double punch of naturalization and reassurance: the chemical diagram adds scientific legitimation as part of the naturalization narrative, while the pleasant scenes of nature and education are reassuring. The landscape scenes have little to do with the actual sites of chemical weapons disposal, while the diagram is scientifically meaningless, because it is unlabeled. The discourses of naturalization and reassurance thus work hard to cover the tracks of chemical weapons disposal.

## *Photography and progress*

These seemingly disjointed pictures, charts and graphs are woven into a particular narrative of reassurance. The visuals of the brochure are part of an argument of (scientific and social) PROGRESS that tries to explain (away) the horrors of chemical weapons in an optimistic and hopeful tone. Progress, here, is a linear movement from the "bad past" (the Dark Ages) upward to a rational solution of the problems, and thus a better life (the Enlightenment). For example, on what would be pages 5 and 6, the chemical weapons disposal program is related to the narrative of progress in a representation of a step-by-step process that moves like an arrow diagonally upward from the lower left to the upper right, thus joining PUBLIC SAFETY (page 5) and MOVING TOWARD OUR GOAL (page 6). The box that is the last step of this visual narrative says "Process complete" and "Goal achieved," before the recurrent eagle flies away from the upper right-hand corner of page 6.

The discourse of progress is also conveyed through the technical means of photography with the juxtaposition of color and black-and-white photography in the promotional brochure. As in *South Pacific* and its promotional brochure, bright colors are for good times. This tactic is most apparent on the cover of the army's brochure, where a black-and-white photo of artillery shells stored above ground in a wooded area is positioned behind a color photo of a different wooded area with no weapons (see Figure 1.2). The story that the photographs tell, once again, has little to do with the brochure title, "The United States Chemical Weapons Disposal Program," that is written above the photos. There is no mention that the shells in the black-and-white photo are the ones that contain nerve gas. Actually, in 1990 the nerve gas canisters were stored underground or in sealed concrete igloos. The army's brochure, however, legitimizes the disposal program by making it appear as if the rockets in the black-and-white photo will just magically disappear, and the natural environment of the forest will then bloom in full color.

*Figure 1.2* Cover of chemical weapons disposal brochure, 1990. Courtesy of the US Army Chemical Materials Agency

Unfortunately, the events have shown that this colorized disappearing act is another of the army's performances of the "magic of the South Pacific": European weapons disappear into the Pacific, while Pacific Islanders have to deal with the problems and the chemical by-products of "chemical demilitarization." "Demilitarization" is actually quite an appropriate and accurate description of chemical weapons disposal. The chemicals do not disappear; they are not completely destroyed. These chemical weapons are honorably discharged to become civilian toxic waste (more below). This myth of an immaculate process of progress is repeated throughout the visual text of the brochure: the only other black-and-white photo is over the first section, HISTORY OF OUR COMMITMENT; it again represents the past according to the trope of enlightened progress. All the other photographs and figures in the brochure are in color, and are generally pleasing to the eye.

## *Science and safety*

The discourse legitimizes the chemical weapon disposal program by concentrating on "Why" and "How" questions that promote the positive and ignore negative consequences. These depoliticized questions of technology naturalize the discourse through "natural science" and scenes of "natural beauty." Here we will examine how the narrative of reassurance uses the rhetoric of expertise and science to naturalize the army's projects in the brochure, in Environmental Impact Statements, and in public hearings.

Logic and probability theory are human-made sign systems that link knowledge to language.[27] The JACADS discourse often utilizes the "objective and neutral" logic of science and probability theory to present the program. Yet scientific discourses, methods and technical language are used only when they are to the army's advantage. The brochure legitimizes the project and reassures the public through the discourse of expertise, stating that "The disposal process has been endorsed and is overseen by the prestigious National Academy of Sciences" (page 2), and that the army has "more than sixteen years of extensive testing and experience in employing environmentally sound methods for disposing of chemical agents" (page 5). However, these statements are misleading. While the army brags that JACADS is the first facility of its kind in the world, this brash statement also underlines how incineration of these types of chemical weapons had never been done before, and had yet to be proven as completely safe. Therefore, the meaning of a "prestigious" organization fully endorsing an unproven technology and the army's claim of "years of experience" when this technology had no record of safe use is less reassuring than it initially appears.

These statements are even more distracting once we recognize the military's messy environmental history at Johnston Atoll. In the 1950s, the US conducted high-altitude atmospheric nuclear tests in the Pacific, including rockets launched from Johnston Island.[28] Just before the Limited Test Ban Treaty came into effect in 1964, the US military again held numerous high-altitude atmospheric nuclear tests at Johnston Atoll; "The effect of these high level explosions lit the sky from Australia to Hawai'i, causing an enormous electromagnetic pulse which put out street lights in Honolulu, 1300 kilometers away."[29] The atoll was heavily contaminated with plutonium from two aborted missile launches in 1963, including one where the nuclear weapon exploded on Johnston Island's launch pad. Large open-air biological weapons tests were conducted just downwind of Johnston Atoll in 1964. In the 1990s, part of the island was still off-limits to personnel because of a spillage of Agent Orange in the early 1970s.

The reassurance narrative of scientific expertise also drowns out JACADS's own troubled history. After it became operational, JACADS was "hampered by flaws in design and operation"[30] that produced what an environmental group called "an impressive record of mishaps, violations, miscues, and disasters."[31] By 1997 there were "four documented releases of nerve agent, a rocket explosion, and many other technical and design problems."[32] These design problems not only resulted in the facility operating at less that fifty percent of its scheduled operating time; technical flaws also led to the death of a worker who was repairing JACADS in 1997.[33] Moreover, rather than cleaning up the environment, JACADS has produced a new range of dangerous pollutants. The Hawaii Medical Association reported that:

> Many scientific studies have shown that the incineration of hazardous wastes with state-of-the-art technology release, in the form of nauseous emissions, residual ash, and effluents of pollution control devices, uncombusted chemicals, heavy metals, and newly formed chemical products of incomplete combustion including polychlorinated dioxins and polychlorinated furans.[34]

In 1990, the official response to questions about the toxic waste of dioxins and furans was, "We do not expect the significant formation of such products."[35]

To overcome its own messy history, the army uses technical language to legitimate the project and reassure the public that the disposal system is safe: the orderly and rational phrases "normal operations" and "standard operating procedures" are often pronounced at public hearings and written in the EIS. But just what are "normal operations" and "standard operating procedures" in this context? Because of hundreds of changes to the incinerator and modifications to the EIS, there was no "standard operating procedure" for the fault that the welder was repairing when he died in 1997. And what happens when something unexpected occurs? The threat of hurricanes is a recurring problem for Johnston Atoll: hurricanes were strong enough to force an evacuation of all military and civilian staff in

1972, 1984, 1993 and 1994. In 1994, JACADS production was disrupted for seventy days to repair hurricane damage.

In brochures and public hearings, the army also uses the phrase "state-of-the-art" technologies to buttress its narrative of reassurance. But this phrase means only that the chosen technology is the best one available of its kind, which does not necessarily mean that the technology is safe. Indeed, state-of-the-art also means experimental. Dr Wayne Landis, formerly head of environmental toxicology at the army's Aberdeen Proving Grounds in Maryland, criticized the army for its unreasonable "failure to consider alternative disposal methods."[36] As the *Marshall Islands Journal*, the Hawaii Medical Association, and people attending the 1990 public hearing all commented, state-of-the-art incinerator technologies may not be safe enough in dealing with lethal chemical weapons.[37]

But such questions cannot be raised within the army's vocabulary, which works to delegitimize chemical weapons disposal techniques that might be safer than incineration. With this management of the discourse, the *Honolulu Advertiser* editorials can state that disposal at Johnston Island is "the best, if not the only, near-term alternative," instead of thinking of long-term responsibilities or asking for whom it is best.[38] However, in a plea for a serious consideration of alternative technologies, *Environment Hawai'i* concluded that the army's mission has changed from destroying chemical weapons to building incinerators; the army thus ignores a number of better, safer options that are available not just for the continental US, but for chemical weapons disposal around the world.[39]

## *Military performances*

The military presented its case at a public hearing in downtown Honolulu on March 20, 1990, deploying the discursive weapons of "science and expertise" loaded with state-of-the-art cultural ammunition. The simple placement of the microphone, the logistics of the room, and other proto-discursive moves show how the discourse of "public opinion" was managed by the army. The uniformed army officers, who were in charge of managing the EIS, sat at the front table, which was raised on a dais above the public. Their presentations were anchored in technical discourse, using highly specialized military language for a lay audience. They used large olive drab overheads to outline their objectives. Although the meeting was billed as a "public hearing," the physical setting for the meeting was arranged in a way that decreased the significance of the large number of people who had gathered to criticize the EIS. The podium with the microphone for the "public voice" was placed so that the "public" would face the committee, not the audience. The moderator, a woman with a southern accent, often mispronounced non-European names, drawing smiles from the brass at the front of the table. As a result, the army's use of language served to delegitimize Pacific Islanders by mispronouncing their names. When people did get a chance to speak, the conversation was limited: the overheads narrowed the discussion to questions that the army was comfortable in answering.

Still, within the strict confines of this technical discourse many disturbing problems with the EIS were raised. Even with the short commentary period of six days, many agreed that the EIS was an incomplete document, with some going so far as to characterize it as "shoddy." Although the army stresses that the atoll is a site of natural beauty rich in wildlife, there is no discussion of how the endangered species located around Johnston Atoll could be threatened by a release of nerve gas into the ocean environment.[40] Although the information paper handed out at the public hearing stated that "The United States is responsible for all security and emergency response functions," the US government did not clearly guarantee it would pay for clean-up and compensation in the case of a major accident.[41]

Last, there was the question of JACADS and international law. Ocean dumping and incineration are already outlawed by the London Convention on the Prevention of Marine Pollution by Dumping Wastes and Other Matter of 1972.[42] Incineration at Johnston Atoll could be seen as ocean incineration, especially since most of its land surface is man-made—bulldozed over living reefs—and thus does not legally count as an island.[43] Yet the army's cultural-technical arsenal managed to discursively overwhelm these critical scientific, policy and legal concerns.

## Silences and safety

The distracting noise of technical discourse disguised the silences of the army's technical narrative on issues of time, place and actor: who, where and when. The army stated that full information had been disclosed regarding the chemical weapons disposal program, and that it was committed to "raising the level of knowledge" of the public. However, in its control of the discourse, the army enforces a division of knowledge that authorizes the narrow range of questions that can be asked about the disposal of the chemical weapons, and excludes broader questions of the timing and spatiality of military activities in the Pacific. At an "information meeting" on August 20, 1990,[44] a common response to the public's questions was, "Sorry, that's outside the area we are prepared to address today," or "We can't comment on matters under litigation."

The army also uses knowledge practices to divide and contain oppositional voices. Rather than writing one document to address the disposal of German-based chemical weapons on Johnston Island, the army produced three separate documents addressing (1) transportation within Germany, (2) ocean transport (The Global Commons Report), and (3) the unloading and incineration of nerve gas at Johnston Island (the 1990 supplemental EIS). By discursively separating these activities, the army made it difficult for resistance groups to protest the whole program. Indeed, a Federal

District Judge denied a preliminary injunction to stop the transport of chemical weapons from Germany to Johnston Island on the grounds that "the plaintiffs were not in the geographical area of the chemical stockpile route from Germany to the territorial waters of Johnston Atoll."[45] By not discussing the accumulated risks of the entire disposal program from Europe to Johnston Island, the army discouraged connections between the resistance groups in Hawai'i and those in the rest of the world. For example, at the public hearing in March 1990, the army only allowed comments on the Johnston Atoll EIS, and not on the other documents.[46] The other two documents were unavailable at the public hearing and were difficult for the general public to obtain due to "national security" concerns. The army would neither reveal the authors of these reports nor tell people how to obtain copies of the report. Although the army is obligated to solicit comments from US citizens regarding the Johnston Atoll EIS, it is unclear who could make comments on the other two documents. Pacific Islanders, who were most affected by the JACADS program, had no legal opportunity to voice their concerns regarding the Global Commons Report, the 1990 EIS for Johnston Island, or transportation in Europe. They suffered the risks without having representation in the decision-making process.

Another rhetorical tactic of the narrative of reassurance pervades the "scientific discourse" of the EIS. The army reversed the "logic" used in a previous decision regarding the disposal of the chemical weapons; therefore, it had to manage the interpretation of its reversal. In the original 1988 EIS, the army stated that the best method was to incinerate the weapons on-site where they were currently being stored, because transportation of the weapons was too risky. The undersecretary of the Department of the Army, James Ambrose, spoke out strongly at the public hearings against the transportation of the weapons held on the US mainland at the other eight storage sites. Major Phil Soucy said: "We feel destroying [the nerve gas] where it is, is the safest way possible to get rid of it. It is much better than moving it all over the planet."[47] But in 1990, the army did just that—moving the weapons all over the planet—without any change in state-of-the-art technology, a stated reason, or even recognition that it had said the exact opposite at another time and place.

The army's promotional brochure, the media and Hollywood movies are all helpful in explaining this double standard. Following the military's image of the South Pacific, the narrative of reassurance relies on an understanding of the Pacific as empty and Johnston Atoll as isolated. When listing the chemical weapons disposal sites, the brochure lists only the continental US facilities by name in the text and on a map. Johnston Island is mentioned only as being a test facility in the remote Pacific: "A full-scale facility will first be operated at the isolated Johnston Atoll in the Pacific" (page 5). When the chemical weapons shipment out of Germany started in July 1990, NBC news anchor Tom Brokaw disclosed the name of the village in Germany, Klausen, but said that the weapons were being shipped "to an island in the Pacific." Klausen has a name, it has citizens who can be photographed. Johnston Island is empty and nameless, and is restricted to JACADS personnel.

This empty notion of the Pacific was first deployed by Euro-American explorers in the eighteenth century who "encountered a place they defined as largely empty in meaning, lacking in culture, but available for western expansion."[48] These explorers, such as Captain Cook, were characteristically part of their nation's military. According to this military logic, the Pacific is not just an empty ocean; even the islands are seen as empty and nameless until soldiers add strategic value. James Michener provides a telling mix of the images of the Pacific and the military in the promotional brochure for *South Pacific*. When Michener names "his island" in the "Pacific backwater," it is not the native name, or even a Euro-American imperialist name, but the US Navy's strategic appellation "CASU-10." Likewise, in the opening lines of the film *South Pacific*, when Joe Cable asks the pilot, "What are those islands over there?," the response is not a name but simply the relevant strategic signifier: "Japanese."

According to American military narratives that are now circulated through tourist promotions,[49] Johnston Atoll was discovered by accident on September 2, 1796; the captain of *USS Sally* thought that it was so empty and insignificant that it did not warrant a name. Although Hawaiians traditionally call it Kalama Island, in 1807 Lt. William Smith of the *HMS Cornwallis* named it after his captain, Charles J. Johnston. The military contractor in charge of JACADS underlines the important presence of absence on Johnston Atoll on its project homepage:

> More than 200 years ago the American brig Sally out of Boston ran aground off an uncharted isle in the Pacific Ocean. Skipper Joseph Pierpont looked at the barren strand of coral and sand and declared it useless, unworthy even of giving it a name. Still he dutifully logged the coordinates and, helped by the tide, kedged his ship off the reef leaving behind an island whose far and distant isolation would one day become its most valuable feature.[50]

The theme of "isolation" is repeated throughout the literature as Johnston Atoll's defining feature. The first lines of army documents, EPA reports and newspaper articles stress this. For example, the EPA's webpage that outlines the "background and history" of JACADS begins, "Johnston Atoll is one of the most isolated land masses on Earth. As the only shallow water and dry land area in millions of square miles of ocean . . . ."[51] Due to this isolation, the contractor states that

> No better place on earth could be found than Johnston Atoll for the US Army to build the prototype integrated chemical weapons disposal

facility that would prove safe enough to serve as a model of design and operation in the continental United States.[52]

The Pacific is thus deemed remote enough to swallow Euro-America's garbage. Just as in the nineteenth century when the US valued Johnston Atoll for its abundant guano deposits, in the late twentieth century Johnston Atoll and the Pacific Ocean are seen as valuable for waste disposal.

Indeed, this rhetoric of isolation and emptiness is not just a problem of the military, for it pervades even critical discussions of the Pacific. For example, while *American Lake: Nuclear Peril in the Pacific* carefully analyzes the horrific plans for nuclear war in the region, the authors talk little about the Pacific Basin itself. Although they are highly critical of US military policy in the Pacific, they basically adopt the discourse of the "South Pacific" as an empty space that is flown over en route to more important things. Their discussion revolves around the Pacific Rim, largely bypassing the islands in the Pacific Basin, in order to discuss the US, Korea, Southeast Asia, Australia and New Zealand. Even though the anti-nuclear movements in Vanuatu, Belau and Hawai'i are mentioned, the sites of these exemplary activities are mentioned only in passing—sometimes as otherwise nameless "island states."[53] They are ignored because the Pacific is still seen as someone else's lake: American Lake, Japanese Lake, Australian Lake, French Lake.[54] Johnston Island and the surrounding Pacific Ocean thus are represented by Euro-American media—military, civilian and critical—as being isolated and empty. Such policies are declared as "rational" and "responsible" because Johnston Island and the other islands are far enough away from "Euro-American shores" to be insignificant.

## Chemical reactions in Oceania

Since the US government declared that it was responsible for the weapons, it was obligated to remove them from Germany. Yet, as this rhetoric of responsibility works against the interests of the Pacific, it is necessary to transform the questions of safety to questions of responsibility and democracy: responsible to whom, and just who is responding? In *South Pacific*, the only islanders of interest are "exotic" women and children who are probably Southeast Asian. So who is deciding where to dispose of European chemical weapons, and who is affected in the new "South Pacific"? The discourse surrounding JACADS shows how the army evades the political aspects of the "Where" and "Who" questions because the decision to incinerate in the Pacific was made in Bonn and Washington, DC. Once again, a North Atlantic problem was solved by sending it to the "South Pacific."

Indeed, the diplomatic performance of "chemical demilitarization" is much like the song and dance in *South Pacific*. Bush sang to Kohl much like (the American) Nellie sings of her problems with (the European) Emile in the film. This song of Euro-American relations is "born on the opposite sides of the sea." Even though the relationship is between North Atlantic powers/lovers, Nellie sings her song by the shore of the Pacific, just as George H.W. Bush sang about toxic waste in the Pacific. Hence, once again, a North Atlantic policy-making process has decided to use the Pacific as a dumping ground for Euro-American problems.

Conversely, rather than negotiating with Pacific Island leaders, Bush, the army, and the State Department merely reported what was being done to Pacific Islanders. Indeed, Australia aided the US Army and used similar diversionary tactics "to 'manage' the debate" at the 1990 annual South Pacific Commission Meeting.[55] Much like the army's performance in the EIS public review process in Honolulu, Australia withheld scientific reports until the last moment, making informed criticism by Pacific Island leaders more difficult. When their criticism persisted, the State Department stated that it was "insulted" by Pacific Island leaders' continued protests after "information sessions."

Concerned citizens in Honolulu also questioned the JACADS program, which some activists saw as another example of a patriarchal and militarized society dumping its wastes in the Pacific far away from Euro-American populations. In testimony at hearings for the extension and modification of the JACADS EIS in 1997 an activist from the American Friends Service Committee recalled that:

> Many of us around the Pacific have been opposed to using the Pacific to experiment with chemical weapons incineration in the first place. The use of the Pacific in this manner by the US government and military was and is continuing to be a clear case of environmental racism. Combined with all of its past exploits of the region and the resulting damage to people and the environment, the message to the US government from the peoples of the Pacific is that "enough is enough."[56]

Since Pacific Islanders did not build or benefit from the construction of these weapons, and were not protected by the weapons stored in Europe, many protestors asked "Why do the Germans have more influence than Pacific Islanders in the Pacific?"

While this may seem a rhetorical question in Washington or Bonn, in Honolulu it was seen as a question of survival. At the public meeting of March 1990, some of the Hawaiian nationalists tried to utilize the power/knowledge dynamic by switching language as a means of resistance. Naming is a method of exercising power, so resistance groups referred to the island by its Hawaiian name—Kalama Island—rather than its Anglo-American name. Indeed, by using the Hawaiian language to express their concerns, some speakers likewise disrupted the army's dominant, jargon-filled discourse. Marsha Joyner, for example, ended her testimony by asking the army to "please listen to our pleas."[57] This was after she had shifted the podium so that she could speak to the audience, rather than just speak to the army brass. This use of language and space served to highlight the racial nature of the program, and thus to consolidate Hawaiian resistance. But it had little impact on the army, whose response to these speakers was no response; the army was not capable of addressing the argument on these terms. It simply ignored these speakers or brushed them aside; in 1990 General Buss thanked Joyner for her "eloquence."

But the army did not hold all the cards. Due to pressure from the public, the commentary periods were much longer for major revisions to the EIS in 1997 and 2000: whereas only six days were allowed in 1990, the army allowed over fourteen weeks in 2000. Moreover, the gains were not just procedural. They were also substantial: after extensive commentary from the EPA and the public, the army was forced to revise its Closure Plans to meet higher safety standards for cleaning up JACADS. As the EPA commented after final approval for the revised plan in 2002: "Several changes have been made to the Closure Plan, thanks to those of you who have sent comments to the EPA. We appreciate your involvement."[58]

Still, in many ways it was a privilege even to air concerns about JACADS. Public hearings were only held in Honolulu, Hawai'i, excluding input by other affected Pacific Islanders. Remembering the nuclear imperialism of the 312 American, French and British tests in the Pacific between 1946 and 1996,[59] Pacific Islanders unanimously opposed the JACADS project. The army's response was: "There's no good reason to hold hearings in Micronesia. There will be no impacts. Even if you're right next to it downwind there's going to be no problem."[60] The South Pacific Commission, the main regional organization of Oceanic states, thought otherwise, drawing its conclusions in terms of a "science of marine environments" as opposed to the army's "science of the continents": "Unfortunately, islands are not totally isolated from the rest of the biosphere. The oceanic and atmospheric systems surround them and link them with the rest of the world."[61] As a doctor reasoned, "It is a real worry that Pacific Islanders, including we in Hawai'i, ... may be vulnerable to contamination via our fish and other migratory creatures."[62] Or as Jean-Marie Tjibaud of the New Caledonian Government Council explained, "The great ocean that surrounds us carries the seeds of life. We must ensure that they don't become the seeds of death."[63]

Resistance to weapons of mass destruction in Oceania thus is leading to theoretical innovations. While the army uses a rhetoric of isolation and emptiness to understand the Pacific as a collection of tiny islands scattered in a vast ocean, Pacific Islanders have been positing new ways of understanding their social and environmental ecosystems as a mode of resistance. Instead of defining the region in terms of the discourse of "Pacific Islands," which highlights small and isolated land surfaces, Epeli Hau'ofa reverses this hegemonic approach to declare that "The world of Oceania is not small; it is huge and growing bigger every day." He argues that:

There is a gulf of difference between viewing the Pacific as "islands in a far sea" and as "a sea of islands." The first emphasizes dry surfaces in a vast ocean far from the centers of power. When you focus this way you stress the smallness and remoteness of the islands. The second is a more holistic perspective in which things are seen in the totality of their relationships.[64]

The Oceanic ecosystem links people not just with the land, but with the water, transforming some of the smallest countries in the world—Kiribati, the Federated States of Micronesia, French Polynesia—into some of the largest countries in the world.[65]

This view of Oceania as "a sea of islands" also refigures human relationships in the region. In the nineteenth century European imperialists drew colonial boundaries in the sea that served to regulate Pacific Islanders as populations by confining them to tiny spaces. According to Hauʻofa's dynamic view of space, Oceania is unhindered by boundaries; it is a fluid space that people constantly traverse in order to build social and cultural networks that facilitate the flow of wealth and power in a new political-economy.[66] The world view of "a sea of islands" thus generates sites of resistance to the hegemonic view of an empty Pacific deployed in the narratives of naturalization and reassurance that justify military policies. Along with other performances such as making technical commentaries on the EIS, refiguring space and speaking Hawaiian at public meetings, thinking of Oceania as "a sea of islands" challenges the hegemonic frame of reference, and thus is a theoretical response to the militarization of the Pacific.

## Conclusion: alternative policy proposals

In 2000, the JACADS facility finished its mission of chemical weapons demilitarization, and in 2004 the plant closure, destruction and clean-up was complete. But at what cost? There was a 550 percent cost overrun for the project, growing from projected costs of $233 million in 1987 to $1.4 billion by the time the facility was shut down in 2001. Likewise, JACADS took much more time than planned to "demilitarize" the chemical weapons: the initial EIS envisioned a ten-year project from 1985 to 1995. But when JACADS finally closed in 2004, the project had taken almost twice as long as anticipated. Moreover, although the clean-up is complete, people are still forbidden from visiting Kalama Island.

Even with the army's elaborate deployment of narrative strategies of naturalization and reassurance that stress "science and safety" in order to overwrite its very contingent and political decisions, certain things are clear: the US Army manufactured chemical weapons, and it is now responsible for their destruction. Rather than limiting the critique of JACADS to what Poka Laenui accurately describes as "a public policy process gone haywire,"[67] it is necessary to examine the army's political responsibility—

in order to make it respond better to affected people. This chapter has argued that a critique of army policy involves confronting not just the discourse of "chemical demilitarization," but also the discourse of the "South Pacific." It is necessary to challenge not only specific military policies, but the wider discourse where the Pacific is constructed in the popular and military imagination as an empty place, a sign that not only needs to be filled with meaning, but with toxic waste as well. To accomplish this analysis, we need to go beyond the army's enticements to focus on the "state-of-the-art" technology of the JACADS incinerators; we need to examine the technology of the "chemical weapons disposal" discourse as it reproduces a militarized Pacific.

In order to better formulate public policy for laudable aims, such as chemical weapons disposal, it is necessary to avoid reproducing the hierarchical relations of power that generated the chemical weapons in the first place. The army should not have such an exclusive control over the environmental impact assessment process. Toxic waste disposal programs need to be produced and reviewed by a more diverse group of organizations—local, national and international—with specific action taken to include Pacific Islanders. Moreover, the EIS should cover all phases of the project, so that a full range of alternatives can be developed and considered by the army, US citizens, non-governmental organizations, international organizations and people from other countries. The EIS should be written by an autonomous organization that solicits input from a variety of reputable sources and should be reviewed by all nations that would be affected by the decision. This appeal to a broader notion of civil society that includes Pacific Asians beyond the boundaries of the nation-state would be very time-consuming and expensive; however, it would lead to a safer and more equitable outcome, and set an example of thinking about environmental problems in global terms as well as challenging the hegemonic representation of the "South Pacific." This solution would shift the knowledge/power relationship, whereby the army would, as Trinh T. Minh-ha writes, "commit [it]self to understanding and by understanding, choosing to share [its] power,"[68] thus changing some of the actors in the "South Pacific," as well as the songs they sing.

# 2 Beauty queens, national identity and transnational politics

In the wake of the Asian financial crisis that devastated the Thai economy, two tales were published in 1998 that addressed a looming Thai identity crisis. In an award-winning short story called "Miss Siam," Thawan Masjarat tells a cautionary tale about the political-economic path taken by Thailand over the past few decades. While the kingdom's political economy shifted first from agriculture to industry, and then to globalization before crash landing in economic crisis, "Miss Siam" traces the experiences of Nommaew, a country girl who follows a similar trajectory through local, national and international beauty pageants. After winning the local Miss Agriculture pageant, Nommaew is recruited by a promoter who changes not only her appearance and manners, but even her name to the more urban and sophisticated Karaket. With this rebranding, Karaket goes on to win Miss Industry and then Miss Siam. She only falls at the final hurdle, losing the "Miss Mega-Universe Pageant" because her English was not fluent. Criticizing Thailand's mad rush for economic development in the 1990s, which that was built on the soft foundation of property speculation, Thawan tells us that the promoter's superficial tutoring did not work to improve the country girl. Just as Thailand begged the IMF to bail it out in 1997, Miss Siam ends up having to sell herself to survive the economic crisis. Thailand needs to reconsider its developmental path of urban industrialization, Thawan tells us; Miss Siam has to reject the material attractions of the city, and go back to "the original root of Miss Agriculture in the rural district."[1]

The second story from 1998 proves that truth is stranger than fiction. In a book called *Boot Camp*, Areeya Chumsai records her experiences on the Thai Army's nine-week basic training course. Although there already were women in the military,[2] Areeya was a special case: she was Miss Thailand 1994. The first lines of her book recognize this oddity: "Who would have thought a girl who's known for posing in high heels with a big smile

---

Based on an article from *Alternatives: Social Transformation and Humane Governance*, Volume 23, Number 1, Jan.–Mar. 1998. Copyright © by Lynne Rienner Publishers. Used with permission.

splashed across her face would trade a glamorous life for grunge, sweat and combat boots?"[3] Areeya, or Lt. Pop, never really answers this question; the book is playful, recording how boot camp not only toughened her up, but also was lots of fun. The entertainment value of the nine-week course was recorded in dozens of color photos of Areeya not only biking, running and kayaking, but shooting pistols, rifles and a bazooka (see Figure 2.1). She thus was more than a simple soldier; Areeya "became the unofficial mascot of my troop and to the Thai army."[4] These pictures were taken not just by her pals in the platoon, but by professionals from *Today's Woman* magazine who deftly wove together the discourses of beauty, national security and consumption.

At a few points in *Boot Camp*, Areeya does get serious. She suggests that she was drawn to the army as part of an identity crisis. Because the military "is the largest dominating presence in Thai history, government and the present way of life. I really believe that to understand the Thai military is to understand a major part of what it means to be Thai."[5] Here, Areeya agrees with her commanding officers, four of whom took time out from their busy schedules to write forewords for her book. They are tickled pink that Miss Thailand would join the army, which the army commander-in-chief tells us is highly selective. It requires "knowledge, ability, strength, perseverance, and willingness to accept the military code ... Lt Areeya Chumsai has all of these qualities."[6] Another general who is the director of Army television agrees that Areeya is the "model of

*Figure 2.1* Miss Thailand in basic training, 1998. Used with the permission of Future Publishing Co. Ltd, Bangkok, Thailand

present day Thai women who are as able as men."[7] The head of Thailand's army reserve credits it to Areeya's American experience (she moved to the US at age four and lived there for seventeen years):

> what impressed me the most is that although Pop speaks her mind like American children, she behaves like a Thai by preserving Thai customs and manners, by showing her teachers and her commanders humility and respect. This is unexpected. Pop or Lt. Areeya Chumsai, Miss Thailand, has proven herself to be a good Lt. for the army.[8]

Lt. Pop went on to have a distinguished career as an English lecturer in the Royal Thai Military Academy—for a few years anyway.[9] While Miss Siam presents a cautionary tale about the risks of straying from national roots, Miss Thailand is a trans/national model not just for Thai women, but for the army and the nation.

Such media productions grow out of a deeply militarized understanding of identity and security.[10] Cynthia Enloe writes that "Militarization relies on distinct notions about masculinity," where the state expends considerable resources to convince boys that military service is a natural part of "becoming a man."[11] This public expenditure to guarantee the congruence of manhood, militarization and nationalism is most obviously seen in recruiting advertisements. But, as we saw in the last chapter, it also works itself out in how the military and police are portrayed on the silver screen and television.[12]

Yet Enloe also argues that such militarized masculine national discourses "have staying power only if they are legitimized by women as well as men."[13] Beyond appointing Queen Sirikit as a full general in the Thai Army and Lt. Pop to the military academy, women act as girlfriends, wives and mothers to support "the boys in green." The state and business in Thailand have each expended considerable resources to shape the Thai identity, including "Thai woman," to meet their shifting needs.[14] While the official model for a Thai man is the heroic soldier, the ideal Thai woman is a beauty queen, who then "naturally" becomes a housewife and mother to complete the iconic narrative of the nation as family. This was comically verified in the first "Mister Thailand pageant" (1994) in ways that revealed the anxieties of Thai masculine identity. Finalists were asked, "If possible, would you rather have been born a man or a woman?" *The Nation* reported that the contestants all "gave similar answers emphasizing male strength and their duty to protect women and their country (by being soldiers)."[15] Like Miss Thailand 1994, Mr Thailand 1994 performed as an odd hybrid of military beauty queen.

This ideal pairing of heroic warrior and beauty queen is not limited to Thailand. Miss America 1944 was painted on a bomber to become the official mascot of the 301st Bomb Group during World War II.[16] The symbolic power of the Marcos dictatorship in the Philippines was supported by the discursive pairing of Ferdinand the heroic soldier with Imelda the beauty queen. In the 1990s, this link between men's national service as a soldier and women's national service as a mother was mooted as government policy in Singapore.[17] Back in Thailand, Field Marshal Sarit Thannarat, who ruled Thailand from 1957 to 1963, was famous for recruiting his mistresses at local beauty pageants.[18] A more ideal marriage of Thai warrior and beauty queen was consummated in the 1980s: Army Commander General Chavalit Yongchaiyudh's wife Pankrua was not just a beauty queen; she was also a judge in the Miss Thailand beauty pageant. Chavalit took this nationalist logic one step further when he became prime minister in 1996. Each of these odd examples underlines how beauty queens serve as role models for women and for the nation, as part of the militarization of civil society.

In this chapter, I will argue that "Miss Thailand" is a high-profile example of gendered national identity production that highlights the tension in civil/military relations between civilizing the military and militarizing society.[19] The institution of Miss Thailand is an interesting example of cultural governance because it does not simply restrict women, but actively serves to create a positive productive image of the "Thai woman" for circulation both at home and abroad. Although their aim is to support militarized nationalism and consumerism, the categories of "Miss Thailand" and "Thai woman" often have an uncomfortable fit. Both Thawan's Miss Siam and Areeya's Miss Thailand suggest that there are slippages and room for resistance.

By focusing on the media's role in constructing the "model Thai woman" we can see how television viewers consume not just programs and products, but a specific range of images, and thus choices for each individual viewer's (national) identity. This is a complex and self-reflexive process: the media constructs the image of Miss Thailand, while at the same time the Miss Thailand beauty pageant with its huge audiences is important in promoting the media, especially the television industry. Simultaneously, Miss Thailand herself serves as an ambassador—a medium—for Thai identity both at home and abroad. Indeed, national beauty pageants now fit into a global political economy of beauty—the main responsibility of Miss Thailand is to go to the Miss Universe pageant. In a strange way, sending a representative to Miss Universe confirms a state's sovereignty in international society in ways that are similar to sending an ambassador to the United Nations. Moreover, just as holding the Olympics is seen as a sign that a country is prosperous and strong, hosting an international beauty pageant confirms that a country is a model world citizen: as part of its entry into international society, Beijing is hosting the 2008 Olympics, and China lifted its fifty-four-year ban on beauty pageants to host the Miss World 2003 pageant.[20]

To discuss this web of representations, I will employ semiotic analysis in two forms. The first section will engage in a synchronic analysis of the

Miss Thailand 1994 pageant to demonstrate how the image is scripted according to male desire. I argue that the televised pageant interpellates Thai women and men into specific gendered identities. But this gendered national identity is neither sure nor static. There are various pressures pushing and pulling at Miss Thailand not just in gendered space, but also in state, national, economic and transnational space. Questions of "authenticity" waver between surveillance over the contestant's Thai cultural characteristics, and whether her costume is strategically padded. Hence, through a diachronic analysis of the history of Miss Thailand, the second section considers the forces that have produced this "authentic" image. Miss Thailand's pockmarked history has curious overlaps with the development of the print and electronic media. Indeed, all are involved in the massification of information and identity; considering the role of television can help us bring out Miss Thailand's role in cultural governance. The third section continues the synchronic analysis of the Miss Thailand pageant to show how the contestants confirm the model of the ideal Thai woman laid out in the first section. Although it is common to see beauty pageants as evidence of Euro-American cultural imperialism, the conclusion argues that Thais are willing participants in this global political economy of beauty. Whereas Thawan's Miss Siam reacts to urban (Western) cultural imperialism with an appeal to the cultural nativism of village life, Thai popular culture is going transnational. Rather than simply promoting essential (and exotic) Thai identity, the pageant has been part of constructing national identity in an explicitly transnational way: Miss Thailand is often the product of the international linkages of mating and education. Thai identity projects thus increasingly appeal to hybrid mixes of foreign and domestic, even selecting a blue-eyed beauty queen in 1996.

## Synchronic analysis of the Miss Thailand 1994 pageant

It wasn't my idea to watch the Miss Thailand 1994 beauty pageant. I had other plans for that Saturday night. It was my wife's desire to see this contest that directed my gaze away from other attractions. This was not an isolated case: the Miss Thailand pageant is one of the most-watched programs in the kingdom; according to the pageant's director, Chin Ampornratana, its audience includes many highly educated urban Thai women.[21] This may seem contradictory, since the hegemonic image of beauty pageants is of "meat markets" where women are defined in terms of the vital measurements of bust, waist and hips, to be paraded as potential mistresses for rich and powerful men. Indeed, it was this criticism that caused the suspension of the Miss Thailand beauty pageant after the October 14, 1973 democratic uprising.

But over the past three decades viewing patterns of beauty pageants have shifted remarkably. Polls in the US show that most people do not see the Miss America pageant as degrading to women, and the Chinese public is more "tolerant" toward them.²² Indeed, the main measures now seem to be talent and intelligence rather than 36–24–36. The Miss America pageant is the largest single source of academic scholarships for women, which can be seen in the names of some state pageants: the Miss Hawai'i Scholarship Pageant.²³ Although there are no scholarships for Miss Thailand, the educational level of the contestants is recorded on the same chart with the "vital statistics," birthplace, age, height and weight in the semi-official program for Miss Thailand 1994.²⁴ Likewise, public opinion polls of Thai youth demonstrate that women and men both support the Miss Thailand beauty pageant.²⁵ Thus, although beauty pageants used to showcase women for men, now the main audience is women.

The television media is a crucial factor in this shift of Miss Thailand's audiences from men to women, and from primarily upper-class groups to a mass audience. The commercial television industry has turned women into the primary consumers of both its programs and its advertisements. Daytime programming in the US is "designed almost exclusively to attract the largest number of women between the ages of eighteen and forty-nine—the proportion of the population that makes the vast majority of consumer purchasing decisions."²⁶ Likewise, Kanjana Kaewthep reports that Thai soap operas have "housewives as the target group."²⁷

This shift occurred because many more women are involved in the public sphere, both as purchasing agents for the family and in paid labor outside the home. Parallel to this is the growth of the sex and pornography industry: men can see more female skin on the street, at the beach or in the massage parlor than at any beauty pageant. Hence, the television audience for the beauty pageant is primarily women looking for fashion tips. The opening of the pageant confirms this with dozens of women marching out in many different styles of fashionable clothing. Thus, rather than men looking at women for flesh value, women are looking at women to see how they can clothe themselves—albeit in revealing ways.

In the early days of the Miss Thailand pageant this fascination with the body was part of state policy to promote hygiene, public health and beauty among Thai women. In the 1930s, the state declared: "Miss Thailand will make Thai women more interested in taking care of their body [because] their upper body is too long and their lower body is too short."²⁸ In recent years the commercial aspect of the pageant constructs this "public health" in order to sell products. The advertisements and sponsors are very gendered: while beer and whisky ads accompany sports programs, commercials for health and beauty aids are directed specifically at women. Colgate Palmolive is the main sponsor of the pageant spending around Bt10 million (US$250,000) in 1994, and other sponsors include Catalina bathing suits and Revlon makeup.²⁹ After the pageant, Miss Thailand is expected to take this commercialized "public health" campaign on the road. As Areeya explained at the end of her reign, "[t]his title means that I have obligations to fulfill and duties to perform such as promoting better oral health out in the provinces for Colgate."[30] Hence, the Miss Thailand pageant is like television where the "programs are really only pre-texts for the real content of television—advertising messages."[31]

However, there are still possibilities for women to achieve greater control over their lives through this very public medium. Beauty pageants even became part of the "women's rights" campaign in Thailand; discussion of equal rights was publicly provoked by a high-profile divorce case involving a former Miss Thailand/Miss Universe.[32] This public uproar generated a political debate that eventually led to a constitutional amendment that guaranteed equal rights for women and men. Beauty pageants, thus, are one arena that reflects the feminist struggle between public and private. Traditionally women are limited to the private sphere of home and hearth to perform the biological duties of sex, mating and child rearing. Men, on the other hand, act in the public sphere of business and the state. Beauty pageants are interesting because they parade women in very public spaces—convention center stages and television screens—in the very private role of "the good woman."

Hence, this has been a problematic route to empowerment for women in Thailand. Much like controversies over the Miss America pageant in the 1920s,[33] the Thai beauty contest was criticized in the mass media as being improper for women when it was initiated in 1934. Organizers recognized that it was shameful and disgraceful for women: "At first society cannot accept the fact that daughters go out in public to have their pictures published in the newspaper."[34] But they went on to say that times had changed; it now would be an honor for contestants "to help the state and the nation" by "sacrific[ing] their own happiness to show people their body in order to enliven the atmosphere of the Constitution Festival." When the bathing suit competition was introduced in 1953, that year's Miss Thailand asked: "Am I brave enough to wear this in public?" The state's Office of the Miss Thailand Pageant responded that it was not shameful, for bathing suits showed how modern and proper Thai women were. The state also said that it would make the contest more "fair" because the bathing suit competition would make it more difficult for contestants to cheat.[35]

The ideology of Miss Thailand works here to bring women into the public sphere, but only in ways that do not challenge the patriarchy. The requirements for contestants have always been very clear: although women are displaying their bodies, they are doing it in a virtuous way that preserves the ideology of virginity. The application rules over the years have stated that women could not be involved in "shameful professions," suffer from unspeakable social diseases, or have a husband. Since marriage in Thailand is not so much a legal status as the social relationship of living together, in the 1980s the marriage restriction was extended to exclude women who had children.[36] The character whom we call "Miss Thailand" thus is constructed in a specific way for a particular patriarchal project that invokes and supports both nationalism and commercialism. As Laura Mulvey tells us, a beauty pageant "is not an erotic exhibition; it is a public celebration of the traditional female road to success."[37]

With television the contestants are displayed not just on the printed page, but are performing before an audience of what film theorists call the "male gaze." Because women cannot return this look, the male gaze defines femininity according to what men desire women to be, rather than according to women's wishes. To put it simply, only a man knows how to be a good woman—and this is seen in such diverse genres as traditional Thai folk drama (Lakorn Nok), Japanese Noh and Kabuki drama, Elizabethan theater, as well as many Hollywood films including *Mrs. Doubtfire*, *M. Butterfly*, *Tootsie* and *Some Like It Hot*. Mulvey explains that female desire is thus dependent on man as the subject and woman as the object:

> Woman ... stands in patriarchal culture as a signifier for the male other, bound by symbolic order in which man can live out his fantasies and obsessions through linguistic command by imposing them on the silent image of woman still tied to her place as bearer, not maker, of meaning.[38]

This gaze is one-way and voyeuristic—that is what makes it political. "To be naked is to be oneself," John Berger writes. "To be nude is to be seen naked by others and not recognized for oneself. A naked body has to be seen as an object in order to become a nude."[39] Although Berger is discussing European art, the same relations hold for print media, film and television worldwide: the female body is semiotically constructed in gendered terms as the object of the male gaze, "the site of multiple male pleasures."[40] Mulvey thus concludes that "[i]n a world ordered by sexual imbalance, pleasure in looking has been split between active/male and passive/female. The determining male gaze projects its fantasy onto the female figure, which is styled accordingly."[41] This logic works in the major themes of modern Thai film with its "emphasis on masculinity and on being the master. The leading actresses were only used to bring out the strength of the heroes."[42] Likewise, in the 1920s the star of the Miss America pageant was not Miss America, but King Neptune; beauty contestants served as Neptune's "mermaids" and "sea nymphs."[43]

The organizers of the 1994 Miss Thailand pageant must have been consulting Mulvey and Berger because the narrative of masculine desire was performed on stage. Between the "evening wear section" and the "bathing suit parade," four young, eligible bachelors sauntered out stage-left to sing us a song: "You are the woman that I always dreamed of." With this song they began to construct the perfect Thai woman. Each time they enunciated their desired qualities, stage-right lit up, and out danced their dream woman. This underlines how the purpose of beauty pageants is to produce "respectable Thai women." Mulvey comments that the 1970 Miss World contest was held light years away from the underground of pornography: this spectacle took place in the very public Royal Albert Hall where:

> The atmosphere was emphatically respectable. . . . The conventionality of the girls' lives and the ordinariness of their aspirations—Miss Grenada (Miss World): "Now I'm looking for the ideal man to marry"—was the keynote of all the pre- and post-competition publicity.[44]

Back in Bangkok, what did the eligible bachelors desire? Women's beauty is for men, but these four white-dinner-jacketed guys are also practical and cosmopolitan. In other words, beauty is necessary, but not sufficient for the ideal Thai woman, who also needs social skills and earning power—in other words, a modern woman who can do it all. This echoes what the Director of Television Channel 7 said as he was reorganizing the Miss Thailand pageant in 1984: "We must admit that the world is shrinking, and these changes affect Miss Thailand too. She cannot be sweetly beautiful as she used to be. She must be good in her figure, her personality and her language."[45]

Back at the Miss Thailand 1994 pageant, Bachelor Number One said his dream girl would be a good housewife, and PING! out spun a former Miss Thailand donning a sparkling white apron tied over her sensible business attire. The choreography of her dance made full use of her wok in one hand and a spatula in the other to promote the products of cooking oil sponsors, as well as the image of a model Thai woman (see Figure 2.2). Just to make sure we understood her mission, she sang "I work all day, and work all night too," with a beautiful smile that spread from the public to the private sphere as she danced for her suitors.

Back to the boys on stage-left: Bachelor Number Two wants to have fun. Out dances a party girl, clothed in a short, bright yellow dress and wiggling her body suggestively in 1960s retro dance steps. She sings lyrics parading her youth and energy, of going out on the town and traveling the world in her own style.

Bachelor Number Three is the dreamer; he wants a woman who is socially aware. The male gaze shifts to the right, and a caring woman dances out the door to sing about helping society. But while social problems —poverty, AIDS, pollution—are characteristically dirty, she miraculously stays clean, perhaps because she is surrounded by a bevy of angels adorned with fluffy white wings. Hence, women are in the public sphere, but only as care-takers and do-gooders in the socialite-style charity work characteristic of beauty queens.

Bachelor Number Four is looking for a strong woman. The producers oblige by spewing out a character who is surrounded by "Old Siam" royal images. The classical Thai music provides a curious departure from the Western soundtrack, at least until she starts singing her "strong

## 52  Beauty queens, national identity, transnational politics

*Figure 2.2* Miss Thailand the professional housewife, 1994. © William A. Callahan

woman" song to the melody of "It never rains in Southern California." The transition in this performance is interesting because it goes against cultural nativist notions of tradition as the core: as the music modernizes (and Westernizes) the dancers step out of their "traditional" costumes into modern street clothes. This could be a simple chronological narrative, but it also suggests that "tradition" is a facade because the Thai soul is "modern."

Although the eligible bachelors sing Billy Joel's "Don't go changing to try and please me" as they dance together with their dream girls, they very clearly laid out a four-point plan for constructing the model Thai woman. The judges—who included two police generals, the wife of the Interior Minister, although none from the Judiciary—obliged, picking the contestant who combined this curious mix of public and private, Thai and foreign. Before we see how they measured up, it is necessary to see the other ideologies hiding in the wings at the Miss Thailand pageant.

## Diachronic analysis: Miss Thailand and television

Beauty may be timeless, but Thai beauty pageants certainly are not. The host of the show told us that the first Miss Siam was crowned in 1934. But what she did not say was that in over twenty-six of the last seventy-one years there has been no Miss Thailand. The announcers tell us of the glorious beginnings, but they never tell of the disjunctures, of when the contest stopped, and why. The unstable history of this national symbol is instructive. It is a history of starts (1934, 1948, 1964, 1984), stops (1940, 1955, 1972) and pauses (1970, 1998) that weave their way through modern Thai history and the ideologies of constitutionalism, nationalism and commercialism—not to mention feminism.

There are three periods of the Miss Thailand Pageant. The first period, 1934–40 and 1948–55, is characterized by state organization and official nationalist ideology. The second period, 1964–72 (excluding 1970), is characterized by a shift from state to private organization, and a commercial ideology. The third period, from 1984 to the present (excluding 1998), is characterized by global capitalist modernity.

The Miss Thailand contest is also intimately intertwined in the history of the mass media as it developed from print to radio to television. Through all its incarnations, Miss Thailand has served as a media for "Thailand," with its message changing as the site of its organization and enunciation shifted. In the first period the contest was organized by the state, so Miss Thailand conveyed state policy and public relations. In the other stages the contest was organized by private groups, usually businesses, so her mission changed to the private sphere of advertising and consumption.

## *Miss Siam and the promotion of the Constitution*

The Miss Siam contest is an important milestone of the early democratic period of Thai history that followed the 1932 revolution. The beauty pageant emerged as a product of the dramatic changes in the 1930s from absolute monarchy to constitutional government to military state that made the decade a watershed of Thai history. Indeed, for the first time Thailand, and much of Euro-America, was shaping political power and mass participation through a management of national history and culture through new popular media.

In 1934 the new state formed the Association of the Constitution to organize a festival to celebrate the political and social legitimacy of the 1932 revolution against Thailand's absolute monarchy. The new state expended considerable resources on this symbolic event, which is noteworthy for two reasons: the Depression hit Thailand hard, and royal extravagance was one of the main justifications for the 1932 revolution. The purpose of the Association of the Constitution's campaign was to make the document "a revered object of national importance," and thus transfer popular loyalty from the monarchy to the constitution.[46] The Constitution Festival thus included religious ceremonies as well as popular entertainment events such as speech contests, singing contests, poems and dancing. The Miss Siam pageant was inaugurated on Constitution Day, December 10, 1934, as a performance "to disseminate democratic ideology." Miss Siam thus served as a "media of entertainment to attract the attention of people to come to the Constitutional Festival" because the contest itself "promote[d] democracy by selecting a beauty to grace the constitution."⁴⁷

In this way, the Miss Siam contest graphically served to undermine royal legitimacy. While the legitimacy and power of the absolute monarchy was shrouded in mysterious rituals such as the "Water Curse," after the 1932 Revolution the representative of Thailand was a "beauty queen"—a commoner chosen by other commoners in a very public forum. Miss Siam was crowned with a hybrid artifact that marked the transition from absolutist to constitutional state: a crown engraved with a picture of the Constitution. The first Miss Siam, Kanya Tiansawang, illustrates the new commoner elite that emerged with the 1932 revolution (see Figure 2.3). Kanya had a high school diploma from an elite school—a very high level of education at the time for women or men. More importantly, she was employed in the honorable middle-class profession of teaching, and was skilled in embroidery, dress-making and cooking—all the marks of a "Siamese lady."⁴⁸

Figure 2.3
Miss Siam crowned, 1934⁴⁹

Although not democratic in the sense of popular elections for political institutions, the Miss Siam contest was representative of Thailand. Interior Ministry officials in local government were instructed to find the beauties in their region and send them to Bangkok. The state sponsored contestants, paying for travel, accommodation and costumes.[50] The pageant was organized by a newly created section of the Interior Ministry called the "Office of the Miss Siam Pageant," which made searching for beautiful women an official duty of government officials. As a lampoon of this practice states:

> to find big busted young women is the big duty of government officials. Anyone who cannot find such a woman will not be promoted because they did not act properly in democracy. Democracy will prosper because we have a beauty contest.[51]

The private sector was also allowed to sponsor contestants starting in 1936, but the field was still dominated by state-sponsored women. The hegemonic media of the day—newspapers—were among the first private sponsors. The responsibilities of Miss Siam included the usual charity work and entertainment, and also included attending parliamentary functions and promoting state policy.[52]

When Field Marshal Phibul Songkram became Prime Minister in 1938 there was a shift of legitimizing discourses from constitutionalism to a militarized nationalism. The Miss Siam contest continued to be held through the Constitution Festival, and helped to build Thai nationalism because young women from all over the kingdom came to Bangkok on equal footing; any citizen could become the archetype for Thai femininity. Thus the contest was emblematic of the new nationalism where Thai identity was constructed more through public performance than through noble birth. But this was a specific form of nationalism. Scot Barmé argues that Thailand adopted a "chauvinistic nationalism according to models provided by Germany, Italy and Japan to create a new, more mass-oriented variety which was deployed on behalf of the new commoner elite that came to power in 1932."[53] Phibul declared that men could not build the Thai nation alone. Women's role in nation-building was to be good mothers and beautiful wives who did not just take care of their families, but also the nation.[54] Once again, while the model for men was the warrior, the model for women was Miss Siam.

The Interior Ministry's Office of the Miss Siam Pageant declared the international aspects of this nationalism: "Miss Siam is the representative of Thai women to show the world that Siam has Miss Siam who is as beautiful as the beauty queens of other countries."[55] Hence, through her physical attributes, Miss Siam is part of the symbolic defense of the Thai nation on the world stage. More to the point, the Miss Siam pageant was part of the very material defense of the regime: the proceeds of the pageant's expensive tickets not only went to promote the constitution and help the poor. The money was also used to purchase weapons for the military.[56]

When Siam became Thailand in 1939, Miss Siam likewise became Miss Thailand as part of the move toward hypernationalism. This name change was the first of the State Conventions (*Rathaniyom*) that guided the increasing militarization of the Phibul regime, which was very gendered. The State Convention on names also required men and women to have suitably "masculine" and "feminine" names. The State Convention on attire prescribed what clothing women and men could wear to specific events. Wichit Wathakan's Dress Committee produced eight dress categories for women, the last of which told beauty pageant contestants what clothes to wear—and what not to wear.[57] In this way, Miss Thailand was instrumental in helping the state promote this unpopular dress policy (which was disregarded even by government officials at the time).

Miss Thailand was also helpful in supporting the Franco-Thai War of 1940–41.[58] Still, the pageant was suspended after 1940 along with the entire Constitutional Festival because World War II came to Thailand. The Miss Thailand pageant was revived in 1948, not so much because the war had ended, but because Phibul returned to power in 1947. Because a coup in 1957 discarded the Constitution, the Constitution Festival was last held in 1956; but the Miss Thailand contest was canceled after the previous year due to moral problems: the contestants had been behaving "improperly."[59]

## *Commercialism: 1964–72*

After nine years without a national beauty queen, the Miss Thailand pageant was revived in 1964. In this short span of time much had happened in Thailand and Southeast Asia that would dramatically affect how the Miss Thailand pageant was organized, and for whom. Most importantly for Thailand and Miss Thailand, the 1957 coup abrogated the Constitution. Indeed, constitutionalism was a severely unstable discourse during the second run of Miss Thailand. There was no Constitution Festival to serve as the venue for the Miss Thailand pageant; hence, the organization of the pageant was taken over by the private sector in the 1960s—although its ties to the Interior Ministry were still strong.

While Miss Siam is firmly placed in the official modern political history of Thailand that begins with the overthrow of the absolute monarchy in 1932, the second incarnation of Miss Thailand is more a part of the social history of Thailand that begins in 1957 with Field Marshal Sarit Thannarat's coup. Indeed, since political activities were tightly controlled under Sarit's despotic paternalism—no Constitution, no political parties, no elections, a tight control of the media—Supatra Kopkijsuksakul argues that people were more active socially. Beauty contests were very popular at this time.[60]

In this political desert people also became very active economically, starting an era of political-economic history that vigorously inserted Thailand into the global political-economy. Although Sarit and his heirs Field Marshals Thanom Kittikachon and Prapas Charusathien put the constitutional system on ice, with help from the World Bank the regime was very active on the economic front. Launching the first national economic development plan in 1961, they dramatically changed state policy from an inward-looking, import substitution program characterized by economic nationalism, to a World Bank-directed, export-promotion strategy that courted international capital. As in Thawan's "Miss Siam" story, the Thai political economy graduated from (Miss) Agriculture to (Miss) Industry to enter capitalist modernity. This authoritarian capitalism further centralized and bureaucratized state policy while extending state intervention for the first time into the daily life of each village in Thailand.[61] As public intellectual Saneh Chamarik concludes: "All of which meant in effect further forced integration of Thai economy into the world market economy. Operation-wise, it was indeed the workmanship of the newly-bred technocracy on its rise to power in the nation's decision-making process."[62]

The growth and spread of electronic media was an important part of this technical approach to the political-economy. Infrastructural development facilitated the state's intervention into daily life because it brought rural Thailand into the modern grid: "Wherever there is electricity, people have access to television. . . . [People] constantly requested electrical service in order to be able to watch television."[63] Desires for electronic media not only brought Thai citizens into the electrical network, but also into the state's network of cultural governance. Indeed, although newspapers were active in the debates surrounding the Miss Thailand pageant, and starting in 1936 were allowed to sponsor their own contestants, Miss Thailand was an important part of the shift in hegemonic media from print to radio to television.

Television loves Miss Thailand much more than other media because beauty is a visual property. Due to its mass-market organization, television also leads to a much wider distribution of the male gaze. Like in the US, the Thai national television network's simultaneity built a national identity shared by the urban elite and the rural masses. Television promoted Miss Thailand and Miss Thailand promoted television: one of the prizes for the winner of the contest was a television. More importantly, both black-and-white television (1955) and color television (1967) were introduced to Thailand through beauty pageants.[64]

To understand the complex relationship between the media and Miss Thailand it is necessary to consider how television constructs "reality." Television is not a simple reflection of reality, but heavily edited and constructed text that structures ways of seeing and pleasure in looking: scopophilia. Mulvey argues that:

> Television revolutionised the conditions of spectatorship associated with mass entertainment . . . to create a home based mode of consumption that was prefigured by radio but without precedent as mass visual entertainment. Whereas the temptation of films was posited on "going out," television appeals to "staying in."[65]

Thus, television brings the world into the living room and, like Miss Thailand, problematizes the public/private distinction. This shift impacts both national and gender identity. Whereas the communal audience for film is limited to the size of a theater, and took place at different times, the use of national relay networks, and then satellites, enabled the television industry to reach all citizens simultaneously for a shared national experience.

The placement of this national medium in the home had a huge effect on women as viewers in the US; television became a force in the 1950s just as "American women were forced back into the home to readjust the unsettling effects of the Second World War on the division of labour between the sexes."[66] Thus, women did not just consume the television programs and advertisements: they also consumed this new image of domestic femininity. "Television condemns us to the Family, whose household utensil it has become," concludes Roland Barthes.[67]

Although the broadcast equipment was imported from the US, the relationship between television and power is different in Thailand. Unlike in America, but much like the Miss Siam pageant, the initial mission of television in the kingdom was not profit, but as a public relations tool for the state:

> television production and broadcasting ha[ve] never been free from political or economic pressure since the beginning of the industry. From the past up to the present time, there were attempts by the governing power clique to control and dictate television operation.[68]

When the first television station, Channel 4, was set up on National Day in 1955, Prime Minister Phibul declared that its goal was "education," not commerce. Although the Miss Thailand pageant had been discontinued, they held a special "Miss Thailand Channel 4 Television Pageant" to launch the channel.

All five television networks in Thailand were set up by autocratic leaders. Because television, much like radio, was under the control of military leaders, the state policy they aimed to promote was actually army policy. The second television channel was set up by Field Marshal Sarit Thanarat in January 1958 just after his first coup d'état in 1957. Its official name was "Army Television Channel 7 (Black and white)," and its purpose was to "create a good relationship and understanding between the army and the people."[69] Although two of the five television stations are leased out to private companies, and new satellite and cable stations invigorated the news environment in the late 1990s, there still is very active control over programming through censorship and self-censorship.[70]

## Miss Vajiravudh becomes Miss Thailand

There were many beauty contests between 1955 and 1964. In addition to the crowning of Miss Thailand on Channel 4 Television, Sarit organized a Miss Thailand Cup in 1957, and a Golden Doll pageant in 1959. But none had the fanfare of the Miss Thailand beauty pageant.

The rebirth of the national pageant was closely intertwined with the workings of the palace. In *Thailand: The Politics of Despotic Paternalism*, Thak Chaloemtiarana argues that after the 1957 coup the monarchy was rehabilitated to displace the Constitution as the main source of political legitimacy.[71] The Thai monarchy was re-imagined from a distant mystical king into people's monarch who traveled the kingdom and the world on high-profile tours. It is curious that the same person—Wichit Wathakan—who created Miss Siam in 1934 as a rival to the monarchy, was crucial to re-inventing the monarchy itself in the 1950s. Rather than having a beauty queen as Thailand's international representative, a beautiful Queen Sirikit traveled extensively as the representative of the Thai nation's "charm and grace" to an international audience.

However, a truly national symbol needed to come from the common people. The most famous beauty pageant at the time was the Vajiravudh College Beauty Queen Contest organized for the Winter Fair of the Vajiravudh College Alumnae Association (VCAA) each November.[72] This fair was held to commemorate the death of King Vajiravudh (Rama VI), who ruled Thailand as an absolute monarch from 1910 to 1926. Thus there is an important shift from the Miss Thailand pageant that the state organized to promote constitutional values, to a contest privately organized by an elite boys' school to commemorate the chief critic of constitutional government. The prizes were very similar, except the crown for the Vajiravudh contest did not have the Constitution engraved on it.

Through a three-year process Miss Vajiravudh was transformed into Miss Thailand. As the World Bank was re-ordering Thailand's national economy to fit into the global political economy, in 1961 another international organization, Miss Universe Inc., came to Thailand to find a suitable contestant for the global political economy of beauty. These representatives first went to the Tourist Authority of Thailand (TAT), who put them in touch with the VCAA. Miss Universe Inc. said that if the VCAA changed the name from the Vajiravudh Beauty Queen Costume Contest to the Miss Thailand pageant, it would pay for the transportation and accommodation of Miss Thailand at the Miss Universe pageant.[73]

Because of criticism from the state and the media Miss Vajiravudh did not become Miss Thailand until 1964. Field Marshal Prapas was a central figure in this transformation since he was both the President of the VCAA and the Minister of the Interior. Even before the re-emergence of Miss Thailand, Prapas used his position to ask government officials to send young women to enter the VCAA pageant, just as in the 1930s. Prapas was powerful, but he was still second in command behind Field Marshal Thanom who became Prime Minister after Sarit's death in 1963. Prapas needed to ask the state for permission to use the "Miss Thailand" brand name for the Vajiravudh contest. In arguing his point Prapas made clear the image of Thai women that he wished to circulate: "To honor Thai women Miss Thailand would never do anything inappropriate. They are properly married and work properly. Beauty Queens with other names are sometimes misled to become mistresses. We must select someone who can protect her own name."[74]

Criticisms of this new Miss Thailand were both economic and political. Newspapers felt that the VCAA just wanted to use the title "Miss Thailand" as an advertising ploy to draw more people to its Winter Fair. As part of a more general power struggle, Thanom also disagreed with the VCAA's plans. He stated that, if the title "Miss Thailand" was used, the pageant should be organized by the state. In 1964 the VCAA Committee, led by Prapas, insisted on using the "Miss Thailand" title without state permission; they only noted that the pageant was sponsored by a private organization. Yet national pride overwhelmed all criticism when the new Miss Thailand 1964, Appasara Hongskunla, was crowned Miss Universe in 1965.

Television was a part of building this broad popular enthusiasm for a national festival and a new national symbol. After the success of the 1964 pageant, the 1965 Miss Thailand pageant was broadcast live on Channel 4. As mentioned above, the inaugural program of color TV on Army Television Station Channel 7 in 1967 was the Miss Thailand pageant. This station obtained the rights from Channel 4 to broadcast the pageant because Prapas was also central in founding Color Television Channel 7 as part of his family business. Indeed, the director of Channel 7 and president of the VCAA are often the same person.

Thus, the second incarnation of the contest was a curious mixture of public and private: through the network power of Field Marshal Prapas, the Ministry of the Interior, Television Channel 7 and the VCAA all cooperated to organize the Miss Thailand pageant. Although it was not state sponsored, Appasara is the daughter of a government official who graduated from Vajiravudh College: like many other elite fathers, he had entered Appasara in the beauty pageant "for the good image of the nation."

But this nationalism had a different character from that in the 1930s and 1940s. Rather than being a state-sponsored nationalism, the second run of Miss Thailand also used nationalism for the profit of business. Both the public and the private sectors profited from Thailand's expanding tourist industry in terms of foreign investment and foreign relations. While Prapas still instructed his government officials to find Thai beauties, there was more private involvement in the second period. Like the television industry in the 1960s, the Miss Thailand pageant began slowly shifting from being a public relations tool of the state to advertising commodities for private consumption. For example, promoters began to look for women to sponsor in the pageant in order to gain commercial benefit. Rather than getting a promotion in the state bureaucracy, the promoters received a percentage of the winnings.[75] Private companies, such as dress-making schools, also sponsored contestants to show off their wares.[76]

The changing responsibilities of the reigning Miss Thailand likewise reflect this shift. Unlike Miss Siam who would attend sessions of parliament, the official state activities of the second period of Miss Thailand were limited to representing the Tourist Authority of Thailand at overseas events. The main activity of Miss Thailand was now charity work.[77]

By the end of the second period Miss Thailand had become a business, as had the beauty contest itself. Yet, we should not exaggerate the commercialization of this period; Miss Thailand herself did few commercials.[78] Actually there was much continuity with the pageant's first run: the judges from the first period were re-enlisted to pick the new Miss Thailand.[79] The major shift was in how Miss Thailand represented the nation. Whereas Miss Siam was largely a medium for domestic state policy, first to legitimize constitutionalism and then hypernationalism, the new Miss Thailand was responsible for promoting the state's foreign policy: making Thailand known to the world. Recall that the idea to change the name of the beauty queen to Miss Thailand came not from the state or Thailand's bourgeoisie, but from Miss Universe Inc. At the time, Thais saw this as an example of the kingdom's close relationship with the US. In 1965 the director of the Tourist Authority of Thailand commented:

> American political policy depends on the people. If more American people know more about the Thai people, they will give friendship to the Thai people. When Appasara became Miss Universe she won not only the judges' hearts, but the people in Miami, America and the World. By obtaining this title, Appasara made the world know Thailand more. It's better than having ten friendship ambassadors. When the American people know the Thai people better, American policy to help Thailand will tighten the friendship between the two countries. Especially in the situation of problems in Asia.[80]

These "problems" led to the Indochina war; American troops were deployed in Thailand beginning in February 1964 with the understanding that they "were in Thailand on the condition that they would move forward into Laos if the situation there threatened Thai security." The armed struggle of the Communist Party of Thailand began in 1965, and the US provided "aid to the military and the police to research projects in the villages."[81] Generally the Miss Thailand contest and the Indochina war worked with each other; the only conflict came in 1970 when the brutalities of the war moved the organizers to cancel the Miss Thailand pageant. But the pageant resumed in 1971.[82]

The second period of the Miss Thailand contest puttered out after the 1972 pageant. It was actually planned for November 1973, but a massive student uprising in October forced Prapas into exile and led to the cancellation of November's VCAA Winter Fair. Without a suitable sponsor, the pageant was cancelled too. In 1974 there was a new Constitution, but holding a beauty contest to celebrate it seemed out of place, especially since this Constitution was the first to guarantee equal rights to women and men. In the newly politicized atmosphere of the mid-1970s, women began to question patriarchal ideology, and criticize beauty pageants for presenting women as sex objects. The class of contestants also had plummeted in the late 1960s from elite daughters such as Appasara, to mistresses for tycoons and government officials. Thus, in the 1970s beauty pageants were criticized as a "sport for rich people who don't have to work."[83]

## Consumerism: 1984 to the present

After twelve years in drydock, Miss Thailand was relaunched in 1984. The purpose of the pageant is no longer nationalism (either public or private), but consumerism. Indeed, while Miss Thailand was reborn in the 1960s because of the Cold War, in the 1980s Miss Thailand was resurrected just as the hypernationalist campaigns of both the military dictatorship and the communist insurgency were exhausting their energies in Thailand. As the power of the Communist Party and the military bureaucracy waned, there was a rise of the business class in Thailand. With rapid economic development since the early 1980s, business groups have become the major extra-bureaucratic force.[84]

Television was an important part of this shift from Cold War politics to market economics. The financial potential of television was recognized in the 1960s; but it was exploited more for corrupt payoffs than in terms of market economics. Petty economics overshadowed political propaganda even on the military stations: "The officers of the company tried to seek profits for themselves. ... The officers sold air-time without forwarding payment to the station."[85] Hence, state propaganda became less blunt; with the rise of the business class and its doctrine of the free market, governance became more diffuse. The Miss Thailand pageant itself was more commercialized and commodified because after the power of television was enhanced with satellite technology in 1979 it allowed the simultaneity of nationwide viewing upon which markets thrive.

### *Miss Thailand rises again*

During the twelve-year break there were numerous beauty contests, including "Miss Thailand Universe."[86] But Miss Universe Inc. wanted an authentic beauty queen for its annual performance, so in 1983 it asked Channel 7 to reorganize the Miss Thailand pageant. Although it was again opposed by mass-media commentators on the grounds that it objectified women, social attitudes toward beauty contests had largely changed. Thus, Channel 7 and the VCAA signed a contract with Miss Universe Inc. to provide a suitable Miss Thailand each year. There were two reasons for this shift in popular attitude toward beauty contests. On the one hand, beauty pageants no longer focused so tightly on the body; judging expanded to consider intelligence, talent, self-confidence and personality.[87] The prospects for Miss Thailand in this new climate also had improved; there was much more social mobility for contestants and winners, especially into business careers. Through the pageant a social space was emerging where women could talk to each other through television to shape what it means to be the "model Thai woman."

Yet, while Thai women are becoming "subjects" who are valued for intelligence and talent, the reincarnation of the pageant under such commercial conditions actually further objectified and commodified women. The rise of the Thai business class fostered not just modernization and industrialization, but the postmodernization of the tertiary service sector, which commodified the (sometimes sacred) culture for tourism, including sex tourism: contestants wear numbers like women in massage parlors and go-go bars. Indeed, remember what fate awaited Thawan's Miss Siam 1998 when she lost the Miss Mega-Universe pageant. Whereas earlier Miss Thailands were involved in state propaganda and foreign policy, now all the contestants were commodified as "a means to advertise products completely."[88] Rather than a meat market for mistresses, the pageant uses the Thai women to sell hotel rooms, beer and real estate. The contestant sponsored by a real estate company, Krisda Mahanakorn, became Miss Thailand 1994. While contestants need commercial sponsors to enter the pageant, the television broadcast was full of commercials for transnational sponsors of the pageant. Colgate Palmolive is the main sponsor of the contest, and one of the most successful commercials for the 1995 pageant showed Miss Thailand 1994 using Palmolive soap. As with the male gaze, women are for sale, not even as themselves, but as curvaceous billboards to sell consumer goods and the middle-class lifestyle. Indeed, the problems of the Miss Thailand pageant in March 1997 presaged the collapse of the Thai economy in July 1997. The contest was anemic because many of the sponsors from the property sector—including Krisda Mahanakorn—were too poor to support contestants.[89]

Although the pageant has wandered far from its official nationalist roots, at times state policy and consumerism overlap in cultural governance. The Miss Thailand 1994 pageant very publicly declared that it was supporting the Ministry of Education's "Thailand Cultural Promotion Year" project. Although the Interior Ministry is no longer directly involved in organizing the pageant, by this time Gen Chavalit was the Interior Minister, and his wife Khunying Pankrua, a former beauty queen, was the head judge who crowned Areeya Miss Thailand 1994. Pankrua continued as head judge when Chavalit rose to become prime minister in 1996.

To sum up the history of the image of Miss Thailand: first, it was organized by the state to promote a certain form of female participation to legitimize the national project; second, it was organized by an elite private boys' school to sell Thailand to the world in Cold War politics; and, third, it was repackaged by Channel 7 to address women as consumers in a global political economy. Although many of the judges are now women, this chapter has shown how they choose the model Thai woman in a very organized, prescribed setting. Although it has now become less apparent, the masculine institution of the military has been a guiding force in each of these scriptings of the "Thai woman" through both institutional and personal networks.

Throughout the history of Miss Thailand there has been a curious economy of tradition/modernity and East/West. When the contest was introduced in 1934 it was an important part of legitimizing the entrance of modern, Western ideas—the Constitution, progress, civilization, nation—against the "traditional" absolute monarchy. Miss Thailand was thus scripted as a "modernizing force." Yet, once this militarized hypernationalism was in place, Miss Thailand is used to defend traditional Thailand against foreign ideas such as "democracy" and "equality." There is one last conclusion to draw from this diachronic analysis: Miss Thailand always survives its sponsoring institutions, and often overshadows them—the Constitution Festival and the VCAA Winter Fair. Each year Miss Thailand is reborn, and thus has a regular opportunity to remold herself as the model Thai woman.

## Synchronic analysis: narratives of the Miss Thailand 1994 pageant

Back on stage the judges have cut the field down to three finalists who will be interviewed a second time in order to choose Miss Thailand 1994. This was the contestants' chance to distinguish themselves through factors that were much more under their immediate control than face and figure: it was a chance to let their talent, intelligence and personality shine. Indeed, in the first synchronic analysis, women's role was spoken by men. In the diachronic analysis I examined how the image of Miss Thailand has been organized by men; especially the military. Now in this question and answer (Q&A) performance we can see how the women speak for themselves with and against the patriarchal "ideology [which] may be slippery or even contradictory" with female roles.[90] Like television dramas, the Miss Thailand performance often contains ironic images of women who are sometimes strong, sometimes weak, both confirming and questioning patriarchal ideology.

Because the women are speaking to the audience, this Q&A reintroduces the issue of the narrative. In the first synchronic section I touched on narrativity to deconstruct how the bachelors narrated their God-like creation of the "Thai woman" (not in six days, but in about six minutes). In its simplest form, the Miss Thailand pageant is an annual recreation of the fairy tale crowning of the worthy peasant girl after an arduous trial.[91] In terms of structure, the contest neatly conforms to the standard storyline of "equilibrium–disequilibrium–new equilibrium" because at the beginning of the pageant there is a reigning Miss Thailand, but then as her time draws near there is the chaos of sixty pretenders to the throne struggling to be chosen as the one true queen. Sometimes this struggle over the title is grotesque: in 1986 the crown was snatched from the new Miss Thailand World by one of the other contestants, and firmly placed on the first runner-up's head.[92] Regardless of any controversy, the contest always ends with a new Miss Thailand being crowned, who re-establishes order and harmony to the realm with her charming smile.

Narratives take on specific forms in the Thai media. Kanjana argues that there are three roles for women in television drama and film: employee, housewife and sex object. She analyzes these roles in terms of family, motherhood, virginity and the "strong woman."[93] The role of "sex object" is relevant to Miss Thailand, considering the power of the ideology of virginity in Thai society and the strict rules prohibiting marriage and children for contestants. Kanjana notes that for a female character in a television drama "losing her virginity is equal to losing control of the direction of one's [sic] life."[94] Lose your virginity in the wrong way, and you risk becoming a prostitute or a mistress, which are scripted as opposites of the model Thai woman.

The roles of employee and housewife need to be contextualized since Miss Thailand contestants are (temporarily) proscribed from both. In Thai narratives there is friction between being an employee and being a housewife, between the public and the private sphere. But Kanjana argues that, unlike in the West, there is no conflict in most Thai narratives: women characters can easily choose between alternatives.[95] If a woman chooses family life and becomes a housewife and mother, then according to the narrative she can expect eternal gratitude from her children, especially her daughters.

The "strong character woman" deals with a view of social life where middle-class women cannot have it all, and must be able to separate "wife" from "house."[96] Through modern education such heroines are more independent and challenge traditional patriarchal values in Thai society. For the strong charactered woman is more than a mother: "a woman's life does not depend on her virginity alone. There are many more dimensions to her life, the same as for a man."[97] Still this "equality as similarity to men" narrative is taken to extremes in Thai dramas, which often turn the woman into a man. Kanjana writes of characters taking on external characteristics of men, for example the female boss having sex with her (male) workers "like other bosses."[98]

These narrative themes and forms can help us understand the Q&A section of the pageant. Although each contestant answered her question in a different way, all three dealt with the tension in the "modern woman" between public and private space in ways similar to these narrative forms. Contestant Number 14 was asked what part of Thai culture was most admired by the world. She deftly put her hands together to perform a *wai*, to the applause of the audience and the approving smiles of the judicial panel: "The wai is part of the Thai cultural identity which is easy to do and anybody who is Thai can do it. And it is admired by the whole world," she explained. Thus she appealed to the image of a private woman, the traditional submissive beauty, the housewife-in-waiting.

But this cultural form has its own politics: the *wai* is a technology of power and prestige. Its performative economy is analogous to the military salute marking out and reinforcing hierarchy—subordinates *wai* superiors. Unfortunately for Number 14, the judges were looking for something a bit more substantive (and perhaps some of the judges remembered that the *wai* is not unique to Thailand)—she came in third.

Number 35, Areeya Chumsai, was asked what she would do if she were crowned Miss Thailand. She quickly answered: "If I became Miss Thailand the first thing I want to do is kiss my mother. Because my mother came back from America to give me moral support. I will embrace my mother and tell her: 'we did it.'" Then she would help out society:

> As for what I would do for society, my father and mother taught me that if I have a high education I will be self-confident and proud of myself. I like teaching and I want everybody in Thailand to have high education so they can help themselves and help Thailand.

Thus Areeya skillfully mixed public and private, traditional deference with modern activism. According to the narrative she was a proper middle-class Thai woman who did not experience the conflict between work and family life. She combined the wishes of Bachelors Number One and Three. She had her priorities set: kissing her mother first showed gratitude. Although this statement seemed to come out of nowhere, Kanjana states that in the Thai narrative it is "fairly impossible to omit the role of 'mother,' even although the mother in the story may have almost nothing to do with the other characters. . . . The mother is an almost indispensable character in Thai literary works."[99] Because Number 35 was clear about her public and private roles, and included the mother figure, Areeya fulfilled all the requirements of the narrative of the model Thai woman—she won. Areeya's combination of East and West, deference and initiative, later led her to the royal military academy to fulfill her dream of being a teacher.

But perhaps the most interesting example was the woman who came in second. Her special question was simple: "What is your dream?" Miss 37 didn't need time to ponder: she wanted to get a master's degree. She confidently said that education is important for women since they cannot just stay at home any more:

> education is important especially since the modern woman can no longer only sit at home, cook and take care of the family. They have to help themselves because they are more independent, more competent and approved by society more. I want to have knowledge, more than just have fun.

The fascinating thing about these earnestly liberal statements is that they went directly against the dreams of the eligible bachelors in section one, and Areeya's plans. A female character's desire here conflicts directly with male desire. And this was no slip of the tongue on Number 37's part. This was actually a continuation of her question in the previous round where she was asked about the relation between beauty and intelligence. She answered that she wanted equality with men: "I want equal rights. Now our country has been developing for a long time. However, in my opinion, it is not developed enough. Women are still taken advantage of and looked down upon." She continued to challenge the dream woman's wok song by questioning whether women should have to work both inside and outside the home: "People expect present day women to both go out and work and take care of the house. I think that it's better to help each other." It seems that Miss 37 has outgrown Bachelor Number Four's strong woman, and thus transgressed the social space of Miss Thailand to become a strong character woman. Although the patriarchy did not award Miss 37 its highest prize, it did not send her into exile either: she came in second.

## Conclusion

As the last example suggests, the purpose of this chapter is not to condemn Miss Thailand, but to trace the institution's unstable history as it performs roles for women (and thus for men) in the present. These roles are complex and contradictory, both restricting and empowering Thai women. Still, it would be easy to dismiss the Miss Thailand pageant as a product of cultural imperialism headquartered in the Pentagon and/or the Los Angeles offices of Miss Universe Inc., as do many cultural commentators,[100] or as an urban distraction from the roots of Thai culture in the countryside, as Thawan does in "Miss Siam."

The current contest itself is an import from the US, complete with organization, music, blocking: America exports a modular form that serves to produce candidates for the Miss Universe pageant. A Thai organizer explained that in the 1980s they "modernized" the pageant so Miss Thailand could better compete for the Miss Universe crown. Although Thai organizers "look for examples abroad, we decide for ourselves."[101] Yet the only Thai culture in evidence at the pageant is in the evening wear section, and even this was special in 1994. Although the MC instructed contestants and viewers to conserve Thai culture as part of the Ministry of Education's "Thai Cultural Promotion Year," much of the "Thai cultural nationalism" displayed was problematic.

One fascinating development in the third stage of the pageant is the transnationalization not just of organizers and sponsors, but of contestants. The first Miss Thailand of the third era actually grew up in the US, only returning to Thailand for the pageant. She was dubbed "Miss Import" by the popular press. In 1988 another American-raised Thai was chosen to represent Thailand at the Miss Universe pageant. There was some discussion in the media about the suitability of someone who was so foreign to represent Thailand: Pornthip's first beauty pageant title was "Miss Teen California 1984."[102] When she won Miss Thailand many commented that "she couldn't speak Thai any better than a tourist." But all objections were silenced when Pornthip won Miss Universe in 1988. Nothing succeeds like success. In 1994 another American-raised woman was chosen to be Miss Thailand, and the First Runner-up had an American father. Now promoters go to foreign countries to scout for Miss Thailand contestants.[103]

What unites these transnational Thais is a fluency in English, which has become an unofficial requirement for Miss Thailand. This puts the proper patriarchal spin on the "education" that the contestants were promoting, for here education does not mean rocket science, but the very gendered area of foreign language training. Although organizers stress that choosing overseas Thai and mixed-race Thai (*luk kreung*) is not a policy (like in the royal military academy), "American experience" is seen as an advantage not only for English but for height and figure as well.[104] One judge commented that "the beauty queen who cannot speak English will be a dumb-mute beauty queen."[105]

Curiously, the issue now is no longer whether contestants are fluent in English, but if they are fluent in Thai. The common defense for Miss Thailand 1994 was that she spoke Thai "so well"—certainly much better than Miss Thailand 1988/Miss Universe 1988! To combat this problem of cultural inauthenticity, in 1995 the pageant organizers asked the Faculty of Arts of Chulalongkorn University (well known as a factory that produces elite Thai women) to design a test to authenticate contestants' knowledge of Thai language and culture. A new prize was created to recognize cultural literacy. Still, in 1995 another American-raised Thai who speaks with a foreign accent was chosen as Miss Thailand, as the newspaper headline put it, "Another American crowned, carries on Miss Thailand torch."[106] In 1996, a blue-eyed Thai who has an American father was chosen as Miss Thailand World, in a trend toward *luk-kreung* celebrities that continues into the twenty-first century.[107]

While considerations of national identity and the state often are reduced to clashes between the twin discourses of cultural imperialism and cultural nativism,[108] Miss Thailand actively participates in both. This dual complicity suggests that, beyond questions of the reigning Miss Thailand's language abilities, the meaning of nationalism itself is changing. It is mutating into hybrid forms, migrating between what Kasian Tejapira calls "Thai" and "Thai-Thai": "whereas *Thai* implies a singular, pure, genuine, authentic, original, definite, narrow and monolithic version of Thainess, *Thai-Thai* connotes a pluralistic, mixed, mutant, altered, simulated, indefinite, broad and differentiated version of the same."[109] Sometimes, the judges go for real "Thai" beauty queens as in 1992 and 2005 when Bangkok hosted the Miss Universe pageant; other times they choose "Thai-Thai" beauty queens who can better juggle the overlapping state, national, commercial and transnational identities. Rather than being the result of Euro-American imperialism, the diachronic analysis suggests that consumerism and mass media of capitalist modernity are the driving force. Actually, televising the Miss America pageant caused similar changes in viewing styles, anxieties and power relations in the US.[110]

Simply put, the production of Miss Thailand further reinforces that identity is a negotiable category. Many of Thailand's neighboring countries have strict discourses of national identity in general and beauty queens in particular,[111] and the Nigerian response to the arrival of the Miss World pageant in 2002 was a riot that killed over 200 people.[112] But neither the Thai state, nor the Thai public, seem to mind having American-raised women representing them as Miss Thailand in international competitions—not to mention representing them at intergovernmental meetings such as forums of the Association of Southeast Asian Nations.[113] This is not to say that nationalism is not important in Thailand, but rather to argue that nationalism, like "beauty," is not a natural category, but one constructed and reconstructed for various purposes—political, military, economic and otherwise. Although this hybrid beauty queen phenomenon may be peculiar to Thailand, Thai cultural governance (and resistance) are not unique in their fluid and ambiguous deployment of domestic and foreign tropes in transnational space. As Areeya's various activities show, Miss Thailand can take on various roles, sometimes being the girl next door, at others a humble teacher, sometimes a beauty queen, at others a soldier. Theoretically, Miss Thailand is also ambiguous as at times she is a prime example of self-Orientalization, and at others a key case of the Occidentalizing of identity through the global beauty industry. Highlighting this pragmatic and ambiguous use of seemingly "national" categories helps us to call into question patterns of cultural governance and resistance in other spaces as well.

Chapter 3 uses the discourse of Asian Democracy to take another critical stab at the relation of media, culture and politics. Curiously, some of the same tropes arise, albeit with a twist. Rather than beauty queen and heroic warrior being the ideal marriage for the nation as family, the beautiful soul vs. the brutal soldier is a guiding image in revolutionary photo albums that commemorate democratic resistance to authoritarian states in Pacific Asia.

# 3 Gender, democracy and revolutionary photo albums

In the 1980s, Pacific Asia became a subject of the world gaze because of its pattern of rapid and equitable economic growth, known to the World Bank as the "East Asian miracle." Researchers and bureaucratic elites talked of a Pacific Asian model of development that is driven more by centralized state planning than by liberal economics. In the early 1990s, Pacific Asia challenged the universals of global order again, but this time in political affairs. In much the same way as the East Asian economic miracle challenged the Euro-American model of capitalism, the mainstream view of democratization is challenged by a Pacific Asian model of political development. Researchers and elite bureaucrats discussed an Asian Democracy that is driven more by the state management of civil society than by liberal ideas of democracy, civil society and human rights.[1] Even after the economic crisis of 1997, the discourse of Asian Values and capitalist utopia persists in both Asia and Euro-America.

Although these debates are characteristically framed in terms of a geopolitics of East vs. West,[2] in this chapter I will argue that the debate often makes more sense when seen in terms of a struggle in domestic politics. Indeed, as Pacific Asia was being hailed for its "miracle" economies, it was also a center of activity for non-violent challenges to authoritarian states.[3] Rather than Asian Democracy being a geopolitical issue of East–West relations, it is a spin doctoring response to Pacific Asia's "people power" movements of the late 1980s and 1990s. These movements struggled against authoritarian rule in very gendered ways as a struggle against patriarchal order. While Chapters 1 and 2 engaged in a thick description of the performances of a specific institution (either JACADS or Miss Thailand), Chapter 3 will offer a more general consideration of gender and democracy that appeals to a variety of examples. While the first two chapters deconstructed the state's cultural governance, in this chapter I will acknowledge and deconstruct both cultural governance and resistance, to show how resistance can easily reproduce new forms of violence.

© *Millennium: Journal of International Studies*. An earlier version of this chapter appeared in *Millennium*, Volume 27, Number 4, 1998, and is reproduced with the permission of the publisher.

## 72  Gender, democracy, revolutionary photo albums

In particular, this chapter will critically examine how "Asian Democracy" is discursively deployed as a mode of gendered cultural governance in two groups of texts. The first section examines official views of Asian Democracy that seek to counter Orientalist images that script Asia as (submissive) feminine in relation to a Western (imperialist) masculine. It will show how Asian Democracy has been used by local elites to reassert the patriarchy that has been problematized by capitalist modernity—the strong-arm tactics of both the state and the IMF address not only the financial crisis, but, as we saw with Miss Thailand in the last chapter, provoked an identity crisis.

The second section thus considers how activists and local journalists have been scripting a different version of democracy in Asia using the popular culture of revolutionary photo albums to commemorate democratic social movements in the Philippines (1986), Burma (1988), China (1989) and Thailand (1992). I will argue that such collages of written and visual texts have their own economy, and produce democracy in Asia using particular gendered grammars and gazes. Gender here does not exclusively refer to women, but is better understood in relation to patriarchy and symbolic politics. This patriarchy is regulated by self/Other relations that include elite men and exclude "women-and-children" along with homosexuals. The photographic narratives, on the other hand, characteristically portray democracy as non-violent and feminine, and the repressive regimes as masculine and violent. But since the gendered images are all too often reproduced through certain stereotypical roles—women as devoted mothers, dutiful daughters, chaste nuns and jaded prostitutes; youth as innocent and idealistic; men as corrupt tyrants and cruel soldiers—these albums risk reinforcing both Orientalism and patriarchy, even as they oppose them. In the conclusion, I will argue that the discourse can easily switch from a feminine democracy of popular politics back to a masculine nationalism of armed struggle, reproducing the complementary relationship between the Beautiful Soul and the Virtuous Warrior that we saw in the last chapter's pairing of beauty queens and heroic soldiers.

These albums raise interesting theoretical questions about interpretation and authenticity, and knowledge and power, that arise in the overlapping terrain of area studies and women's studies. Both institutional formations are engaged in issues of identity politics that emerge from the tension between identity and difference. Is the goal of women's studies/Asian studies to find the true subject, or to allow for different ways of being? In both spaces the struggle is about who can speak, and whether the legitimacy of their utterances is determined by essential traits, or is the product of social and cultural construction. In this chapter, I will consider these issues through an examination of how the transnational politics of democracy and gender are negotiated in specific social movements. I will argue that the masculine and the feminine are very unstable concepts in Pacific

Asia: they are revalued with each successive utterance. Although it is common to assume that the East is feminized by a hypermasculine West,[4] gender distinctions are not so stable: the Goddess of Democracy, who was the symbolic focus of the Tian'anmen Square democratic movement in 1989, was herself originally the opposite: a Soviet man. The chapter will show how certain albums, as part of their democratic project, appeal to hybrid notions of identity to efface the binaries of feminine/masculine, peace/war and Orientalism/Occidentalism. Hence, in the conclusion I will examine the interrelation between the "politics of issues" and the "politics of rhetoric" in the construction of Asian Democracy to argue that the masculine and the feminine are very unstable concepts in Pacific Asia. Hence, while we should be wary of reproducing a rhetorical politics of domination, we should also be wary of discarding images of difference in Pacific Asia and among women.

## Asian Democracy and the logic of patriarchy

An instrumental use of terms such as democracy is nothing new. In many ways it mirrors the ambiguous and multicoded uses of the concepts of civilization, modernization, development in the past, and the debates over Asian values and human rights in the present. Although it is fashionable to see such debates as peculiar to the post-Cold War era, the discourse of democracy has been defined, used and redefined in Thailand by various groups—including politicians, non-governmental organizations (NGOs), and even the military—since the 1932 revolution against absolute monarchy.[5] Indeed, in the 1940s Mao Zedong spoke of "New democracy." In the 1950s Sukarno talked of "Guided democracy" for Indonesia, while in Bangkok Field Marshal Sarit Thanarat promoted "Thai-style democracy." In the 1970s General Park Chung-hee spoke of "Korean-style democracy." From the 1970s to the 1990s, Suharto promoted "Pancasila democracy" in Indonesia.

These conflicting discourses of democracy are part of a very gendered notion of East/West relations that needs to be read in terms of its history. As we saw in the Introduction, in *Orientalism* Edward Said argues that the relation of Europe and Asia was one of self/Other. The grand imperial project was not just a matter of conquest, occupation and administration of the East. It was also a matter of identity politics that created "the East" as the imperfect mirror image of the West. East/West relations were typically in a hierarchical form with the West on top, and the East as the willing servant waiting to be civilized. There are important parallels between images of the East in Orientalism and images of women in patriarchy: both are defined as irrational, child-like, different, homogeneous, mysterious, derivative and subjects of the gaze.[6] Indeed, the prototype of international affairs is Western man and Oriental woman: the new Miss Thailand is often the product of a Euro-American father and a Thai mother.[7]

As we saw in the last chapter, such a complementary pair has been reproduced in popular culture from recent films to colonial postcards as well as literary works: "This is especially evident in the writings of travellers and novelists: women are usually the creatures of male power-fantasy. They express unlimited sensuality, they are more or less stupid, and above all they are willing."[8]

This politics of patriarchy persists beyond the era of formal imperialism. Many of the postcolonial regimes in Pacific Asia have constructed their identities through a simple reversal: the East used to be feminine, so now it has to be masculine. Such nation-building regimes are caught in the relation between colonization and decolonization. As Said suggests, colonization imposes boundaries of self/Other, civilized/barbaric, traditional/modern, empire/nation and male/female. Decolonization typically accepts these boundaries and organizes resistance around their reversal in an "emancipation through mirroring" that entails a "mix of defiance and mimesis."[9] Hence, rather than Orientalism, where Western imperialists script submissive identities for Asians, now we have Occidentalism. Occidentalism takes the Orientalist categories for granted, and simply mirrors them: Orientals used to be defined as lazy in relation to the Protestant work ethic, but now Pacific Asian elites complain about lazy Westerners who lack the Confucian work ethic. Such a combination of Occidentalism and decolonization, then, continues to reproduce the power of domination, and reasserts the power of the patriarchy.

Patriarchy is a sticky term, and to some inappropriate to Pacific Asia since its "Western" connotations are seen as overwhelming: the position of Thai, Philippine, Burmese and Chinese women is very different from the lot of Euro-American women. Yet Rey Chow turns this familiar question on its head. Recognizing the historical power of the patriarchal discourse of Confucianism in China, she refigures the oppression of women into "a significant clue to modern Chinese society" and thus an opportunity for understanding modern China better: "Because women are the fundamental support of the familial social structure, the epochal changes that historians document are most readily perceived through the changing status of Chinese women."[10]

In this context, patriarchy becomes the guiding ideology not just for women's oppression but as a key to the organization of the selected Pacific Asian societies themselves. Much analysis in feminist theory looks at how social groups, such as the working class, are *feminized* in the patriarchal spaces of the capitalist market and the bureaucracy.[11] This expands the use of feminist theory beyond women into symbolic politics, for feminized means that the working class is put in a similar position of exploitation in the economy as women-and-children are put in the patriarchal family.

We would expect this patriarchy to rely on authoritarian tropes, such as hierarchical Confucian values.[12] But what is interesting about current reassertions of patriarchy in Pacific Asia is that they have also appealed to the idea of democracy: Asian Democracy. Asian Democracy is part of the grand decolonial project of imagining Asia as a community separate from the West. The oppositional nature of Asian Democracy is demonstrated by the title of a Japanese bestseller: Malaysian Prime Minister Mahathir Mohamad and Japanese ex-parliamentarian Shintaro Ishihara's book *The Asia That Can Say No: A Policy to Combat Europe and America* was translated into English as *The Voice of Asia: Two Leaders Discuss the Coming Century*.[13]

This particular East/West distinction uses democracy to assert the moral superiority of Pacific Asia against a degenerate West:

> Datuk Seri Dr Mahathir Mohamad has asked Malaysians not to accept Western-style democracy as it could result in negative effects. The prime minister said such an extreme principle had caused moral decay, homosexual activities, single parents and economic slowdown because of poor work ethics [*sic*].[14]

Responding to the threat of transnational media flows, Mahathir was likewise quite clear as to the decadence of the liberal free press: "Today they broadcast slanted news, tomorrow they will broadcast raw pornography to corrupt our children and destroy our culture."[15]

The gendered construction of Asian Democracy also emerges in the speeches and interviews of Singapore's Senior Minister Lee Kuan Yew. He only discusses women as a political problem that needs to be solved:

> Democracy's assumptions have some weak points. Men and women are assumed to be equal, or should be equal. Therefore, there is one person, one vote. But is equality real? If it is not, then insisting on equality is sure to lead to a step backwards.[16]

Rather than taking away the rights of women, which Lee recognizes as difficult to justify, he productively uses cultural governance to further institutionalize the privileges of patriarchs:

> I'm convinced, personally, that we would have a better system if we gave every man over the age of 40 who has a family two votes because he's likely to be more careful, voting also for his children. He is more likely to vote in a serious way than a capricious young man under 30.[17]

Democracy thus has to be reformed to support the patriarchy. Asian Democracy is thereby limited to electoralism, discursively excluding civil society, dissidence and human rights. After the elections the answer is an authoritarian state: "we need strong governments and strong leaders."[18] Asian Democracy is used in cultural governance as a device to buttress a patriarchal state that feminizes and youth-izes society: transforming citizens into capricious "women-and-children" who cannot be responsible for their actions.

These speeches and writings are volleys in the battle over identity in Pacific Asia. They define the East in conflict with the West, using a highly gendered vocabulary. In scripting Asian Democracy the leaders portray themselves as the true bearers of Asian tradition, and thus local critics and opposition parties are redefined as un-Asian or alien.[19] When people argue for a broader notion of democracy that includes civil society they can be excluded by being "depicted as traitors to their own cultures, or not real members of society."[20] This discourse of Asian Democracy is more than just talk. The ideas work themselves out into state policies that continue to make homosexuality illegal in many of these states, and justify negative discrimination toward women, particularly single mothers.[21] The spectacular downfall in 1998 of Mahathir's deputy prime minister Anwar Ibrahim, who favored a more open relationship to liberalism and Euro-America, is telling: Anwar was not just charged with (and convicted of) corruption, but sodomy.

Since the economic crisis of 1997, the arguments about Asian Democracy have not been as convincing in Euro-America; but Asian Democracy is being reasserted in Southeast Asia,[22] and is mutating into other cultural forms of democracy in Northeast Asia through an Asian Values debate in South Korea[23] and discussions of "Democracy with Chinese Characteristics" in China,[24] both of which look to "Confucian democracy."[25] (I will develop this point in Chapter 4.) In each of these cases, the solution to the 1997 economic/financial/identity crisis is not less Asian Democracy, but more Asian Democracy. These culturally informed understandings of democratization all share a central role for the state in politics, with political reform coming from the educated elite rather than from the masses.[26]

## Popular images of democratic struggle

There are many ways to critically analyze these conceptions of Asian Democracy. Some criticize the logic of unchangeable East vs. immutable West, which is supported by essentialist notions of family, men and women. They note that cultures and roles are inherently changeable. Others point to the cultural construction work that characterizes "Asian values" and "Asian Democracy," in order to argue that these are myths that need to be dispelled in the service of clarifying the truth of "Asia."[27] But I would argue that, once we start to discuss Asian Democracy, we are already entering the discourse, and thus producing truths. Rather than looking at myths as false images that need to be corrected, I follow Roland Barthes to examine how myths are involved in truth production.[28] If we can see how the patriarchal myth of Asian Democracy produces certain conceptions

## Gender, democracy, revolutionary photo albums  77

of Pacific Asia that exclude discourses of civil society, feminism and local dissent, then we can also look at how alternative truths are produced.

The alternative truths considered in this section point to more robust and people-centered images of democracy in Pacific Asia. It turns out that, regardless of the theoretical debates about democracy in Pacific Asia, in 1986 the Philippine people took to the streets and overthrew a dictator who had ruled the country through martial law for fourteen years. This democratic movement spread to other countries in the region as part of both very local uprisings and quite international movements in South Korea (1987), Taiwan (1987), Burma (1988), China (1989), Thailand (1992) and Indonesia (1998).[29] These unarmed insurrections have produced not only reams of primary sources and commentary, but also a set of photographic albums that pay tribute to the struggle: *Bayan Ko! Images of the People Power Revolt* from the Philippines,[30] *Burma's Revolution of the Spirit: the Struggle for Democratic Freedom and Dignity*,[31] *June Four: A Chronicle of the Chinese Democratic Uprising*,[32] and *Catalyst for Change: Uprising in May* from Thailand.[33] Rather than making speeches or writing books, the activists who put together these volumes chose to represent their popular struggles through the popular culture of photo albums. While the subalterns cannot necessarily speak, their struggles are graphically displayed in full color in these revolutionary photo albums.

Revolutionary photo albums are typically a special publication put together by newspaper reporters and photographers, and thus constitute a blend of official and unofficial information. Each is a coffee table book where the written text and the photographic images are intertwined: written text captions the photos, while the photos caption the written text. Each of these texts is written in English, as an international language, which means that they are directed toward both a domestic and an international audience.

A question of authenticity arises since only the Thai text was produced in its native land: the Chinese and Philippine volumes were published in Hong Kong, while the Burmese volume came out in New York and Bangkok. Still, we should not be limited by national boundaries in our interpretation of texts; because of the logistics of stillborn revolutions it was impossible to publish the Burmese and Chinese albums on home turf. Hence, they are directed more at an international audience. Many would point out that "international" characteristically means "Euro-American," and critical scholarship could conclude that this is yet another example of Euro-America universalizing its own particular values. But in this case we should understand that international audience here means more than Euro-American audience. We cannot take it for granted that the use of English reconstitutes imperial relationships, for English is increasingly being used by Asians who wish to communicate with other Asians in a regional civil society.[34] Indeed, Mahathir and Ishihara's *The Voice of Asia* was translated from Japanese into English—not Malay.

The best way to understand these albums then is not in terms of the colonial and decolonial essences of East/West, woman/man, domestic/foreign, but in terms of transnational postcolonial projects. In this way we can get out of the straitjacket that binds both interpretation and action, to more ironic and productive understandings. The postcolonial has a more fluid relation to boundaries than the confrontation and reconquest characteristic of both the colonial and the decolonial: "to those who have experience crossing them, boundaries become a matter of play rather than an obsession. The element of play opens possibilities for innovation beyond the logic of opposition-through-imitation."[35] Unlike the patriarchal Asian Democracy described above, activists in the albums are not limited to a pure authentic essence of race, language or culture. As the examples of resistance discussed below will show, politics consists of using various identities—gendered, religious, national, traditional, modern—as tactics in a struggle for the project of democracy whose legitimacy already has been established.

Actually, these albums show that, in order to reach the widest possible audience both at home and abroad, written language is effaced—photography is seen as the most important genre. In his preface to *Burma's Revolution of the Spirit*, Sein Win, the Burmese Prime Minister in Exile, makes clear that:

> These photographs will bring the world's attention back to the suffering of our nation. People of the world must see beyond the military-sponsored mass rallies ... *Burma's Revolution of the Spirit* provides a true window into Burma. It helps the international community understand the undying spirit of revolution.[36]

In Thailand, there were dozens of books that put together photographs with journalistic-style written text in Thai language; a careful examination of these albums shows that they write basically the same photographic narrative as the *Bangkok Post*'s English version. These representations of the democratic movements in Asia are thus part of a post-literate revolution where people get ideas and images primarily from the visual cultures of television, film and pictures, rather than the written culture of books and newspapers. Although they are certainly written in earnest, the photo albums often function as a souvenir, a keepsake that people casually flip through, rather than an object of critical study. As artifacts of postcolonial play, revolutionary photo albums are exemplary texts that illustrate and reinforce popular memories.

The various revolutionary albums are also interesting because they go beyond structural arguments to popular politics; they purport to document popular struggles in Pacific Asia that claim to be both democratic and Asian. This is not to say that such albums are purer or truer than texts such as *The Asia That Can Say No*. Rather, they form an alternative discourse that has its own rules and logic, its own set of inclusions and exclusions. Just as Mahathir and Lee Kuan Yew pick virtuous things to define Pacific Asia and degenerate things to define the West, each of the revolutionary albums contains a careful selection of images to tell a certain story. The acknowledgments section of *Burma's Revolution of the Spirit* tells us that the album's 120 pictures have been chosen out of over 3,000 photographs.[37]

Such constructive editing is common with the discourse of history, where historians emplot the narrative to tell a story of a particular kind.[38] It becomes more complex with photo albums that are engaged in their own writing of history. This is not an obvious thing. As Michael J. Shapiro writes, "Of all modes of representation, [photography] is the one most easily assimilated into the discourses of knowledge and truth, for it is thought to be an unmediated simulacrum, a copy of what we consider the 'real.'"[39] Alan Trachtenberg further explains:

> The historian employs words, narrative, and analysis. The photographer's solution is in the viewfinder: where to place the edge of the picture, what to exclude, from what point of view to show the relations among the included details. . . . [Thus] the viewfinder is a political instrument, a tool for making a past suitable for the future.[40]

The creative editing of meaning with photographs does not stop with the viewfinder. Another stage of cultural construction occurs when we gather photos into an album. Album means white or blank in Latin; it needs to be filled up to be meaningful. This process is seen in the everyday practice of creating photo albums of a wedding or a vacation: the photographic album is first composed of blank sheets of paper that we fill up with our own photos in order to write our own personal history. Coffee table books of photographs followed this logic in the nineteenth century. Photos were basically postcards; they were numbered for ordering, but each viewer could construct their own order and their own view of history in the albums: "Organized into a catalogue or a sequence, single images can be viewed as part of a presumed pattern, an order, a historical totality."[41] Indeed, a similar unbound album of war photographs to "commemorate the 60th anniversary of the world anti-fascist war" was published by the Chinese Communist Party's Central Party School in 2005.[42] Thus, with the viewfinder, the ordering of the photos, and written captions we construct a particular meaning, and our own particular truth.

War albums are a tried-and-true genre of photography, appearing in the early days of the practice. In his chapter "Albums of War," Trachtenberg looks at the grammar of photography as it recorded the American Civil War.[43] Specifically, he shows how it helped people to remember their terrible sacrifices in suitable ways, often as a sacred memory. This quest for a sacred memory has much in common with the revolutionary albums of Pacific Asia; both sets of texts deal with divided societies that are fighting for unity. One photographic album of the American Civil War is praised for paying "'tribute' to that 'American character' that proved itself by surviving fratricidal battles and reestablishing national unity."[44] Revolutionary albums from Asia are also involved in this quest for unity and order.

The revolutionary photo albums, like most histories, reproduce generic narrative structures.[45] Following Northrop Frye's theory of genres, Jeffrey Wasserstrom argues that Chinese narratives of the protest movement are characteristically romances, while Euro-American political representations are tragedies.[46] In a technical sense, romance refers to a quest involving two main characters: a hero and an enemy in an unironic struggle. In this adventure tale, the hero represents youth, angelic spirit, spring, dawn, order, fertility and vigor, while the enemy is the opposite: old age, demonic, winter, darkness, confusion, sterility and moribund life.[47] The four revolutionary photo albums generally comply with Frye's notion of romance. The trope of the sacred conflict is evident, in very gendered ways.

To those familiar with debates about gender and international relations, such a story is not new. In the 1980s, Jean Bethke Elshtain warned us about the discursive economy of reducing gendered politics to stereotypes of the "Virtuous Warrior" and the "Beautiful Soul."[48] Women in peace movements have characteristically been represented (and self-represented) as the Beautiful Soul. This narrowed the definition of women in public life to roles that reinforced a "purity and innocence about the historical course of the world."[49] This "socially sanctioned innocence" reinforced male/female typologies, and Elshtain counsels us to be wary of such stereotypes. Indeed, how are we to make sense of the violence of female leaders such as Margaret Thatcher, Golda Meir, Indira Gandhi, Madeleine Albright and Condoleezza Rice?[50] Elshtain suggests that we challenge the grand narrative not with the peace of a Beautiful Soul, but with the politics of a "chastened patriot." These are the politics not of "solemn deed doers but of zestful act takers, experimenting with new possibilities playfully but from a deep seriousness of purpose."[51]

In other words, a chastened patriot must look at politics not just in terms of issues, but in terms of rhetoric. Using similar metaphors, Shapiro notes the similarities between religious piety and political piety in photographic practice. Here, piety involves a support for established codes regardless of whether they are religious, social or political norms. Shapiro dares us to be impious in our understanding of photography, challenging us to question the images' piety:

> the tendency to either reproduce dominant forms of discourse, which helps circulate the existing system of power, authority, and exchange or to look at them on the basis of their tendency to provoke critical analysis, to denaturalize what is unproblematically accepted and to offer thereby an avenue for politicizing problematics.[52]

## Gender, democracy, revolutionary photo albums 81

In the remainder of this chapter I will interpret the romance of photographic narratives in terms of age and gender. I will argue that the Burmese and Philippine photo narratives highlight women as sacred heroes, while the Chinese and Thai photo narratives revolve around tropes of sacred youth. Although still romantic, the albums' narratives go directly against patriarchal forms of Asian Democracy. While reading these narratives, I will relate them to the discourses of Orientalism and the Beautiful Soul; while we should be wary of reproducing a rhetorical politics of domination, we should also be wary of completely discarding images of difference in Pacific Asia and among women.

### Gender and power in images of Burmese Revolution

*Burma's Revolution of the Spirit* is interesting for two reasons. First, along with *Bayon Ko!*, it is the most sophisticated of the revolutionary albums, deftly interweaving visual and written texts. Second, *Burma's Revolution of the Spirit* provides an interesting case study because it actually meets the needs of the patriarchal Asian Democracy considered above: free and fair elections. The mass uprisings of 1988 led to the election of 1990, which was won by Aung San Suu Kyi's National League for Democracy (NLD). It thus shows how instrumentally the category of Asian Democracy is used by its promoters in Malaysia, Singapore and Indonesia, because they have consistently supported the military junta, the State Law and Order Restitution Council (SLORC), through both economic investment and (specifically Singapore) illegal arms transfers.[53] The promoters of Asian Democracy again supported SLORC by inviting Burma into the Association of Southeast Asian Nations in July 1997.

While the patriarchs set up an analytical opposition between East and West, *Burma's Revolution of the Spirit* is emblematic of the discourse of these revolutionary albums because it locates the conflict firmly within domestic space where nationalism and democracy intertwine. The name of Aung San Suu Kyi's political party is the *National* League for *Democracy*. "Bayan Ko!," which means "My Country," is the name of the nationalist anthem from 1928, which was originally directed against the American colonial regime. But, rather than being part of a de-colonial struggle with a Euro-American Other, these albums are part of a postcolonial project that is organized around groups of people rather than the institutions of nation-states.

The cover of *Burma's Revolution of the Spirit* makes the defining opposition clear: a sacred woman in conflict with violent men. The cover is a collage that is constructed from pictures that are in the volume separately: a small color picture of a smiling Aung San Suu Kyi is placed over a grainy black and white photo of Burmese soldiers with helmets on and bayonets fixed (see Figure 3.1). Suu Kyi invites us into the text, attractively smiling directly at the viewer, while the soldiers are all nervously looking away to guard the entrance to the text. The narrative of the cover, as with the album, suggests that the democratic women led by Aung San Suu Kyi will prevail over the face-less men in the military.[54] As we saw in Chapter 1 with the JACADS brochure, the grammar of these photos is temporal: the juxtaposition of (progressive) color over (repressive) black and white leads us out of the dark past of military dictatorship into a future of feminized democracy. The chapters of *Burma's Revolution of the Spirit* are organized to portray a harmonious Buddhist society that has been ravaged by military excess. Aung San Suu Kyi plays the role of savior to

*Figure 3.1* The cover of *Burma's Revolution of the Spirit*

re-establish Buddhist harmony through non-violent struggle in a curious mixture of colonial and postcolonial images.

This romantic framing of beautiful women as heroes and male soldiers as the enemy provides a fascinating counter-discourse to patriarchal versions of Asian Democracy and the ideology of Miss Thailand. Both *Bayan Ko!* and *Burma's Revolution of the Spirit* employ a reversal of the logic of moral Eastern autocracy vs. degenerate Western democracy. In *Bayan Ko!*, Marcos is represented as degenerate both morally and physically. There are numerous photos of him in ill health with a dazed look on his face, his hands wrapped in bandages.[55] His election campaign is presented as immoral in two ways: first, his goons with their prominent pistols—phallic symbols extraordinaire—are shown threatening voters.[56] Second, scantily clad women are pictured as an important part of the entertainment at his election rallies[57] (see Figure 3.2). Thus the images of women and sexuality are central to the cultural governance of the revolutionary narrative. They

*Figure 3.2*
At a Marcos rally. *Bayan Ko!*, page 71

appear as both hookers and nuns, as sex objects for corrupt cronies and as chaste symbols of purity in the democratic social movement.

Marcos's opponent, Cory Aquino, not surprisingly comes in on the side of purity. She is represented as a deeply religious woman, combining religious and political piety into a Beautiful Soul. The album is dominated by the religious framing of Cory and her campaign, including a full-page picture of her kneeling in prayer at her private chapel.[58] This image follows from the dominant portrayal of Cory as a reluctant savior, a widow who only entered the political stage because her husband Senator Benigno S. Aquino was assassinated by Marcos's thugs in 1983 as he returned from exile. Religious piety thus is converted into political piety. Likewise, *Burma's Revolution of the Spirit* stresses the link between religious and political piety through Orientalist photographs of Buddhist temples and monks. These images form the basis of harmony before, during and after military dictatorship.[59]

A careful reading of the texts shows that the struggle is not just between democracy and oppression. The conflict is also between violent and non-violent protest once full-scale military power was deployed in August 1988. The set of religious images in the introduction and first chapter of *Burma's Revolution of the Spirit* is replaced by images of struggle and violence in "Chapter 2: A Nation Explodes." One two-page set of photographs is particularly instructive; it shows a confrontation between students and soldiers, all of whom are men. The students on page 38 appear to be yelling at the soldiers on page 39, while the soldiers on page 39 look like they are pointing their bayonets at the students on page 38 (see Figure 3.3). But these are two separate photographs that have been juxtaposed to construct a conflict. The image on page 39 is familiar; although it is in color here, it was reproduced in grainy black and white on the album's cover. This is a fascinating construction of meaning that recycles images in slightly different contexts. While the soldiers are juxtaposed with Aung San Suu Kyi on the cover, the same photo is paired with male student activists to narrate a violent conflict. The violence in the Burmese uprising is characterized as masculine: there are no women in the fourteen images of "A Nation Explodes." While Lee Kuan Yew and friends see women as a "problem," this album's photographic narrative reverses the equation: men are a problem for democracy in Pacific Asia.

The narrative of the album takes a radical turn with "Chapter 3: Grace Under Pressure," to complete its first cycle of non-violence/violence/non-violence, and women/men/women. Aung San Suu Kyi appears here for the first time in *Burma's Revolution of the Spirit*, taking the role of savior to recreate the calm of the mystic Buddhist past. Much like *Bayon Ko!*'s distillation of all that is virtuous and non-violent into the image of Cory, this chapter switches from the morality of Buddhism to that of the non-violent campaigning of Suu Kyi.[60] Here, Suu Kyi and Cory represent a particular non-radical form of democracy: parliamentary democracy.

# Gender, democracy, revolutionary photo albums 85

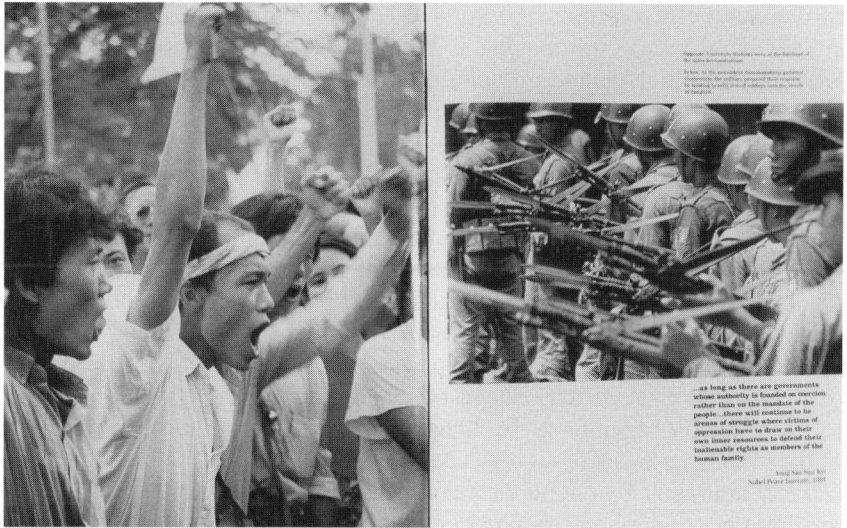

*Figure 3.3* Constructions of male violence. *Burma's Revolution of the Spirit*, pp. 38–9

Neither was a central organizer of the popular politics of mass movements or NGOs; both led political parties in a struggle for state power. Chapter 3 of *Burma's Revolution of the Spirit* focuses on Suu Kyi's election campaign, pushing the narrative progressively from unwieldy mass demonstrations to the disciplined institutional practices of electoral politics. This is ironic since Suu Kyi points out that women constituted only three percent of the candidates for the parliamentary elections of 1990, and only fourteen women were elected.[61]

But the struggle did not end with the arrival of the savior. The following chapter's photographic narrative tells how the non-violent democratic struggle led by women did not succeed. After SLORC arrested Suu Kyi and canceled the results of the 1990 elections, students and dissidents fled for refuge along Burma's mountainous border with Thailand. Although Suu Kyi maintained her non-violent stance, the last photo of the chapter shows members of the Coalition Government of the Union of Burma, which brought together Burman dissidents with ethnic minorities in an armed struggle against the Burmese junta.[62] This confirms the change of character of the struggle from women back to men and from non-violence back to violence. This shift to violent struggle is represented through page after page of images of armed insurgency. Perhaps in reference to the chaotic situation in Burma, the photographic discourse loses the plot, and degenerates into a haphazard collection of the social and political problems that Burma faces under SLORC rule.

The narrative cannot end with this chaos, however. The Epilogue of *Burma's Revolution of the Spirit* seeks to re-establish the non-violent logic of democratic revolution. The collage of pictures is complemented by a collage of chapters, introducing for the first time a foreign element: the 1993 meeting in Thailand of Nobel Peace Laureates to support Aung San Suu Kyi. A connection with the "peace and harmony of Burma" is re-established through the Buddhism of the Dalai Lama and the non-violence of the other Nobel Peace Laureates. There is no East or West—only comrades in a transnational peaceful revolution. The last person pictured in the album is Aung San Suu Kyi; with the same photo as on the cover. Although the struggle has not yet ended for Burma, the narrative of the album has come full circle again via *deus ex machina*. The non-violent savior is reasserted in both an original written text by Suu Kyi, "Towards a True Refuge," and her picture on the opposite page. The final photo of the album is of an ancient statue of the Lord Buddha, bringing us back to the peaceful, harmonious Buddhist society set out in the "Introduction" of the volume. The sacred unity is restored, much like that in the American Civil War albums, by paying tribute to an exotic Burmese character. Hence the album reasserts a romantic essential form of identity that risks supporting patriarchal versions of Asian Democracy.

### *Revolutionary youth in* **June Four**

Although all four albums carry the same basic narrative of gendered democracy, there are important technical and conceptual variations on this theme. The four albums can be divided into two groups, not only according to the issue politics of winners and losers, but also according to the rhetorical politics of their format and focus. While the Burmese and Philippine albums are definitely published in the coffee table book format, the Chinese and Thai albums are more in the format of a newspaper's special publication. They came out very soon after the events, are A4 sized with soft covers, and are generally less expensive than the more traditional coffee table books: the Thai albums cost between US$1 and US$4, the Chinese album cost about US$5, while the Burmese album cost US$25, and the Philippine album about US$30.

They also contain a different selection of elements for their collage. While *Burma's Revolution of the Spirit* employs a thematic narrative that is loosely based on time, the Chinese album, *June Four*, strictly utilizes a chronology to order its discourse, starting with the death of Hu Yaobang on April 15, 1989, and ending with Deng's justification of the massacre on June 9. It is not a smooth format. As the opening statement of *June Four* attests, it was not a smooth time: "*June Four* is a diary, beginning and ending abruptly, as the uprising did."[63] There is no slick cyclical narrative of harmony/disharmony/harmony as in the Burmese album. As a diary, it is presented as a series of events, the unvarnished truth that aids its impact. Even though we know the tragic ending, this organization of meaning does not lead us in any specific analytical or political direction.

While *Burma's Revolution of the Spirit* tells us a history of Burma as a background in its opening chapter, the other albums assume the viewers' knowledge of such a historical background. For example, the Beijing protest movement of 1989 was immersed in a commemoration of a number of other defining events of modern Chinese history: the 70th anniversary of the May 4th movement, the 40th anniversary of the founding of the People's Republic, and the 150th anniversary of the Opium War, which was China's first major contact with capitalist modernity. Thus, the Chinese album often uses phrases such as "history will judge," presuming that viewers know the past as shared memory, and are looking forward in time: history points to the future.

Because of this heavy historical burden, the Chinese photo album carries a more intense function of "evidence" of the patriotism and purity of the student movement: "People will never forget" is the caption on the first color photo page of *June Four*. In addition to the diary and photographs, *June Four* contains a host of documents: photos and translations of newspaper editorials, official eulogies, transcripts from televised meetings, photos of posters and placards, transcripts from radio broadcasts, the martial law declaration, signed petitions, announcements, declarations, interview transcripts, photos of photo exhibits, press releases and official statements. Thus, there is a relationship between written and visual texts; the photographs take on an important evidence function.[64] Shapiro notes that photography has historically been involved in such knowledge practices, and argues that photographs thus tend to reinforce existing practices and structures of power, authority and exchange.[65] The People's Liberation Army, for example, published its own bilingual counter-revolutionary photo album—*Quelling the Counter-revolutionary Rebellion in Beijing*—to highlight the heroism of the army and the violence of the students.[66] The revolutionary photo albums such as *Burma's Spirit of Democracy* and *June Four* could also support counter-hegemony, as evidence to buttress the legitimacy of a future more democratic regime.

The second difference between the texts involves how gendered images are deployed. On the one hand, it seems that women and the feminization of democracy are obvious in the Chinese album as well as in the Chinese rebellion. One of the three main student leaders was a woman—Chai Ling was commander-in-chief of the demo. The guiding image of Tian'anmen was also female: the Goddess of Democracy. The gendering of this statue was quite deliberate. The students from the Central Academy of Fine Art took a figure of a Soviet-style peasant man grasping a wooden pole with both hands, and transformed it into a woman by lengthening the hair, adding breasts and softening the facial features.[67] Woman, thus, was the image of defiance used to resist both China's feudal past and Mao's puritanical communism. The Goddess of Democracy was strategically positioned to stare straight into the face of the grand patriarch himself, the portrait of Chairman Mao over Tian'anmen.

But images of women and a feminized democracy are not hegemonic in the Chinese and Thai revolutionary photo albums, as they are in the Burmese and Philippine texts. There actually is a denial of the importance of gender in China and Thailand. Rey Chow's first reaction to the horror of the Tian'anmen massacre in 1989 was:

> I heard a feminist ask: "How should we read what is going on in China in terms of gender?" My immediate response to that question was, and is: "We do not, because at the moment of shock Chinese people are degendered and become simply 'Chinese'."[68]

A Thai feminist, Jiranand Pitpreecha, gave a similar answer at the height of the unrest in May 1992: "It's not a matter of gender. We can classify demonstrators by their age. Most of them are graduates and mature. In this fighting, from the leaders at the top to the bottom—there are women."[69] Even though women are not central, patriarchy is still ordering the discourse. As Jiranand suggests, we need to look beyond the gendered relations of patriarchy to the generational relations: youth. Recall that Lee Kuan Yew was not just doubtful of the reliability of women, but worried about giving power to "capricious young men under 30."

Here youth is not being used in a demographic or economic sense, but in a symbolic sense. This youth has little to do with the material measures of age, marriage and full-time employment, which are commonly used to distinguish young people from adults. Symbolically, youth refers to the subordinate position of certain people in a system of social hierarchy. In such a patriarchy, people—regardless of age—are treated as irresponsible youth who must rely on the wisdom and experience of their elders. A case in point is the conversation between Chinese Premier Li Peng and student leader Wu'er Kaixi in their first dialogue during the students' hunger strike:

> LI PENG: The Party and the government are very concerned about the students' health. ... You are all so young—twenty-two or twenty-three at most. My own children are older than you. I declare that none of my children is involved in guandao [official corruption]. ...
>
> WU'ER KAIXI: Time is running out quickly. We're sitting here comfortably while our fellow students are starving outside, so please pardon me for interrupting.[70]

Li asserts the hierarchy by comparing the protesters to his children; like a good father he is most concerned about their health—not their political opinions. Wu'er Kaixi plays the rebellious youth by impatiently interrupting this speech with a sarcastic "pardon me."[71]

Students are archetypal members of this youth. Since they led the massive nationwide demonstration against imperialist aggression on May 4, 1919 Chinese students carry a heavy symbolic load on their shoulders as the soul of the nation. This romanticization of youthful idealism is iconic in China, and has strong resonance in other countries around Pacific Asia and Euro-America: 1998 produced many revolutionary photo albums commemorating the 30th anniversary of mai '68 in France.[72] Thai and Chinese activists deal with this "youth-ization" in different ways. As Jiranand suggests, Thai activists generally tried to deny youth in the 1992 demonstrations. Although students were active, along with the working classes and urban poor, the dominant image of the May events in Thailand was of middle-class protesters. They take the patriarchal categories for granted and try to separate themselves from failed student movements in the past: "the 1976 victims [of the military crackdown] were relatively inexperienced youths. Now the main targets of the propagandists are shrewd and popular politicians."[73]

The struggle for the identity of the demonstrators quickly shifted from categories such as "youth" and "student" to competing definitions of "the mob" in a curious construction of new symbols out of old. While the Thai army was using traditional definitions of the mob as "lower class, rabble, uncultured and illiterate," Bangkok newspapers redefined the word "mob" as part of the middle-class success story: "The typical member of the 'mob' was a well-off, well-educated, white collar worker."[74] The demonstrators and sympathetic media avoided the designation of "students" because the army claimed that such impressionable youth could be manipulated by outsiders. They employed the strange category of "middle class mob" to represent the movement as responsible, rational, mature, non-violent, middle-aged, and thus democratic.[75]

Chinese protesters, on the other hand, did their best to avoid the label of mob and the related term "turmoil" pasted on them by the *People's Daily* on April 26.[76] This pivotal editorial was an official statement that raised the two fears that captivated the party-state's leadership in Beijing. Youth was a problem for the leadership, both because of their memories of the murderous student movements of the Cultural Revolution, and of the hooligans who roamed the streets in the 1980s.[77] China's aged leaders were afraid that the youth's activities—by definition—would get out of hand, "stirring up trouble using the methods of the Cultural Revolution."[78] Other official statements from the party-state are full of references to an excitable youth who need to be controlled: "Considering that the majority of the people were in mourning, and that youngsters may overreact when they are excited, the Party and the government exercised the utmost restraint and tolerance."[79] The state's discourse assumes that students are being manipulated either as a part of factional struggles or foreign influence.

Unlike the Thai protesters, Chinese demonstrators did not deny or avoid being named student. Their aim was to have the government retract statements suggesting that they were not patriotic. Rather than seeking to widen their constituency—to include workers and professionals—Chinese demonstrators took this youth-ization to the next level of hyperbole, exaggerating

90  *Gender, democracy, revolutionary photo albums*

it by distributing hyper-images of hyper-youth. Thus, the logic of the images in *June Four* is regulated by age. The bulk of the 200 pictures in the album are of young people. They are not depictions of rowdy hooligans or murderous Red Guards, but of youth who are the innocent and idealistic soul of the nation. The politicization of images is deliberate: youth is not defined by age to include the young soldiers and police who were on the opposite side of the barricades—they had to get their own official album that commemorated the sacrifices of youthful soldiers.[80]

The revolutionary youth were framed as "romantic heroes" through photographic practice: they were often photographed against the backdrop of the Monument to People's Heroes in Tian'anmen Square, where they set up their headquarters. To stress their romantic heroism the album's first photo actually constructs this image: photos of the various student leaders are inset against the background of a photo of the Monument (see Figure 3.4). The next two-page photo spread is also at the Monument,

*Figure 3.4*
Revolutionary heroes at Tian'anmen.
*June Four*, p. vii

and shows more happy and engaged students. Other photographs emphasize the innocence of youth: June 1 is Children's Day, and there are numerous photos of cutely dressed young children supporting their "older brothers and sisters."[81]

Once the hunger strike started in Tian'anmen Square on May 13, the innocent children trope went into romantic overdrive. One picture has a student holding a poster that says, "Mama, I'm hungry, but I'm too concerned to eat."[82] The Hunger Strike Declaration repeatedly uses the idealistic youth trope:

> We are young, but we are ready to give up our lives. . . . But we know that we are still children, the children of China. Mother China, look at your children. . . . We say to our dear mothers and fathers, do not feel sorry for us when we are hungry. . . . Farewell, father and mother, forgive us that we're being unfaithful as your children; we must be faithful first to our country.[83]

Thus children of individual parents are symbolically inflated to become children of the nation, the soul of the nation in this romantic narrative.

According to the written and visual texts middle-aged people were not at the center of the action; Vera Schwarcz explains that most university professors were off at conferences to discuss the 70th anniversary of the May 4th movement.[84] Middle-age was measured not in years, but by profession: middle-age generally meant middle class. There are many pictures of different groups of people marching with banners—journalists, workers, professionals. Thus, like in Thailand, the category "middle age" overlaps with the category "middle class." But unlike Thailand, where the middle class played a central role, middle-aged demonstrators were merely supporting actors in the Chinese performance. As their banners tell us, they are not, in fact, demonstrating for themselves, but "supporting the students." In addition to supporting the students rhetorically, they aided the students through donations of food, drink and shelter in Tian'anmen Square. In their petitions, and even hunger strikes near the end of the demonstration, these middle-aged professors and professionals called for an "end to old man government," and liberally used images of emperors.[85]

The government is portrayed as a group of elderly patriarchs—reviving the term gerontocracy that previously had been used to criticize the pre-Gorbachev Soviet leadership. But even old age had both a positive and a negative spin. There are scattered images of the older heroes of the movement—Hu Yaobang and Zhao Ziyang—as good elders. When Hu died, he was grouped with Zhou Enlai as an honest and caring official. There is also a picture of a smiling Hu posing with Tibetan children in June 1980, and Zhao is humanized through a photo of him with his grandson.[86] But the dominant image of old people portrays them as the opposite of the virtuous official—the corrupt bureaucrat who is stiff and authoritarian.

Thus, the trope of age worked differently in Euro-American and Chinese texts: while Euro-American media explained the conflict in terms of communist tyrants, Chinese texts pointed not to ideology, but to age. Much like the representation of Marcos, where his moral corruption was buttressed by images of his physical decay, the Chinese leaders are old and infirm not just physically and morally, but in terms of ideas. One placard reads, "We're through with the politics of old men," a banner: "End the rule of the old men." There are many placards that compare the communist government to the imperial state: "step down last emperor."[87]

Thus the Chinese and Thai albums, much like the Burmese and Philippine albums, switch the logic of patriarchal Asian Democracy. This simple reversal values youth rather than age, instead of feminine over masculine, to script a romantic revolutionary narrative.

## Conclusion

This chapter has argued that Asian Democracy is part of identity construction in Pacific Asia. There are struggles both in language and on the streets over how to define democracy, thus combining rhetorical politics with issue politics. Since both elite bureaucrats and popular social movements are using the same basic democratic vocabulary, the politics lies in how democracy is constructed and performed. In the first section, I argued that elite views of Asian Democracy use a patriarchal reading of politics to frame the issues in a decolonial East/West framework. The rhetorical politics of this East/West conflict is directed at policing the identity of domestic groups: the Voice of Malaysia radio broadcast quoted above made it clear that Western-style democracy is traitorous and corrupt. In other words, the patriarchal discourse of Asian Democracy, which arose in places such as Singapore and Malaysia after 1993, was a reaction to the very real democratic events in the neighboring countries of the Philippines, South Korea, Taiwan, Burma, China and Thailand.

The revolutionary photo albums examined in the second section frame the discourse quite differently to commemorate these democratic movements. Rather than appealing to the geopolitical or inter-civilizational grammars of East/West, they aim their discursive cannons at specific actors in their own society, while appealing to a transnational civil society. The revolutionary photo albums use a different set of distinctions from the patriarchs to produce their own concepts of democracy. This chapter has argued that the discourse is gendered as women-and-children vs. patriarchy, and is supported by related distinctions such as non-violence vs. violence, unarmed demonstrators vs. heavily armed soldiers, parliamentary democracy vs. military dictatorship, mass demonstrations vs. coups, virtue vs. corruption. It should not be surprising that gender forms a guiding part in the construction of these democratic memories. Just as women-and-children's labor has formed a central part in Pacific Asia's economic development, women and students have been central in democratic movements. Thus, in terms of the politics of issues—democratic social movements struggling against authoritarian regimes—the conflict represented in revolutionary photo albums is clear.

The political rhetoric of the photo albums is more complex. On the one hand, there is a shift in textual practice. While the official texts are literate, the texts representing popular politics use popular culture: photography. These visual narratives are politically impious because they challenge the patriarchy in Pacific Asia. Even so, the albums ooze a different sort of political piety. The visual narrative is characteristically sentimental, highlighting the internal states and spirits of Beautiful Souls, rather than the actions and structures of chastened patriots (or in this case, matriots): Aung San Suu Kyi talks of a revolution of the spirit and freedom from fear, while the Chinese students constructed a Goddess of Democracy out of styrofoam. Rhetorically, the albums' narratives correspond well with Frye's notion of romance that pits a hero against an enemy in an unironic struggle of divine vs. demonic. The photographic narratives characteristically portray democracy as non-violent, feminine and young, while the repressive regimes are violent, masculine and old. The concept of the savior is very important to these texts; in a proper romance mode the savior collects the heroic virtues of non-violent democracy together to fight the corrupt military patriarchy.

In terms of the politics of rhetoric, the problems with romance narratives are manifest. The hyper-youth-ization of students in China risked reproducing the power by replacing the essence of communist revolution with another essence of students as the soul of the nation. Cory Aquino and Aung San Suu Kyi likewise transformed their religious piety into a political piety. The gendered images were scripted into certain stereotypical roles—women as devoted mothers, dutiful daughters, chaste nuns and jaded prostitutes; youth as innocent and idealistic; men as corrupt tyrants and cruel soldiers. Thus, these albums risk reinforcing both Orientalism and patriarchy, even as they oppose them. As we saw in *Burma's Revolution of the Spirit*, the discourse switches all too easily from a feminine democracy of popular politics to a masculine nationalism of armed struggle, from the Beautiful Soul to the Virtuous Warrior. The Chinese album likewise romantically glorifies bloodshed and sacrifice as the key to political change: its original Chinese title is *The Tragically Heroic Movement: An Extremely Peaceful Beginning, an Extremely Bloody End*.

But is this curious combination of romance and Orientalism necessarily problematic? Or is the appeal to the opposite of Romance—Satire—even more problematic? Some argue that social science analysis in the Satirical mode, which emphasizes the politics of rhetoric and the acid tools of deconstruction, can lead to a paralysis in the politics of issues.[88] Thus both gender and democracy risk being delegitimized as productive discourses and mobilizing forces.[89] To put it another way, Mahathir, the *Ming Bao* newspaper, and the American Buddhist editors of *Burma's Revolution of the Spirit* all Orientalize/feminize the subjects of their texts, but in different ways and for different aims. In *Occidentalism* Chen Xiaomei argues that, since the essences of East and West are cultural creations rather than essential truths, there is nothing inherently wrong with either Orientalism or its reverse, Occidentalism. Rather, she argues that:

> it is the use to which these terms are put by those who articulate them, and by those who hear and receive them, that determines their social— and literary—effects. . . . The Orient can anti-imperialistically use the Occident to achieve its own political aims at home.[90]

Hence, Chen praises the 1988 Chinese television series *Heshang*, which juxtaposed fancifully positive images of the West (i.e. Occidentalism) with grotesquely degenerate images of China (Orientalism). The authors were not actually criticizing the Chinese people, Chen argues. Rather, the program was pushing for political reform since the image of an "inferior China" was a metaphor for the single-party state.[91] Chen's argument brings us back to issue politics, and sees the politics of rhetoric in terms of a set of tools that are used to struggle for particular goals. According to this logic, it is right and proper for *Burma's Revolution of the Spirit* to use Orientalist images of Buddhist harmony as a technology of resistance in the service of a popular democratic movement that is directed against authoritarian state power. Since the Burmese and Chinese activists are quite sure about the morality of their democratic project, using Orientalist images and the Beautiful Soul for this aim are acceptable if they work.

But do they work? Occidentalism as a form of resistance in post-Tian'anmen China has not worked. Occidentalist images of an evil and corrupt West have nourished the official nationalism of the Chinese state, as well as xenophobic identities in Thailand, Malaysia and Singapore. As Dai Jinhua argues:

> The Occidentalism of the late 1970s and the 1980s, which offered a critical perspective or held out promise for social cohesion, has fundamentally disappeared. Nationalism, or self-Orientalism, as an instrument of the officials, has become the only effective measure for social cohesion.[92]

I think that the problem with Chen's analysis is more than temporal; although she repeatedly states that dividing the world up in a binary fashion into Occidental/Oriental is problematic, her arguments keep deploying and thus reproducing this particular binary mode. This reassertion of a dichotomy of essentials amounts to a battle of stereotypes that leads us farther away from Chen's stated concerns with the everyday life of the Chinese "back home."[93] As the well-known Chinese literary critic Li Tuo argues, by conjuring up such clear stereotypes and romantic structures, Chen risks falling back into the Maoist trap that she most desperately seeks to avoid. He describes his own struggles with writing:

> It was as though I had to classify matters in which I had an interest with written words—the "best," the "worst," the "absolutely right," or the "utterly wrong"—before I could rest easy. ... I have called this style the "Mao style," and it is a unified system of language style that has extended its grip on all realms of discourse.[94]

The hyperbole of MaoSpeak is evident in the Chinese photo album's title—*The Tragically Heroic Movement: An Extremely Peaceful Beginning, an Extremely Bloody End*. To resist the Maoism of romantic decolonial discourses of opposite extremes, Li tells us that we have to resist this Mao-style of discourse production.[95] This brings us back to the politics of rhetoric as it informs issue politics.

Similar moves were taking place within the Chinese protest movement. Toward the end of the demonstration, and later in exile, criticism of the student movement that relied on the image of a savior began to gain force.[96] According to the Hunger Strike Declaration of middle-aged intellectuals on June 2, 1989, the political task was to break out of the cycle of emperors and saviors:

> For thousands of years, Chinese society has been circling from one emperor to another. We overthrew the old emperor only to establish the crown of another. History has proven that the replacement of an unpopular ruler by a popular one does not resolve China's political problems. What we need is not a perfect savior but a good democratic system.[97]

This declaration combines rhetorical and issue politics to begin the shift from a politics of *deus ex machina* that relies on the pious spirits and catchy slogans of the Beautiful Soul, to the action and organization of chastened patriots. As Li argues, we must beware of simple reversals; recall that Elshtain concludes that chastened patriots need to be "zestful act takers, experimenting with new possibilities playfully but from a deep seriousness of purpose"[98] if they are to avoid producing another romantic mode.

What is necessary is a switch from Romance not to Satire, but to Comedy. Whereas Romance emplots the story of good triumphing over evil, and Satire points out the ultimate folly of human endeavor, Comedy organizes action according to the hopeful narrative of temporary triumph and the occasional reconciliations of the forces at play.[99] Zhang Hongtu's "Chairmen Mao" series of paintings provides a cogent example of how to resist power through irony and play in the Comic mode. Rather than discarding the Mao image and thus denying the past, or reproducing it in kitsch form to commodify the past,[100] Zhang plays with power by recontextualizing iconic photos of Mao in multiple and impious ways.[101] Of the many meanings of Mao, some highlight gendered themes: one painting replays the iconic image of the Tian'anmen Square confrontation where the Goddess of Democracy stared down Mao's official portrait. Zhang's retextualization has a lecherous Mao leering back at the Goddess, saying "Babe!" Another painting resists the power of Mao by mixing metaphors of both age and gender: the Chairman is transformed (much like the Soviet peasant into the Goddess of Democracy) into a school girl by adding chubby red cheeks and pig-tails[102] (see Figure 3.5).

*Figure 3.5* Chairmen Mao #3 (1989), by Zhang Hongtu. Collage and acrylic on paper. Used with permission

The best way to understand these albums, then, is not in terms of the colonial and decolonial essences of East/West or woman/man, but in terms of postcolonial struggles. In this way we can evade the romantic straitjacket that binds both interpretation and action to more ironic understandings of political possibility. Rather than being limited to a search for pure opposition, the examples of resistance cited above demonstrate that politics consists of using various identities—gendered, religious, national, traditional, modern—as tactics in a struggle against the state's cultural governance and power as domination. In this instance, the struggle is for the project of democracy whose morality already has been established. At other times, we could take gender for granted, in order to question democracy.

When seen in this way, resistance is not simply a matter of using patriarchy to fight patriarchy, and thus reproducing power as domination. For example, Bishop Desmond Tutu playfully used gendered identity to fight the military patriarchy in Burma: "We hope very much that the military junta which is scared of a little woman is made to shake in its boots because, in our mission, we have said 'the world is watching you. Watch out!'"[103] Likewise, for tactical reasons Cory Aquino wrote "housewife" as her occupation when registering her candidacy for president—even though she actually was quite worldly as the manager of her family's vast plantation holdings.[104] Aung San Suu Kyi at various times switched from prioritizing gender when other discourses were more politically useful: she often undermined the guiding discourse of peaceful women vs. violent men by playfully pointing to her fond memories of how well the Burmese army had taken care of her in her youth.[105]

Hence, like Chapter 2's analysis of Miss Thailand, this chapter has argued the masculine and the feminine are unstable concepts in the region: they are revalued with each successive utterance. Revolutionary photo albums provide a useful resource for examining the politics of popular culture in Pacific Asia. They suggest that questions of authenticity and artificiality, upon which the more official texts rely, do not lead us to easy answers about political and social movements in Pacific Asia. Simply put, there is a lot of cross-dressing going on: in addition to Mao with rosy cheeks and pigtails, the Goddess of Democracy was originally the opposite: a Soviet man. And, of course, in Chapter 2 we saw how Miss Thailand at times dressed up as a soldier, complete with bazooka. But rather than seeing hybridities as a problem, these impertinent metaphors are part of a solution both in terms of the politics of issues and the politics of rhetoric. They can be politically impious, and thus help us to escape from the essentialized binaries of feminine/masculine, peace/war, Orientalism/Occidentalism, colonial/postcolonial to a more productive view of politics. By questioning the rhetorical politics of these essential categories we can work on the politics of issues: to resist power as domination wherever we find it.

Chapter 4 will jump right in and question the category of civil society, the virtue of which has been taken for granted in this chapter. Instead of valorizing civil society as an essential part of democratization, Chapter 4 will differentiate it from social movements. Using examples from South Korea, China and Taiwan, it will argue that, while civil society can be effectively used in elite state policies of cultural governance, social movements are better able to resist power and promote popular politics in the broad arena of capitalist modernity.

# 4 Popular politics, civil society and social movements

While Chapter 3 described how politicians and activists battled over the meaning of democracy in Pacific Asia, this chapter will consider academic debates over the meaning of democratic concepts. Chapter 3's consideration of democratic uprisings tended to blur together the concepts of civil society and social movements, hence this chapter will consider the important theoretical questions raised by this distinction. In particular I will examine how the debate over the meaning of democracy in Pacific Asia has been framed in terms of certain binary oppositions—civil society/state, East/West—to argue that this ordering of the discourse misses out on the multiple and ironic identities and institutions that operate in the region. I argue that the search for civil society in the region is often misplaced. The question is not whether there is an authentic civil society in the states that make up Pacific Asia; the main issue is how different groups are using the concept of civil society in very political ways. Although civil society is often assumed to be progressive and democratic, the first section of the chapter will show how it is often used by elites as a mode of cultural governance to control popular political movements. Civil society is deployed as part of the state policy of democratization, which limits popular participation to familiar procedural forms of electoralism, rather than a broader social and economic democracy.[1] I use examples from South Korea and China to illustrate this conservative notion of civil society.

But this is not to say that Pacific Asia is doomed to conservatism as the scholars who study the political culture of Confucian democracy and Asian values often conclude.[2] Indeed, in spite of many states' durable conservative hegemony, as we saw in Chapter 3 there have been vibrant social movements in Pacific Asia. Actually both political leaders and well-known theorists have noted that we cannot rely on philosophers—either Greek or Pacific Asian—for democracy. Rather, we must bracket our preoccupation with the (comparative) study of utopian ideals, in order to more clearly appreciate the struggle of people in social movements.[3]

The second section then makes the theoretical shift from the singularity of civil society to the multiplicity of social movements, and the third section uses examples from China, Taiwan and South Korea to demonstrate a more multiple, decentered and ironic practice of cultural governance and resistance. I argue that, when we challenge the guiding binaries of civil society/state and East/West that frame the debate over civil society in Pacific Asia, we can open up space for a re-examination of the popular politics of social movements that struggle with and against capitalist modernity. Thus, the analysis of this chapter pushes us from the politics of stability (of civil society) to the politics of possibility (of new social movements).

## Civil society and the politics of stability

In the late 1990s, the *Korea Journal* commissioned a series of articles to discuss the concept of civil society in the South Korean context.[4] Although the "transition to democracy" narrative's goal is political stability,[5] this debate over civil society in South Korea showed how stability is not just institutional, but epistemological. In other words, most analyses of civil society are obsessed with finding stable definitions of institutions and identity. David Steinberg's discussion of civil society in South Korea is exemplary of this search for stability: in addition to often using the word "define," his discussion of orthodoxy liberally deploys the concepts of "singularity," "unity," "unique," "homogeneity" and "totality."[6] In a way familiar to cultural nativists, Steinberg discusses Korean society's uniquely homogeneous nationality, culture, ethnicity and language. Steinberg thus argues for the enduring strength of orthodoxy in post-Confucian South Korea to warn of the problems that civil society faces.

Hahm Chaibong also seeks to define Korean society as a way of discussing civil society.[7] Unlike Steinberg, who traces the enduring influence of Confucianism in modern Korea, Hahm argues that the ideology and the institutions of the South Korean state diverge from authentic Korean culture. Although political parties and parliament call themselves "democratic" in South Korea, Hahm reasons that Confucianism is actually the correct mode of understanding South Korean politics. He argues that the twisted politics of reform in South Korea make much more sense in terms of a Confucian "rule of man" rather than a liberal "rule of law." Hahm's thought-provoking analysis again relies on a search for stable definitions of comparative political theory: the short title for his article is "Confucianism and Democracy." Although Hahm's stated aim is to explain the politics of reform in South Korea, he spends the bulk of his time defining idealized forms of Confucianism as Korean (and thus authentic), and idealized forms of liberalism as Western (and thus foreign). The debate between Steinberg and Hahm demonstrates the discursive framing of civil society; regardless of whether one is pro- or anti-Confucianism, pro- or anti-civil society, all contributions to the debate engage in the epistemic performance of nailing down the meaning of civil society.

The politics of the meaning of civil society in Pacific Asia characteristically involves the issue of "translation." After a thorough search, scholars tell us that there are no ancient concepts in Korea or China that we can use to translate "civil society": "These linguistic explorations suggest that it is hard for Chinese discourse to translate precisely concepts that as yet have no corresponding experience and reality. This does not eliminate the possibility for innovation."[8] Thus scholars have had to make their own creative translations of "civil society." Steinberg and others touch on this problem of the multiplicity of "civil society" in Chinese and Korean translations (which use the same characters)—but only as an afterthought.[9] Shu-Yun Ma considers different translations to show how the discourse of civil society was framed in mainland China, while Wang Hui and Leo Lee devote an entire article to the question of translation.[10] Curiously, recent mainland Chinese discussions of civil society also are concerned with nailing down a stable definition; yet they do not frame translation as a cultural problem, but as a political problem of how to maintain the stability of the state.[11] If nothing else, these long lists of possible translations (from English to Chinese and back again) show the fruitful ambiguity of the concept of civil society.

Yet this search for stable definitions and simple word-for-word translations assumes that "civil society" is a natural concept in European discourse, and it is foreign to Pacific Asia. Definitions and translations both suggest that civil society is a finished product (much like twentieth-century views of "democracy," "development" or "civilization" in Euro-America), rather than a site of contestation in the process of political and social change. Thus it is not surprising that many of the academics unapologetically state that they are involved in a narrative of discovery: many of the titles of books and articles include the phrase "In search of . . .," which is again reproduced in the text.[12] This search is part of a narrative of disjuncture—civil society was on track, being developed some time in the not-too-distant past, but unfortunately there was a break in this historical process of development. The task then is to go in search of civil society's past, which can lead us to its future: a future that always is assumed to be democratic.[13]

This rupture occurs at different times in different countries. In China, pre-revolutionary history is taken as the benchmark.[14] Civil society was developing normally in late Qing and Republican China, only to be interrupted by the Communist Party and its 1949 revolution. The logic of this "break" asserts that civil society did not disappear forever. In mainland China, scholars tell us, civil society began to reappear with the economic reforms of 1978.[15] The history of civil society, and its break, is slightly different in Taiwan. Civil society was repressed by the Guomindang (GMD) military state in the late 1940s, specifically with the February 28 (1947) movement, which brutally suppressed local intellectuals and leaders.[16] When the GMD changed its tactics in the 1980s from coercive martial law to political liberalization, civil society began to reappear.[17] In South Korea, Cho Hein tells us, civil society was developing in the late Choson period (1392–1910) through independent Confucian organizations of "backwoods scholars"— but it was brutally interrupted by the Japanese colonization of South Korea in 1910.[18] The debate over civil society thus is displaced from the present; it is now located somewhere in the past to determine whether or not there are authentic roots of civil society in national tradition.

This search for civil society suggests two assumptions about historiography: history is seen as linear and progressive, while the germ of civil society is seen as a finished product waiting to be (re)discovered after being hidden because of grand historical tragedies. In other words, the task for scholars is to mine the past for the golden nuggets called facts, looking—desperately at times—for the mother lode of civil society. Indeed, Adrian Chan characterizes the whole academic pursuit of civil society in China as a comical "search for the holy grail," which ends up "pushing square pegs into round holes."[19]

Before discarding the notion of civil society in Pacific Asia altogether, it is helpful to interrogate the assumptions of stability and unity. Habermas reminds us the concept of civil society is far from unambiguous. In his "Translator's Note" to Habermas's *The Structural Transformation of the Public Sphere*, Thomas Burger warns of the difficulties of matching concepts in English and German: is *Bürger* "bourgeois" or "citizen?"[20] In the first sentence of this classic, Habermas warns that "The usage of the words 'public' and 'public sphere' betrays a multiplicity of concurrent meanings."[21]

Discourses and practices of history and society in South Korea and China are likewise far from clear-cut. The past is not a stable "thing" that is waiting for us to discover it. Rather, history is a narrative that has its own particular rules of inclusion and exclusion.[22] In South Korea, as in China, historiography has been not progressive and linear, but circular. Andre Schmid questions the familiar unities of time, space and race in South Korea by comparing traditional Confucian historiography with Sin Ch'aeho's revisionist historiography. Confucian patterns of historical scholarship privileged the royal court, and were engaged in the task of "identifying the legitimate dynasty ... then recounting how the rulers attained, maintained, and lost the Mandate of Heaven through a moral appraisal of their actions."[23] On the other hand, Sin's historiography, which set the standard for later Korean historians, shifted from focusing on the court (and then the state) to *minjok*: the racially defined nation. Much like the narrative of civil society, Sin does not specifically define *minjok*, but rather used "the rhetoric of rediscovery," which assumes that the racial purity of South Korea is self-evident. In this way, Sin was able to shift the definition of Korean space from the peninsula to include Manchuria. Schmid thus concludes that even "the most concrete feature of Korean national identity, territory, has in fact been open to contestation."[24]

The search for civil society often bleeds into the search for identity in its various forms: national, regional, local. As Steinberg, Hahm and Schmid suggest, analyses of political change in Pacific Asia do not just seek out a stable definition of civil society, but also end up defining the rest of intellectual and social practice: orthodoxy, unity, authenticity, civilization, territory and race. But these debates about democracy in Pacific Asia also suggest the problems of this "in search of civil society" mode of analysis: as Nietzsche taught us, we usually find what we are looking for, because we ourselves put it there in the first place (and then forgot we put it there, and then forgot that we forgot).

## Political culture and civil society

Civil society is a hot topic around the globe, but most specifically in two geographical areas: Eastern Europe and Pacific Asia. These two areas are also associated with activity among political culture scholars who deal with post-communist and post-Confucian societies.[25] In this section, I will examine how civil society is part of the discourse of political culture, which has become quite powerful in the field of Pacific Asian politics.[26] Simply put, political culture describes a subfield of political science that tries to account for the diversity in world politics that rational-choice approaches miss. The practice of political culture research often involves the search for core values and basic institutions that define the range of choices for a particular society. These norms and institutions are typically located in the past; they are the product of history, but once fully formed they are frozen. Hahm's "Confucian Political Discourse and the Politics of Reform in Korea" is a good example of political culture research. It does not look for democracy in contemporary social movements or parliamentary elections, so much as in the seventeenth- and eighteen-century European texts of Hobbes, Locke and Montesquieu. It finds Confucianism in ancient texts rather than in the New Confucian movements of the late twentieth century.[27]

Although framing analysis with terms such as "post-communist" and "post-Confucian" suggests it engages in new ways of analyzing political change, the civil society texts reaffirm very familiar discourses of political science: East/West relations. Sinologists look to the ideological definition of East and West to compare communist China with post-communist Eastern Europe, while Korean studies texts employ Orientalist definitions of East/West to compare Confucian East Asia with the liberal democratic West. This dual East/West debate shows how similar political events in China and South Korea are explained in different ways.

## China: East/West as left/right

In the discussions of civil society, China is not compared with the post-Confucian society of South Korea, or even Taiwan, but with the post-communist societies of Eastern Europe. The year 1989 guides and organizes this discourse for three reasons. The first two are obvious: there were successful democratic revolutions in Eastern Europe and an unsuccessful social movement in China. Even though the students and other demonstrators were looking to Asian examples of successful democratic transitions in Pacific Asia, scholars have been captivated by Eastern Europe's transition from communism. Richard Madsen begins "The Public Sphere, Civil Society and Moral Community" with a quotation from Vaclav Havel.[28] McCormick, Su and Xiao look to the Polish experience to explain social organization in China, while Xiaoqin Guo concludes that the Hungarian model is most apt.[29] Ma and Su Shaozhi each argue that China has more similarities with Eastern European countries than East Asian ones; Su concludes with three possible models for democratic transition: the Polish model, the Hungarian model, and the Romanian model.[30] Many note that the notion of civil society was revived in Eastern Europe in the 1970s and 1980s to guide the eventual revolutions.[31] Chinese intellectuals in exile after 1989 thus increasingly looked to Eastern European examples and definitions.[32]

Unfortunately, there is a chronological problem with using Eastern Europe to explain China. The fall of the Berlin Wall came five months after the massacre at Tian'anmen Square. Indeed, it makes more sense to use "the Chinese model" to explain post-communist Eastern Europe than vice versa. But it is easy to see why the discourse of civil society in Eastern Europe is so attractive. Its narrative also relies on a violent break with tradition—first from Nazi Germany and then from the communist "revolutions" of the 1940s—and the consequent search for civil society that is part of a return to pre-war Enlightenment values.[33] Indeed, one of the books that Ma cites from Eastern Europe is also called *In Search of Civil Society*, and another prominent volume is entitled *The Reemergence of Civil Society in Eastern Europe and the Soviet Union*.[34]

The third reason for the focus on 1989 is more discursive than historical—although still European. Jürgen Habermas's 1962 classic about civil society, *The Structural Transformation of the Public Sphere: An Inquiry into the Category of Bourgeois Society*, was published in English for the first time in 1989.[35] This book guides most of the discussion of civil society in China,[36] which uses Habermas's analysis to distinguish between public and private, and the state and civil society. Beyond the guiding ideas, many of the civil society articles look to Habermas for a checklist of the institutions and practices necessary for civil society. While Habermas argues that coffee houses were an important meeting place for civil society in eighteenth-century Europe,[37] there is a heated debate over whether Chinese tea houses are a functional equivalent.[38] William T. Rowe tentatively points to Laoshe's novel *Teahouse*, and Lu Xun's story "In the Wineshop" as early twentieth-century depictions of the institutions of civil society in China.[39] In response to this popular argument, Madsen argues that

Just because Habermas tells us that coffee houses played a key role in the development of a bourgeois public sphere in eighteenth-century England, we should not assume that teahouses might play the same role in China! What matters is not the consuming of a beverage but the fostering of a certain quality of relationship.⁴⁰

But, after noting the problems with using European concepts in a Chinese context, Rowe looks to standard definitions of civil society. He seems to go through a Habermasian checklist of items necessary for a thriving civil society: capitalism; an institutionalized public purse, public utilities and public management; literacy, publishing and the print culture; urbanization and sites for collective discussion of "public affairs"; autonomous organizations; social contract; natural rights; a theory of proprietorship; individualism; civility; and public opinion.⁴¹ In an exemplary case of a political culture method of searching for the pre-conditions for democracy, Rowe compares each of these institutions, ideas and practices with Chinese examples to see if they work—and he admits that they do not work very well.

## *South Korea: East/West as tradition/modernity*

Although Sinologists characteristically look to Eastern Europe and Habermas to understand civil society in China, South Koreans look elsewhere. Certainly, Habermas is not unknown in South Korea. His 1997 visit to the country became a media event, and has produced an edited volume where Habermas and his South Korean colleagues discuss various social issues, including civil society.⁴² Habermas has entered the South Korean debate on civil society through Han Sang-Jin's influential article "The Public Sphere and Democracy in South Korea."⁴³ Yet, Habermas is largely absent from other discussions of civil society in South Korea because the debate shifts from Europe to East Asia. Although Cho and Steinberg discuss the "Habermasian concepts" of autonomy and checks and balances, they do not look to European examples—as do the Sinologists. Rather, Cho and Steinberg debate whether Confucian society in Korea was orthodox or pluralistic. Hahm more directly shifts from framing South Korean politics in terms of left vs. right to consider political change in terms of the relation of tradition and modernity. Hahm, thus, is not satisfied with the mainstream view of South Korea as a liberal democratic state whose "ideology has provided the bulwark against ideological as well as military encroachments of Communist North Korea."⁴⁴ Rather than looking to communist counter-examples, many Korean scholars are looking away from them. But they are still involved in an East/West discourse. Rather than focus on ideology as the defining feature, they increasingly look to civilization to frame South Korean politics. Hence the alternative to the individualism of liberal democracy is no longer the communist values of socialism, but the communal values of Confucianism. Hahm sets up liberalism and Confucianism as polar opposites. Like the Southeast Asian leaders discussed in Chapter 3, Hahm argues that the "essential differences" of liberalism and Confucianism are incommensurable.[45]

## The politics of multiplicity

At first, the description of civil society in terms of East/West, tradition/modernity and individual/family is quite persuasive. But, on closer study, serious conceptual problems arise for this framing of social and political change in terms of binaries such as state/civil society.[46] This is part of the critique of the project of modernity that is a search for the cognitive unity of truth, the cultural unity of tradition, the moral unity of the common good, and the geopolitical unity of the nation-state. These unities are constructed through mutually exclusive binary oppositions. Although social scientists try to measure the "autonomy" of civil society, civil society does not make sense unless it is seen in opposition to the state—albeit in a complementary way.

In practice many of the articles cited thus far have "methodological caveats," admitting that the binaries do not always work.[47] This is because society in South Korea and Pacific Asia is characterized more by multiplicity than by binary distinctions.[48] Han exemplifies this multiplicity in his discussion of different kinds of public spheres: the bourgeois public sphere, the proletarian public sphere, the peasant public sphere, and the feminist public sphere.[49] But the complex logic of South Korean society goes far beyond the usual sociological categories of class, race and gender, which again make neat pluralistic divisions to add up into the whole of society. Rather, identity in Pacific Asia is characterized by overlapping and multilayered discourses and practices.

Thus, standard sociological techniques have problems measuring and quantifying South Korean society. This can most easily be seen in polls taken about religious affiliation. Although many are quite comfortable stating that Korean society is Confucian, the public opinion polls do not unequivocally bear this out. Depending on which poll you choose, either one percent of South Koreans are Confucian or 91.7 percent are Confucian.[50] This statistical problem arises not because South Koreans cannot make up their minds, but because religious identity and practice in South Korea is multiple rather than exclusive: people commonly are a combination of Shamanist, Buddhist, Confucian and/or Christian. According to one of the polls, Buddhists are 100 percent "Confucianized."[51] These polls thus show how South Korean identity is not pluralistic, as in civil society, where all the differences add up to a 100 percent whole. Rather, it is multiple, going beyond any simple unity: when you add up all the figures, the sum of identities is far more than 100 percent. As Robert Weller concludes, the difficulties in understanding popular politics in the region "speak less to the inadequacies of Chinese culture in the modern world than to inadequacies of the concept of civil society."⁵² Thus, we have to look beyond binary ways of defining social practice to open up and appreciate the hybridity of society in Pacific Asia.

## *Confucian and Foucauldian multiplicities*

Although many scholars like to frame Confucianism as an orthodoxy in a binary relation with liberal democracy, there is also multiplicity in Confucianism. Indeed, rather than being organized into binaries of state/civil society or individual/society, social practice in Pacific Asia is not just multiple, but holographic. As we saw in the Introduction, the Confucian classic *The Great Learning* describes an environment where people seek fulfillment in ways that join the personal, familial, communal, political and cosmic. These orthodox Confucian practices transgress dichotomies to make the individual, civil society and the state coterminous and mutually entailing.⁵³ Likewise, the Chinese term for humanity—*ren*—"refers to human beings, both collectively and individually, both male and female, both physically and spiritually."⁵⁴ Rather than focusing power in the family, as Confucian democracy promoters advocate, Confucianism also diffuses power; it comes from many nodes, sometimes in harmony, sometimes in creative tension.

There are interesting parallels between *The Great Learning* and Foucault's concept of "governmentality," which argues that power is not just found in state institutions. Rather, Foucault argues that power is more pastoral and multiple:

> the practices of government are, on the one hand, multifarious and concern many kinds of people: the head of a family, the superior of a convent, the teacher or tutor of a child or pupil; so that there are several forms of government among which the prince's [external] relation to his state is only one particular mode; while on the other hand, all these other kinds of government are internal to the state or society.⁵⁵

Rather than state and civil society being distinct, and in opposition, the various forms of governmentality interweave the state and society with other spaces.

Both *The Great Learning* and Foucault's governmentality show how framing political change in terms of the state/civil society relations misses the multiple practices of power. Rather than being reduced to definitions of civil society, both texts lead us toward an ironic politics that resists simple definition. These hybrid forms mix discourses, to lead us away from simple binary distinctions of East/West. Although Chen Xiaomei's *Occidentalism* claims that the main way to be anti-government is to be pro-Western,⁵⁶ there is a history of ironic resistance in China that ranges from the ancient texts such as the *Zhuangzi* that have Confucius saying "un-Confucian" things, up through contemporary novels that have Marx criticizing Marxism in China.[57] Although the ritualization of student protests in South Korea often reproduced traditional state orthodoxy,[58] Chinese students resisted the state in 1989 by playing with state ritual as well as ironically laughing at inappropriate times.[59]

When power is multiple, then resistance is multiple as well. Such multiple practices of resistance are evident in popular politics in Pacific Asia that question the category of civil society: old social movements, new social movements, political opposition, private volunteer organizations, non-governmental organizations and extra-parliamentary activity. Although it may seem daunting to have so many categories for making sense of political change, Foucault argues that such multiplicity is indicative of power relations.[60] The relation between power and resistance is not clean or pure, but sticky. Thus, for social movements, "independence" and "cooptation" are relative terms. Chung Chulhee's analysis of South Korean social movements shows the ironic and sticky nature of power where there is an overlap of formal and informal activities, parliamentary and extra-parliamentary politics, and violent and non-violent tactics.[61] NGO activities often overlap with state policy; while some NGOs have been coopted, others cultivate a relationship to power where their "independence" is "fostered" by the state.[62] Rather than being simply autonomous (or not), South Korea's new social movements have a relationship of "conflictual cooperation" with the state.[63]

South Korea does not just have multiple identities, but has a very vibrant discourse of "Confucianism" and "democracy" that gives rise to multiple interpretations. While Han states that different civil societies can be formed under different historical conditions,[64] we can push this argument further to say that within history there are competing concepts of civil society. Hence, the question is not whether there is an authentic civil society in South Korea or China, but how different groups are using this concept in very political ways. The following sections re-examine political change in China and South Korea to see how conservative groups have quite successfully used the discourse of civil society for cultural governance, while progressive groups have used the concept of social movements to resist capitalist modernity.

### *Conservative uses of civil society*

Although many see a contradiction between civil society and Confucianism, often those who promote civil society are the same scholars who advocate Confucianism in Pacific Asia. Although Adrian Chan sees this as an American conspiracy to subjugate China,[65] many of these dual promoters are Chinese and South Korean. In this section I will examine examples of seemingly odd discourses of civil society. Indeed, there is nothing inherently "progressive" or "democratic" about civil society; each social movement needs to be evaluated on its own terms. Specifically, I will trace how certain elite groups have used the concept of civil society first to limit democratic reform, and second to strengthen the power of the state and corporate business in capitalist modernity.

While the pro-democracy movement of 1989 provoked Sinologists to discuss civil society in China, discussion of civil society started in mainland China in 1986, and Taiwan in 1985–6.[66] While Ma describes a vibrant and diverse civil society discourse in mainland China, he notes that it did not rely on radical division between civil society and the state. By 1988, the state had actually domesticated the concept of civil society for its own purposes. Through debates over definitions of the concept of "citizenship"—actually over the translation of *Bürger* that bothered Burger—the concept of civil society shifted from describing a "politicized" bourgeois society to constitute a "neutral" citizen's society. The task for civil society theorists then was to determine how to transform the undifferentiated and potentially chaotic Chinese "mass" into an active and responsible "citizenry." Ma thus argues that "civil society was seen as the creation of a modern citizenry through the inspiration of civic awareness by the state among the people"[67] in a top-down mode of cultural governance. Here, civil society is not posed in opposition to the state, for this civil society theory recognizes the "inevitable existence of the state."[68] Thus, civil society is not a social movement emanating from the grassroots, so much as a creation of top-down state policy. The party-state has not limited its action to merely colonizing civic organizations in a corporatist model of Chinese society; rather, it has worked to colonize the idea of civil society itself. This cooperative conception of civil society was welcomed by conservative groups in the Chinese regime, who published an official "handbook for citizens" in 1988.[69] In ways familiar to Lee Kuan Yew, this handbook guided the discussion of civil society away from freedoms to responsibilities, social discipline and public security. The party thus is playing both the East/West games to make a civil society that has both Chinese characteristics and socialist characteristics.

Although the discussion about civil society published within China stopped between 1988 and the mid-1990s, and most of the dissidents went abroad in 1989, sociological explorations have confirmed that such elite views of civil society persist in post-Tian'anmen China.[70] White, Howell and Shang's detailed research into civil society in China concludes that the reformers in China are largely counter-elites: entrepreneurs who are not radically opposed to the state. They have benefited from the reforms and are against rapid political change.[71] NGOs in China are better described as GONGOs (government-oriented NGOs) because of their close links with the state.[72] An awards ceremony held in 2004 is instructive: the Ministry of Civil Administration, which regulates civil society, decided to commend outstanding NGOs for the first time in China. The ministry invited NGO leaders to a grand ceremony at the Great Hall of the People on Tian'anmen

Square, where the minister himself gave a speech to list their achievements. Not surprisingly, the minister praised NGOs for serving as a "bridge that connects the people with the Party and the state." NGOs hence facilitate the implementation of the official goals of "economic development, social progress, and an all-around development of people." Moreover, the NGOs were commended for "using Deng Xiaoping theory and [Jiang Zemin's] Three Representations as their ideological guide to implement the objectives of the Party Central Committee and the State Council." Last, the minister declared that NGOs "must serve the state, serve society, and serve the people"—presumably in that order.[73]

Other more scholarly sources agree that the role of civil society in China is to serve the state; its role is to provide solutions to the social problems raised by economic reform that cannot be resolved by the state or the market. Although NGOs are necessary in reform China, scholars in prominent journals argue that the state has to keep a close eye upon them, and clarify the rules and regulations. The state needs to effectively manage these semi-independent organizations because "stability is the overwhelming responsibility in China."[74] Far from contesting state power, this concept of civil society legitimates the need for state power—in both theory and practice. The state uses civil society not as a means of sharing power, but for a "more effective control of society."[75] In the early twenty-first century, civil society in China is framed as an appendage of the state, as part of a strategy of top-down democratization.[76] Indeed, one writer argues that civil society is useful because it "strengthens the state's authority," and thus is a "resource for the state's legitimacy."[77]

## South Korean elites

The Chinese use of civil society mirrors tactics of Asian Democracy analyzed in the last chapter that sought to limit democracy to electoralism. In South Korea there are interesting examples of a "Confucianization" of civil society that limits the discussion of political issues to the elite in the business leaders, top universities and the media. Indeed, Steinberg does not even include the mass media in his definition of civil society.[78] This narrowing of civil society has facilitated a middle-class political consolidation that limits democracy to its procedural forms, rather than encouraging popular participation in political, social and economic arenas.

This section will examine three prominent examples of Confucian civil society: the Songgyun'gwan Confucian Foundation, the journal *Tradition & Modernity*, and the activities of the Hyundai Corporation's Asan Foundation. It will argue that these elite civil society groups are not acting against the state; they are involved in social engineering projects that seek to redefine the natural, and thus the social. Alongside their activities that encourage state power, the mass media, corporate business and academics also encourage each other in their support of capitalist modernity.

The Songgyun'gwan Foundation is commonly taken as the representative of Confucianism in South Korea because of its traditional historical position. Songgyun'gwan is the name of the official Confucian academy founded by the first ruler of the Choson dynasty in 1398. This traditional Confucian academy has grown into Songgyun'gwan University (founded in 1895), which includes programs in natural science and engineering in addition to humanities and social sciences. The university has the highest concentration of Confucian scholars in South Korea. It hosts an Institute of Confucian Philosophy, which is located next to the ancient ceremonial buildings where Confucian priests conduct the proper rituals (see Figure 4.1).

In response to what they saw as disorderly student movements, the Confucian Foundation met in 1991 to discuss how to modernize the foundation and popularize Confucian teachings.[79] This revival included declaring Confucianism a "religion" in 1995, and using summer camps, public lectures and teacher training courses to instruct young people in Confucian ethics.[80] More than just reasserting tradition, Confucian associations altered their ritual culture to expand participation: "In principle the ritual is observed only by Confucians, but it was opened to high school students in order to give them an opportunity to be exposed to their tradition and history."[81] Kim Kwang-Ok thus argues that this regeneration of Confucian culture is changing the nature of tradition that was previously "the exclusive asset of [a] particular privileged class."[82] As a voluntary association, the Confucian Foundation is transforming itself into a working element of civil society through this revival project.

*Figure 4.1* Confucian temple at Songgyun'gwan, 1997. © William A. Callahan

Sometimes the Confucian Foundation is a very powerful element: it protested when the South Korean Supreme Court struck down the provision in the marriage law banning marriage between people from the same clan, stating that: "The ruling is an outright challenge to the only remaining instance of public morality handed down for centuries. We, the ten million Confucian followers, will fight against it, resorting to all possible means."[83] Although these "Confucian fundamentalists" seem to be appealing to orthodoxy, they are actually working as an example of a Confucian civil society. The Songgyun'gwan Foundation is a "pressure group" in mainstream South Korean politics, even protesting in front of the National Assembly: "In the face of fierce opposition from staunch defenders of Confucian values such as the *yulim* 'fundamentalist' Confucians who continue to exercise a great deal of influence in rural areas, the National Assembly has decided not to act on the amendment."[84] Still, it is a very elitist form of civil society; Kim Kwang-Ok's detailed ethnographic study of local Confucian associations shows that distinguishing between the Confucian elite and the masses continues to be one of their main activities.[85]

*Jontong gua hyundae* (*Tradition & Modernity*) is another example of Confucian civil society. The first issue of this quarterly journal was published in June 1997. It is an important departure from the above-mentioned revival of Confucianism, which was dominated by conservative old men. *Tradition & Modernity* brings together young academics who are using their elite education to reconsider the value of Korean tradition in a modern context. Although it is managed and written by university professors, its target audience is much wider: Korean intellectuals, especially middle school and high school teachers. Its purpose, according to the editor-in-chief Hahm Chaibong, is to "reintroduce Confucianism into public discourse," because Confucianism has been ignored by social scientists and politicians alike since the fall of the Choson dynasty.[86] It appeals to the logic of "In search of civil society," because it also relies on a historical break in tradition so that Confucian civil society can reassert itself—but this rupture is from a liberal democratic era, rather than an authoritarian one.

Much like Hahm's discussion of Confucianism and democracy examined above, *Tradition & Modernity* seeks to shift from framing South Korean politics ideologically, in terms of left vs. right, to understand it in terms of the relation of tradition and modernity. The inaugural issue of *Tradition & Modernity* contains eight specially commissioned articles on Confucianism in the modern world: "Confucianism and Globalization: Problems of Particularity and Universality," "Anti-Confucian Politics: Contradictions of Political Argument in South Korea," "The Possibilities and Limits of Confucian Capitalism," "Can Confucius Be Revived?," "Modern Moral View and Confucian Moral View," "Education of Leaders in the Choson Dynasty" and "Universal Education in Modern Times."

As these article titles suggest, rather than resisting East/West discourse, *Tradition & Modernity* switches from a Cold War East/West discourse to an Orientalist East/West discourse, where the goal is to replace Euro-American modernity with Confucian tradition. Unfortunately, it seeks to limit the scope of civil society even as it acts as a member of civil society. A discussion of "Confucian capitalism" disqualifies social movements and labor unions from commenting on state policy, for civil society is limited to the neo-mandarins in the media and the university.[87] In a similar vein, Hahm boldly states that:

> Liberal democracy has been the ideal for the majority of South Koreans in name only. Very few Koreans understand either the theoretical assumptions or the normative standards which undergird liberal democracy and its institutions. Moreover, once they are explained to them, few would espouse liberal democracy with as much ardor and enthusiasm.[88]

Much like the "youth-ization" discourse analyzed in Chapter 3, here scholar-officials see the nation as a family where scholars are patriarchs who have to lead the common people as children. In this sense, scholar-officials do not need to find out what the people want, but are tasked with acting in their best interests.[89]

The last example of Confucian civil society is the Asan Foundation (the charitable arm of the Hyundai Corporation); its activities show how corporate conglomerates are likewise asserting a restrictive view of civil society. Along with sponsoring international conferences on Eastern Ethics, and funding academic research projects on traditional Korean culture, the Asan Foundation gives out the Filial Piety (*hyo*) Award. This award emerged from an Asan Foundation symposium on problems of the elderly, retirement, the family and women, and is a good example of how business conglomerates employ traditional culture to advance their corporate aims. Hyundai is not alone in such activity: Samsung Corporation is well known for its newspaper advertisements praising filial piety, while Daewoo funds *Tradition & Modernity*. In the same spirit, the semi-official Academy of Korean Studies elevated filial piety to new heights with its 1995 international conference on "Filial Piety and Future Society," which was co-sponsored by the Korean Broadcasting System and the Samsung Welfare Foundation.

The Asan Foundation's Filial Piety Award, which was created in 1991, aims to promote "the expansion of the culture of filial piety," which Hyundai founder and Asan chairman Chung Ju-Yung sees as the "prime virtue of our tradition."[90] Yet, due to rapid industrialization and urbanization, the number of people who practice filial piety is declining with the disappearance of the extended family. This is not just a moral problem, but a political economic problem: since the nuclear families do not include grandparents, people are no longer taking care of their elderly parents. Thus Chung Ju-Yung established the Filial Piety Award, which distributed

148 awards of between 10 and 20 million Won each for a total of 1,277,030,000 Won (US$1,596,278) in its first five years.[91]

Along with a political economy of age, the Hyo Award governs a political economy of gender. Although the Confucian classics tell us that the filial relationship is between fathers and sons, many of the prizes go to dutiful daughters-in-law who live in extended families, respect parents and elderly people, and teach the culture of filial piety to the next generation. This project is a direct reaction to the break-down of patriarchy, which depends on the unpaid labor of women; rather than using the stick of cultural and legal sanctions—which serve business leaders well in controlling female workers—now the business conglomerates are appealing to the carrot of material rewards. Thus, as in the Chinese diaspora, "Filial piety has been bent and channeled to serve the governmentality not only of the family, but of global capitalism as well."[92]

These examples of elite civil society suggest that Pacific Asian Confucian societies are naturally conservative patriarchies. Yet they also show how difficult cultural governance is: the state and corporate groups have to work very hard and spend large amounts of money to maintain an ideology that naturalizes their particular vision of society.

## Social movements and modernity in South Korea and China

Foucault writes that, wherever there is power, there is resistance. The elite civil society examined above is often involved in a geopolitical resistance to globalization and Westernization: "The revival of Confucianism is also a reaction against the process of modernization based on American-style pragmatism and economic wealth modeled on Western standards."[93] The state and corporate groups must struggle against Euro-American cultural imperialism in order to preserve their tradition from the invasion of foreign cultures. Prominent sociologist Kim Kyong-Dong argues that Korean business conglomerates must help the country "survive the onslaught of cultural imperialism," which brings with it "degradation, vulgarity, obscenity, violence and ... demoralization."[94]

Yet, the problems highlighted by the Confucian Foundation, *Tradition & Modernity* and the Asan Foundation are not limited to liberalism—and thus easily criticized as "Westernization" or "cultural imperialism"—but are more characteristic of capitalist modernity that no longer has territoriality. As Chung Ju-Yung himself said, the problems come from industrialization and urbanization. Still, few question the grand project of modernization, and the rapid economic growth that it has brought to South Korea. Rather, they are seeking to use Confucianism as an ideological crutch to deal with the problems created by rapid industrialization and urbanization.

John Tomlinson's discussion of cultural imperialism can help us make sense of cultural governance and resistance in Pacific Asia. He suggests that the process that we call "cultural imperialism" is actually the practice of capitalist modernity. Modernity impacts not just individual cultures or the economics of capitalism; it affects the world itself. Tomlinson thus argues that cultural imperialism is best explained in terms of a broad shift from tradition to modernity. In so doing, he switches analytic focus from place to time, and thus from the geography of East/West to the temporality of tradition/modernity. In this sense, Tomlinson agrees with the editors of *Tradition & Modernity* that it is more productive to look at issues of temporality than those of left/right ideology. Although *Tradition & Modernity* often switches back to the geographical ideology of East/West, Tomlinson argues that recognizing the time dimension challenges the concept of cultural imperialism as one culture dominating another; of Euro-American culture dominating South Korea. The most useful way to talk about cultural imperialism is not in terms of a battle between national cultures, but as the spatio-historical spread of modernity itself.[95]

Tomlinson thus asks in what sense are all cultures condemned to modernity. Modernity is more than modernization; it is a system that defines our everyday life. Rather than searching for historical and philosophical roots of tradition, Tomlinson discusses the "lived culture of modernity" that is transmitted through the main socio-economic institutions of Euro-America: the capitalist market, bureaucracy, science and technology, and mass communication. The cultural governance of modernity employs the discourse of development and its guiding concepts of progress, expansion and growth.[96]

Although these modern institutions and ideas originated in the Europe, they no longer represent the choices of Euro-America either. Indeed, although the South Korean state policy in the late 1990s was to globalize Korean culture, economy and society,[97] modernity has its own inertia—it proceeds regardless of individual state policies.[98] Cultural imperialism then is not an invasion of weak cultures (of the Third World) by stronger ones (of the First World), so much as a spread of cultural crisis from Euro-America to the rest of the world. Cultural imperialism, as the spread of capitalist modernity, is a loss for everyone because modernity "weaken[s] the cultural coherence of *all* individual nation states, including the economically powerful ones—the imperialist powers of a previous era."[99]

Modernity, here, refers to more than just modernization or globalization, but "-ization" itself as the whole "process of becoming." This presents problems for East and West alike: marketization, industrialization, urbanization, secularization, occupational specialization, media-ization and democratization. Foucault thus uses "-ization" language to shift from state policy to broader practices of governmentality: "Maybe what is important for our modernity—that is, for our present—is not so much the *étatisation* of society, as the 'governmentalization' of the state."[100] This "-ization" phenomenon is not limited to French- and English-language texts; the Korean/Chinese suffix *hwa/hua* (-ization) is omnipresent in Pacific Asian discourse as well. Since Confucian civil society's response to capitalist modernity is Confucianization and civilization, Tomlinson would argue that it is resisting the outward forms of modernity, while playing into the discourse of capitalist modernity.

Still, it would be a mistake to lament the onset of modernity as a total loss. There have been many economic benefits, as well as significant improvements in public health and education. The question, then, is how to criticize modernity's problems while recognizing its comforts, and thus avoid romanticizing tradition as the Confucianizers often do. Tomlinson suggests that, although modernity is a hegemonic system, its cultural governance is not monolithic, and thus can be resisted in various ways. He points to "new social movements" as examples of a critique of modernity, because they defend endangered ways of life: women's movements, environmental movements, indigenous rights movements, regional and ethnic struggles and religious movements.[101] Rather than search for the roots of civil society, he suggests that we examine how new social movements have been challenging capitalist modernity, and thus resisting power in its multiple forms.

Considerations of social movements always risk exaggerating their power and impact; even more so in Pacific Asia where states are strong and often unsympathetic. Even naming them as "social" and "movements," as opposed to political institutions, suggests that they are not very significant. As Rob Walker argues, they are "merely social, always moving"; as "mosquitoes on the evening breeze," some social movements are deadly, but most do not present much of a challenge to the institutionalized power of the sovereign state and the practice of capitalist modernity.[102] Still, just because of their slippery nature, social movements can pose a challenge, not just to particular regimes, but to the whole political imagination that relies on modernity for its self-understanding.

The rest of the chapter will switch from searching for the roots of civil society, to examine the multiple forms of resistance in social movements. While civil society often is used in cultural governance by the elite, the popular democracy of new social movements emerges from the grassroots in multiple sites of resistance.

## Chinese social movements

Many scholars have noted it makes more sense to talk of resistance in Pacific Asia in terms of the informal politics of social movements rather than the institutions of civil society.[103] White, Howell and Shang argue that, since structural analysis focuses attention too much on the formal aspects of politics, it is necessary to consider informal social relationships.[104] In an exhaustive study of civil society in China, White *et al.* recognize the heterogeneity of resistance that "contain[s] sectors which are traditional and modern, incorporated and oppositional, urban and rural, national and grass-roots, political and non-political, respectable and sinister, liberal and ultra-leftist, open and underground."[105]

The Tian'anmen Square democracy movement of 1989 seems an obvious starting point for analysis, but actually social movements in Taiwan provide better examples of a post-Confucian society struggling with modernity. The discourse of civil society emerged in 1985–6 in Taiwan, as part of the rapid political liberalization of 1986–8. At this stage, civil society was helpful in framing three strategic goals: (1) situating opposition relations on the main axis of state vs. society, to avoid the ideologically charged issue of independence vs. unification with China; (2) unifying social forces and countering the state apparatus that was dominated by the ruling party (the Guomindang); and (3) opposing the monopoly of state capitalism to push economic liberalization.[106]

Yet many Taiwanese questioned an approach to social change that was guided by the state/civil society dichotomy: civil society theory assumes that there is a center, and that all coalitions have a common basis, when actually this "center" is created by the state–civil society binary opposition.[107] This centralizing tendency did not match with the reality of social movements in Taiwan that were multiple and often contradictory: consumer protection, anti-pollution, environmental, women, aboriginal rights, students, New Testament Church, labor, peasants, human rights of teachers, handicapped and social welfare, veterans' rights, rights of political victims, exiles, anti-nuclear power, Hakka culture, non-homeowners, February 28 Event memorial, anti-military, educational reform, traffic accident victims, Taiwan independence, prostitutes' rights, newspaper boycott and purification of elections.[108]

Drawing on many Euro-American theorists such as Alain Touraine and Manuel Castells, and grassroots experience, Taiwanese scholars switched from figuring resistance in terms of civil society to employ theories of popular democracy and new social movements that decentered power and resistance.[109] These new approaches worked against any attempt to form a movement center because this risked reproducing the power by establishing a new hegemony in the process of opposition. Rather than working for a new organic whole, they viewed politics in terms of the multiplicity of social movements: grammatically, civil society is singular, while social movements are plural. Unity is not a question of permanence and natural organic coherence, but of contingent and temporary coalitions of specific social movements that do not have to subscribe to a new whole.[110] The main battlefield of popular democracy exists in everyday life, and these coalitions form against specific dominations in political, economic, social and cultural space.[111]

In addition to questioning the binary logic of civil society theory, the Taiwanese experience also helps us question cultural arguments that rely on the binary logic of Confucian East and liberal West. Weller argues that Confucianism has not been an obstacle to democracy so much as rigid ideas of civil society. In other words, Chinese culture has enabled democratic change: "Taiwan has not abandoned Chinese culture. ... In fact, there is something of a cultural renaissance going on, with everything from a religious revival to tea houses to a new Confucianism developing in opposition to Lee Kuan Yew's."[112]

Indeed, while corporate conglomerates give out Filial Piety Awards to buttress the patriarchy in South Korea, filial piety is a basis of resistance in Taiwan: "the idea of filial piety helps to justify protest in widely held and politically acceptable values ... visible commemoration of the debt owed to ancestors and the obligation owed to children."[113] Confucian culture thus is not monolithic, but is multifaceted and adaptable:

> democratization in a postcolonial context encompasses multiple practices, ideals, and institutions that shade into, clash against, and spill over conventional boundaries between "liberalism" and "Confucianism," "dissent" and "loyalty," "representation" and "reality," "democracy" and "authoritarianism."[114]

Politics in Taiwan is not derivative of Chinese tradition, Western democracy or the European Enlightenment, but represents an "alternative civility."[115]

Because of China's corporate colonization of civil society, which requires formal registration and limits horizontal ties between groups, resistance is much more difficult. Rather than standing in opposition to the state, social movements thus concentrate more on "chipping away from state's authority" in order to create new social spaces.[116] The real activity does not take place in the peak national organizations that are formally regulated by the state, but in local organizations that have developed "small-scale sets of informal ties beyond the gaze of the state."[117] Although these groups are hard to study because they are also often beyond the gaze of researchers, Odgen argues that there are

> over 200,000 interest groups and professional associations at county, prefectural and provincial level. These represent constituencies as diverse as commercial entrepreneurs, lawyers, doctors, women, businesspeople, importers and exporters, accountants, consumers, environmentalists, trade groups, shareholders, parent-teacher associations, artists, sports clubs, television and movie producers, computer groups, *qigong* practitioners, dancers, workers, musical societies, religious groups, retired workers, sportsmen, industries, and anti-tax groups.[118]

These groups in China's villages and urban neighborhoods can be much more confrontational than their corporate cousins, "often push[ing] at the outer limits of policy" through small-scale demonstrations, letter writing campaigns and even blockades.[119] While formal associations in both

Taiwan and the People's Republic of China (PRC) are more "easily coopted or simply repressed," informal community groups in villages and urban neighborhoods are often much bolder, and much more difficult for the state to manage.[120] Weller explains that, contrary to stereotypes of Confucian patriarchy, many of the most militant grassroots social movements in Taiwan are led by women, while Ogden points to the successful activities of NGOs associated with the All-China Women's Federation.[121]

Rather than being a top-down technical problem of reforming institutions and creating civil society through cultural governance, democracy thus is an ethos that fosters non-violent political conflict: "it is precisely the uneven, unwieldy nature of politics in Taiwan that, conversely, offers a ray of hope: in destabilizing the political environment, it pushes society to consider more (and possibly alternative) understandings of the common good."[122]

The informal community-based new social movements, then, are not limited by the reigning political imagination, but are looking for alternatives: new lifestyles, new meanings, new culture and new identities as well as new norms and values.[123] By cultivating community relations via horizontal ties of trust, these social movements are political in a wider sense of "quality of life" issues, and need not have specific "party political" goals.[124]

Of course, this understanding of social movements risks becoming yet another romantic view. But what is interesting about these social movements is that they are not just reactive to state power, but constructive of alternative social meanings. Here, we are moving from the politics of stability (via civil society) to the politics of possibility (via new social movements), from political culture to the politics of popular culture.

## South Korean social movements

Likewise, in South Korea resistance has been becoming more decentered over the past three decades. It has moved from the grand organic opposition against the state exemplified by the *minjung* (popular masses) movement of the 1970s and early 1980s, through old social movements of workers and students in the 1980s, to the new social movements of the 1990s.[125] These three stages of social movements also trace a familiar pattern of addressing the problems of capitalist modernity: in the 1970s there were struggles against the capitalist model of development and the modernity of the bureaucratic-authoritarian regime, first in a general populist mode, and then in a specific class struggle. But, once capitalism was firmly established in the 1980s, social movements refocused on pursuing social and economic justice as part of a reform movement rather than a political revolution.[126]

The June Uprising of 1987 was a turning point in South Korean social movements because it appealed to both unity and diversity. Unity was necessary to oust the military dictatorship, but it was not an organic unity of *minjung*—the popular masses—as it was earlier in the decade. Rather, Chung's structural analysis shows how the National Council for the Democratic Constitution (NCDC), which organized the June Uprising, was a coalition among social movement organizations. The NCDC successfully formed an alliance to exert a unified challenge to the authoritarian regime, despite all the differences and conflicts in strategy, ideology and goals of its constituent groups. This unity produced an array of mass mobilizations, for a total of 3,362 demonstrations that attracted over one million participants in June alone.[127] This shows how South Korean social movement organizations were able to use oppositional consciousness to forge an effective unity that resisted any appeal to orthodoxy.[128]

But, after the end of the military dictatorship in 1987, democratic issues lost much of their focus. Although the confrontational tactics of labor and student groups effectively mobilized social movements against military authoritarianism in 1987, these same tactics did not work in the post-authoritarian era. In the more open quasi-democratic society "[s]ince 1988, the strategic focus has changed [from mass antigovernment demonstrations] to consensus mobilization through public discourse in the media."[129]

After 1987 NGO numbers mushroomed in South Korea, growing to 6,159 by 2000.[130] These new NGOs increasingly shifted political focus from the state to a whole range of issues that are critical of modernity. The Citizen's Coalition of Economic Justice (CCEJ), which in 2003 won the alternative Nobel Peace prize, the Right Livelihood Award, is a key example of this trend.[131] The CCEJ is a typical NGO in that it is a voluntary, non-profit organization that is not seeking to seize state power. Rather, it pursues a "politics of influence" not just with the state, but with business conglomerates, the media and so on. Although new social movements are typically led by the middle class, the CCEJ is also known for working on transclass issues. Its social justice agenda is issue-based around consumption and quality of life concerns: environmentalism, feminism, consumer rights and human rights.[132]

The CCEJ was founded in July 1989 when it was clear that the state was not meeting popular aspirations for a more balanced approach to industrial growth, social welfare and the environment. Thus, the social costs of rapid industrialization and urbanization remain an issue, but the focus and methods have changed from an ideologically charged struggle for economic equity and democracy, to the promotion of diverse agendas that extend beyond strictly economic and political objectives.[133] Although it might not be as radical as student and labor movements because it does not directly challenge the state, the CCEJ is radical in the sense that it questions the discursive foundations of capitalist modernity. Rather than being extremist, Han Sang-jin describes these new social movements as examples of the "middling grassroots."[134] Han has developed the concept of the "middling grassroots" as an alternative to a politics that is polarized into binaries of left and right. It helps us to describe social movements that attract specific sections of the middle class that have maintained a grassroots identity acquired in university even after they enter fulltime employment. Their social movement organizations are neither captive to the state, nor projects of romantic revolutionaries.[135] Thus, there is an important difference here from *Tradition & Modernity*'s shift from the left/right dichotomy to an elite politics of traditional modernity; Han's middling grassroots shifts from ideological extremism in order to open up space for grassroots activity.

To understand the middling grassroots, Han suggests that we shift from a structural analysis of social movements to the cultural analysis of identity politics. Rather than seeing identity politics in terms of Confucianism, Han looks to the countercultural *minjung* movement, which emerged from a collapse of traditional family values in the face of industrialization and urbanization. The *minjung* movement sought to break up the orthodoxy and question elitist conceptions of self through subaltern discourse that examined identity from the viewpoint of the non-elite and stressed radical openness, solidarity and justice.[136] It moved from elite Confucian culture to popular culture to revalue Shamanism, peasant music and dance as positive progressive forces.[137] It questioned the Confucian elite's responsibility of being "the voice of the people," to encourage the people to speak for themselves. Although Chinese entrepreneurs and academics are very suspicious of subaltern discourse because it reminds them of the ravages of the Cultural Revolution,[138] South Korea's middling grassroots is able to make cross-class links.

The best examples of this subaltern discourse are popular culture movements that reconsider history and culture from the point of view of popular sovereignty. Kim Kwang-Ok's analysis of the role of *madangguk* in the popular culture movement shows how the new social movements did not just challenge mainstream society, but also created new social meanings. *Madangguk* is an eclectic style of popular drama that is both anti-establishment and develops new ways of expressing socio-cultural experiences.[139] It was originally developed at universities in the 1960s in opposition to Park Chung-Hee's authoritarian modernization policy, which framed tradition as a barrier to development.[140] As an oppositional force, *madangguk* celebrated peasant culture, but not as a static nostalgic experience, for it combined modern culture and traditional peasant culture in a deliberate construction of symbolic community.[141] When it developed in the 1970s and 1980s *madangguk*'s purpose was subaltern in the sense that it replaced the power elite's stories with those of the powerless majority. *Madangguk* thus represents a new dimension of subversion where participants construct their own world of resistance, an alternative world that elevates humble everyday life experience into sacred revolutionary art.[142] After 1987, *madangguk* continued to be popular; although it has spread from alternative venues to mainstream theaters it is still "adopted by various civil movement and student rallies" as a mode of resistance to cultural governance.[143] Such a constructive view of culture and identity also includes Confucianism, not as the hegemonic discourse, but as part of anti-state movements that mix Confucianism and Shamanism.[144]

Scholars and activists in China are also framing Confucianism in a way that is supportive of critical social movements. The director of the New Confucianism Research Center at the Chinese Academy of Social Sciences argues that the New Confucian movement that emerged in the 1980s has a new approach to the relation of Confucianism and society. While the imperial scholars worshiped Confucius, and liberal and socialist scholars reviled Confucius in the twentieth century, in China's period of reform and opening after 1978, scholars can examine Confucianism anew. They can critically evaluate Confucianism, to use it where it is useful, and disregard it where it is not.[145]

In *Tradition & Modernity*, Lee Seung-Hwan takes a similar critical view of Confucianism by warning against a simplistic division of philosophy and practice into tradition and modernity, East and West, and suggests that hybrid forms of Confucianism, liberalism and other discourses are necessary to meet the needs of contemporary South Koreans.[146] Han Sang-Jin also addresses the question of how to use postcolonial strategies to get beyond the East/West dichotomies that he criticizes as fundamentalist. Han seeks to imaginatively use Confucian norms as a tool to criticize modernity.[147] Tu Weiming and Kim Dae-Jung, for example, suggest that Confucianism with its emphasis on humanity being integrated with nature can be useful in environmental movements.[148] These arguments signify a promising start, and more work needs to be done to see if Confucianism can be helpful for new social movements in resisting the cultural governance of capitalist modernity.

## Conclusion

This chapter has deconstructed the discourse of "civil society" to argue that the concept of "new social movements" is more helpful for understanding popular politics in Pacific Asia. Through a discursive analysis of the defining regime of civil society, I have shown how the search for definitions often requires a political and epistemic stability that does not adequately account for the varied and ambiguous practices that civil society seeks to describe. One way of dealing with this theoretical problem of civil society is to search for a more precise definition of this important term. But, rather than join the debate over the definition of civil society in order to draw my own, more correct, boundary between civil society and the state, and East and West, I found it more useful to examine the political practices of cultural governance and resistance in Pacific Asia. The chapter shows that civil society is not simply part of a grand project for democracy; it has been used quite effectively as a mode of cultural governance by elite conservative groups to domesticate opposition and restrict dissent.

Although civil society discourse is hegemonic in discussions of democratic transition, I found it more productive to examine the fruitful ambiguity of political and social change through the optic of new social movements. While I risk creating yet another dichotomy of civil society vs. new social movements, the strategy seeks to question such an organization of political space. As categories, civil society and new social movements certainly overlap in interesting ways. But this chapter encourages a shift in tactics to examine politics in the wider frame of the struggle with capitalist modernity. New social movements differ from hegemonic definitions of civil society because they are not focused on contesting state power, and thus avoid reproducing the power of the state. Rather than being limited to national issues in official space, they construct and deconstruct identity in various arenas. As we saw, the search for civil society is also a search for identity. But while civil society tends to limit us to national identity, new social movements allow us to look to other spaces and practices, including subaltern identity and Confucian civil society. Rather than tautologically being part of a democratization process—as with civil society—the concept of new social movements allows us to examine each event specifically, where we can judge its utility and morality against our own specific values as argued in Chapter 3. Some new social movements will be democratic, some will not; others need to be understood in a different way entirely. Indeed, if the events of 1989 in Eastern Europe taught us anything, it is to be ready for surprises and to not neglect alternatives to mainstream understandings.

# 5 Corruption, political reform and the deferral of democracy

Although promoters of Asian Democracy argue that corruption is an essential feature of the West (see Chapter 3), corruption certainly is a major issue in most Pacific Asian countries. It has defined key events throughout the region, including the anti-Marcos movement in the Philippines, the 1989 democratic movement in China, the 1991 coup in Thailand, the 1998 downfall of Indonesia's Suharto regime, the 2000 election of the opposition party in Taiwan and so on.[1] At the height of the Indonesian social movement that ousted Suharto from power in 1998, an activist explained that "Our crisis is not only economic but also political and psychological. People are fed up with the same government that is corrupt, nepotistic and full of cronies."[2] Because corruption attracts the attention of public intellectuals, opposition parties and the media, anti-corruption campaigns can and have led to real political change as part of political reform movements. Indeed, in Pacific Asia "reform" is the new ideology that defines late twentieth- and early twenty-first-century politics in places as diverse as post-Mao China (*gaige*), post-crisis Malaysia and post-Suharto Indonesia (*reformasi*) and post-1991 coup Thailand (*patirup*).

Yet corruption and reform also have been important theoretical topics in the debate about the "East Asian miracle" and its unraveling. Luminaries such as Chalmers Johnson and Lucian W. Pye have argued that corruption in Pacific Asia is not a problem—it is actually the secret of the region's success. Many Asian studies scholars ask whether "corruption" is merely a Euro-American concept that has dubious utility in Pacific Asia. Indeed, in Thai the word for "corruption" is the phonetic loan-word *kawrupchun*, suggesting that it is not an indigenous concept or concern.[3] As we saw with "civil society" in Chapter 4, using the concept of corruption is not necessarily helpful in understanding social grammar in Pacific Asia. For example, in the 1980s Johnson argued that what some criticized as "structural corruption" in Japan was certainly "structural," but not necessarily "corruption."[4] Like Pye, Johnson went on to argue that corruption actually has been a key part of the democratization of the bureaucratic state.[5] Since the sale of access in such large state structures is "unavoidable," Johnson reasons that scholars should change their analytic questions to ask "what is the overall performance record of any given strong bureaucratic state? How is the purchased access actually used? And does the citizenry tolerate the sale of access?"[6] He answers these new questions by rehearsing the story of Japan's broad-based economic success where patterns of what some call "corruption" have actually redistributed income from rich to poor, and opened up the secretive ministries of the Japanese state to parliamentary scrutiny. The only hesitation Johnson had with this line of analysis in 1986 was to state that the Japanese public felt that corruption had gone too far.[7] Yet, when Johnson republished this article in 1995, he added a paragraph at the end that completely undermined his democratization argument: corruption was no longer helpful, but had become a disease rampant not only in politics, but in the bureaucracy and business.[8] Because corruption dominated all corners of society, citizens became disillusioned with parliamentary democracy, and the Japanese economy fell into the doldrums in the early 1990s.

Japan is not alone in suffering from structural corruption that has spread to contaminate the whole society. It is common to hear that vote buying is the key issue for Thai politics. Indeed, vote buying—which used to be just one of many campaign tactics—in the 1990s became emblematic of Thailand's "political disease." The political disease of vote buying, according to prominent commentators, not only corrupted Thailand's election system, but (like in Japan) plagues Thai society more generally. Stopping vote buying, as we will see, was one of the main goals of Thailand's reform movement that produced the "People's Constitution" in 1997. However, in this chapter I want to question such dominant understandings of Thai politics, and use the issue of vote buying to criticize political reform movements more generally. Although the meaning of "political reform" and "vote buying" seem obvious, this chapter will question the concept of vote buying and its slippery relationship with political reform. Simply put, what is the bigger problem: vote buying or the political reformers' obsession with it?

To be clear, I am not trying to turn the common understanding of vote buying on its head by applauding corruption as a democratizing development strategy, or by presenting vote buying as the only redistribution method that actually benefits villagers. Neither will I join those who furrow their brow in a relativist questioning of Orientalist definitions of "corruption." Although I agree with Johnson and Pye that there is a link between democracy and corruption, I see it as a vicious relation rather than a virtuous one. Hence it is necessary to trace what the discourse of vote buying reveals and conceals. To do this, it is necessary to shift analytical attention from vote buying to examine just what this focus on vote buying stops us from seeing. The topic is not just what vote buying research reveals about Thai politics, but what the discourse of vote buying *conceals* about political reform movements.

Following from Chapter 4, which offered a critical view of the conservative workings of civil society in Northeast Asia, this chapter will consider the relation of civil society and social movements in Southeast Asia to argue that the Thai political reform movement uses the discourse of civil society as a means of cultural governance. In particular, I will examine the politics of the 1997 Constitution and the 2001 general election in Thailand to argue that the focus on vote buying conceals the antidemocratic nature of many reform campaigns. I will show how the discourse of vote buying not only points to legal and structural problems, but, in an ideological legerdemain, political reform's focus on constitutions and good governance conceals a host of cultural and socio-economic issues. The political reform movement's attention to corruption thus is a form of cultural governance that directs attention away from bourgeois hegemony, and the deeper issues of rural poverty and the institutional corruption of the Thai civil service. In other words, vote buying is more than just the red flag of Thai politics. The discourse of vote buying is also a red herring that distracts attention away from structural and ideological contradictions of capitalist modernity. Simply put, anti-vote buying campaigns characteristically defer democracy; this cultural governance of the political imagination emanates not just from the state, but also from hegemonic social groups.

This chapter will explore how and why vote buying has become such an important issue in Thailand. It will argue that vote buying now describes more than a simple transaction whereby some cash is exchanged for the promise of a vote in an election. Rather than assuming the coherence of vote buying as a category of electoral activity, here I follow Michel Foucault's analysis of how a grand narrative of "rationality" is not a universal value, but only takes shape when distinguished from the various historical practices designated by the negative category of "madness."[9] Rather than seeing vote buying as a singular and coherent "thing," I likewise will examine how vote buying takes shape as a discourse through a series of distinctions from liberal democracy. The positive ideals of a "democratic civil society" and "good and able leaders" only make sense when contrasted with their opposite: gangsters using money politics to manipulate the elections in patronage-ridden villages. In this way, we can trace how the varied practice of political corruption has been reduced to the curious gerund phrase "vote buying," which then becomes a key subject-category to be described, measured, debated—and ultimately destroyed.

The chapter is divided into four sections to examine how vote buying structures the popular understanding of democracy and politics in Thailand. Using sources from academic discourse and popular media, each section looks to a narrative—law, technocracy, political culture, political economy—to move from a legalistic and institutional concept of democracy, to a political-cultural notion of civil society, and then to a structural analysis of the Thai political economy. Through its implementation of the concepts of law, "good and able leaders," gangsters, the middle class, civil society and village life, vote buying tells us much about identity production in Thailand. Liberal political reformers see relationships as contributing to the clientelism that leads to vote buying. Their goal is to ensure autonomy, with individuals interacting independently in civil and political society. But I agree with those analysts who see identity not as autonomous and essential, but as produced in relation to difference and Other. Again, "vote buying" defines Thai political identity in this negative way: the positive ideals of a "democratic civil society" take shape when contrasted with their opposite: the money politics of patronage-ridden villages. This relationality is not crony capitalism's collusion between corrupt government and business elites; rather, the relations are between a series of Others that are necessary to produce both vote buying and the Thai democratic self. The solution to the problem of vote buying, I argue, changes from severing relations in the name of autonomy to reconsidering the form that these intersubjective ties take.

Here Thailand is participating in a more general cultural governance of corruption and anti-corruption. Although corruption is usually understood as the exception to the rule of lawful social activity, Peter Bratsis argues that, regardless of ideological perspective (right, left, populist, technocratic, religious, secular), "[i]t is striking that so many disparate and competing political discourses all agree that corruption is the problem, oftentimes *the* problem."[10] Focusing on corruption as the key political problem is not just a local problem, as an exception to the rule of good governance. Rather, it is a theoretical problem in the sense that corruption is bound up with the contradictions of capitalist modernity.[11] Like other forms of corruption, vote buying is produced by specific relations between political and economic power, urban and rural power, official and unofficial power, and public and private power. To challenge vote buying, one needs to challenge the dynamics of these relations—not sever the relations, as the political reformers demand. This follows from an understanding of politics where corruption does not stem from the exchange of money for votes, so much as how unbalanced relations between wealth and power endanger democratic processes and values.[12] Hence, the chapter uses a broad notion of democracy to interrogate how both the moral problems and the technical solutions of the discourse of vote buying are discursively produced in struggles between cultural governance and resistance.

## Constitutionalism and good governance

The 2001 general election in Thailand was important not just for choosing a new government. It also ushered in a raft of new processes and procedures that dramatically reshaped both institutions and civil society in Thailand. These rules were not imposed from above (as in the past), but were the upshot of years of campaigning among political and social groups, which in 1997 resulted in a new "People's Constitution."

This Constitution was the product of a decade of political successes and failures in Thailand. Throughout the 1980s Thailand was seen by scholars and policy-makers alike as an example of a successful transformation from authoritarian bureaucratic polity to more democratic liberal corporatist polity.[13] Through a fortuitous combination of ethnic Chinese business and supportive Thai public policy, Thailand experienced four decades of uninterrupted economic expansion, with an average annual GDP growth rate of over 10 percent, and an increase in per capita GDP from US$100 in 1961 to $2,750 in 1995.[14]

At the same time, Thailand's political institutions were gradually becoming more democratic, moving from the semi-democracy of an unelected prime minister over an elected parliament in the early 1980s, to the more full democracy of an elected prime minister in 1988. But, in 1991, the Thai military seized power in its first successful coup in fourteen years. Political unrest then erupted in May 1992 when the coup leader tried to legitimate and extend his rule by becoming an unelected prime minister. After a brutal military crackdown on democratic mass demonstrations, the army leader was forced to step down in favor of Anand Panyarachun, a care-taker prime minister who organized elections that put an elected government back in power in September 1992.[15]

Although democracy in Thailand was back on track, a loose group of elites commonly known as the "Political Reform Movement" were not satisfied. To the reformers, having an elected government was not enough. There were still structural problems in the Thai body politic, most notably the military-imposed constitution that was still in force even after the coup-makers had been ousted from power. As a key reformer wrote in 2001, "It came as no surprise that one popular demand in May 1992 was the complete revision of the Constitution. The Events of May [1992] set off a political reform process, which is still unfolding to date."[16]

Hence, after 1992 a loose alliance of business leaders, politicians, bureaucrats and public intellectuals started discussing how to reform Thai politics through rewriting the Thai Constitution. This alliance of conservative, liberal and progressive activists built upon a tradition of democratic activism that went back to the 1970s. Members of the group had formed the Campaign for Popular Democracy to protest the 1991 coup, and then in 1992 joined PollWatch, a monitoring organization that fought electoral corruption. Through PollWatch reformers spread civil society activity outside the metropolitan center to include activists in provincial towns. Many of PollWatch's members pressured the government to institute political forms, hence the government appointed them to the Democratic Development Committee (DDC) in 1994, which was charged to study possible reforms to the Thai political system. The DDC included voices from the provincial middle class, as well as from elites from the center. The DDC facilitated the election in 1996 of the Constitution Drafting Assembly, which drafted the 16th Thai Constitution, presented to Parliament for approval in 1997.

While political problems were being solved, Thailand was soon engulfed in economic problems. Due to a combination of internal mismanagement, corruption and external pressures, in July 1997 the Thai economy abruptly slipped from four decades of uninterrupted growth into a world-class depression.[17] The resulting East Asian economic crisis spurred the Thai government to secure a $17.4 billion rescue package from the International Monetary Fund (IMF). While the crisis sparked anti-Chinese riots and anti-Western demonstrations elsewhere in Asia, it aided the ongoing critical self-examination of social and political institutions of Thailand. Although it was the result of various factors,[18] many blamed the crisis on inept and corrupt politicians who had bankrupted the country's decades of economic growth in a few short months. Reformers thus turned the crisis into an opportunity to institute far-reaching political reforms; against the opposition of politicians and bureaucrats they were able to push Parliament to approve the 16th Constitution of Thailand in October 1997. The new rules and institutions created by this Constitution were first tested in the general election of January 2001.

Although there are many ways of explaining the sources of Thailand's political problems, it is noteworthy that both activists and analysts pointed to vote buying as a key problem for the 16th Constitution of Thailand to solve. Former election commissioner and prominent democratic activist Gothom Arya explains: "One of the objectives of the present political reform is to stem vote buying. Many provisions of the Constitution were drafted having this problem in mind."[19] Thailand's foremost expert on electoral politics, Sombat Chantornvong, agrees:

> The drafters of the new constitution appeared to be convinced that they had solved the problems of legitimacy and efficiency that had long destabilized the Thai political system. The practice of vote buying by competing politicians was the source of many of these evils.[20]

Since vote buying was the most common fraud in Thai elections, reformers targeted it as a way of instituting "a better electoral process [that] would produce a better political system."[21]

As vote buying is technically illegal, reformers looked to the legal system for solutions. Institutional reforms of the Constitution were seen as necessary in an appeal to "good governance." Good governance is a term that often refers to a neo-liberal governance of the global political economy. It takes a rational view of modern society that stresses the role of formal institutions, the rule of law and transparent administration. Starting in 1996, the IMF used the phrase "good governance" to describe and proscribe economic and political reform projects that are part of structural adjustment.[22] This is where the reform movement's constitutional logic overlaps with the IMF's structural adjustment logic. As Bratsis argues, "The question of corruption has remained largely a technocratic one, involving managing things properly so that everything stays where it should be."[23] According to this framing of the issue, money politics and vote buying are diseases that need to be surgically removed from the body politic through legal and institutional reform rather than through political debate and popular participation.

But good governance is not just the ideology of transnational neo-liberal institutions. It also became popular in pre-1997 Bangkok when it was promoted by the three heavyweights of Thai public life: Anand Panyarachun, Prawase Wasi and Thirayuth Boonmi. Although Thirayuth distanced himself from IMF definitions of good governance by expanding the concept—which he translated into Thai as *thammarat* (virtuous state)—to include democratic civil society and non-governmental organizations (NGOs), the rational logic is still the same. Good governance, according to Thirayuth, is "the collaboration between public, social and private sectors to create governance and administration that are transparent, legitimate, accountable, and effective."[24] Good governance also received an important institutional cachet when it was chosen as the topic of the Thai Development Research Institute's year-end conference in 1998. The prime minister adopted good governance official policy in 1999, thus initiating it into the charmed circle of elite civil society examined in the last chapter.

According to good governance, the rational impartiality and universality of law can combat the irrational bias of politicians. Reform is instituted through constitutional politics. The title of a 1994 bestselling book that set the agenda for the 1997 Constitution is telling: *Constitutionalism: The Solution for Thailand*.[25] This view of the "salvation" powers of constitutions is not new in Thailand. Two decades ago, Chai-anan Samudavanaija wrote that Thai politics was mired in a vicious circle of corruption, coups, constitutions and elections.[26] Constitutionalism is part of the rational project in that it depends upon the belief that *this* time will be different: *this* constitution will be "the solution for Thailand" that, "unlike all previous constitutions, will be fail-safe, foolproof, cast-iron, lasting and eternal."[27]

Since vote buying is framed as a legal problem in this narrative, the People's Constitution was crafted as the technical solution. Democracy here is framed in the Schumpeterian procedural terms of free and fair elections rather than a broader notion of popular participation and socio-economic justice. In this context the problem of vote buying is simple: gangster politicians buy their way into office as a way to take advantage of the riches of the country. As ministers, they warp the system to direct state resources to friends and relatives in their home province, while protecting their own illegal businesses of smuggling, logging, gambling and so on. For such politicians, business and politics are two complementary activities: they use proceeds from illegal business to buy votes to get into power, and then use that power to expand and protect their illegal ventures.[28]

According to the discourse of reform, the constitutional solution to this problem is two-fold: (1) to sever the link between elections and government ministries, and (2) to change election procedures to restrict vote buying. These separations and restrictions show the rationality of the Thai elite: the aim of reformers is to plug the legal loopholes in a search for perfection. Under previous constitutions, the Senate was not elected, but appointed by the sitting government. It was an enclave of the military-bureaucracy that was suspicious of the electoral politics of parliamentary democracy. The House of Representatives was elected from multiple-member constituencies.

The 1997 Constitution dramatically re-formed the National Assembly into three kinds of elected representatives: senators, constituency members of Parliament (MPs) and party-list MPs. The Senate was directly elected from each province. It was meant not just to be an upper house for legislative scrutiny, but also to function as a separate apolitical body that would be above rough-and-tumble partisanship. As Sombat explains: "The charter writers wanted the new senate to be completely free from politics."[29] Senators had to be "pure": candidates could not be members of political parties, and there were heavy restrictions on election campaigning.[30]

The House of Representatives was divided into two sorts of MPs: 400 constituency MPs and 100 party-list MPs. Ministers could not be constituency MPs. Hence they either had to be elected from the party-list, or they had to resign their seats and pay for the by-election for their vacated seat. The purpose of this elaborate constitutional solution was two-fold. Not allowing constituency MPs to become ministers was seen as a clever way of cutting the corrupt link between vote-buying politicians and lucrative ministries.[31] The party-list ballots also would encourage voters to think of politics in terms of parties and policy rather than personalities and vote buying. Constituency MPs, according to the constitutional reforms, would be elected from smaller single-member constituencies. This would encourage a closer bond between the representative and the represented. All three kinds of representatives had to meet stricter criteria. Candidates for office now had to possess at least a bachelor's degree, and could not be drug addicts.[32] The Constitution also made voting compulsory, hoping that expanded electoral participation would make vote-buying too expensive.[33]

To enforce these new rules, the Constitution created an independent organization, the Election Commission of Thailand (ECT), to run the elections instead of the Ministry of the Interior. The remit of the ECT as an independent non-partisan organization was to run "clean and fair" elections by "sever[ing] the crucial ties that exist between politicians and the civil servants responsible for administering elections."[34] Most importantly, the Constitution and the Organic Election Law gave the ECT teeth: it was empowered to investigate and disqualify candidates for election fraud, and to call for a rerun of elections when there were irregularities.

In many ways, the reforms were a success in the popular imagination: the ECT received the "Best Government Reformer" award from *Asiaweek* magazine in 2000.[35] A prominent election-monitoring NGO concluded that, for the first time in a generation, vote buying was down; its press release after the 2001 general election declared that "money and intimidation no longer produced the desirable results."[36] Because the election was organized by a neutral organization—the ECT—candidates were disqualified for the first time in history. The reforms, which were crafted to encourage party voting rather than personality voting, were reasonably successful. According to a survey by the ECT, 41 percent of the electorate voted for constituency MPs on the basis of parties and platforms. On the party-list ballot, 59 percent chose according to party and platform.[37]

Thaksin Shinawatra's Thai Rak Thai (TRT) Party nearly won a clear majority in the House of Representatives, and much of this support came from rural voters choosing the TRT on the basis of its party platform, which stressed a redistribution of resources to the villages. As it is difficult to buy votes for the party-list ballot, many newspaper commentators concluded that the TRT's success showed that it was not able to simply purchase the election. Columnists and academics both felt that the reforms encouraged parties to be more serious about writing policy platforms, and made political parties more of a national institution than a cobbling together of regional warlords[38] (see Figure 5.1).

But this celebration of the success of the political reform movement was premature, since there were also serious problems with the elections. The ECT was successful in using its powers to disqualify candidates and rerun elections, but this quickly became a farce as in the end it took five rounds of elections to fill the Senate, producing the longest election process in world history. According to ECT figures, voter participation over this period rapidly declined from 71 percent to around 30 percent. The ban on political party membership and the restrictions on campaigning were twisted by prominent politicians to their advantage: over one-third of the senators turned out to be members of political families. Rather than the intended separation of powers between House and Senate, the Senate chamber was turned into a "politician's wives' club" and an "assembly of clans and dynasties" when relatives of prominent members of the House of Representatives were elected.[39]

Despite hopes that the new Constitution would end the common practice of electoral fraud, vote buying continued in the 2001 general election. While an NGO declared that vote buying was in decline, a bank survey noted that during the campaign the flow of cash increased to 25 billion baht—five billion more than for the 1996 election.[40] Campaigning and vote buying in Sumaleeburi province started early, before the House was dissolved on November 9, 2000, and thus were legal.[41] In addition to buying votes according to the usual methods—cash to individual voters, trips for local groups, donations to temples and so on—vote buying adapted to the

*Corruption, reform, deferral of democracy* 133

new situation. Due to increased scrutiny, harsher penalties and a stiffer enforcement of the law, it was more difficult to buy votes. Hence canvassers in Sainsburi province used a more subtle "direct sales method" to buy votes from relatives and close friends who were unlikely to turn them in to the ECT. Rather than buying votes directly, some candidates expanded on a method used earlier in the 1990s to simply recruit most of the village as small-scale canvassers. Hence, rather than buying votes, candidates employed the voters themselves in a strategy of "saturation recruitment."[42]

While political reformers hailed the success of party voting, canvassers used this modernizing trend to buy votes in different ways. In addition to paying voters directly for their support in cash or in kind, canvassers bought

*Figure 5.1*
Campaigning under the mango tree.
© William A. Callahan

voters by recruiting them as party members. This turns the ideology of grassroots political parties on its head: party members do not pay membership fees to finance the local and national branches of a democratic party. The party pays them. Nationwide, the TRT was proud to note that it had recruited 11 million new members—roughly equal to the number of votes its party-list received. In Sumaleeburi, the Democrat candidate urged voters to join his local candidate's party club and the national political party: 20,000 joined the club and 10,000 joined the national party. In Sainsburi, the TRT recruited 30,000 members, and the New Aspiration Party was active as well. The candidates and canvassers were able to enforce the link between party membership and voting through a campaign of disinformation. Since the election system was new, few people knew the rules. Voting was compulsory, and canvassers fraudulently told the voters that they were legally bound to vote for their new party.

Hence, the political reform movement, which sought to elect a more legitimate government by eradicating vote buying through structural reform, was only partially successful. Vote buying continued in new forms, although in smaller numbers. It is a flexible practice that adapts to new rules, no matter how rational they are. The best example of electioneering adapting to new conditions is in the role of political party membership. Low membership in the kingdom's informal and non-ideological parties has often been listed as one of the pathologies of Thai politics. The reforms were crafted to encourage "real political parties" that have "mass membership, sophisticated administrative structure, local branches, representative leadership, ideological cohesion and concrete policy platforms."[43] But the 2001 election showed how vote buying morphed into political-party membership buying. The TRT Party's 11 million members voted for it on the party-list, thus electing it to government.

But the new reformist institutions missed many of these twists, because the ECT and the press concentrated on vote buying to the exclusion of other forms of electoral fraud. Vote buying makes great headlines; it sells newspapers and adds to the legitimacy of the ECT. Moreover, it directs attention to the legal issues of the fraud committed by a few criminal politicians. Yet the Senate Working Group Report concluded that "The Electoral Commission centrally assigned so much importance to [vote buying] that they neglected other issues of electoral abuse."[44] Although vote buying was often investigated by the ECT, problems of spoilt ballots, fake ballots, vote counting and corruption among government officials were largely ignored, even when evidence of fraud was overwhelming.

Hence one has to ask the more theoretical question: What is concealed by the search for technical solutions to vote buying? The legalistic problematizations that define this discourse of vote buying encourage an elitist view of politics, and lead us away from the deeper structural issues of institutional corruption and socio-economic justice. Moreover, the political reform movement shows how non-state groups can also use cultural governance campaigns—in this case, an anti-corruption campaign—to change state institutions. This certainly is a form of resistance to state power, but, as we will see, it resists power in such a way as to reproduce state power.

## Good leaders and the *coup de technocrats*

Although the reformers were happy that the new Constitution, the Organic Election Law and the ECT were able to clean up the 2001 elections, they were unhappy with the election results. Thaksin's TRT Party was able to win a landslide victory with what many saw as an old-style party structure that cobbled together existing factions and veteran MPs from other parties.[45] This makes clear that the reformers were not simply concerned with the legal problem of arresting vote buyers. It was a leadership problem: the 2001 elections did not produce the "high-quality" politicians envisioned by political reform. Here the discourse switches from good governance to the search for "good and able" leaders. Although the phrase does not appear in the Constitution, "good and able people" (*khon di mi khwamsamart*) became a catchphrase for the goal of constitutional reform. The Constitution shifts here from being a rational-legal document setting down universal standards, into a means by which the moral problem of elections can be solved by "good people." According to Thai political scientist Prudhisan Jumbala, the party-list was not only intended to deter vote buying and strengthen the party system; it was crafted to "encourage knowledgeable candidates who are not good at campaigning."[46]

Anand Panyarachun, the diplomat-turned-business executive who became prime minister at the invitation of the junta in 1991, is the poster boy of the good and able people. Anand, who became prime minister again in 1992 after the Black May democratic uprising, has never been elected. But the first and second Anand governments are seen by many as the most effective and efficient in Thai memory: a business magazine declared with glee that the 1991 military putsch was a "coup de technocrats," since Anand's cabinet was the "dream-list" of the World Bank.[47] After he left office in 1992, Anand became "the unofficial leader of conservative activism" and "the pin-up hero of the good governance set," who in 1996 was chosen to be chairman of the Constitutional Drafting Committee.[48]

This desire for government by good and able technocrats makes sense of many of the Constitution's more elitist sections. Electoral reforms such as the bachelor's degree requirement were meant to "encourage better-known and more respectable personalities to enter politics."[49] The restrictions on campaigning for the Senate would encourage virtuous metropolitan technocrats who lacked the popular charm to woo the masses. The conservative branch of the reformist movement therefore was motivated by what Duncan McCargo calls a "desire for technocracy" that was "only shallowly rooted in democratic principles."[50]

Reform was not so much about including more people in the popular democratic spirit, as it was about including a certain kind of person: the virtuous technocrat. This was accomplished not just through positive measures, but through negative ones as well. The Constitutional requirement for a BA, for example, actually excluded 95 percent of the Thai electorate, and 99 percent of the farmers, from contesting office. To put it another way, the excluded were not simply criminals, but politicians in general. As the president of the Constitutional Drafting Assembly put it: "Let's behead a few politicians so our country can be better."[51] The leader of the political reform movement likewise stated, "The public felt a mixture of loathing and exasperation concerning the behavior of politicians."[52] Speaking as the chairman of the Constitutional Drafting Committee, Anand made the intention of the charter clear: political reform "is not an attempt to make bad people good, but it is a seeking of preventative ways to stop bad people having the opportunity to hold governing power."[53]

Thus, in the conservative discourse of vote buying, politicians are, by definition, evil and corrupt. Although they are often distinct, the discourse collapses the categories of gangster politician, local godfather (*jao pho*) and provincial MP into one identity.[54] Indeed, the 2001 election was framed by election-monitoring NGOs and political commentators as a "showdown" between good and able technocrats and the vote-buying politicians, between metropolitan gentlemen and the crass outsiders of the provincial *nouveau riche*.[55] Provincial businessmen-politicians were seen as warping the nation's governance with their money politics. Rather than clean and fair elections, the discourse points to the dirty vote buying of the provincial tycoons.[56] The legalistic checks and balances, such as the division of constituency MPs and ministers, were meant to separate not just the executive branch from the legislative branch, but economic from political power. Thus, it is not just that the public loathes politicians; technocrats likewise loathe the public: "the elite do not like submitting themselves to popular scrutiny and rejection."[57] As with the promoters of Asian Democracy, here Thai bureaucrats also find it "highly offensive" that they can be called to account by the public.[58]

Indeed, rather than moving from a bureaucratic polity to a bourgeois polity, a coalition of bureaucrats and metropolitan businesspeople used the discourse of vote buying to craft a constitution that asserted a technocratic polity that restricts representative democracy. In this way, Thailand's Anand-style good governance follows Singapore's Asian Democracy model of a managed society, which limits popular sovereignty to participation in regular elections in an elite technocratic single-party state. As McCargo concludes: "Such a technocratic polity would not simply clean up electoral politics, but would effectively by-pass such politics altogether."[59] The Thai technocratic-style Constitution thus does not just build walls between the executive and legislative branches, but also between politics and economics, and the political and anti-political. The reforms instituted an elite notion of democracy that sought to limit the powers of elected representatives. It is part of a class politics whereby Thailand's royalists and metropolitan bourgeoisie try to delegitimize, and thus limit, the growing political-economic power of provincial capital. In this way, political reform was not a departure from old-style politics, but a return to Thailand's pre-democratic anti-politics that were dominated by the military-bureaucratic elite.

## The political culture of followership

While the conservative reformers saw Thailand's political pathology as a leadership problem to be solved by the 1997 Constitution, liberal reformers framed the issues as a "followership problem." Their main concern was not vote buying, but vote selling. Why, these critics ask, do voters sell their voice? Rather than being a technical problem for lawyers or a moral dilemma for good people, liberal political reformers look to the socio-economic issues of clientelism that foster vote selling. Since the frameworks of law and good people neither made sense of the problem nor led to reasonable solutions, a theoretical reform was needed, the liberals say. The main analytic division of this clientelist understanding of vote buying is not simply patron/client but urban/rural: the urban middle-class civil society and rural patronage networks. This is not simply regional politics; instead, it is another manifestation of class politics. As we will see, urban middle-class liberals are trying to civilize/modernize the rural peasantry.

Anek Laothammatas popularized the urban/rural view of politics in a bestselling book, *A Tale of Two Democracies*, which caused a media sensation that caught the attention of Thai public intellectuals in 1995.[60] Anek questions the received wisdom that the main political division in Thailand is between the civilian middle class and military dictators (who, for example, clashed in the democratic uprising of 1992). Rather, he argues that it is between the urban middle class and rural patronage networks. This is an important political issue because, even though the rural constituencies elect governments through their control of 90 percent of the seats in parliament, urban citizens bring down governments through their vocal criticism of public policy. Although the urban middle class argued that vote buying was a perversion of democracy, Anek tells us that the middle class needs to better understand rural life. Rather than villagers simply engaging in "shameful vote buying and perverted electoral behavior" that elected unqualified politicians, he writes that election campaigns in rural Thailand are deeply normative activities.[61]

Vote buying is part of the social network of village life; canvassers are not the criminals described above by conservative reformers, but local leaders who achieve influence through philanthropy. For example, a street food vendor and a grocery store owner are two of Chiangmai city's powerful canvassers—hardly the image of hoodlum politicians promoted by conservative reformers.[62] While the aim of the conservative political reform movement is to get "good and able people" into office, in rural areas the patrons who buy votes are usually seen as "good people"[63] (see Figure 5.2).

Hence the moralistic approach that the urban middle class uses to damn the villagers is not only unhelpful, but inaccurate according to the discourse of liberal reformism. In vote buying, villagers are "acting morally within the existing social norm."[64] The problem, according to liberal reformers, is that the urban middle class is imposing its idealist view of democracy on rural life that is still organized according to a hierarchical patron–client relationship. Villagers give their votes as a "favor" to candidates supported by canvassers who are local worthies. Such campaigning, then, is not an economic transaction of money for votes. For a vote seller, the cash is largely symbolic, "confirm[ing] the social ties that link him and the local leaders."[65] The problem therefore is not the moral bankruptcy of the villagers, but the socio-economic gap between urban and rural sectors. Anek's solution to the problems of vote buying—in a famous phrase that has been repeated many times—is to "turn patronage-ridden villages into small towns of middle-class farmers or well-paid workers."[66]

*Figure 5.2*
A "godmother" describes how to buy votes in rural Thailand.
© William A. Callahan

In the liberal discourse of political reform, democracy takes shape as an urban practice of the middle class in civil society when it is contrasted with the corruption of rural patronage networks. Although the village in Thailand is often portrayed as the essential site of authentic Thai life, here the countryside is the dystopian foil against which utopian middle-class democracy is produced. Liberals use the urban/rural distinction to argue that "we"—the urban middle class—need to improve the lot of rural dwellers through development programs. Anek, once again, is advocating a top-down rural development policy reminiscent of previous military-bureaucratic regimes.[67]

This generalization of urban vs. rural is a common way of ordering society. But, as Raymond Williams argues in *The Country and the City*, urban and rural are heavily loaded categories:

> On the country has gathered the idea of a natural way of life: of peace, innocence, and simple virtue. On the city has gathered the idea of an achieved center: of learning, communication, light. Powerful hostile associations have also developed: on the city as a place of noise, worldliness and ambition; on the country as a place of backwardness, ignorance, limitation. A contrast between country and city, as fundamental ways of life, reaches back into classical times.[68]

Thailand shows that this binary coding of social space endures not just across time, but across cultures. Whereas in English "the country" refers both to the whole nation and a rural part of it, Thai is very urban-centric. "City-*muang*" refers both to the city and the whole nation. Although the village is the dominant image of the country in Thailand—*ban* means both home and village—in official discourse, the moral weighting of the division between the royal capital and the rest of the country is clear. Everything outside the metropolitan area is *dang jangwat*: upcountry, or the Other provinces. The problem with the urban/rural distinction, Williams argues, is that it is very unstable. Meaning has to be continually constructed, not with the city and country as autonomous spaces, but as relations in tension.

Likewise, in the discourse of vote buying, democracy takes shape as an urban practice of the middle class in civil society only when contrasted against the corruption of rural patronage networks. Although the village in Thailand is often portrayed as the essential site of authentic Thai life, for Anek the rural countryside is the dystopic foil against which a utopia of middle-class democracy is produced. Rather than being a legal problem for the entire country, vote buying is figured as a cultural problem of rural life. The solution, according to Anek and the good governance theorists, is not just to write new laws, but "to develop new values and consciousness."[69]

Actually, rather than being the standard by which democracy is judged, the Thai middle class is famous for being fickle: it applauded both the coup in 1991 and the mass demonstrations in 1992.[70] It has historically valued stability and prosperity over democracy. Rural businessmen are demonized as godfathers and barons, so metropolitan businesspeople can take their interests as the national interest. But after the economic crisis of 1997—brought on in large part by the dodgy deals and crony capitalism of metropolitan business—it can hardly be argued that the Bangkok elite engage in the accountable and transparent activities that their good governance demands of provincial politicians.

On the other hand, rural areas have produced the most interesting recent democratic social movements in Thailand. Since the mid-1990s, most of the important social issues have pitted the urban middle class against rural dwellers. This is the upshot of Thailand's industrial development drive since 1960, which industrialized the city on the back of the countryside's cheap labor, cheap food and export revenue. But, once industrialization was successful, the middle class blamed farmers for being poor and backward. In response, rural social movements have been active. In other words, rather than the rural northeast being the prime location of the pathology of vote buying, it has been the source of Thailand's major democratic social movements, such as the Assembly of the Poor and the Small Farmer's Assembly of Isarn.[71] Rather than being poor because they are lazy, villagers are very active because they are poor.

Alongside the reform movement, a localism/nationalism movement has gained currency since 1997 as another response to the moralistic promotion of urban civil society. This localism recodes the city from being the seat of civilization to be the source of corruption, also reversing the image of the village from dystopia to utopia. Rather than looking to official knowledge from the urban center—which they see as foreign cultural governance—the localists look to rural wisdom. Instead of the political culture of patron–client relations being a problem, the "community culture" of the Thai village was seen as the solution to both political and economic crises. Local knowledge is used to create alternative development strategies that do not rely on the central planning of the state. In this sense, Thawan Macharat's "Miss Siam," discussed in Chapter 2, is a member of the community culture school because, after her bad experience with capitalist modernity, she rejects the material attractions of the city, and returns to "the original root of Miss Agriculture in the rural district."[72] Contrary to liberal reformers' prescriptions, localists do not wish to modernize rural life. Urbanization, industrialization and consumerism are seen as the main problems with the dominant development paradigm. While urban civil society is seen as a combination of Euro-American and Chinese lifestyles, community culture is seen as the truly authentic Thai-style way of life. Like reformism, this localism comes in both conservative and progressive forms. The conservative bureaucrats use it to fight against foreign/Euro-American influence, while the grassroots democrats use it to decentralize power away from state institutions.[73] This positive moral coding of rural life involves romanticizing and (self-)Orientalizing the Thai village as a harmonious organic society guided by Buddhist values of caring and sharing. This is a very complex movement, but it is noteworthy that vote buying and electoral politics are topics that are conspicuously absent from the community culture group's discussions. More generally, these examples of urban corruption and rural mobilization show how using the urban/rural distinction to frame vote buying and democracy breaks down under scrutiny.

## Anti-vote buying as democratic deferral

Received wisdom tells us that vote buying is a pathology of rural life that displaces democracy. In this last section, I would like to make the controversial argument that vote buying itself is not as big a problem as is our obsession with it. The concentration of media and academic attention on vote buying—often to the exclusion of all other forms of electoral and institutional corruption—significantly narrows the understanding of politics in Thailand. For example, as the restrictive sections of the 1997 Constitution show, reform politics easily becomes a neo-liberal anti-politics. In this section, I will argue that democracy involves not simply constitutionalism or electoral reform, but a reform of political-economic relations.

First, vote buying only became an issue in the late 1980s as Thailand shifted from being a semi-democracy—an elected parliament led by an unelected military prime minister—into a parliamentary democracy. Vote buying had been around since elections began in the 1930s, and became rampant with the 1983 by-election in Roi-Et province. Before the 1980s, electoral corruption was characterized by government officials stuffing ballot boxes. It only became an issue of popular concern in the late 1980s as political power was privatized, shifting from the military-bureaucracy to provincial capitalists.

The liberalization of politics was accompanied by a liberalization of the media, especially the popular press.[74] Michael Kelly Connors argues that, with a few notable exceptions, this was part of a shift in analysis from radical structuralist criticism to reportage about vote buying and corruption: "Analysis of forms of vote buying became a new academic pastime and a form of journalistic scoop. Military radio constantly lampooned the capitalist politicians."[75] Thus, the stories of vote buying were often tied to the even more graphic headlines of gangsters and *jao pho*. Through this media process, the image of corruption was privatized from government officials to focus on civilian politicians. The military-bureaucracy profits from this discourse of vote buying, since it shifts criticism from the widespread corruption and nepotism of the military to target civilian politicians.

Second, the reason for the rise of vote buying, *jao pho* and provincial politicians is more than simply an issue of law and (moral) order; they are an important part of the success of the Thai political-economy. Due to a combination of the shift in the development model to an export economy and infrastructure projects sponsored by the US in the Vietnam War era, the provincial economy took off in the 1960s.[76] But, because of a weak legal system, this frontier-style capitalism depended on close relations between local entrepreneurs and local officials. The *jao pho* needed to cultivate local officials to receive protection from the police as well as access to government concessions. The officials—who as part of the Thai bureaucratic system were always from another province—also needed to cultivate local sources of wealth and power in the marketplace.

The *jao pho* pattern of political and economic activity is actually quite familiar: it stems from the pariah capitalism of diasporic Chinese in Thailand, who were conscious of their vulnerability as foreigners. (This will be explored more in Chapter 6.) Thus, it is not surprising that many of the *jao pho* are first- and second-generation Chinese immigrants who were preyed upon by Thai government officials. In other words, the corruption does not come just from the illegal activities of provincial capital, but from the political-economic relations forced upon them by government officials. Although the conservative reformers analyzed in the first section were very confident about the rational distinction between the legal and the illegal, provincial businessmen and villagers often see law as an instrumental exercise of arbitrary power.

In the 1970s, the *jao pho* became more powerful than local officials. Thus, when parliamentary politics became profitable, metropolitan business leaders came to the *jao pho* in the provinces to organize local party branches because national political parties lacked local contacts.[77] There is an important parallel here between local branches of banks and political parties. Previously metropolitan banks had also come to the local elite—including *jao pho*—to serve as compradors for Bangkok financial interests in the provinces.[78] Thus, with the rise of parliamentary democracy, the *jao pho* became canvassers who pieced together a local election network much as they had pieced together a local financial network. In the 1980s, the *jao pho* themselves increasingly became actors on the national scene by sponsoring MPs—this is when gangster politicians and vote buying became a story. Hence, vote buying is one upshot of the extra-legal dynamic of pariah capitalism and official corruption. Contrary to the popular view of vote buying as a problem of civilian politicians in the provinces, the practice is tied into networks with both corrupt government officials and Bangkok business. Provincial capital was mainly reacting to the situation where the rule of law was arbitrary and the bureaucracy was corrupt.

The discourse of vote buying likewise defers us from understanding the problems and solutions of rural life. Rather than legal or cultural issues, they are largely structural problems. But the popular view of the rural idiocy of vote buying displaces any analysis of the political and economic structures that contribute to this poverty. To transform clients into citizens, more is needed than the "alternative political culture" that I suggested in a previous book about elections and democracy in Thailand.[79] Many reformers note that vote buying is necessary because there is a lack of local party branches and constituency support. I would argue that the problem is not one of political parties; rather, vote selling is an upshot of the arbitrary nature of public services. According to a World Bank report, over 40 percent of government positions in Thailand are secured through bribes.[80] Many have noted a decay in the abilities of government officials. Hence, much like in the urban American political machines of yesteryear, Thai people have to depend on patrons and *jao pho* for help. Viengrat Netipho argues that, without a change in the distribution of social welfare, ordinary people will still depend on the canvassers' networks to provide social services.[81] The way to fight vote buying in the villages and the urban slums is to fight official corruption, and have a more regular and equitable distribution of resources to rural areas.

Some liberal and grassroots activists frame the problems in this way to stress empowerment. In the early 1990s, NGOs used the elections and special funds from the election-monitoring NGO PollWatch to emphasize specific issues and mobilize people from urban slums and rural villages.[82] As part of the political reform movement in the late 1990s, they pushed for a more open government, whereby Thai people could assert the rights of individuals and communities against the state. The Constitution institutionalized this through the Administrative Court, the Ombudsman, the Human Rights Commission and the freedom of information law. Transparency applies here not just to politicians, but to the bureaucracy. Even so, grassroots democratic activists are increasingly less interested in the political reform of Thailand's constitutional structures and anti-vote buying strategies; since 1997 NGO groups have been working less on elections and more on developing a grassroots civil society, which encourages the empowerment of local communities. In this way, they are more interested in promoting democracy through expanded debate and political participation, rather than through good governance's technical solutions.[83]

The point here, again, is that the discourse of vote buying displaces attention from many of the issues of grassroots social movements. Indeed, a focus on vote buying leads one away from a consideration of rural poverty. Thaksin and the TRT's metropolitan business bail-out policies have rightfully been criticized as an appeal to the poor to bail out the rich. It is resulting in a narrower political-economic oligopoly. But the TRT's rural policy platform of a three-year debt moratorium for farmers, low-cost healthcare and a development fund for each of Thailand's 60,000 villages does much to address villagers' needs. More importantly, Thaksin implemented these policies in his first year in office. It is not surprising that he received a majority of party-list votes in 2001—and an even larger one in the 2005 general election. Sadly, Thirayuth and others dismiss such policies as yet another form of vote buying.[84] This shows how middle-class reformers restrict democracy to a legalistic process that highlights their own sectoral issues rather than a popular movement that could substantively benefit villages with what grassroots activists call "edible democracy"—democracy that is not simply political or procedural, but also economic and social. More importantly, the rise of Thaksin shows how money politics is transforming again, away from issues of vote buying to a much more pervasive use of public power for private gain.[85] To criticize and resist the TRT political machine, both the media and academia need to get beyond the discourse of vote buying.

## Conclusion: a true *coup de technocrats*

In this chapter I have taken a contrarian stance, but not the expected one that questions mainstream concepts of corruption as Orientalist misunderstandings. Rather than lamenting the pox of vote buying on the body politic, I have questioned the popular concern with this particular political practice. I have argued that such a tight focus on vote buying—as a legal infraction of good governance, an ethical dilemma of good and able leaders, or a cultural practice of village life—is misleading. Although I certainly do not dispute that money politics is problematic, I have also argued that an exclusive examination of the commercialization of politics leads to other political problems, many of which are class-based: legalistic delusion, elite technocracy, a neocolonial exploitation of rural areas, and a new system of anti-politics. The focus on vote buying, as a mode of cultural governance that produces this specific set of problems and solutions, warps our view of Thai politics. Democracy becomes elections, and campaigns become headline-grabbing showdowns between good technocrats and evil gangsters in the popular media.

Rather than simply hunting down vote buyers, it is helpful to consider who benefits from this particular problematization of Thai politics: metropolitan business, bureaucrats and the military. Vote buying, therefore, is more than a problem that can be excised from the Thai political system; the discourse of vote buying is actually quite useful to reformers as an ideological crutch to both gain legitimacy and distract Thai voters from other issues. Certainly, the bourgeoisie only gains short-term benefits from the discourse of vote buying, as the flow of capital ultimately depends on the legitimacy of parliamentary democracy. Thus, the contradiction: bourgeois-led political reform risks undermining bourgeois hegemony.[86]

At the practical level, vote buying does not occur in a vacuum: it must be aided by local government officials and supported by metropolitan business. Indeed, elected politicians need to have relations with both local worthies (including *jao pho*) and government officials to be successful. I have argued that, rather than the *jao pho*'s vote buying producing corrupt politics, it is the corrupt bureaucratic system that produces *jao pho* and vote buying. Thus, corruption is not an ethical problem of autonomous individuals (*jao pho*) or communities (the village), but grows out of specific relations between political and economic, urban and rural, public and private, official and unofficial power. But I argue that the solution to vote buying is not to cut social relations, and thus turn rural clients into proper liberal autonomous rational individualist citizens. Rather than reform leading to a privatization of social life, the relations need to be transformed from clientelism to something else—rural civil society or community culture—which better addresses these relations of power, and thus better empowers Thai people. Although they are not prominent in the discourse of good governance, NGOs and social movements have been promoting aspects of the People's Constitution that decentralize power and make the state more accountable.

Unfortunately, the tight focus on the discourse of vote buying misses this point. It is not a coincidence that anti-vote buying campaigns characteristically coincide with anti-democratic moves by conservative military-bureaucrats. While it is true that the 1997 Constitution is "a symbol of urban desire,"[87] fulfilling this desire has involved the displacement of a host of important political-economic issues, and the practice of participatory democracy. It is unlikely that a grand cleansing of society will solve the problem of corruption once and for all, as the reformers hoped. Political corruption is part of the contradictions and tensions of capitalist modernity and must be addressed in that spirit. We need to develop policies and practices that refocus attention on bourgeois hegemony and the deeper issues of rural poverty and the institutional corruption of the civil service in Thailand. To resist this mode of cultural governance, we thus need to question not just the practices of corruption and vote buying, but also the discursive production of their complementary opposites, political reform and bourgeois democracy.

# 6 Cosmopolitanism, nationalism and diasporic politics

It is popular to see globalization as the spread of a homogeneous political economy that challenges the legitimacy and efficacy of the nation-state. This global political economy is attended by a cultural dominance characterized as Westernization or Americanization. But resistance to such economic and cultural governance is not limited to a reassertion of the boundaries of the nation-state or protest actions by cosmopolitan social movements. Another group of texts examines the highly successful "culture of capitalism" in diasporic Chinese networks to argue that they are an authentically Asian form of globalization. Hence, rather than discussing a global political economy, many now talk of a distinctly Chinese modernity that has its own unique economic-culture.[1] While earlier chapters have pointed to social movements as one mode to resist cultural governance, here we have "moving societies"—diasporas—resisting the state by generating a range of alternative modernities.

Although Arjun Appardurai hails diasporas as postnational groups who challenge the cultural governance of both state sovereignty and global capitalist modernity,[2] overseas Chinese identity itself has been radically unstable for the past 150 years. Beyond simple hyphenations such as Sino-Thai and Chinese-American, the diaspora was called "domestic overseas Chinese" in imperial China,[3] "foreign Orientals" in the Dutch East Indies,[4] and "artificial Chinese" and "noble-ized Chinese" in Thailand.[5] Since the 1980s the new generation of immigrants are considered "pseudo-Chinese" in the People's Republic of China (PRC).[6] Although the overseas Chinese network is seen as an "invisible empire" that "knows no borders,"[7] this chapter will look to the Sino-Thai experience to see how diasporic Chinese have been involved in defining borders: provincial, national and transnational.

Most research on Sino-Thai identity, like diaspora research in general, begins and ends with a comparative examination of Chineseness and Thai-ness. The two national cultures are related according to the distinction of assimilation/multiculturalism to ask whether the essential "Chinese identity" has been assimilated into Thai culture—or not. Thus, diasporic Chinese are studied as an "ethnic problem" in the new states of postcolonial

Southeast Asia; like many Jewish communities in Europe they have been criticized as a pariah entrepreneur group who profited from European imperial regimes. Politics is thus reduced to questions of the loyalty of these "essential outsiders" to their Chinese homeland or their adopted nation.[8] Sino-Thai history therefore is not autonomous, but is absorbed into the national historiography of either China or Thailand.

Critical studies of diasporas seek to question the cultural governance of the assimilation/multiculturalism distinction by arguing that cosmopolitan ethnic communities should not be defined by either countries of origin or host countries. Donald M. Nonini and Aihwa Ong, for example, argue that diasporic Chinese have their own "third culture" that is neither purely Chinese nor essentially Thai, but mobile: "different ways of being Chinese are not based on the possession of reified Chinese culture, but on the propensity to seek opportunities elsewhere."[9] This critical examination of diaspora and cosmopolitanism has highlighted the intimate and specific linkages between the global and the local as well as the interplay of gender, class and ethnicity.[10] As Wang Gungwu—the doyen of overseas Chinese studies—argues, the diaspora is no longer tied to China, but is engaged in a "quest for autonomy."[11]

But the response of diasporic Chinese to the rape and murder of ethnic Chinese in Indonesia in 1998 makes us question such a clear distinction between cosmopolitanism and nationalism. Many of the diasporic Chinese websites that now serve as networks for a cosmopolitan community—the World Huaren [Chinese] Federation's www.Huaren.org, for example—were initially organized as a response to anti-Chinese atrocities in Indonesia. These diasporic cyber-networks also interacted with mainland Chinese cyber bulletin boards to pressure the Chinese state in Beijing to respond more forcefully to these events.[12] Hence, cosmopolitan networks are here used for nationalist issues, in an interplay of influence: while elite diasporic cosmopolitans (in Southeast Asia, Australia and North America) were providing information to pressure the Chinese state, elite mainland Chinese nationals were pressuring the same state in support of diasporic Chinese (in Indonesia). Rather than global civil society, which appeals to universal rights to argue for justice, these groups framed their resistance in terms of defending Chinese ethnicity in a diasporic public sphere. Thus cosmopolitanism, nationalism and diaspora are mutually produced first in cyberspace and then in state pronouncements—cyber-campaigns from both inside and outside the PRC pushed Beijing to depart from its policy of diplomatic non-interference to condemn the Indonesian state.

In this chapter, I will argue that, although such essentialized notions of identity—either for nation-states or for diasporas as an autonomous third culture—are useful for the cultural governance of mobile populations, they are not helpful for explaining transnational politics. I will question how nationalism and cosmopolitanism are formulated by arguing against the increasingly popular notion of diasporic Chinese as a postnational cosmopolitan community of "transnational yuppies" who are constantly in motion.[13] Instead of searching for the true Sino-Thai "third culture" in relation to some stable notion of Thai-ness and Chineseness, this chapter will show how diasporas resist such nationalized cultural governance in ways that both construct and deconstruct the seemingly opposing forces of nationalism and cosmopolitanism. Although diasporic Chinese capitalism is often figured as a Pacific Asian form of globalization, which erodes national borders in Southeast Asia, I will argue that diasporic Chinese populations are intimately involved in defining borders as well as calling them into question. To achieve this, the chapter will not merely deconstruct the nation or the cosmopolitan, but show how diasporas are necessary for the mutual production of nationalism and cosmopolitanism.

To understand the transnational politics of diaspora, we need to move beyond sociological approaches to international politics that focus on national identity, norms and formal institutions. Examining the politics of diasporas is helpful for they are often seen as "social problems" by states because they do not fit in homogeneous notions of territory and identity. While "Nationalism involves fixing fluid identities, refashioning their representations, and rigidifying the perception of boundaries between the self and the Other," diasporas challenge the natural linkage between nation and state.[14] Thus, because diasporas—almost by definition—lack political status, they present epistemological and ontological problems for social and political theories that are regulated by the concepts of the state and international regimes.[15] Hence, I argue that the positivist/postpositivist debate in IR theory is not exhausted by the sociological turn of Constructivism seen in books such as Peter J. Katzenstein's *The Culture of National Security*.[16] Other critical international politics scholars are turning to anthropology and ethnographic methods to show how borders of territory and identity are negotiated in the social relations of identity and difference.[17]

This ethnographic approach encourages us to look in different places for international politics, shifting away from state actors to transnational non-state actors, from geopolitics and International Political Economy (IPE) to economic-culture, and from law and institutions as the foundations of international society to the less formal organizations of diasporic public spheres. Instead of discovering a coherent national culture that is easily essentialized as a discrete "substance" that affects state policy, Weldes, Laffey, Gusterson and Duval argue that culture is multiple and "composed of potentially contested codes and representations, as designating a field on which are fought battles over meaning."[18] Whereas the sociological approach searches for "norms" as positive values, anthropological approaches foreground how communities are formed by excluding difference: security depends upon insecurities. Negotiations between identity and difference thus are not simply clashes between the specific norms of national identities; insecurities also come from conceptual differences such as nation/diaspora and nation/cosmopolitan.

The detailed and decentered analysis afforded by an ethnographic approach enables us to examine how the identity of diasporic Chinese is meaningful not just as an "ethnic problem" in the post-Cold War world. The Chinese diaspora has been crucial for global capitalism, national identity, and provincial politics for over a century. Diasporas are useful, in other words, just because they are strange. The analysis of diasporic Chinese politics will show that what China and Thailand share is not a common normative identity, but a common set of differences against which their particular national identities are constructed. In the context of IR theory, diasporas show the relations of power that constitute both national identity and alternatives to it.[19] This ethnographic approach to the transnational politics of diasporas allows us to look in different places for evidence. For example, the reigning paradigms for the political economy of Pacific Asia typically do not emphasize cultural elements—developmental state theory and neoclassical economics are transfixed by struggles between the state and the market.[20] This chapter builds on recent studies that highlight the interplay of political economy and culture in regional and transnational politics to examine diasporic economic-culture.[21] We are often told that overseas Chinese capitalism, also called Confucian capitalism, relies on the economic-culture of "a positive attitude toward the affairs of the world, a sustained lifestyle of discipline and self cultivation, respect for authority, frugality, and an overriding concern for stable family life."[22] The small and medium-sized family firms of Chinese capitalism are noted for flexibility and quick decision-making. Together these values describe a network capitalism that works according to *guanxi*-relationships between diasporic Chinese entrepreneurs and officials in the PRC. The comparative advantage of the diaspora's Confucian capitalism is that cultural ties lower the transaction costs of doing business in China where the legal system is underdeveloped. Rather than just looking to formal institutional regimes, which are state-based, economic-culture also allows us to examine how the informal practices of everyday life produce nationalism and cosmopolitanism.[23]

Yet economic-culture, as a set of "core values," is conceptually problematic: it has been used as shorthand to explain both the unique transnational characteristics that produced the Asia economic miracle and the unique Thai values that resist globalization.[24] But, when we use the anthropological approach, which examines politics in terms of the tension between identity and difference, we can see the *guanxi* network of relationships is not simply between ethnic Chinese and for economic gain. Cultural governance regulates diasporas not just through "the individual," but in other spaces as well: kinship networks, public and private schools, the capitalist workplace, the nation-state, and transnational networks. An examination of the relations between identity and difference shows how diasporic insecurities produce identity in both its nationalist and cosmopolitan forms. As we will see, these boundaries are not territorial, but cultural and economic; power is not measured just according to military force and economic growth, but according to the diasporic public sphere's "cultural arsenals" of temples, fraternal organizations, newspapers and schools.[25] Economic-culture therefore is a useful way of describing culture as a set of practices rather than a set of ideas.

Still, to understand how diasporas both construct and deconstruct nationalism and cosmopolitanism, we need to employ a critical use of the anthropological approach. The weakness of an anthropological approach is the opposite of a sociological approach: it tends to bypass the state by jumping directly from the tribal to the postnational, from the local to the global. Hence, this chapter will examine nation-states as well as mobility and flexibility. The first two sections of this chapter will deconstruct essential notions of nation-state and diaspora to show how overseas Chinese have been crucial in the production of Chinese and Thai nationalism. While cosmopolitan Chinese activities involve transnational flows of capital, populations and information, they are not only postnationalist disjunctures that call boundaries into question. In China, overseas Chinese are used not just as a financial resource to fund political revolutions in the past and economic reforms in the present; they have been an important symbolic resource in the construction of Chinese nationalism. The second section will show first how diasporic Chinese were the main insecurity against which Thai nationalism was constructed in the twentieth century. Second, it will argue that in the late 1990s Sino-Thai shifted from resisting nationalism to producing it: they have been among the main promoters of neo-nationalism in Thailand. Hence the diaspora does not just challenge the nation-state, but is an important cosmopolitan part of nationalism.

The third section will highlight how the diaspora forms a set of new communities and thus new borders among Sino-Thai in Thailand. Although they may seem national, we should be clear that these borders are not the juridical-legal territorial borders of the nation-state, so much as economic and cultural borders of various communities in the national centre of Bangkok, the transnational node of Phuket, and Mahasarakham province. Rather than being mobile, "seeking opportunities elsewhere," the ethnography of these three sites will show how diasporic Chinese respond to political, economic and cultural opportunities in these contexts. Rather than assimilating or separating themselves from mainstream life, the chapter will show how Sino-Thai communities tend to colonize identity formation in the various local economic-cultures, both responding to and developing the prevailing practices of cultural governance. In Bangkok, they are national nodes for inter/national activity. In coastal Phuket, they are transnational nodes for regional activity. In rural Mahasarakham they are provincial centers for mercantile capitalism. The flexible economic-cultures of diasporic Chinese, thus, are key elements in the construction of social and economic borders. These new borders are not simply symbolic constructions; the third section will show how Sino-Thai communities are supported by the informal organizations and networks of a diasporic public sphere. The chapter thus highlights both the dynamic interaction between Chinese, Thai and Sino-Thai identity construction, and the mutual production of cosmopolitan and national politics.

To understand how nationalism and cosmopolitanism, the global and the local work, we need to see how the outsiders—in this case, diasporas—are necessary for constructing communities and producing boundaries. Diasporas thus are not just an economic resource for home and host countries, but are a symbolic resource in the production of cosmopolitanism, nationalism and localism. Diasporas thus help us question the structures of world politics that look to the opposition between cosmopolitanism and nationalism. Hence "think[ing] of ourselves beyond the nation" is not enough;[26] we also have to think of ourselves beyond the cosmopolitan. This chapter will conclude that diasporas are interesting beyond the curious details that they provide as examples of resistance to the nation-state and Euro-American capitalist modernity. By resisting the state's cultural governance in indirect ways, diasporas generate their own modes of cultural governance that, in turn, can regulate both state and non-state practices.

## Chinese identity: neo-nationalism and diaspora

The Chinese diaspora has always been a problematic concept. As either nationalists or cosmopolitans, overseas Chinese have been measured against the norm of a single and coherent culture. The policy choices of assimilation and multiculturalism both look to a core of Chinese culture that is either modified or preserved. Wang Gungwu's problems in even naming this population are indicative: the first substantive footnotes in many of his essays lament the difficulty of defining "Chineseness" or naming the overseas Chinese.[27] But, rather than trying to define overseas Chinese as a coherent "thing," we need to understand their identity as a relation. This section argues that the nation and the diaspora are not separate autonomous "substances" with core identities; Chinese nationalism and diaspora take on meaning in relation to each other. Indeed, the concepts of "nationalism" and "overseas Chinese" both appeared at the end of the nineteenth century, and I argue that this was not a coincidence: nationalism and cosmopolitanism produced each other in tension. In this section then, I will first examine how Chinese nationalism is not regulated by a collection of core values as many texts tell us; identity has been produced against the difference of Euro-American empire, Chinese empire and diasporic Chinese. This is not simply a history lesson, for the dynamic of nationalism and cosmopolitanism is again producing Chinese identity in familiar ways. For the past fifteen years, PRC policy has been not simply to recruit overseas Chinese as patriotic investors, but to re-educate the diaspora in its "national" history.

Since the 1990s, nationalism has once again become a major topic in Chinese politics, with many security studies analysts searching for the guiding norms of Chinese civilization. The hyperrealism of Chinese foreign policy, for example, needs to be understood not just according to the economic analysis of the Chinese state as a rational actor, but according to exotic culture and history.[28] In both academic and popular culture within China itself, the rise of nationalism has likewise been accompanied by a rediscovery of China's glorious 5,000-year civilization. National Studies Fever—*Guoxue re*—in the 1990s stressed the achievements of the Chinese nation in a positive way. But this new nationalism also created new enemies: *Guoxue*'s nativist search for "authentic" ways of being Chinese can be both anti-modern and anti-Western. The Chinese state, for example, uses Confucian nationalism as a mode of cultural governance to "cure the 'diseases' of modernization."[29]

The timing of this rediscovery of Chinese nationalism is important. In the early 1990s, the PRC faced political and economic crises both domestically with the Tian'anmen massacre, and globally with the fall of the Soviet Union. Although the economic reform policy was reasserted in 1992, the political struggle was resolved in favor of a neoconservative nationalism. The PRC has particular ways of promoting this new form of nationalism. While positive notions of identity have proliferated through *Guoxue*, a more negative production of identity has also been prominent. The 1990s also saw the reappearance of the discourse of National Humiliation as part of the party-state's patriotic education policy.[30] Like *Guoxue*, it first became prominent in the 1910s and 1920s as China faced the twin challenges of imperialism and modernity. While *Guoxue* addressed the problems of modernity, National Humiliation—*Guochi*—addressed the problem of imperialism.[31] To understand neo-nationalism and national security, it is necessary to understand national insecurities. In other words, we need to reverse Paul Kennedy's famous thesis about "the rise and fall of the great powers," to examine the "fall and rise" of China.

The Chinese state is quite blunt in the cultural governance of its patriotic education policy. Textbooks characteristically talk of the "Century of National Humiliation" to define modern Chinese history and to celebrate the foundation of the PRC in 1949. National Salvation thus does not make sense separate from National Humiliation. The discourse of National Humiliation recounts how, at the hands of foreign invaders and corrupt Chinese regimes, sovereignty was lost, territory dismembered, and the Chinese people thus humiliated. The Opium War whereby the British navy pried open the Chinese empire to Euro-American capitalism is usually seen as the beginning of the century of national humiliation, and the communist revolution in 1949 as the end. As a key patriotic education textbook puts it: "Never forget national humiliation. . . . The invasion of the imperialist powers and the domestic reactionary ruling class's corrupt stupidity together created the roots of this catastrophe."[32]

Thus, the foreign Other is not the only focus of national humiliation. The Chinese self has its problems too. The primary contradiction of foreign imperialism was exacerbated by the ineptitude of the various regimes that preceded the PRC: the misdeeds of the Qing dynasty and the Republican regime are summarized as "domestic corrupt stupidity."[33] This is not simply a battle against a different race (the Qing were Manchu) or different ideology (the Republican leaders were from a rival political party) because both of these groups are condemned as *Chinese* traitors who "sold out the nation." The conclusion that the discourse of national humiliation draws is that the Chinese people need a strong state to save the nation from evil imperialists in the past, present and future. This discourse is very popular in both official and popular culture in China. Long after the century ended in 1949, national humiliation springs up in conversation and public opinion to explain diplomatic crises such as the bombing of the Chinese embassy in Belgrade (1999), campaigns to host the Olympics (1993 and 2001), the crash of the US's EP-3 surveillance plane in China (2001), and anti-Japanese riots in Chinese cities (2004, 2005). Thus, National Humiliation discourse uses modern Chinese history to secure the Chinese people to a particular territory. This essentialist construction of identity takes both Chinese people and Chinese territory as self-evident categories. National Humiliation forcefully reasserts the hyphen between nation and state.[34]

## *Diasporic identity*

There was also a rebirth of overseas Chinese identity in the late 1980s because of two factors that accompanied Deng's economic reforms. The open door policy allowed a host of "new immigrants" to leave China.[35] It also invited the older generation of wealthy overseas Chinese to return and invest in their homeland as part of the economic network of "Greater China."[36] Overseas Chinese identity has been involved in a cosmopolitan dynamic, which largely bypasses not just Southeast Asian nation-states, but the PRC as well. Popular business authors such as John Naisbitt and noted scholars such as Tu Weiming have both stressed that Greater China and overseas Chinese economic success need to be understood separately from Beijing's centralized political control. Naisbitt writes, "It is not China. It is the Chinese network," to explain the grand shift in economic activity from nation-states to networks. In the early 1990s, Tu likewise noted the "glaring absence of the PRC" in East Asian success stories, and argued that now the "periphery [that is, the Chinese diaspora] sets the agenda for the center."[37]

Yet, because mainland China has been very successful in the past decade, we also need to consider how diasporic identity is produced in relation to the nation-state. The PRC's cultural governance policies labor to see "Chineseness" as an essential identity tied to its state. The relation of overseas identity and domestic nationalism is shown in the creation of the term for overseas Chinese, *huaqiao*. Although Chinese have been traveling abroad for millennia, the creation of a single term to name this group is quite recent, taking form at the same time that nationalism gained currency in China. Before 1893, there was a legal ban on unofficial overseas travel. The state saw these unofficial travelers as "vagabonds, fugitives, or outlaws" who risked punishment as criminals on returning to China.[38] The constitution of *huaqiao* identity is not just part of the production of Chinese nationalism, but is related to national humiliation. Historically, Chinese only migrated in large numbers as a result of the economic and political dislocation that started with the "invasion of foreign countries' capitalism" after the Opium War.[39] As Wang argues, the term *huaqiao* was crafted by the Qing regime "to encourage sojourners to identify with China and Chinese civilization."[40] The constitution of *huaqiao* identity thus is part of the gelling of the concept of National Humiliation in China: "it was not until after several decisive defeats by the European powers in the second half of the nineteenth century that a name for these Chinese and their misfortunes and achievements was found."[41] Although *huaqiao* was a new word, it had an ancient pedigree that framed the overseas Chinese as an "elegant and respectable" group.[42] Thus, in the late nineteenth century, overseas Chinese were transformed from outlaws into honored mandarins as part of an imperial nationalism. Evidence of this transformation can been seen in the Sino-Thai exhibit of the Roi-Et National Museum in rural Northeastern Thailand: it has a grand portrait in imperial dress of Pridi Kasemsap, a prosperous overseas Chinese who returned to China to take up an official post.

Since the late twentieth century, overseas Chinese are again being recruited into the narrative of National Humiliation as patriotic "sons of the Yellow Emperor" who thus form "a part of China's history that is splattered with blood and tears."[43] Thus the Chinese state is trying not only to lure overseas Chinese investment into the PRC, but also to culturally govern the diaspora by re-educating it with National Humiliation history. Official National Humiliation texts are increasingly co-published in Hong Kong in traditional Chinese characters for overseas distribution. Specialized texts have been directed squarely at Hong Kong and diasporic audiences to knit them into official nationalism. For example, in the preface to a slick National Humiliation text, the Director of the Chinese Revolutionary History Museum in Beijing explains that the book "will help overseas Chinese, especially our young friends overseas, to understand this period of the motherland's history."[44]

Mainland descriptions of the overseas Chinese experience neatly mirror the logic of National Humiliation discourse. Similar to Guo Qifu's patriotic education textbook cited above, Ren Guixiang and Zhao Hongying list the reasons for the diaspora as stemming from both foreign invasion and domestic corruption:

> among the foreign reasons we must stress the frenzied plunder of China's cheap labor by the foreign invaders, among the domestic

reasons we must stress the basic corruption and ineptitude of the Qing state, which was powerless to protect our people from the foreign invaders' human trafficking.[45]

Chinese identity thus expands through National Humiliation from being defined according to citizenship and territoriality to a wider transnational view of the Chinese race: "China is not just the most populous country in the world; it also has the most populous diaspora."[46] According to these sources, the 25 million diasporic Chinese constitute the third largest economy in the world. Overseas Chinese, therefore, are characteristically figured as a financial resource for the Chinese nationalist project.

As the popular verses of the "Song of Revolution" (1903) show, diasporic Chinese communities felt an anxiety about their wealth, and the risks it posed to diluting their authentic Chinese identity. It thus calls on overseas Chinese merchants to finance the nationalist revolution to reclaim their identity:

> Let me call again to the *Huaqiao* overseas,
> Compatriots to the distant ends of the earth! ...
> What use is the accumulation of silver cash?
> Why not use it to eject the Manchus? ...
> It is hard to be happy all one's life,
> You need but little conscience to feel shame.
> What then is the most shameful matter?
> To forget one's ancestors deserves the greatest hate!
> If not that, then to register as a foreign national
> Forgetting that you come from Chinese stock.[47]

This ditty, which was widely distributed between 1903 and the republican revolution in 1911, shows how economy and identity are closely linked: overseas Chinese merchants are enjoined to finance the revolution—or risk losing their Chineseness. Indeed, the "Father of the Chinese nation," Sun Yat-sen, is not only known for gathering financial and political support from abroad during this period; he grew up overseas in Hawai'i (see Figure 6.1).

Such financial aid also has lent the various revolutions and regimes added symbolic legitimacy: the PRC and Taiwan still struggle for the loyalty of overseas Chinese as part of their transnational national reunification strategies.[48] Both Taipei and Beijing have Overseas Chinese Affairs Offices to coordinate such propaganda.[49] Thus, one of the activities of Chinese regimes in both Taipei and Beijing has been to "re-Sinicize" overseas Chinese populations through education and cultural activities.[50] In 2005, for example, the Chinese state opened 100 Confucian Institutes around the world to teach national language and culture, like Germany's Goethe Institute. Yet, while the task of the Goethe Institute is to spread German

*Figure 6.1*
Sun Yat-sen memorial statue in downtown Honolulu.
© William A. Callahan

language and culture to foreigners, the Confucian Institute targets overseas Chinese as well.

The national shame, therefore, is not just about the loss of the Chinese body politic where imperialist powers divided up China's "sacred territory," but of the loss of many Chinese bodies. The key to cleansing National Humiliation in both general narratives and in overseas Chinese stories was revolution against the Qing and an anticolonial struggle against the imperialists. The purpose of founding a strong nation was not just to reunify China, but to protect diasporic Chinese who otherwise "deeply know the shame and pain of a weak country." Hence, according to mainland sources, overseas Chinese understand that "their own destiny is wrapped up in the destiny of the motherland."[51] Indeed, the language of National Humiliation is key in mainland understandings of diaspora. Persecution of Chinese overseas during the century of National Humiliation was not just physical or financial, but a question of "respect"—or the lack of it: "If Chinese people were bullied locally, that was because China received no respect internationally."[52] The rape and murder of ethnic Chinese in Indonesia were seen as a measure of the diplomatic weakness of the PRC. Overseas Chinese experience thus not only becomes a chapter in the history of National Humiliation textbooks as a problem to be solved, but as a "reflection of the development of modern Chinese history" itself.⁵³

Diasporic Chinese, therefore, are not simply a financial resource for China. The dynamic of diasporic persecution and National Humiliation is used as a symbolic resource for producing Chinese national identity. Curiously, these financial and symbolic resources, which are transnational and deterritorialized in diaspora, are used to consolidate the identity of the Chinese nation. The more obvious the national difference abroad, the greater the need for a strong Chinese state to protect the diaspora both diplomatically and militarily. It is common to conclude that diasporic Chinese nationalism ended in the 1950s, with the end of immigration from the PRC and the rise of postcolonial nationalism in Southeast Asia. But nationalism continues to grow both at home and abroad. Over the last century, a series of atrocities provoked national outrage among new and old immigrants: at the turn of the twentieth century by anti-Chinese immigration policies in North America and Australasia, in the mid-twentieth century by the Anti-Japanese War and the Rape of Nanking, and at the turn of the twenty-first century by the rape and murder of ethnic Chinese in Indonesia. In each of these cases, the national and the cosmopolitan produce each other, regardless of whether it is the diaspora protesting national problems, or the nation protesting diasporic problems. In other words, although we often assume that nationalism is defined by positive norms, there is nothing like a humiliating atrocity to unite a diverse and dispersed population into a community.⁵⁴ In addition to gathering around glorious Chinese civilization, diasporic Chinese communities increasingly identify with the national humiliation of such atrocities. As Ian Buruma sarcastically concludes: "It is, it appears, not enough for Chinese-Americans to be seen as the heirs of a great civilization; they want to be recognized as heirs of their very own Holocaust."⁵⁵ Hence, overseas Chinese not only network for economic gain in a mobile "third culture," but for social and political projects, to produce a transnational form of nationalism.

In the next section, I will turn these questions around, first to see how diasporic Chinese have been used in a negative way to produce Thai nationalism, and second to examine how Sino-Thai have been among the most vociferous supporters of an inclusive neo-nationalism since 1997. This argument will reconfirm how nationalism depends upon cosmopolitan Chinese, and how the diaspora is more than a financial resource. It has had considerable symbolic power in constructing and deconstructing the Thai nation.

## Diaspora and neo-nationalism in Thailand

Nationalism in Thailand has a time-honored tradition of using diasporic Chinese as the Other against which the "Thai-ness" is defined. Overseas Chinese were not just the fifth column of republican and then communist revolution in China. They also have been a key element in the formation of Thai nationalism. While Chinese nationals banded together with the diaspora to fight against Euro-American imperialism in the Century of National Humiliation, in Thailand Chinese have been used as a symbolic resource in national identity construction in a negative way: the "essential outsider" against whom a national self is constructed.[56] After the Chinese republican revolution of 1911 and again after the communist revolution in 1949, the Thai elite questioned the loyalty and utility of Thailand's large urban Chinese population. To stem the spread of republican revolutionary ideas in the 1910s and communist ideology in the 1950s, the Thai state strengthened its policy of regulating the Chinese population, especially Chinese education. Most famously, King Rama VI wrote "Jews of the Orient" (1914) as part of Thailand's transition from a multiethnic empire into an exclusive nation-state.[57] According to Thai officials, "Sino-Thai" was a contradiction in terms: you had to be one or the other. Diasporic Chinese nationalism thus both preceded and provoked nationalism in Thailand, Malaysia and the Philippines.[58]

Most studies of overseas Chinese identity overlook this negative use of the diaspora by highlighting how Thailand has been accommodating to diasporic Chinese as fellow Buddhists—at least when compared with harsher regimes in the neighboring Islamic societies of Malaysia and Indonesia. For example, Prime Minister Gen. Chaovalit Yongchaiyut tried to blame Sino-Thai capitalists for the 1997 economic meltdown, calling them "the nation's problem." Although this was a very successful diversionary measure in other countries—the state encouraged anti-Chinese riots in Indonesia to save Suharto—it did not work in Thailand. After a public outcry, Chaovalit apologized and complained that he had been misunderstood, which was actually a reasonable excuse since Chaovalit is well known for being incomprehensible.[59]

This rapid about-face showed the power of the Sino-Thai who are now not only business people, but also journalists, academics and civil servants. Actually, it is easier to study diasporic Chinese in Malaysia where difference has been institutionalized into the official corporate ethnic categories of Malay, Chinese and Indian. But I argue that Thailand is a useful site to examine diasporic Chinese identity production just because of the ambiguous nature of the distinction between Chinese and Thai. As Chaovalit's awkward experience shows, people have to work hard to make distinctions between the Chinese, Thai and Sino-Thai populations.

While neo-nationalism arose in China to address a political crisis—the end of the Cold War and the Tian'anmen massacre—in Thailand neo-nationalism became an issue because of an economic crisis. Due to a range of factors that have been well analyzed elsewhere, the Thai economy abruptly slipped from four decades of uninterrupted growth into a serious depression in July 1997.[60] Once the Thai Baht was floated on international currency markets it lost half its value, spurring the Thai state to secure a

$17.4 billion rescue package from the International Monetary Fund (IMF). These funds came with the conditionality of a structural adjustment of the Thai political-economy that stressed policy and institutional reforms, which would promote open markets and good governance. The Thai government passed a raft of bills to reform bankruptcy and foreclosure laws, and to loosen up restrictions on foreign ownership. The result was the closure of three-quarters of the finance companies and the nationalization of four of Thailand's major banks, which altogether wiped out one-third of Thailand's financial system. Sixty-nine thousand other companies needed debt restructuring. Multinational corporations (MNCs) from Japan, Singapore, Taiwan, Europe and the US bought Thai assets at "fire sale" prices. At the nadir of the crisis in 1998, the economy contracted by 9 percent, poverty rose by 20 percent, and unemployment to more than 2 million.[61]

## *Economics and neo-nationalism*

The first political reaction to the 1997 economic crisis in Thailand was not the expected nationalism that would target the usual suspects, the overseas Chinese. As we saw in Chapter 5, the economic crisis spurred Thailand's political reform movement and facilitated the passage of the 16th Constitution. Even so, a different sort of identity politics soon emerged from the crisis. Thai public intellectuals also created a new set of Others: liberals and the West. According to the neo-nationalists, the solution to the 1997 economic crisis was not a financial restructuring, but a reassertion of Thai national identity and economy. Thai neo-nationalism trumpeted the notion of economic and cultural self-sufficiency that often romanticized the Buddhist village community as part of its rejection of urbanism, consumerism and industrialism. Neo-nationalism thus was part of the reaction to the elite moves of the political reform movement examined in the last chapter.

Neo-nationalism in Thailand thus employs a similar set of images to Chinese neo-nationalism: patriots as slaves to foreigners, the semi-colonialism of economic imperialism, and immoral foreign robber barons. While treaties signed between 1842 and 1949 were seen as unequal and thus illegitimate in China's Century of National Humiliation, Thai foreign debt in 1997 was framed as illegitimate. Once again, foreign invasion and domestic corruption: the debts that the Thai public had to pay were created by the exploitative policies of the West in collaboration with the corrupt elite in Bangkok.[62] The purpose of Thai neo-nationalism is to "save the nation" from such corrupt traitors who risked "selling out the nation." Indeed, the United Thai for National Salvation Club was formed in 2000 to argue this case. This Club sponsored a special issue of *Setthasart kanmuang-Political Economy*, "The Declaration of Neo-Nationalism," which was published to influence the political campaign for the January 2001 general election—which was won by a "nationalist" party.[63]

Although it is easy to write off Thai neo-nationalism as a knee-jerk populist reaction to a painful crisis that was used instrumentally by some political parties, it is important to understand it in its full complexity. Like the political reform movement, this neo-nationalism gathered together an often contradictory group of promoters from political, economic and civil society: the monarchist/bureaucratic elite, national business leaders and progressive grassroots activists all called for a return to a national/local economy. Some criticized economic liberalization to promote social justice for the poor and oppressed; others—including businesspeople—expanded the criticism of globalization to target the immorality of capitalism and consumerism more generally.[64] Utopian views of the Thai Buddhist village community culture can serve two purposes. On the one hand, they have been part of this localist notion of economic-culture, but on the other, they were used by conservative institutions to promote the authoritarian linkage of "Nation, Religion and Monarchy" first proposed by King Rama VI. For example, in 1998 the Ministry of the Interior tried to turn the grassroots social democracy of neo-nationalism into yet another top-down development strategy.[65]

Actually, the neo-nationalists did not engage in a debate about the merits of alternative development strategies—they did not present an economic plan.[66] Even the "nationalist" prime minister who was elected in January 2001 did not have a coherent nationalist economic policy: sometimes Thaksin Shinawatra praised self-sufficiency, other times he promoted foreign investment and an export-oriented economy. But, rather than looking at what divides these various strands of neo-nationalism, it is important to see how neo-nationalism only makes sense in terms of its relation to the Other. The progressive, bourgeois and reactionary nationalists—who fundamentally disagree about most issues in Thai politics—are unified here by a common target: foreign capitalism, specifically the IMF. As one newspaper columnist put it, "This new nationalism is the child of the IMF's [Managing Director] Michel Camdessus."[67] According to this argument, the issues are not about the political-economy of class and capitalism, but the economic-culture of territory and citizenship. The president of the Thai Senate proclaimed, "the poor, struggling, indebted Thai are threatened by rich, foreign creditors."[68] Thus Thai business, even if it is a "monopoly or oligopoly" is seen by neo-nationalists as virtuous because the wealth still stays in the country.[69] Likewise, all the neo-nationalist groups looked to Malaysian Prime Minister Mahathir Mohamad's strong mercantilist response to the crisis. Malaysia's capital controls were praised more for their ideological meaning than their economic efficacy: Mahathir was hailed because he did not bow to the IMF. This support for Mahathir was a major shift for many of the progressive neo-nationalists who previously had been critical of his authoritarian politics.[70]

Those in Thailand who questioned the efficacy or ethics of neo-nationalism were summarily dismissed as "naïve," "weak, stupid, and morally cowardly," "crazily following Western slogans of liberalization, globalization, and accountability," "stupidly following foreigners," "being brainwashed by foreigners," "childishly liberal," "alarmist and frankly intolerant" and "blindly following the global system."[71] In its more extreme form, neo-nationalism dismisses those who supported a liberal political-economy not only as stupid, but as un-Thai traitors who wish to "sell the country."[72] One commentator approvingly notes how traitors who sold out the country to Burma in the eighteenth century were beheaded under King Taksin.[73]

## *Democracy and neo-nationalism*

The Thai do not have to go back 200 years for examples of the violent cultural governance of nationalism. Many of these same activists and opinion-makers were victims of the Thai state's criminalization of difference in the recent past. Up until 1973, nationalism in Thailand was largely used as a tool by a series of military dictatorships to repress left-wing movements. Even after the popular democracy interregnum of 1973–6, progressive politics has largely been understood as anti-military or pro-democracy rather than as pro-nationalist.

Memories of a repressive anti-Chinese nationalism were still fresh just before the economic crisis in 1997. Reacting to renewed calls for a right-wing nationalism that excluded Sino-Thai as communists, Kasian Tejapira wrote:

> Thai has many forms. There are communist Thai, fascist Thai, democratic Thai, dictator Thai, Free Thai, and tyrant Thai. Now I am no longer a communist, but I want to insist that communists are also Thai in the same way as fascists are Thai. Therefore Thai who have different ideas should try to express their ideas peacefully instead of shooting M16s from helicopters or firing rounds from tanks.[74]

Here, Kasian is part of the general movement among a new generation of Thai neo-nationalists to be more inclusive and democratic. It is noteworthy that many of the essays go out of their way to cite as authorities progressive nationalist heroes such as Pridi Phanomyong, rather than militant nationalists such as Field Marshals P. Phibulsongkram (Phibul) and Sarit Thanarat. Indeed, many of the same people who were pushing for liberal or grassroots democracy in the early 1990s (against military dictatorship) now argued for a democratic nationalism (against economic neocolonialism). In this way, the criticisms of corruption are not simply defining domestic enemies, but entail a critical engagement with reform politics and extra-parliamentary popular politics. Many of the more thoughtful writers are trying to pry nationalism away from the military and bureaucratic elite to guide popular democracy. The nation thus is redefined by the elements of the people, liberty and justice.[75]

### Race and neo-nationalism

Certainly, Thai nationalism has been involved in racial politics. This can be graphically seen in the change of names by the militarist regime in 1939: "Siam" named a multiethnic country, while "Thai-land" is racially exclusive. Neo-nationalists are quite aware of the anti-Chinese history of their ideology. But their reaction since 1997 has not been to reject nationalism, as had many progressives in the past, but to embrace an explicitly inclusive form of Thai nationalism. Unlike in China where neo-nationalism is closely related to ethnicity, the key here to being Thai is not pure Thai blood, but citizenship and participation in Thai life. Thus "genuine nationalism" is differentiated from racism.[76]

Part of this shift toward toleration is practical. Even if the Thai elite desired to once again discriminate against diasporic Chinese, logistically it would be very difficult—as Chaovalit saw in 1997. In the past "Chinese" lived in certain communities—Chinatowns—and engaged in certain businesses. But now Chinese and Thai have intermixed to such an extent that they are difficult to differentiate. Authentic Thai-ness is not just an ideological non-issue, but a racial non-issue as well. As Kasian, a key theorist of both neo-nationalism and Sino-Thai identity, argues:

> The ultra-nationalist history cannot blame the economic crisis of the 1990s on the Sino-Thai because Thailand in 1998 is much different from Thailand during Phibul era of sixty years ago. During Phibul's era, the nationalist movement was anti-Chinese. The imaginary lines that divided between Thai and Chinese were possible. But by now, "Chineseness" has been assimilated into "Thai-ness" and cannot be easily separated. Therefore now it is difficult to draw a line to divide *Jek* [Chinese] from the Thai and claim that *Jek* are the national enemies. The boundary of the definition of Thai-ness has already expanded to include *Jek* to unite with the Thai.[77]

But this seemingly cosmopolitan nationalism is not completely differentiated from racism. While Sino-Thai commentators extended the shared norms of Thai national identity to include Chinese and other non-Thai ethnic groups, this expansion of the self has necessitated the creation of a new Other. The new racism targets the West, and is often anti-American.

Like in China, this new Occidentalism emerged in a specific historical context: in 1998, parliament debated the new bankruptcy and foreclosure laws at the same time that it modified the Alien Business Law. Although many of the buyers were from fellow Pacific Asian countries, such as Japan, Singapore and Taiwan,[78] most Thai felt that the government was simply selling Thailand to Euro-American MNCs—and cheaply. Furthermore, it is not just foreign firms that are preying on a prostrate Thailand. Thai firms have also gone transnational: Thailand's CP Group is the largest foreign investor in China.[79] Likewise, a "Manifesto of Neo-nationalism" laments that the Thai have lost their transnational capitalist opportunities: "I see that Singaporeans, Hong Kongers and Taiwanese own many businesses in our neighbouring countries such as Burma, Cambodia and Laos. What a pity that the Thai have lost these opportunities."[80] But such political-economic arguments miss the point, because the issue was the economic-culture of Thai identity that was framed in racial terms: neo-nationalism was not simply anti-American, but anti-White. Rather than talking about the Yellow Peril of a Chinese threat to Thailand, as King Rama VI did in 1914, now there are warnings of the "White Peril."[81] Similar to National Humiliation in China, the problem is not simply the IMF or liberalism, but the barbaric White race that is trying (once again) to subjugate the vulnerable Asian masses.[82]

Thus, a new Thai self is produced by a new Occidentalized Other in much the same way as National Salvation in China needs National Humiliation. With the economic crisis of 1997, neo-nationalism arose not as a positive movement hailing the glories of the core values of Thai culture—Nation, Religion and Monarchy in official discourse—but in relation to difference. Much the same logic and vocabulary was used as in previous incarnations of Thai hypernationalism, but this time with a twist: Sino-Thai activists were among the most prominent promoters of an inclusive and democratic neo-nationalism. But this new broader nationalism still depends upon difference; the Other is the "White Peril" of the IMF and Euro-America. Thai neo-nationalism, therefore, is similar to Chinese neo-nationalism in terms of its logic, which produces identity through relations of exclusion, if not in terms of content—this national unification is of the Thai citizenry rather than the Chinese race.

## Diasporic Chinese in Thailand

The first two sections deconstructed essential notions of nation-state and diaspora to show how diasporic Chinese have been crucial in the production of Chinese and Thai nationalism. While cosmopolitan Chinese activities involve transnational flows of capital, populations and information, they are not only postnationalist disjunctures that call boundaries into question. In the previous sections, I showed how cosmopolitanism and nationalism produce each other. This section will highlight how the diaspora forms a set of new communities and thus new borders. Although they may seem national, we should be clear that these are not the territorial borders of the nation-state, so much as economic and cultural borders of various communities. Thus, the ethnographies will show how identity is produced through constructing borders of self and Other, not just for the most obvious case of national identity, but in relations of exclusion in local and transnational contexts as well. The new borders are not simply symbolic constructions; as I will illustrate, they are supported by non-state actors' "concrete institutions and networks."[83]

More importantly, these communities will show how problematic Thai and Chinese neo-nationalism are in these contexts. Even though neo-nationalism was at the height of its popularity in Bangkok during my fieldwork period in 2000–1, it was not an issue that excited interest among diasporic Chinese educators, businesspeople, politicians and clan organizers. The neo-nationalist debate is largely restricted to elite groups in Bangkok who are looked upon with suspicion by provincial businesspeople and grassroots organizers alike. They fear that anti-urbanism and anti-capitalism could easily again target ethnic Chinese merchants.[84] This last section uses fieldwork in Thailand to demonstrate how economic-culture is constructed in three very different contexts: the national center in Bangkok, a transnational node in Phuket, and the rural province of Mahasarakham. I chose these three sites because they should best exemplify nationalist, cosmopolitan and local economic-cultures in Thailand. But the complex ethnographies of these three sites will show how the diaspora calls into question neo-nationalism, globalism and localism. Thus, the identity politics is not simply between nationalism and cosmopolitanism, as most research on diasporas states, but between diaspora and context in national, transnational and local spaces.

### *Diasporic Chinese in Bangkok*

Comparing two global conventions of overseas Chinese in Bangkok shows the inter/national nature of diasporic Chinese activity in the capital that produces national boundaries in new ways. The Seventh World Huang Clan Association Convention, held in Bangkok in 1999, functioned quite differently from the World Chinese Entrepreneurs Convention held in Bangkok in 1995. Rather than gathering individual businesspeople into a transnational network, as the cosmopolitan diaspora narrative would suggest, the World Huang Clan Association conference gathered *national* Huang clan associations.[85] Indeed, the world body was created and promoted by the Taiwanese Huang Clan Association in 1980 as part of Taiwan's informal diplomacy of national reunification since it was ejected from the United Nations in 1971.[86]

Certainly, the World Huang Clan Association is one of the transnational bodies that exemplify the invisible empire of the overseas Chinese. The Huang clan even has its own anthem, which sings of bringing together brothers from around the world. Glorious civilization is praised in familiar ways: "our country is the country of manners." But it is not clear whether they are referring to Chinese civilization or Huang civilization. While standard Chinese texts celebrate 5,000 years of glorious Chinese civilization, the Huang clan convention program states that "for more than 4,000 years our people have not forgotten their Huang roots." The unification of the various peoples from ancient times is not simply to unify the motherland in 1949, but to unify the transnational Huang clan in 1980.[87]

But the convention also shows the intensely national nature of the association: the Huang associations are not anti-national or postnational, but look to Thai national leaders and national symbols as part of clan identity. While World Chinese Entrepreneurs conventions are "patronized by prominent Chinese transnational entrepreneurs, with the blessing of [non-Chinese] local [that is, national] political leaders," the World Huang Clan Association's program makes sure to celebrate the powerful Thai national politicians who are members of the Huang clan.[88] More to the point, the Thai organizers of the Huang convention made sure to appeal to national symbols: the first page of the program has an official photograph of the Thai king and queen. The genealogy of illustrious Huang ancestors comes second. In a more prosaic sense, the mission of each Huang association is national: the Bangkok-based group is a charitable organization that takes care of Huang clans-people in Thailand. Cosmopolitan activities are organized according to the borders of the host nation-state.

This nationalization of clan organizations is part of the firming up of Thai borders in the past decade. While there has been much talk about globalization breaking down the borders of the nation-state, since the 1980s the Thai state has been solidifying its physical and economic borders. Huge construction projects have spent scarce resources to build roads to clarify Thailand's borders with Burma and Malaysia, and embankments along the Mekong River to stabilize its riparian border with Laos.[89] Likewise, years before neo-nationalism emerged in 1997, the state has been rationalizing/nationalizing customs and immigration procedures to assert central Bangkok control over the national political-economy. Thailand is involved in a global network economy. But the main Thai node of this network is Bangkok, the capital of the nation-state.

The cosmopolitan Chinese associations in Bangkok work according to this inter/national logic. Here, they provide evidence for standard views of overseas Chinese politics: Sino-Thai organizations serve as bridges between China, Thailand and other nation-states. For example, in 1998 the fifty-five clan associations of Thailand sent letters both to the Indonesian embassy to protest the atrocities against ethnic Chinese, and to the Chinese embassy to demand action for Chinese compatriots.[90] This shows how the Chinese clan associations based in Bangkok work according to the diplomatic logic of the nation-state: even though they represent transnational groups, they still gathered together in 1998 according to Thai boundaries to petition the nation-states of Indonesia and the PRC. National clan associations thus serve as a gateway for inter/national flows of people, information, capital and charitable relief. They certainly take care of their own domestic Sino-Thai constituency, but they diverge radically from Thai neo-nationalism. They are an inter/national form of nationalism rather than a nativist neo-nationalism. Academic analysis of overseas Chinese communities also characteristically follows this nation-state formula: research is conducted on overseas Chinese society "in" Thailand, "in" Malaysia, "in" Indonesia, "in" the US and so on. But, as we have seen, cosmopolitanism is produced in the tension between nation-states in Thailand and abroad.

### Diasporic Chinese in Phuket

Sino-Thai economic-culture in Phuket is different from that in Bangkok. In Bangkok, anti-Chineseness is a non-issue because the Chinese have mixed with the Thai to such an extent that you cannot easily tell one from the other. In Phuket, neo-nationalism is not a problem because the Chinese dominate the province, constituting 70 percent of the population. Phuket is both the smallest and the richest province in Thailand. In this way, Phuket is a prosperous ethnic Chinese enclave more similar to Singapore and Penang than its fellow Thai provinces of Chiangmai and Khon Kaen.

It is not a coincidence that Phuket has a similar regional economic-culture to Singapore and Penang. The three island-cities are linked in a historic network of Chinese migration facilitated by the European empires in Southeast Asia. While most of the Sino-Thai in Central, Northern and Northeastern Thailand came to the kingdom through Bangkok, most came to Phuket along the "southern route" to work in the island's tin mines. This itinerary joined southern China, Hong Kong, Singapore, Penang, Phuket and southern Burma together in a circuit of diasporic Chinese migration, trade and culture.[91] The itinerary bypassed Bangkok not for political reasons, but because of economies of transport: until recently it took four days to travel overland to Bangkok, while it took just sixteen hours to sail to Penang.[92]

Rather than being produced in relation to the nation, the diaspora is produced in relation to the British Empire as a community of Southeast Asian overseas Chinese, the Nanyang [South Seas] Chinese. Diasporic Chinese activities were organized more around these British imperial nodes than according to Thai national borders. Although mainland Chinese national historiography employs overseas Chinese as an important source of anti-imperialist Chinese national identity, diasporic Chinese were also an integral part of Euro-American imperialism. Another new word, comprador, was coined to describe the Chinese middlemen who facilitated imperial governance. Although Chinese people suffered from the opium and indentured labor regimes, Chinese merchants were also key figures in the network economy of the opium and labor trades.[93] When Thai nationalism made Chinese culture a problem in the 1940s and 1950s it was common for ethnic Chinese from Phuket to follow the empire's circuits to send their children to Penang for schooling. Likewise, books for Phuket's Chinese school initially came from Penang and Hong Kong; only later did Taiwan compete with the PRC for influence through patriotic nationalist education.

Phuket has been a prosperous node in a transnational political-economy since the mid-nineteenth century, first through its tin mines, and then its tourist industry. Trade was conducted not just within the diasporic Chinese network facilitated by the British Empire, but directly with North America, Europe and Australia. Now, because of the consolidation of the Thai state, borders are firmer, and most trade goes through Bangkok. Still, the mayor of Phuket City wished to decentralize state power from Bangkok back to Phuket to encourage both a cosmopolitan economy and good governance. The point is not simply to join a Greater Chinese network—most of the Hokkien Chinese majority who dominate Phuket have little interest in mainland China—but to encourage Phuket as a node in a more transnational economy.[94]

One way to measure the strength of the Chinese community is to examine the success of Chinese schools. According to this method, the overseas Chinese have been quite successful in Phuket. The Thai-Chinese (*Thai-Hua*) school celebrated its ninetieth anniversary in 2000. The alumni of the school are proud to note that Thailand's first private Chinese school was founded in Phuket, not Bangkok. Chinese education has also survived better in Phuket than in other provinces, most probably because of Phuket's high concentration of diasporic Chinese and their political influence in the capital.[95] While alumni are proud that their school has survived, they are also humiliated at the school's suffering. The foundation of the school in 1910 puts it firmly in the trend of the growing nationalist consciousness among overseas Chinese.[96] Yet the timing was also unfortunate: Chinese became a "problem" when the Thai monarchy was threatened by China's 1911 republican revolution. The Thai state thus had much the same view as the various Chinese regimes: overseas Chinese schools were seen as centers of political influence. The Thai state needed to control such activity, and hence Chinese schools were either closed down or closely regulated.

Like overseas Chinese history more generally, the school's ninety-year history is hardly stable: it has opened and closed again and again, changing its name several times. Initially it was called the Zhonghua (Chinese) School, and when it was re-opened in 1948 it was called the Thai-Hua (Thai-Chinese) School. It was seen as a threat to Thai nationalism in the Phibul era (1938–44 and 1948–57), and as a communist threat during the Sarit-Thanom-Prapas era (1959–73). Alumni told how, during the 1930s and 1950s, when students heard a state inspector coming, they had to burn their Chinese books. As with diasporic Chinese in general, the humiliation suffered in Phuket was not an epic humiliation of the Chinese nation, but day-to-day harassment. As state control of Chinese education was only liberalized in 1992, memories of anti-Chinese policies are still fresh.[97] Although respondents at the Thai-Hua School did not take the threat of neo-nationalism seriously, their history of humiliation and suffering made them wary. They wanted their remarks reported anonymously, which suggests that they still fear that Thai nationalism entails anti-Chinese activity.

Chinese schools are not just for educating children, but, like the clan association examined in Bangkok, they are a center of community activity.

Two other centers for community activity in Phuket are the Chinese temples and Rotary/Lions clubs. The Chinese temple in Phuket is especially noteworthy as it is at the center of the world-renowned Vegetarian Festival. It draws many tourists from Euro-America, but the Festival also is part of a pilgrimage circuit for ethnic Chinese believers. Therefore, diasporic Chinese relations are reversed. Here, the Sino-Thai are not sojourners who long to return to China. Connections between Phuket's Kathu temple and temples on mainland China are very weak. The main relationship is with a Chinese temple in Malaysia that was founded in 1850 as an offshoot of the Kathu temple. This was only rediscovered in 1993, when the president of the Taiping temple in Malaysia traced its origins back to Phuket. Hence, rather than homecoming being directed at hometowns in China, as standard overseas Chinese narratives tell us, here the center is in Phuket.[98] Sino-Thai in Phuket are not pseudo-Chinese in need of re-education in Chineseness by the PRC, but a source of Chinese culture that is produced in relation to nodes of transnational activity in Southeast Asia.

Similar regional communities have been formed through petit bourgeois social clubs. Although the Rotary and Lions clubs are both middle-American in origin, they have a very loyal following in Southeast Asia that is largely, if not exclusively, overseas Chinese. A noteworthy Sino-Thai politician, Phichai Rathakul, was president of the Rotary International Club in 2002. As with schools and temples, most of the networking is not with China or Taiwan, but with neighboring Southeast Asian nations.[99] Their solidarity is with compatriots in Malaysia and Indonesia. Even so, it is not like Thai neo-nationalism that looks to Mahathir as an anti-Western ally. It was clear from interviews that the solidarity is with fellow ethnic Chinese who gather against a perceived Islamic threat exemplified by Malaysian and Indonesian society.

The Phuket experience shows how overseas Chinese still engage in transnational networks, often in conflict with the central government in Bangkok and neo-nationalist ideology. These transnational networks have grown out of a Nanyang Chinese economic-culture fostered by the British Empire, which persists in postcolonial Southeast Asia. But, as the major civic institutions of Phuket—the Chinese school, the temple and the petit bourgeois social clubs—show, these networks are not closely linked with China. Rather, they are involved in transnational microcircuits of education, pilgrimage and conventioneering within Southeast Asia, especially with Chinese communities just over the border in Malaysia. As they cross national borders, they produce new communities not just in distinction to states, but as part of a relation of Chinese and Islamic economic-cultures. Thus, cosmopolitan Chinese groups in Phuket are not evidence of a "third culture" that is independent of nationalisms. The diaspora takes on meaning in regional networks of economic-culture rather than in either homogeneous national communities or a coherent cosmopolitan culture.

## Diasporic Chinese in Mahasarakham

The Sino-Thai situation in the rural northeastern province of Mahasarakham is in many ways the opposite of that in Phuket. It is involved in neither a national nor a transnational economic-culture, but as we will see it takes shape in relation to outsiders from other provinces. The community is small. It is one of the poorest provinces in the country. Although ethnic Chinese have been in the area for nearly two centuries—first settling in the neighboring province of Roi-Et in 1836—not much is going on in Mahasarakham. The Chinese school lasted only from 1944 to 1949 when it was shut down by the state. Clan associations are absent; interested Sino-Thai have to go to the closest city, Khon Kaen. Likewise for the Rotary and Lions clubs.[100]

The main "Chinese" institution in the province is called the Mahasarakham Association, and it was founded relatively recently in 1982. Unlike the Thai-Hua school in Phuket, this Association has not had to struggle for recognition from the state. Quite the opposite: as part of cultural governance, the state instructed the local Sino-Thai community to found the association to celebrate the ruling Chakri dynasty's bicentennial. Diasporic organizations thus were formed at the provincial level to legitimate royal nationalism. Strangely, the Chinese committee of Mahasarakham decided to name the association and its building after its Thai province rather than anything Chinese or royalist.

Unlike in Phuket, Mahasarakham is not part of any transnational network—unless you count the communist insurgency that raged in the region up into the 1980s, and was led by ethnic Chinese. It would be hard to argue that Mahasarakham is even part of a national network because the railroad and super highway both bypass the province. The most cosmopolitan aspect of the province is the University of Mahasarakham, which forms a strong cultural center for the community. (Phuket with all its wealth and influence still lacks a proper university.) Business in Mahasarakham, on the other hand, is local. Economic activity is almost exclusively trade and commerce: there is no industry in the province. The most prominent Sino-Thai owns the Toyota dealership. A past president of the Mahasarakham Association is a shopkeeper who sells picture frames. Sino-Thai business is generally represented by the Chamber of Commerce, which has the same membership as the Mahasarakham Association, that is, it is ethnic Chinese. The diaspora's limited "economic horizon" in Mahasarakham, which focuses on trade rather than manufacturing, is common among provincial business in Thailand's remote northeastern region.[101]

Sino-Thai life, as with life in general in Mahasarakham, is best described as "provincial" in both the geographical and the pejorative sense. The mission statement of the Mahasarakham Association underlines this:

> The objectives of the association are: to be a meeting place for the Mahasarakham people, to create unity among the Mahasarakham

people, to support secure jobs for Mahasarakham people, to be the intermediary between government officials and the people, and to promote education, sports, religion, and traditional customs.[102]

Such provincial capitalism, which was dominated by Sino-Thai business, was one of the keys to the successful Thai political-economy before 1997 (see Chapter 5). But a recent controversy testifies to the parochial nature of the economic-culture in Mahasarakham. In 2001, the Chamber of Commerce was up in arms because its members were being undersold by extra-provincial caravan traders. Competition from these outsiders was driving the Mahasarakham traders out of business; the outsiders' prices were lower because they did not have to pay local taxes, the Chamber of Commerce complained.

Rather than promoting a transnational network and a liberal trade regime as in Phuket, Sino-Thai business in Mahasarakham organized demonstrations to protest against a national free market.[103] Globalization was not the problem here, so much as any national economy—Sino-Thai business demanded that the provincial governor restrict interprovincial trade and enforce a Mahasarakham mercantilism. The irony is that overseas Chinese used the caravan trade in the nineteenth century to penetrate markets in northeastern Thailand. Such an anti-entrepreneurial attitude among the diasporic Chinese is one reason why Mahasarakham is not as prosperous as its neighbors. Sino-Thai in Mahasarakham are wary of investing money, and prefer to deposit it in banks—none of which is based in the province.[104]

Sino-Thai in Mahasarakham thus show how diasporic Chinese adapt to, and develop, local economic-culture. In this way, they are the only diasporic Chinese I interviewed in Thailand who correspond with Bangkok's neo-nationalist mercantilism thematically, if not in terms of content. They see outsiders as immoral competition, and wish to construct and guard economic borders. They complain that the system is unfair, and see the problem as more political than economic. The state—in this case, the governor and mayor—is either too weak to defend their interests, or has shown its corrupt nature by selling out the province to outsiders. The province is an economic backwater—even when compared with its neighbor Roi-Et, let alone Bangkok or Phuket—and successful overseas Chinese traders reflect this very narrow view of business. Rather than being evidence of an invisible empire of diasporic Chinese entrepreneurs who constitute the third largest economy in the world, or of a neo-national economic-culture, this group of businesspeople is simply trying to keep the caravan traders out. Once again, the diaspora is necessary for producing economic and cultural borders in Mahasarakham. Its community takes shape against the mobile and flexible capitalism of the extra-provincial caravan traders.

These three ethnographies certainly demonstrate the diversity of Sino-Thai experience—sometimes national, other times transnational, and still others provincial—and how it is formed in distinction to a set of Others:

for example, anti-Indonesian in Bangkok, anti-Muslim in Phuket and anti-caravan trader in Mahasarakham. But we can generalize from this analysis. In all three sites, Sino-Thai are not at the periphery of either Thai or Chinese economic-culture. They are not the sojourners of old who defined themselves in terms of China's standards of civilization, or immigrants who have assimilated to Thai nationalism. Rather, these groups are busy networking for three particular forms of capitalism: international, transnational and provincial. The key to understanding their activity is that they are all networking in similar ways: constructing diasporic identities against difference encountered in their specific contexts. Hence, diasporic identity in Thailand functions in similar ways to national identity: it is not a culture of shared norms, so much as a set of common differences defined by particular economic-cultural contexts.

The ethnographies thus help us to question cosmopolitanism: none of these three diasporas is evidence of an autonomous "third culture" of Sino-Thai identity that "seeks opportunities elsewhere." Rather than being flexible and mobile, as Nonini and Ong argue, these three ethnographies show how the diaspora is flexible but not necessarily mobile. Thus, arguments that point to the fluid cosmopolitanism of diasporas only apply to the limited case of wealthy "transnational yuppies." Instead of being a transformative force for a new style of globalization, evidence shows that diasporic Chinese adapt to particular economic contexts. Rather than seeking opportunities elsewhere, they creatively respond to and develop opportunities in context. They are very successful at colonizing and governing particular economic-cultures: inter/national capitalism in Bangkok, transnational capitalism in Phuket and provincial capitalism in Mahasarakham. They are not nationalist in Phuket or Mahasarakham simply because most of the inter/national economic opportunities are concentrated in the Bangkok area; they are less cosmopolitan in Bangkok than expected for the same reason: it is the national economic node. Diasporas, thus, are not the pure agency of mobile capital, but flexibly respond to specific economic-cultural contexts according to relations of difference. In each case, the diaspora has responded to the state's cultural governance in a creative way that does not directly oppose it, so much as colonize it for the diaspora's benefit.

Hence, to understand diasporic politics in Thailand, we need to do more than chart out the specifics of each particular experience in Bangkok, Phuket and Mahasarakham. Rather than each being a prime example of nationalist, cosmopolitan and local identity—as expected—the ethnographies show how economic and social activity is produced in a common logic of difference. Although the content of each economic-culture is different in the three sites, the cultural governance of identity formation through exclusion is the same. These varied experiences demonstrate how identity is produced through constructing borders of self and Other, not just for the most obvious case of national identity, but in relations of exclusion in local and transnational contexts as well.

## Conclusion

As this and previous chapters have shown, "globalization" does not simply describe a process whereby Euro-American capitalism and popular culture dominate the world, and erode both state sovereignty and local culture. This chapter has demonstrated how Chinese capitalism and culture have been key in building borders and producing communities through their own modes of cultural governance. But, rather than substituting "Chinese" for "American" to describe this process, I have used diasporas to question popular understandings of the global versus the local to argue that cosmopolitanism and nationalism produce each other in relations of identity and difference. Hence, diasporas not only loosen any essential link between nation and state, but also can illuminate the informal cultural governance of the relation between the global and the local, the self and the Other.

Although diasporic Chinese capitalism is often figured as a Pacific Asian form of globalization that erodes national borders in Southeast Asia, I have shown how diasporic populations are intimately involved in defining borders. Neo-nationalisms in China and Thailand share a similar logic: a highly territorialized identity, an economic-cultural understanding of neo-imperialism, and an Occidentalizing of Euro-America. Both have a strong notion of National Humiliation that relies on a foreign/domestic dynamic: foreign invasion aided by domestic stupidity and corruption. Both have used diasporic Chinese as a resource to construct a nationalist self and a foreign Other. Although Thai nationalism has been constructed against a Chinese Other in the past, now neo-nationalism not only includes Sino-Thai, but is largely formulated by them.

I have also questioned how nationalism and cosmopolitanism are formulated by arguing against the popular notion of diasporic Chinese as a cosmopolitan community that resists state power. The ethnographies both added to and problematized critical considerations of diasporas by examining the diversity of Chineseness as it is articulated in different economic-cultural spaces in Thailand. Fieldwork in Bangkok, Phuket and Mahasarakham demonstrated that ethnic Chinese populations do not simply constitute a third culture. Although internally coherent to people in Bangkok, Phuket and Mahasarakham, each ethnography called the others into question, adding to our critical view of national identity. Diasporas thus both construct and deconstruct the dynamic of nationalism and cosmopolitanism. Rather than assimilating to Thai nationalism, diasporic Chinese are involved in colonizing the prevailing economic-culture, be it national, transnational or provincial. It is noteworthy that, on the one hand, many of the Bangkok elite who write neo-nationalist manifestos are Sino-Thai, and, on the other hand, a provincial diasporic Chinese institution is called the "Mahasarakham" Association. Diasporas thus work both with and against the state, employing their own extra-state modes of cultural governance.

To understand how nationalism and cosmopolitanism, the global and the local work, we need to see how the outsiders, such as diasporas, are necessary for constructing communities and producing boundaries. Diasporas thus are not just an economic resource, but a symbolic resource for the cultural governance of cosmopolitanism, nationalism and localism. What China and Thailand share is not a common identity, but a common set of differences—in this case, diasporic Chinese and Euro-American imperialism—against which their particular national identities are constructed. By shifting the analytical focus from unitary norms to the multiplicity of difference, we are better able to consolidate an anti-essentialist view of identity and understand the complexities of cultural governance and transnational politics. In this way, diaspora research is part of a movement in IR from a tight focus on "inter-national," to an attention to "relations"—the relationality of identity. Diasporas thus are a theoretical issue that helps us question the hegemonic structures of world politics that are governed by the binary opposition between cosmopolitanism and nationalism.

# Conclusion

This book's strange journey through the political curiosities of Pacific Asia has addressed many of the issues of comparative politics: civil/military relations, revolutions and reform movements, elections and political parties, civil society and social movements, development and political culture, and the role and rights of ethnic minorities. But this odd itinerary through the region also has used the thematic of cultural governance and resistance to highlight a different set of issues: imaginative geography, the culture of technology, popular culture and national identity, gender and patriarchy, corruption and democracy, formal and informal politics, and the curiously national/transnational politics of diasporas. The case studies of JACADS, Miss Thailand, Asian Democracy, Confucian civil society, vote buying and the Chinese diaspora exemplify both specific political problems, and broader trends of global capitalist modernity. As this book has shown, cultural governance is more than a state practice, thus it is important to see resistance in terms of its relations with the multiple forms of governmentality in various spaces. This Conclusion will revisit some of the substantive and theoretical issues raised throughout the book by examining the contact zone of the "politics of issues" and the "politics of rhetoric," not only to summarize answers, but to raise new questions.

## The politics of issues

Although it is common to argue that Pacific Asian politics is dominated by hegemonic factors such as "US imperialism" or the "China threat," I contend that such issues are largely a distraction. They impose a state-centric binary framework that often narrows our understanding to judgments that are pro- or anti-American, pro- or anti-Chinese. I have framed the book's analysis to examine how Pacific Asia works with and against global capitalist modernity to trace how practices of cultural governance and resistance have emerged in the region.[1]

While this book can be seen as a catalogue of the unique absurdities of Pacific Asian politics, generalizations about important issues can be made. While we characteristically understand the military in terms of the power of its destructive force, and study hardware that kills people and destroys environments, I have reframed military power into a productive force that generates civilian identity in the context of problems and solutions that perpetuate the militarization of political life. The US military bakes cakes and publishes brochures to guide our understanding of its chemical weapons disposal project. The Thai military recruited Miss Thailand first to show its humane (feminine?) side, and then to promote a certain view of women and men in Thai society. The Chinese military not only invades its own capital city, as in June 1989, but publishes coffee table books to commemorate the crackdown. While cultural governance works in very different ways in the US, Thailand and China, all three countries increasingly frame security threats according to a common theme: Islamic fundamentalism.

The policies of the US's "war on terror" are well known, and it is necessary to understand how China's and Thailand's Islamic insurgencies emerged from their own particular histories long before September 11, 2001. Although in the People's Republic of China (PRC) much is said about a coming post-Cold War conflict between China and America,[2] Beijing has been fighting wars to assert hegemony over its Central Asian frontier for centuries. China's recent labeling of independence movements in its northwest region of Xinjiang as "Islamic terrorists" is less about global geopolitics than it is about a local policing of borders of identity and territory.

Thailand, likewise, has had a bloody relationship with the Muslim populations along its southern frontier with Malay states for centuries. The unrest that erupted in January 2004 when insurgents raided an army depot, stealing 300 weapons and killing four Thai soldiers, shattered an atmosphere of political calm and compromise that had reigned for decades. Rather than framing this as a political or criminal issue, the Thai government responded with military force, attacking mosques and killing 84 people in one day, including 78 who died while in custody. Needless to say, the state's reaction to this southern unrest has exacerbated an already dire situation: over 850 people were killed between January 2004 and August 2005.

As in China, political groups that used to be classified as "separatist" or "independence" movements are now labeled as terrorist. While Chapter 6 examined how the Chinese diaspora is often seen as a victim, it is also important to note how China and Thailand are increasingly militarizing relations with their Islamic citizenry. Pacific Asia is participating in the war on terror, but not simply as one of many military fronts in a global conflict led by the US. Conflicts in China and Thailand grow out of historical self/Other dynamics—recall that the main "Other" for Sino-Thai identity in the south is not Thai Buddhist, but Malay Muslim. The issue is less about military hardware than the militarized software that frames political issues in ways that convert difference into Otherness. The militarization of identity not only limits the options of Muslim populations, but as in Euro-America has consequences for civil society at large—in 2005 the Thai government passed emergency legislation that would limit protests not only in the south, but in Bangkok itself. The military in Pacific Asia, thus, is important far beyond issues of "national security," for it continues to militarize society at large—recruiting national icons from reigning monarchs to beauty queens as part of its cultural governance performances.

Another key issue explored in the book is the relation between the state and civil society. The first few chapters examined modes of cultural governance and resistance by charting state policies and civil society's reaction to them, such as the resistance to the US Army's chemical weapons program on Johnston Atoll or to Pacific Asian states' illiberal form of Asian Democracy. Yet, the analysis also has shown how the state and civil society are not opposites struggling against each other: each depends upon the other for existence in a complementary self/Other relation. Later chapters push beyond understanding the complementary nature of the state and civil society to argue that civil society itself is often complicit with state-led cultural governance. Rather than assuming that civil society is a site of resistance, I argued that civil society can easily be a conservative force that helps states preserve the status quo in the face of radical opposition. The discourses of chemical demilitarization, national and international beauty queens, Asian Democracy, Confucian civil society and anti-vote buying reform are all useful ideological crutches that promote the legitimacy of the state and distract citizens from other important issues. In this way the state and certain segments of civil society work together through cultural governance to stabilize national and regional identities at the expense of other possibilities. I used examples of social movements in Pacific Asia that were multiple and often contradictory to take a critical view of the workings of civil society. The conclusion is that political resistance does not simply oppose the state, but engages capitalist modernity in various social, economic and cultural spaces.

Considering the politics of rhetoric in Pacific Asia will help us better understand this shift of political issues; asking the rhetorical questions of "how" discourse is produced will help us answer the "what" questions of specific political problems. To appreciate the contingency of governance and resistance, and the links between rhetoric and issues, it is important to leave the "summary mode" to argue these points through a case study that affects both China and Pacific Asia: the discourse of Mao Zedong. As we will see, the politics of the Mao image is far from clear. Long after his death in 1976, Mao continues to influence both rhetorical and issue politics. As Dai Jinhua cryptically states, "the Mao era has been 'an enormous inheritance and debt' that society has found it difficult to acknowledge."[3]

## Framing Mao

In the Introduction, I impiously equated the influence of Miss China with the impact of the Chinese Communist Party (CCP). In a similar spirit, I think that, to properly understand the influence of Mao on China and the world, it is important to free him from being seen as either a revolutionary God or a totalitarian devil. While Zhang Hongtu paints Mao leering at the Goddess of Democracy and Geremie R. Barmé compares the cult of Mao to the cult of Elvis,[4] I think it is helpful to compare Mao to Miss Thailand—less in terms of beauty and popularity than in terms of the institutional power of their images. According to many Chinese intellectuals, including those who are critical of him, "Mao was the quintessential representation of China, the embodiment of the nation."[5] In the early 1960s Mao-chronicler Edgar Snow recognized how Mao was more than a political leader; Mao had "become an Institution of such prestige and authority that no one in the Party could raze it without sacrificing a collective vested interest of first importance."[6] Examining the institutional politics of the Mao image will help us explore the sticky relation between the politics of issues and the politics of rhetoric.

While Miss Siam emerged with the revolutionary regime that overthrew absolute monarchy in the 1930s, Mao came to prominence as China was negotiating its shift from the imperial system to a republican system. The institutions of Miss Thailand and Mao both have represented the state at large, sometimes as part of cultural governance, and at others as part of resistance. Like the rise, fall and rise again of Miss Thailand over the past seven decades, Mao's political history has been uneven. As with Miss Thailand, he always survived his time in the political wilderness, coming back to set the tone for each new age. Even after Mao died in 1976, he was reborn through a posthumous cult in the 1990s that both reflected and promoted a new consumer culture. Just as Miss Thailand first represented the state, and then national capitalism, and finally global capitalist modernity, Mao's institutional career as an image has emerged in three distinct eras that have migrated from the communist party, to the socialist state, to capitalist modernity (in a curious reversal of the Marxist trajectory). The Mao image was first institutionalized at the revolutionary base of Yan'an when Mao consolidated his power over the CCP (1936–47). The Cultural Revolution is the second age of Mao (1966–76). The third age of Mao began in the early 1990s, and continues to the present. The aim here is not to write a political biography, or examine the importance of Mao Zedong Thought, but to consider the impact of Mao discourse as it has changed over the decades (see Figure 7.1).

### *Mao as leader in Yan'an*

Among scholars, Mao is not known as a significant theorist; the meaning of his speeches, which were later gathered into the canon of *Selected Works*,

*Figure 7.1*
Reconstructing the Mao statue in Shenyang, 2005.
© William A. Callahan

comes more from the rhetorical form they took than from their intellectual content. Mao was more a revolutionary messiah than a party organizer. In *Revolutionary Discourse in Mao's Republic*, David E. Apter and Tony Saich thus argue that Mao gained power less through force of arms or intellectual persuasion than through textual practice. Using a revolutionary form of cultural governance, Mao's speeches and writings sought to "change the world by reinterpreting it," and thus create "a utopic republic [that] came to represent the moral moment of the Chinese revolution."[7] Rather than texts being an objective record of events or sacred founding documents, for Mao they were "instigators and the objects of struggles in CCP."[8] Mao worked as a storyteller, "transforming the main episodes of war and revolution into turning points for both a narrative of history and a projection of truth" that formed the canon that guided Chinese politics for decades.[9]

Maoism thus framed much journalistic and academic writing in China from the 1940s to the 1980s in a very graphic way: quotes from Mao characteristically were placed in the introduction and conclusion of all publications.¹⁰ The cultural governance of Mao as an image also began at Yan'an. Mao's portrait representing him as the savior of China was published for the first time in 1937. Mao badges, often recycled from toothpaste tubes, first appeared in 1945.¹¹

Although the Yan'an period ended in 1947, the Yan'an spirit that canonized Mao's image continued to animate the party-state's cultural governance long after the PRC was established at Tian'anmen in 1949. The discursive community of Yan'an cadres, which continued to dominate the leadership in the 1980s, still argued for the primacy of rhetorical power: the control of "pens and gun barrels" was the key to defending the revolution.¹² The battle over Tian'anmen Square in 1989, according to Apter and Saich, was between a new generation of Chinese leaders and the retired Yan'anites who were struggling for relevance in the era of economic reform.¹³ Mao's image thus congealed at Yan'an into a powerful force through a rhetorical politics that shaped the strategy of the revolution, and the politics of the PRC.

## *The Mao cult and the Cultural Revolution*

Although Mao is credited with defeating the imperialist powers and founding the PRC in 1949, his power and influence suffered a serious setback after the disaster of the Great Leap Forward (1958–60). Yet the power of Mao's image not only persisted, but grew. According to Snow, to the Chinese people in the early 1960s, Mao was "not just a party boss but . . . a teacher, statesman, strategist, philosopher, poet laureate, national hero, head of the family, and greatest liberator in history. He is also Confucius plus Lao-tzu plus Rousseau plus Marx plus Buddha."¹⁴ While Michel Foucault would list these various roles to exemplify the dispersion of pastoral power in cultural governance,¹⁵ during the Cultural Revolution Mao's image gathered them all together in a reassertion of an organic mode of governance that looked to an omnipotent God-King. Because traditional religious institutions had been outlawed in socialist China, people put their faith in Mao not necessarily as a vote of support for his policies, but because adoring Mao was the only sanctioned form of worship.¹⁶

The power of Mao's image framed the politics of everyday life during the Cultural Revolution, where all utterances were required to include references to Mao or the Chinese revolution. A typical conversation at the market would go something like this:

> "Serve the people. Comrade, could I have two pounds of pork, please?"
> "A revolution is not a dinner party. That makes 1.85 yuan all together."
> "To rebel is justified. Here you are."
> "Practice frugality while making revolution. There's your change, and there's your meat."¹⁷

People learned this language style from studying the little red book and Mao's *Selected Works*. During the ten years of the Cultural Revolution, 40 billion volumes of Mao's works were in circulation, amounting to over "fifteen copies of Mao's works for every man, woman and child in China."[18] A story told by a prominent newspaper editor underlines how the politics of rhetoric trumped the politics of issues during the Cultural Revolution: he nearly got into serious trouble when an article he wrote used a quote that could be attributed to Lin Biao (who was then out of favor), and was only saved when he found the same phrase in the Mao canon. The content of the quote did not matter, the main issue was the rhetoric of its scriptural provenance.[19]

As in Yan'an, Mao discourse was not limited to texts, but produced posters, clocks, books, stamps and, most famously, badges. The volume of these artifacts is startling: 2.2 billion portraits of Mao were printed. As for Mao badges, one source tells us 4.8 billion were produced between 1966 and 1970, while another reports that 2.2 billion had been minted by 1969.[20] According to a famous story, Mao lamented the production of so many badges because the badges consumed enough aluminum to build 39,000 fighter jets.[21]

Here, Mao is missing the point of the Mao image, for the badges were important not for their material value, but as sacred objects; according to the contemporary etiquette, you wore the badge over your heart to generate revolutionary credibility. As artist Zhang Hongtu explained in the 1980s, the image still emitted its own living power:

> The Mao image has a charisma of its own. It's still so powerful that the first time I cut up an official portrait of Mao for a collage I felt a pang of guilt, something gnawing away inside me. Other people, in particular other Chinese, may well feel the same.[22]

The Cultural Revolution's cultural governance of Mao's image was so strong that it was still difficult for Zhang to resist in New York City a decade after Mao had died.

While it is common to dismiss the Mao cult as something peculiar to China and the Cultural Revolution, the power of Mao's image also captivated people in Euro-America at this time.[23] On the right, Cold War scholars studied the Mao canon as the key to understanding the PRC. Alongside Kremlinologists, a cadre of Pekinologists emerged to study and translate the Mao canon as a way of gaining purchase on Chinese politics in particular, and communist revolution in general. The Mao canon's prominence in Euro-America was largely due to a political-economy of textual scarcity: from the 1950s to the 1970s few outsiders could travel to China, let alone live there. Chinese sources could be found in only a few places: Harvard University, the Hoover Institute and the Universities Service Center in Hong Kong. In this way, Mao became China and China

Conclusion   181

became Mao in the 1960s not just for Red Guards in the PRC, but for scholars in the Euro-American academy.

For many progressive scholars and activists, the PRC was seen as an example of an alternative to liberal capitalist Euro-America; through Mao's writings and carefully guided tours of the mainland, China was presented to European scholars as a utopian republic (like Yan'an). As Dutton recalls, "An entire generation of great philosophical minds in the West . . . who subsequently informed many of the theoretical developments in such fields as cultural studies . . . began their academic careers entranced or excited by the Chinese Cultural Revolution."[24] For example, after a three-week tour of the PRC, Julia Kristeva used "Chinese women" as a wedge to critique patriarchal workings of capitalist modernity in Europe. Like many of her Euro-American contemporaries, Kristeva was not really interested in understanding China; the PRC was Orientalized so as to criticize the West.[25] Rey Chow cites such examples to argue that Maoism, with its focus on oppression, victimization, subalternity, is a key source of critical cultural studies.[26]

Battles over Maoism as a revolutionary discourse persist into the twenty-first century—often beyond China and Europe. During the 1990s, Pacific Asian struggles were displaced to Peru where the Maoist "Shining Path" fought against ethnic Japanese President Alberto Fujimori, who declared that "only Asian values can save my country." In Thailand many of today's key intellectuals spent their early twenties in a jungle-based Maoist insurgency, before coming back to the cities in the early 1980s. The greatest threat to the Nepalese monarchy is a Maoist insurgency. The best place to purchase Mao texts from the Cultural Revolution era is not in China, where they have been pulped, but in the US. Because of an ideological split over Deng Xiaoping's revisionist repudiation of Mao, the Revolutionary Communist Party, the US still sells Mao literature and images at its chain of "Revolution Books" stores.[27] The power of Mao captivated people around the world during the Cultural Revolution, and persists long after his death.

*Posthumous Mao as a folk god*

During the Cultural Revolution, Mao was all things to all people. Even after he died in 1976, and the Cultural Revolution was criticized, Mao was still seen by the CCP as "great Marxist, founder and leader of CCP, PLA, and the PRC."[28] Since the 1990s, Mao "remains a patriotic leader, martial hero, philosopher-king, poet, calligrapher."[29] Yet, there is an important shift here from Mao as the omnipotent God, as in the Cultural Revolution, to Mao as a folk god in China's polytheistic pantheon.[30] Whereas in the second era Mao's image covered all the bases, now it is different things to different people. Like Miss Thailand, Mao as image is framed in various ways: teacher, soldier, beauty queen and bad girl.

Actually, Mao went out of style in the 1980s as people were recovering from the Cultural Revolution. Rather than framing him as the guiding light, the CCP declared that Mao's role in Chinese history was "70 percent positive and 30 percent negative." In the late 1970s, there was a cleansing of discourse to linguistically root out the Mao cult. Still, the CCP did not end its tight management of discourse; often it merely moved terms from the list of appropriate words to the list of inappropriate words, and vice versa.[31] For example, the Confucian term for loyalty, *zhong*, was used during the Cultural Revolution to signify loyalty to Mao and the Revolution.[32] In the late 1970s the Party's Central Department of Propaganda started a process of "the Disposal of Extant Objects Related to 'Loyalty'."[33] This was not a simple change in appropriate formulations, for the Mao cult generated a huge number of material artifacts that continued to incur enormous economic costs. One army warehouse was filled with 2,300 kilograms of Mao badges. Publishers' warehouses were piled high with Mao texts and portraits. For both ideological and economic reasons, these mountains of sacred artifacts needed to be destroyed. The Mao canon from the Cultural Revolution thus was pulped. By the early 1980s, 90 percent of Mao badges had been "recycled."[34]

But Barmé notes that, just as the party-state was pulping Mao, the Chinese masses started to demand Mao's image: "In 1989 a mere 370,000 copies of the official portrait of Mao had been printed. In 1990 the number rose dramatically to 22.95 million, of which 19.93 million were sold."[35] This Mao revival was more spiritual than ideological; Mao was re-deified as a folk god in popular culture, rather than as a political savior in official culture. According to a popular urban myth, the Mao craze started in Southern China with a horrible car accident that killed many, but spared the driver who had a small Mao portrait on his dashboard. Thus, after 1991, people began to "seek the protection of the Mao-God when they build houses, engage in business, and drive vehicles."[36] In anticipation of his centenary in 1993, Mao's portrait was laminated in the style of a folk god talisman, dangling with red tassels and gold ingots, and labeled with good luck slogans such as "May you have happiness and prosperity" (see Figure 7.2).

This popular deification of Mao was not politically orchestrated by the party-state as a mode of cultural governance. While the Mao centenary was an official media event, most of the activities that defined the Mao craze took place in popular culture. While wearing the Mao badge over one's heart generated revolutionary credibility during the Cultural Revolution, these laminated Mao talismans are consumer items that focused on personal luck rather than party loyalty. The Mao mausoleum in Tian'anmen Square is now less a sacred site than a tourist destination that it is commemorated with the kitsch culture of tea towels (see Figure 7.3). In this way, the popularization of Mao in folk culture often threatened the state's control over cultural governance.[37]

*Figure 7.2* Mao talismans in Shaoshan, 1999. © William A. Callahan

*Figure 7.3*
Mao mausoleum tea towel, Beijing, 1985.
© William A. Callahan

Shaoshan, Mao's home village in central China, is also cashing in on this consumer pilgrimage trend: in the early 1990s, the Shaoshan Mao Badge Factory started producing Mao badges again, a 10.1-meter-high bronze Mao statue was unveiled, and a Mao paraphernalia market thrived. The Mao Family Restaurant, which was established in the 1980s by one of Mao's distant relatives, spread to China's major cities.[38] At the entrance of a Beijing branch, a Mao bust serves as a shrine, mixing Cultural Revolutionary icons with practices of Chinese folk religion (see Figure 7.4).

The party-state tried to capitalize on this new Mao craze by producing books, comics, films, television shows and popular music. But this official culture was behind the curve of popular culture. The new interest in Mao was often a criticism of the new inequalities, official corruption and gross materialism produced by Deng Xiaoping's economic reforms. As Barmé explains, the Mao craze emerged out of a "deep dissatisfaction with the status quo and a yearning for the moral power and leadership of the long-dead Chairman."[39] Like the rise of non-traditional religions in the United Kingdom in the nineteenth century and the United States in the twentieth century, the Mao craze is a reaction to rapid social and political-economic change. As the following ditty shows, Mao is seen as the god of itinerant workers, the floating population that has been uprooted by China's economic reforms:

*Figure 7.4* Shrine in Mao Family Restaurant, Beijing, 1999. © William A. Callahan

> Beijing relies on the Center,
> Shanghai on its connections,
> Guangzhou leans on Hong Kong,
> The drifting population lives by Mao Zedong Thought.[40]

In addition to an icon of nostalgia for the underclass, Mao is framed by artists and writers as an authority to be resisted. Rather than Mao being revered as a god, critical intellectuals talk of a "Mao malady" that still captivates many Chinese.[41] As we saw in Chapter 3, one way to resist Mao is to resist the hyperbole of MaoSpeak that frames politics in terms of the grand battle between good and evil. In *Please Don't Call Me Human*, Wang Shuo satirizes this language by inflating the hyperbole. The people of a Beijing neighborhood address, for example, their local Party functionary as "Respected wise dear teacher leader helmsman pathfinder vanguard pioneer architect beacon torch devil-deflecting mirror dog-beating club dad mum granddad grandma ancestor primal ape Supreme Diety Jade Emperor Guanyin Boddhisattva commander-in-chief." They refer to themselves as "little people knaves the black haired scum you children grandchildren tufts of grass little dogs and cats a gang of hooligans."[42] Although this is entertaining, it is difficult to know if this satire is an effective mode of resistance, as it restates and thus reaffirms MaoSpeak.[43] As we saw in Chapter 3, the task is to stop looking for a savior and take responsibility for your own politics.

Zhang Hongtu's "Chairmen Mao" series of paintings, which recontextualizes iconic photos of Mao, is more effective at resisting cultural governance. Zhang erodes the Mao cult through a multiple representation of the official image, sometimes as a lecherous old man, other times as a young school girl, sometimes as an Asian tiger, others as Joe Stalin. When they were reproduced on t-shirts and Vivienne Tam's line of fashion clothing these paintings made it into popular culture, for a broad circulation beyond art galleries.[44] Zhang's irony and play helps us to question the power of the Mao image in particular, and the savior theme of revolutionary politics more generally. But serious resistance to the regime of Mao images is still scarce.

In the late 1990s, the state was more successful at tapping into the power of Mao's image. Mao made another comeback as part of the official commemoration of the 50th anniversary of the founding of the PRC on October 1, 1999. Shorn of his communist persona and Cultural Revolutionary activities, Mao was re-presented as the patriotic nationalist who saved China from the ravages of imperialism (rather than capitalism). As conservative commentator He Xin said, "today the Chinese are rediscovering patriotism. Mao Zedong is the symbolic figure who led China to achieve international recognition and historical respect in the twentieth century."[45] In the lead-up to National Day on October 1, old patriotic films were re-broadcast on national television, as were new biographical

186  *Conclusion*

teleseries of Mao himself. Newspapers and magazines had numerous stories each day tying Mao to liberation. The PLA's song-and-dance troupes were busy touring the country (and being broadcast on provincial and national television) singing the praises of Mao and the revolution (see Figure 7.5).

Most dramatically, the Mao image is now framed by currency in China. To celebrate fifty years of the PRC, the national bank issued a new bank note with a new denomination: 100 yuan with Mao's visage on the front. This was the first time official currency celebrated an individual: before 1999, currency portraits celebrated China's collective leadership, social

*Figure 7.5* PLA dancing for Mao, Shaoshan, 1999. © William A. Callahan

classes and national minorities. Currency images have always been important for identity politics in the PRC: whereas Cultural Revolutionary notes pictured workers, peasants and soldiers, the new 50 yuan note in 1986 celebrated workers, peasants and intellectuals.[46] This was seen as recognition of the value of intellectuals and the mistakes of the Cultural Revolution. Now Mao is framed by the 100 yuan bill (see Figure 7.6). The meaning of "value" thus is changed from moral and political to instrumental and exchange. Mao is reincarnated not just as the Kitchen God, but as a capitalist guru who inspires pop business books in China, and adorns newspaper advertisements for transnational capitalist organs such as *Forbes Global*.[47] In China, the commercialization of Mao became so grotesque that in 1994 the party-state banned the use of Mao's image in commercial advertisements.[48]

For the past seventy years, Mao's image has served as currency in numerous ways. In Yan'an, and again during the Cultural Revolution, Mao's words were currency to argue for and justify political action, and his image generated revolutionary credibility as a sacred icon. In the current era, Mao's image is exchanged in a commercialized popular culture. Since 1999, the image itself is currency—adorning all denominations of Chinese money—to buy material goods in a capitalist economy. Mao is used in this new political economy in three ways: popular culture (Mao icons), commercial culture (television) and official culture (legal tender). Whereas before people in China and Euro-America used the Mao canon to gain purchase on China and communist revolution, now we can use Mao as part of an economy of cultural consumption. Maoism as an orthodoxy and Mao as an image thus are good examples of the mutually entailing relationship between cultural governance and resistance in Pacific Asia.

But as Barmé concludes, "the most fearful thing about the Mao cult may be that it has become a permanent part of China's cultural landscape, and

*Figure 7.6* New Mao currency, 1999. © William A. Callahan

nothing, be it economic development or political upheaval, can alter this."[49] In the 2000s political debate in China is still largely limited to pro- and anti-Mao arguments in the sense that those who criticize the current economic reform policy characteristically look to Mao texts and Mao images for support. To resist the cultural governance of Mao it is not enough to resist state sanctioned images; it is important to recognize how the savior regime of Mao discourse continues to guide mass culture and identity politics in China. Like Miss Thailand, the Mao image is a floating sign that is used in contradictory ways by various groups as both a vehicle for the state's cultural governance and resistance to it. As national identity has shifted in Thailand and China, Miss Thailand and Mao have survived as patriotic images. Although Miss Thailand never had sovereign power over life and death like Mao, now both sets of images circulate in global capitalist modernity, guiding lifestyles and consumption—if not life and death.

## The politics of rhetoric

The multiple meanings of Mao show that we cannot assume the coherence of one leader's identity, let alone the coherence of any national or regional identity. Rather, it is necessary to historicize these discourses to show the contingent workings of cultural governance and resistance in Pacific Asia. While the US Army deployed the idea of "safety" to calm the public's fears about chemical weapons disposal, Chapter 1 traced the uneven and messy history of the military's safety record in the Pacific. Likewise, other chapters questioned the received categories of diaspora, national identity, electoral corruption, civil society and Asian Democracy by tracing the contingent history of these practices: like the Miss Thailand beauty pageant, the Sino-Thai school in Phuket has opened and closed again and again, changing its name several times. Mao shifts from being a revolutionary messiah in Yan'an, to a sacred icon in the Cultural Revolution, to currency for economic exchange in the twenty-first century. These diverse examples show how identity and difference are very unstable concepts in Pacific Asia, being revalued with each successive utterance. The discussion of Mao discourse underlined how the politics of rhetoric frames the politics of issues: "what" people said in Cultural Revolutionary China often mattered less than "how" they said it. Although the Mao image presents an extreme example, the politics of rhetoric certainly is not peculiar to China. While the US Army directed our gaze to the technology of the JACADS incinerators, we examined the technology of the "chemical weapons disposal" discourse to deconstruct state power. Other examples presented in this book have shown how myth-making sets the limits on what can (and cannot) be discussed.

Rhetoric here means more than simply theory; as the chapters have shown, the state uses the rhetoric of technology to stabilize and regularize its cultural governance of political life. Chapters 1, 2 and 3 each examine how the state uses the technical marvels of photography to guide our understanding of problems and solutions: both the US Army and pro-democracy forces in Burma juxtapose black-and-white pictures with color ones in a narrative of progress to naturalize their political projects. The national identities of (Miss) China and (Miss) Thailand are both shaped by the techniques of their television production. Rather than taking these techniques and their products as natural, I have deconstructed and historicized them to show that they are modes of cultural governance that can be resisted.

As with the discussion of issue politics above that aimed to avoid the binary figurations of Pacific Asian politics as pro- and anti-American or pro- and anti-Chinese, here I would like to avoid debates that try to prove or disprove Orientalism, Occidentalism or postcolonialism. While these theoretical optics generally focus on contradictions in national and civilizational space, this book has used the wider optic of self/Other relations to see how culture and politics work to constitute various spaces in global capitalist modernity: international space, national space, domestic space, gendered space, electoral space, family space and transnational space. Since each of these spaces is involved in cultural governance it has been necessary to refigure analysis away from the state-centered rhetoric of comparative politics to examine governance and resistance as activities in self/Other relations. The aim, as we saw in Chapter 4, is to criticize capitalist modernity without romanticizing the unfreedoms of traditional societies.

This is not to say that Orientalism, Occidentalism and postcolonialism are incorrect or insignificant. They each constitute an important mode of analysis. My argument is that they are insufficient for understanding Pacific Asian politics; indeed, one postcolonial theorist admits as much by discounting the struggle for democracy in Burma because it is pursing what he judges to be "western liberal ideology."[50] This underlines how the politics of domestic and regional struggles in Pacific Asia can be erased by figurations that limit the definition of conflict to East vs. West. Struggles are not just between grand continental territories or civilizational bodies; but take place in political nooks and crannies, the details of everyday life, such as those examined in this book. Hence, I have refigured the rhetoric of analysis to consider politics of self/Other relations in the contact zone where the politics of issues and the politics of rhetoric overlap. In this way we can evade the romantic straitjacket that binds both interpretation and action, and open analysis up to more ironic understandings of political possibility. Rather than being limited to a search for pure opposition, the examples of resistance cited in this book demonstrate that politics consists of using various identities—gendered, religious, national, regional, traditional, modern—as tactics in a struggle against capitalist modernity's cultural governance.

## Conclusion

One of the problems with arguing against essentialism is that in criticizing essentialism you risk grounding your analysis on yet another essential foundation. Rather than set up a new foundation of knowledge from which to critically analyze Pacific Asian politics, the technique of analyzing power in terms of cultural governance and resistance is flexible. Chapters 1, 2 and 3 used examples of civil society to critically deconstruct the state's cultural governance. Chapters 4 and 5 shifted to use the concept of social movements to criticize the epistemological stability of the state/civil society relationship. Finally, Chapter 6 used moving societies to deconstruct the notions of social movements and diasporas. The question is not whether there is authentic civil society or real social movements in Pacific Asia; the main issue is how different groups are using these concepts in very political ways. Since both elite bureaucrats and activists in popular social movements are using the same basic democratic vocabulary, the politics lies in how democracy is constructed and performed. I used gender to deconstruct state power in Chapter 2, while criticizing gender politics from the stance of popular democracy in Chapter 3. The transnational production of Miss Thailand called into question discourses of national identity in Chapter 2, while the intimate links between nationalism and transnationalism were deconstructed in Chapter 6.

As a technique, semiotics has no inherent politics. It can be used to deconstruct anything, and thus risks deflating opposition movements by focusing on their contradictions and their complicity with power. Although poststructuralism is often criticized for being depoliticizing, I have shown how poststructural analysis can be very political in terms of both the politics of issues and the politics of rhetoric. Chapters 1 and 5, for example, ended with policy proposals about how to address the problems of chemical weapons disposal and vote buying in ways that are more participatory and open to difference. For scholars, the politics comes not just from theoretical approach or positionality, but from the decision of what we choose to study, and which power we choose to deconstruct: the state or opposition movements, the IMF or economic nationalism, the United States or China? My argument throughout the book is that, if we are going to take the politics of Pacific Asia seriously, it is necessary to critically understand the dynamics of power and resistance in the region, not framing Pacific Asia as a set of subalterns, but as a group of peoples who have their own subjectivity and power relations. I have deconstructed US power specifically in Chapter 1, and more generally throughout the book. But the main focus has been on how Pacific Asia operates with and against global capitalist modernity, generating cultural governance and resistance in local, national, regional and transnational spaces, addressing issues of age, gender and ethnicity in both official and popular culture. To appreciate the politics of Pacific Asia it is necessary (as argued in Chapter 3) to switch from the romance of East/West battles, not to a destructive rhetoric of satire, but to comedy. Whereas romance emplots the story of good triumphing over evil, and satire points out the ultimate folly of human endeavor, comedy organizes action according to the hopeful narrative of temporary triumph and the occasional reconciliations of the forces at play. The goal of resistance to capitalist modernity is not to find a final solution, or discover a political vocabulary that accurately describes political life. Rather, it is to carve out space for a more contingent politics that allows difference to thrive.

To put it in another way that recalls the questions raised in the Introduction, I would like to conclude this book by arguing that things are not problematic because they are foreign. People, institutions and ideas often become a problem when they are "foreignized," when difference is converted into Otherness in self/Other relations. We must resist global capitalist modernity not because it is foreign—but when it is unjust.

# Notes

**Introduction**

1. Elisabeth Rosenthal, "Here She Comes! (Will China Ever Be the Same?)," *New York Times*, 16 July 2002.
2. See David E. Apter and Tony Saich, *Revolutionary Discourse in Mao's Republic*, Cambridge, MA: Harvard University Press, 1994, pp. 94–5. Apter and Saich go on to argue, in a way that also applies to the Miss China pageant, that "Thus the 'founding' as an event has a dramatic episode inside it. The party has a 'miraculous birth', floating on the waters in a boat, the dry land around it a hostile sea swarming with spies and enemies" (ibid., p. 94).
3. "Beauty Pageants Gaining Popularity in China," *China Daily*, 16 August 2003.
4. "Miss China Beauty Pageant Opens," *China Daily*, 21 January 2005.
5. "Beauty Pageants Gaining Popularity in China," *China Daily*.
6. "India Beauty Pageant," *New York Times*, 26 November 1996; also see Barbara Crossette, "An India Less Than Congenial," *New York Times*, 24 November 1996.
7. "Beauty Pageants Gaining Popularity in China," *China Daily*.
8. Rosenthal, "Here She Comes!"
9. Ibid.
10. Alastair Iain Johnston, "Is China a Status Quo Power?," *International Security*, 2003, vol. 27: 4, 12–14.
11. The reaction of Miss Taiwan was to join the presidential campaign of the pro-independence party that seeks to legally separate Taiwan from China (Oliver August, "Taiwan Beauty Joins in Independence Struggle," *The Times* (London), 19 March 2004, p. 17; Melody Chen, "Miss Taiwan in Beauty Pageant Shocker," *Taipei Times*, 11 July 2003).
12. "Split Over Tibetan Beauty Pageant," *The Australian*, 12 October 2004.
13. "Miss Tibet Expelled from Miss Tourism World due to Chinese Pressure," www.MissTibet.com (accessed on 29 June 2005).
14. Seth Myans, "Vietnam: Beauty in the Eye of the Government," *New York Times*, 28 March 2002.
15. See Geremie R. Barmé, *Shades of Mao: The Posthumous Cult of the Great Leader*, Armonk, NY: M.E. Sharpe, 1996.
16. See Rodney Bruce Hall, "The Discursive Demolition of the Asian Development Model," *International Studies Quarterly*, 2003, vol. 47, 71–99.
17. See Richard Curt Kraus, *The Party and the Arty in China: The New Politics of Culture*, Lanham, MD: Rowman & Littlefield, 2004; Michael Schoenhals, *Doing Things with Words in Chinese Politics: Five Studies*, Berkeley, CA: Institute of East Asian Studies, University of California, 1992, pp. 1–29; Michael Kelly Connors, "Ministering Culture: Hegemony and the Politics of Culture and Identity in Thailand," *Critical Asian Studies*, 2005, vol. 37: 4, 523–51.

18 Ien Ang, "Desperately Guarding Borders: Media Globalization, 'Cultural Imperialism,' and the Rise of 'Asia'," in Yao Souchou (ed.) *House of Glass: Culture, Modernity, and the State in Southeast Asia*, Singapore and London: Institute of Southeast Asian Studies, 2001, p. 36.
19 For a key text see Masao Miyoshi, *Off/Center: Power and Culture Relations Between Japan and the United States*, Cambridge, MA: Harvard University Press, 1991.
20 See Geremie R. Barmé, *In the Red: On Contemporary Chinese Culture*, New York: Columbia University Press, 1999.
21 See Arif Dirlik, "Introduction: Pacific Contradictions," in Arif Dirlik (ed.) *What is in a Rim? Critical Perspectives on the Pacific Rim Idea*, 2nd edn, Lanham, MD: Rowman & Littlefield, 1998, pp. 3–14.
22 Rey Chow, *Writing Diaspora: Tactics of Intervention in Contemporary Cultural Studies*, Bloomington, IN: University of Indiana Press, 1993, pp. 18–20.
23 James Scott, who wrote *Weapons of the Weak*, is a Southeast Asianist (James C. Scott, *Weapons of the Weak: Everyday Forms of Peasant Resistance*, New Haven, CT: Yale University Press, 1985).
24 Cynthia Enloe, whose path-breaking work *Bananas, Beaches and Bases* founded the field of feminist IR, is originally a Southeast Asianist (Cynthia Enloe, *Bananas, Beaches and Bases: Making Feminist Sense of International Politics*, Berkeley, CA: University of California Press, 1989).
25 One of the leading figures in poststructuralist IR, Michael J. Shapiro, argues that his positionality in Hawai'i greatly informs his research on international politics (see Michael J. Shapiro, *Methods and Nations: Cultural Governance and the Indigenous Subject*, New York: Routledge, 2004, pp. 1–31).
26 One of the leading figures in the study of nationalism, Benedict Anderson, was born in China and is an expert in Southeast Asian studies (*Imagined Communities*, revised edn, London: Verso, 1991).
27 Arif Dirlik, one of the key critics of postcolonialism, is a historian of China.
28 Edward Said, *Orientalism*, New York: Vintage, 1978.
29 See Tzvetan Todorov, *The Conquest of America: The Question of the Other*, New York: Harper & Row Publishers, 1984, p. 10.
30 Said, *Orientalism*, pp. 2–3.
31 Ibid., p. 3; also see Edward Said, "Orientalism Reconsidered," in A.L. Macfie (ed.) *Orientalism: A Reader*, Edinburgh: Edinburgh University Press, 2000, p. 346.
32 For a good introduction to the issues see Ania Loomba, *Colonialism/Postcolonialism*, New York: Routledge, 1998.
33 Robert J.C. Young, *Postcolonialism: A Very Short Introduction*, Oxford: Oxford University Press, 2003, p. 17.
34 Robert J.C. Young, *Postcolonialism: An Historical Introduction*, London: Routledge, 2001, p. 57; Young, *Postcolonialism: A Very Short Introduction*, p. 2; also see Ankie Hoogvelt, *Globalization and the Postcolonial World*, 2nd edn, London: Palgrave, 2001, p. 165.
35 Young, *Postcolonialism: An Historical Introduction*, p. 65.
36 Ibid., pp. 65, 66.
37 Castle's *Postcolonial Discourses*, for example, takes a regional view of the literature that excludes Pacific Asia (Gregory Castle (ed.) *Postcolonial Discourses: An Anthology*, Oxford: Blackwell Publishers, 2001).
38 See Rey Chow, *Woman and Chinese Modernity: The Politics of Reading between East and West*, Minneapolis, MN: University of Minnesota Press, 1991; Allen Chun, "An Oriental Orientalism: The Paradox of Tradition and Modernity in Nationalist Taiwan," *History and Anthropology*, 1995, vol. 9: 1, 27–56; Chow, *Writing Diaspora*; Trinh T. Minh-ha, *Woman Native Other*, Bloomington, IN: Indiana University Press, 1989.

39 Chen Xiaomei, *Occidentalism: A Theory of Counter-Discourse in Post-Mao China*, 2nd edn, Lanham, MD: Rowman & Littlefield Publishers, 2002, p. 2.
40 Jinhua Dai, "Foreword," in Chen Xiaomei, *Occidentalism: A Theory of Counter-Discourse in Post-Mao China*, 2nd edn, Lanham, MD: Rowman & Littlefield Publishers, 2002, p. x.
41 Chen, *Occidentalism*, p. 3.
42 Dai, "Foreword," p. xiv; also see Chun, "An Oriental Orientalism."
43 Chen, *Occidentalism*, p. 5; also see Dai, "Foreword," p. xix.
44 Arif Dirlik, *The Postcolonial Aura: Third World Criticism in the Age of Global Capitalism*, Boulder, CO: Westview, 1997, p. 118.
45 Apter and Saich, *Revolutionary Discourse in Mao's Republic*, p. 92.
46 Carl A. Trocki, *Opium, Empire and the Global Political Economy*, London: Routledge, 1999.
47 Arif Dirlik, "Culture Against History? The Politics of East Asian Identity," *Development and Society*, 1999, vol. 28: 2, 167.
48 Ibid., pp. 187–8.
49 Also see Kwame Anthony Appiah, "Is the Post- in Postmodernism the Post- in Postcolonial?," *Critical Inquiry*, 1991, vol. 17: 2, 336–57; Sun Ge, "Globalization and Cultural Difference: Thoughts on the Situation of Transcultural Knowledge," *Inter-Asia Cultural Studies*, 2001, vol. 2: 2, 261–75; Dai, "Foreword," p. xiii.
50 Dirlik, *Postcolonial Aura*, p. 121.
51 Ibid.; also see Chun, "An Oriental Orientalism," pp. 28–9.
52 Aristotle, *The Politics*, New York: Penguin Classics, 1981, pp. 217–18; also see Donald K. Emmerson, "Singapore and the 'Asian Values' Debate," *Journal of Democracy*, 1995, vol. 6: 4, 96.
53 Herodotus, *Histories*, New York: Everyman Library, 1964, pp. 1–13.
54 William A. Callahan, *Contingent States: Greater China and Transnational Relations*, Minneapolis, MN: University of Minnesota Press, 2004, pp. 25–55; Zhang Guolong, *et al.*, *Wenming yu yeman* [Civilization and Barbarism], Beijing: Shehui kexue wenlian chubanshe, 1998; Ian Buruma and Avishai Margalit, *Occidentalism: The West in the Eyes of Its Enemies*, New York: Penguin, 2004; Stefan Tanaka, *Japan's Orient: Rendering Pasts into History*, Berkeley, CA: University of California Press, 1993.
55 Dirlik, *Postcolonial Aura*, p. 122.
56 Ibid., pp. 1–22.
57 Jan Nederveen Pieterse and Bhikhu Parekh, "Shifting Imaginaries: Decolonization, Internal Decolonization and Postcoloniality," in Jan Nederveen Pieterse and Bhikhu Parekh (eds) *The Decolonization of the Imagination: Culture, Knowledge and Power*, London: Zed Press, 1995, p. 11; also see Loomba, *Colonialism/Postcolonialism*, pp. 1–19.
58 Pieterse and Parekh, "Shifting Imaginaries," p. 11.
59 Pal Ahluwalia and Peter Mayer, "Clash of Civilizations—or Balderdash of Scholars?," *Asian Studies Review*, 1994, vol. 18: 1, 30.
60 See Wang Jisi (ed.) *Wenming yu guojizhengzhi: Zhongguo xuezhe ping Huntingdunde wenming chongtulun* [Civilization and International Politics: Chinese Scholars Comment on Huntington's Clash of Civilizations thesis], Shanghai: Shanghai renmin chubanshe, 1995; Daniel A. Bell and Hahm Chaibong (eds) *Confucianism for the Modern World*, Cambridge: Cambridge University Press, 2003; Christopher R. Hughes, "Globalization and Nationalism: Squaring the Circle in Chinese IR Theory," *Millennium*, 1997, vol. 26: 1, 110.
61 Pieterse and Parekh, "Shifting Imaginaries," p. 11.
62 Ibid.
63 For example, see L.H.M. Ling, *Postcolonial International Relations: Conquest and Desire between Asia and the West*, New York: Palgrave, 2002.

64 Arjun Appadurai, *Modernity at Large: Cultural Dimensions of Globalization*, Minneapolis, MN: University of Minnesota Press, 1996, p. 14.
65 See, for example, Daniel A. Bell, *East Meets West: Human Rights and Democracy in East Asia*, Princeton, NJ: Princeton University Press, 2000.
66 Michel Foucault, "Afterword: The Subject and Power," in Hubert L. Dreyfus and Paul Rabinow (eds) *Michel Foucault: Beyond Structuralism and Hermeneutics*, New York: The Harvester Press, 1982, p. 209.
67 Michel Foucault, "Governmentality," in Graham Burchell, Colin Gordon and Peter Miller (eds) *The Foucault Effect: Studies in Governmentality*, London: Harvester Wheatsheaf, 1991, p. 91.
68 Also see David Campbell, *Writing Security: United States Foreign Policy and the Politics of Identity*, rev. edn, Minneapolis, MN: University of Minnesota Press, 1998, pp. 41–2.
69 Foucault, "Afterword," p. 215.
70 Ibid., p. 214.
71 Ibid., p. 213; Michel Foucault, *The History of Sexuality*, vol. 1, New York: Vintage, 1980, p. xv.
72 This translation is based on that in Roger T. Ames, "Continuing the Conversation on Chinese Human Rights," *Ethics and International Affairs*, 1997, no. 11, 197.
73 Ibid., 198.
74 Foucault, "Governmentality," pp. 91–2.
75 Foucault, *The History of Sexuality*, p. 95.
76 Ibid., pp. 95–6; also see Foucault, "Afterword," pp. 211–13.
77 Shapiro, *Methods and Nations*, p. 49.
78 Ibid., p. 34.
79 Ibid., p. 49, xvii; also see David Campbell, "Cultural Governance and Pictorial Resistance: Reflections on the Imaging of War," *Review of International Studies*, 2003, vol. 29 (Special Issue), 57–73; Mitchell Dean and Paul Henman (guest eds) "Governing Society Today," a special issue of *Alternatives*, 2004, vol. 29: 5, 483–618; Michael Dillon, "Culture, Governance and Biopolitics," in Francois Debrix and Cynthia Weber (eds) *Rituals of Mediation: International Politics and Social Meaning*, Minneapolis, MN: University of Minnesota Press, 2004, pp. 135–53; Kathy E. Ferguson and Phyllis Turnbull, *Oh, Say, Can You See? The Semiotics of the Military in Hawai'i*, Minneapolis, MN: University of Minnesota Press, 1999.
80 Shapiro, *Methods and Nations*, pp. xi–xii.

**1 Culture, the military and the "South Pacific"**

1 This chapter is based on an essay co-authored with Steve Olive: William A. Callahan and Steve Olive, "Chemical Weapons Disposal in the *South Pacific*," *boundary 2*, 1995, vol. 22: 1, 263–85. I would like to thank Steve for allowing me to republish this article.
2 Kurt Schock, *Unarmed Insurgencies: People Power Movements in Non-democracies*, Minneapolis, MN: University of Minnesota Press, 2005, pp. 18–19; David Campbell, "Cultural Governance and Pictorial Resistance: Reflections on the Imaging of War," *Review of International Studies*, 2004, vol. 29, 57–73.
3 Jiefangjun huabaoshe [People's Liberation Army Pictorial] (ed.) *Beijing pingxi fangeming baoluan—Quelling the Counter-revolutionary Rebellion in Beijing* [bilingual], Beijing: Changchung chubanshe, 1989; also see Zheng Nianjun, *Zai jieyande rizili* [In the days of enforcing martial law], Beijing: Jiefangjun wenyi chubanshe, 1989.
4 See Richard Curt Kraus, *The Party and the Arty in China: The New Politics of Culture*, Lanham, MD: Rowman & Littlefield, 2004, pp. 42–3.

5 According to regulation 40 CFR 270.42(f), the US Army and the US Environmental Protection Agency (EPA) are required to set up and maintain public mailing lists for the distribution of documents concerning the environmental impact of JACADS. For more information on the chemical weapons disposal project contact the EPA at www.epa.gov/region09/features/jacads/ (accessed on 2 June 2005).
6 Kathy E. Ferguson and Phyllis Turnbull, *Oh, Say, Can You See? The Semiotics of the Military in Hawai'i*, Minneapolis, MN: University of Minnesota Press, 1999, p. xiii.
7 See Hesh Kestin, "They May Not Be Weapons at All," *Forbes* (18 September 1989), 45; also see a report by one of the army's auditors, the Henry L. Stimson Center, Washington, DC, "Chemical Weapons Destruction Completed on Johnston Atoll," *CBW Chronicle*, 2000, vol. 3: 2.
8 Michael Dillon, "Sovereignty and Governmentality: From the Problematics of the 'New World Order' to the Ethical Problematic of the World Order," *Alternatives*, 1995, vol. 20: 3, 330.
9 Joshua Logan, director, and Buddy Adler, producer, *South Pacific*, South Pacific Enterprises, Inc., 1958; *South Pacific*, Burbank, CA: Buena Vista Home Entertainment, 2001.
10 James A. Michener, *Tales of the South Pacific*, New York: Macmillan Company, 1947; James A. Michener, *The World Is My Home: A Memoir*, New York: Random House, 1992, p. 52.
11 George [H.W.] Bush, "Text of Remarks by the President at the Conclusion of the United States-Pacific Island Nations Summit," Honolulu: East-West Center, 27 October 1990, 1.
12 *South Pacific*, n.p.: South Pacific Enterprises, Inc., 1958.
13 Michener in ibid., n.p.
14 Even its spelling varies from Michener's book—Bali-h'ai—to the film brochure's rendering of Bali Ha'i.
15 Charles Johnston, Interview, University of Hawai'i, January 1991.
16 The first public map defining "Southeast Asia" was published by National Geographic during World War II (see Pekka Kornhonen, "Monopolizing Asia: The Politics of Metaphor," *Pacific Review*, 1997, vol. 10: 3, 347–65).
17 Michener, *The World is My Home*, p. 184.
18 Ibid., p. 52.
19 Also see Campbell, "Cultural Governance and Pictorial Resistance"; Krause, *The Party and the Arty*, p. 134.
20 See US Environmental Protection Agency, "JACADS: Permit history," www.epa.gov/region09/features/jacads/permit.html (accessed on 2 June 2005); also see Joris Janssen Lok, "Erasing agents," *Jane's International Defence Review*, 1 March 2001; Washington Group International, "Johnston Atoll Chemical Agent Disposal System (JACADS)," www.wgint.com/project.php?id=22 (accessed on 2 June 2005).
21 Ferguson and Turnbull, *Oh, Say, Can You See*, pp. xiii, 3.
22 Roland Barthes, *Image/Music/Text*, New York: Hill and Wang, 1977, p. 165.
23 Roland Barthes, *Mythologies*, New York: The Noonday Press, 1972, p. 142.
24 Umberto Eco, *A Theory of Semiotics*, Bloomington, IN: Indiana University Press, 1976, p. 7.
25 United States Army, "The United States Chemical Stockpile Disposal Program," Program Manager for Chemical Demilitarization, Office of the Chief of Public Affairs, Aberdeen Proving Ground, Maryland, 1990.
26 See "Closure of JACADS to be celebrated," Press Release: US Army Chemical Materials Agency, 23 October 2003.
27 Michel Foucault, *The Order of Things: An Archaeology of the Human Sciences*, New York: Pantheon Books, 1970.

28 *New York Times*, 26 April 1955; *New York Times*, 24 May 1959.
29 *WISE news communiqué*, 20 October 2000, www.antenna.nl/wise (accessed on 2 June 2005).
30 *New York Times*, 29 April 1991, A1.
31 "JACADS Demonstrates Need for Alternative Treatments," *Environment Hawai'i*, 1997, vol. 7: 9.
32 Kilali Alailima, American Friends Service Committee, "Pacific Peoples say 'Enough is Enough'," *Common Sense*, September 1997. This article is based on Alailima's testimony at 27 August 1997 public hearing for an extension and modification of the JACADS EIS.
33 "Pacific Island Incinerator Employee Dies on the Job," *Common Sense*, April 1998, Chemical Weapons Working Group, www.cwwg.org (accessed on 2 June 2005).
34 Resolution of the Hawaii Medical Association, 10 December 1990.
35 US Environmental Protection Agency, "Johnston Atoll: Questions and Answers," Region IX, no. 1 (December 1990), 2.
36 "The Battle for Johnston Atoll," *Pacific Islands Monthly*, September 1990, 7.
37 *Marshall Islands Journal*, 1985, 16: 38, 4; Resolution of the Hawaii Medical Association, 10 December 1990; and Public Hearing (20 March 1990).
38 *Honolulu Advertiser*, 13 August 1990, A8.
39 "JACADS Demonstrates Need for Alternative Treatments," *Environment Hawai'i*, 1997, vol. 7: 9.
40 See Alfred Picardi, "Greenpeace Review of Johnston Atoll Chemical Agent Disposal System (JACADS) 1988 Final Draft Supplemental Environmental Impact Statement," Washington, DC: Greenpeace International, 1989.
41 Ian Anderson, "Destruction of Chemical Arms Comes Under Fire," *New Scientist*, August 1990, p. 4.
42 See "Convention on the Dumping of Wastes at Sea," *Journal of World Trade Law*, 1973, vol. 7, 485, and Ursula Wasserman, "Attempts at Control Over Toxic Waste," *Journal of World Trade Law*, 1981, vol. 15, 410.
43 Testimony of Jon M. Van Dyke, Professor of Law, William S. Richardson School of Law, and Director of the University of Hawai'i Institute for Peace, Public Hearing Testimony (20 March 1990); also see the Law of the Sea Convention that came into effect in 1994.
44 The meeting was to address the extension of the permit allowing the storage of chemical weapons under the Resource Conservation and Recovery Act (RCRA).
45 *Greenpeace USA v. Stone*, United States federal district court, Hawai'i, 748 F. Supp. 749, (28 September 1990), paragraph 4.
46 Department of the Army, "Final Second Supplemental Environmental Impact Statement for the Storage and Ultimate Disposal of the European Chemical Munitions Stockpile," Program Manager for Chemical Demilitarization, Aberdeen Proving Ground, Maryland, 1990.
47 The Bureau of National Affairs, *Environmental Reporter*, 1988, vol. 18, 37.
48 Ferguson and Turnbull, *Oh, Say, Can You See*, p. 6.
49 The army's narrative of Johnston Island and JACADS has been cut and pasted onto the website of Pacific Island Travel. This is odd, since the public is restricted from travelling to the atoll (www.pacificislandtravel.com/micronesia, about_destin/marshall_johnston.html (accessed on 2 June 2005)).
50 Washington Group International, "Johnston Atoll Chemical Agent Disposal System (JACADS)," www.wgint.com/project.php?id=22 (accessed on 2 June 2005).
51 Environmental Protection Agency, "JACADS: Background and history," EPA Region IX, www.epa.gov/region09/features/jacads/ (accessed on 2 June 2005); also see "Johnston Atoll: United States Nuclear Forces," a report by a

Washington think-tank, Global Security, www.globalsecurity.org/wmd/facility/johnston_atoll.htm (accessed on 2 June 2005).
52 Washington Group International, "JACADS."
53 Peter Hayes, Lyuba Zarsky and Walden Bello, *American Lake: Nuclear Power in the Pacific*, New York: Penguin, 1986, pp. 10, 404, 420.
54 Epeli Hau'ofa, "Our Sea of Islands," in Rob Wilson and Arif Dirlik (eds) *Asia/Pacific as Space of Cultural Production*, Durham, NC: Duke University Press, 1995, pp. 86–98.
55 Karen Mangnall, "A Tale of Two Hotels," *Pacific Islands Monthly*, September 1990, 11.
56 Alailima, "Pacific Peoples say 'Enough is Enough'."
57 Testimony of Marsha Joyner (20 March 1990).
58 "EPA Approves JACADS Closure Plan: Notice of Permit Change," US EPA, Region IX, 4 September 2002.
59 See Joni Seager, *Earth Follies: Feminism, Politics and the Environment*, London: Earthscan, 1993, pp. 61–8; Ferguson and Turnbull, *Oh, Say, Can You See*, p. 211.
60 *Marshall Islands Journal*, 20 September 1985, vol. 16: 30, 16.
61 South Pacific Commission Environmental Newsletter, 1980, no. 3, 11.
62 Testimony of Steven Moser, M.D., EPA Public Hearing, (11 December 1990), Honolulu, Hawai'i, 3.
63 Hayes *et al.*, *American Lake*, p. 393.
64 Hau'ofa, "Our Sea of Islands," pp. 90, 91.
65 Ibid., p. 96.
66 Ibid., p. 92. This alternative view of the Pacific is popular in theoretically informed texts on military politics and cultural politics (see Ferguson and Turnbull, *Oh, Say, Can You See*, p. 66; Arif Dirlik, *The Postcolonial Aura: Third World Criticism in the Age of Global Capitalism*, Boulder, CO: Westview, 1997, pp. 137–40).
67 See Mary Adamski, "Johnston Island Gas-burning Foes Fear Contamination via Food Chain," *Honolulu Star-Bulletin*, 12 December 1990, 3.
68 Trinh T. Minh-ha, *Woman Native Other*, Bloomington, IN: Indiana University Press, 1989, p. 86.

## 2  Beauty queens, national identity and transnational politics

1 Thawan Masjarat, "Nangsao Sayam" [Miss Siam], in *Mednangrak*, Bangkok: Tonor 1999, Inc., 1998, p. 104. Siam was Thailand's official name before 1939. Many thanks to Ms Kesinee Chutavichit for bringing this story to my attention.
2 For a novelistic description of problems that women have in the Thai military see Wanlaya Phuphinyo, *Tho so ying* [A Female Adjutant Officer], Bangkok: Air Force News Press, 1998.
3 Areeya Chumsai, *Muat Pop* [Lt. Pop] (English title: *Boot Camp*), Bangkok: Future Publishing, 1998, p. 18.
4 Ibid., p. 112.
5 Ibid., p. 22.
6 General Chetta Thanajaro, Army commander-in-chief, in ibid., p. 6.
7 Gen. Paeng Malakun na Ayutthaya, director of Army television, in ibid., p. 7.
7 Lt. Gen. Phanom Jenawijarana, head of the Army Reserve, in ibid., p. 8.
9 Areeya's flirtation with the military worked for a while, but in the end it was too restrictive; Areeya resigned from the cadet school after a few years. Rumor has it that she quit after a scandal emerged when she posed in a slinky dress for a fashion magazine—the army felt that this was not the "proper" image of a model teacher at the cadet school.

10 See Kathy E. Ferguson and Phyllis Turnbull, *Oh, Say, Can You See? The Semiotics of the Military in Hawai'i*, Minneapolis, MN: University of Minnesota Press, 1999.
11 Cynthia Enloe, *The Morning After: Sexual Politics at the End of the Cold War*, Berkeley, CA: University of California Press, 1993, pp. 3, 53.
12 Annette Hamilton, "Cinema and Nation: Dilemmas of Representation in Thailand," *East-West Film Journal*, 1993, vol. 7: 1, 81–105.
13 Enloe, *The Morning After*, p. 3.
14 See Michael Kelly Connors, "Ministering Culture: Hegemony and the Politics of Culture and Identity in Thailand," *Critical Asian Studies*, 2005, vol. 37: 4, 523–51.
15 Saneepong Prombunpong, "A Farce in Three Acts," *The Nation* (Bangkok), 2 November 1994, C3. I would like to thank the librarians at *The Nation* (Bangkok) newspaper who have compiled articles on "beauty contests" since 1985.
16 Barney Oldfield, "Miss America and the 301st Bomb Group," *Air Power History*, 1990, vol. 37: 2, 41–4.
17 Also see Geraldine Heng and Janadas Devan, "State Fatherhood: The Politics of Nationalism, Sexuality, and Race in Singapore," in Andrew Parker, Mary Russo, Doris Sommer and Patricia Yaeger (eds) *Nationalisms & Sexualities*, New York: Routledge, 1992, p. 348.
18 Thak Chaloemtiarana, *Thailand: The Politics of Despotic Paternalism*, Bangkok: Thammasat University Press, 1979, p. 337.
19 See Paul Virilio, *Speed and Politics: An Essay on Dromology*, New York: Semiotext(e) Foreign Agents Series, 1986, p. 62.
20 "Beauty Pageants Gaining Popularity in China," *China Daily*, 16 August 2003; "China set for Miss World Contest," BBC News, 6 December 2003.
21 Chin Ampornratana, Secretary to the Managing Director of BBTv Color Channel 7, Interview in Bangkok, 27 October 1994.
22 "Few Americans Think Miss America Pageant Degrading," *Gallup Poll Monthly*, 1 September 1990, vol. 300, 53; "Beauty Pageants Gaining Popularity in China," *China Daily*.
23 Laurie Peterson, "Sizing Up Miss America," *Adweek's Marketing Week*, 23 September 1991, vol. 32: 39, 9; A.R. Riverol, *Live from Atlantic City: The History of the Miss America Pageant Before, After and in Spite of Television*, Bowling Green, OH: Bowling Green State University Press, 1992.
24 *Yodpatoo '37* [Top Woman '94], *Miss Thailand 1994*, Bangkok: Yodpatoo Entertainment Co., Ltd, 1994, p. 74.
25 NJ Survey, "Do You Agree with Beauty Pageants?," *The Nation Junior* (Bangkok), 1–15 May 1994, vol. 2: 42, 22; Kawalpreet Kaur, "It Takes Brains to be Beautiful," *The Nation Junior* (Bangkok), 1–15 September 1993, vol. 2: 26, 26.
26 Robert C. Allen, "Talking About Television," in Robert C. Allen (ed.) *Channels of Discourse: Television and Contemporary Criticism*, Chapel Hill, NC: University of North Carolina Press, 1987, p. 14.
27 Kanjana Kaewthep, "'East' Meets 'West': The Confrontation of Different Cultures in Thai T.V. Dramas and Films," in Nitaya Masavisut, George Simson and Larry E. Smith (eds) *Gender and Culture in Literature and Film East and West: Issues of Perception and Interpretation*, Honolulu, HI: University of Hawai'i Press, 1994, p. 182.
28 See Supatra Kopkijsuksakul, *Kan Prakuat Nangsao Thai (B.E. 2477–2530)* [Miss Thailand Contest: 1934–1987], unpublished Masters Thesis, Bangkok: Thammasat University, 1988, p. 60.
29 Chin, Interview.

30 Areeya Chumsai, "The Year that Changed a Life," *Bangkok Post*, 14 March 1995, 27.
31 Allen, "Talking About Television," p. 8.
32 Opas Boonlom "High-stakes Divorce Case Sparks Women's Rights Debate," *The Nation* (Bangkok), 15 February 1995, A8.
33 Riverol, *Live from Atlantic City*, p. 1.
34 See Supatra, *Miss Thailand Contest*, p. 76.
35 Ibid., pp. 54, 94, 96. The Miss America Pageant, on the other hand, grew directly out of Bathing Beauty Contests, which began in the 1880s. Still, the main reason that the pageant was canceled in 1928 was "moral concerns" (Riverol, *Live from Atlantic City*, pp. 9, 24).
36 Supatra, *Miss Thailand Contest*, pp. 78–9, 81, 170, 221.
37 Laura Mulvey, *Visual and Other Pleasures,* Bloomington, IN: Indiana University Press, 1989, p. 3.
38 Ibid., p. 15.
39 John Berger, *Ways of Seeing*, New York: Penguin Press, 1977, p. 24.
40 Teresa de Lauretis, *Alice Doesn't: Feminism, Semiotics, Cinema*, Bloomington, IN: University of Indiana Press, 1985, p. 149.
41 Mulvey, *Visual and Other Pleasures*, p. 19.
42 Kanjana, "'East' Meets 'West'," p. 182; also see Rey Chow, *Woman and Chinese Modernity*, Minneapolis, MN: University of Minnesota Press, 1990, pp. 3–33.
43 Riverol, *Live from Atlantic City*, pp. 13, 20.
44 Mulvey, *Visual and Other Pleasures*, p. 3.
45 Cited in Supatra, *Miss Thailand Contest*, p. 246.
46 Scot Barmé, *Luang Wichit Wathakan and the Creation of a Thai Identity*, Singapore and London: Institute for Southeast Asian Studies, 1993, p. 111.
47 Supatra, *Miss Thailand Contest*, p. 49.
48 Ibid., pp. 83, 85.
49 In Orasum Suthisakhorn, *Dokmai khong chat: Jak wethi khwamngam su wethi chiwit, album chiwit 13 Nangsao Thai yuk raek* [Flowers of the nation: from beauty stage to life's stage, the album of the first 13 Miss Thailands], Bangkok, 1990, p. 20.
50 Supatra, *Miss Thailand Contest*, p. 117.
51 Cited in Supatra, *Miss Thailand Contest*, p. 77.
52 Ibid., p. 118.
53 Barmé, *Luang Wichit Wathakan*, p. 8.
54 Supatra, *Miss Thailand Contest*, p. 59.
55 Ibid.
56 Ibid., p. 54.
57 Ibid., p. 63.
58 Ibid., p. 122.
59 Ibid., p. 52.
60 Ibid., p. 136.
61 See Pasuk Phongpaichit and Chris Baker, *Thailand: Economy and Politics*, 2nd edn, New York: Oxford University Press, 2002.
62 Saneh Chamarik, *Democracy and Development: A Cultural Perspective*, Bangkok: Local Development Institute, 1993, p. 14.
63 Hamilton, "Cinema and Nation," p. 83.
64 Chin, Interview.
65 Mulvey, *Visual and Other Pleasures*, p. 63.
66 Ibid.
67 Cited in Sandy Flitterman-Lewis, "Psychoanalysis, Film, and Television," in Allen, *Channels of Discourse*, p. 188.

68 Paradee Kiatpinyochai, *The Thai Television Broadcasting Industry: Its Economics & Politics*, unpublished Masters Thesis, Bangkok: Thammasat University, 1990, p. 71.
69 Ibid., p. 12.
70 See Duncan McCargo and Ukrist Pathmanand, *The Thaksinization of Thailand*, Copenhagen: NIAS Press, 2005, pp. 188–97; William A. Callahan, "Media and Society: Chermsak," *The Nation* (Bangkok), 12 February 1993, A6.
71 Thak, *The Politics of Despotic Paternalism*.
72 Supatra, *Miss Thailand Contest*, p. 141.
73 Ibid., p. 158.
74 Ibid., p. 147.
75 Ibid., p. 170.
76 Ibid., p. 165.
77 Ibid., p. 198.
78 Ibid., p. 200.
79 Ibid., p. 163.
80 Ibid., p. 158.
81 Surachart Bamrungsuk, *United States Foreign Policy and Thai Military Rule 1947–1977*, Bangkok: Editions Duang Kamol, 1988, pp. 118, 119.
82 Supatra, *Miss Thailand Contest*, p. 148.
83 Ibid., p. 151.
84 Pasuk and Baker, *Thailand: Economy and Politics*.
85 Paradee, *The Thai Television Broadcasting Industry*, p. 25.
86 Supatra, *Miss Thailand Contest*, p. 155.
87 Ibid., p. 246.
88 Ibid., p. 3.
89 Yuthana Priwan, Ekarin Petsiri and Busarin Treerapongpichit, "Ugly Economic Realities Mar Pageant: Sponsors Shy Away from Miss Thailand during Tough Times," *Bangkok Post*, 1 April 1997.
90 Mimi White, "Ideological Analysis and Television," in Allen, *Channels of Discourse*, p. 153.
91 See Vladimir Propp, *Morphology of a Folktale,* Austin, TX: University of Texas Press, 1970; Sarah Ruth Kozloff, "Narrative Theory and Television," in Allen, *Channels of Discourse*, pp. 47, 48.
92 *The Nation* (Bangkok), 22 September 1986.
93 Kanjana, "'East' Meets 'West'," p. 180.
94 Ibid., p. 181.
95 Ibid., p. 184.
96 Ibid., p. 189.
97 Ibid., p. 194.
98 Ibid., p. 193.
99 Ibid., pp. 187–8.
100 See, for example, M.G.G. Pillai, "West's Idea of Beauty Ignores Rest of the World," *Bangkok Post*, 22 February 1995, p. 5.
101 Chin, Interview.
102 *The Nation* (Bangkok), 4 April 1988.
103 Supatra, *Miss Thailand Contest*, p. 232.
104 Chin, Interview.
105 See Supatra, *Miss Thailand Contest*, p. 246.
106 Seneepong Prombunpong "Another American Crowned, Carries on Miss Thailand Torch," *The Nation* (Bangkok), 5 April 1995, C1, C2.
107 See Seth Mydans, "Thais with a Different Look, Flaunt Your Genes!," *New York Times*, 29 August 2002; Craig J. Reynolds, "On the Gendering of Nationalist and Postnationalist Selves in Twentieth-Century Thailand," in Peter A.

Jackson and Nerida M. Cook (eds) *Genders and Sexualities in Modern Thailand*, Chiangmai: Silkworm Books, 1999, pp. 269–71.
108 Rey Chow, *Writing Diaspora: Tactics of Intervention in Contemporary Cultural Studies*, Bloomington, IN: Indiana University Press, 1993, pp. 1–26; L.H.M. Ling, *Postcolonial International Relations: Conquest and Desire between Asia and the West*, New York: Palgrave, 2002, pp. 145–69.
109 Kasian Tejapira, "The Postmodernization of Thainess," in Yao Souchou (ed.) *House of Glass: Culture, Modernity, and the State in Southeast Asia*, Singapore and London: Institute for Southeast Asian Studies, 2001, p. 166.
110 Riverol, *Live from Atlantic City*.
111 Miss Indonesia only became a full contestant in the 2005 pageant; Miss Indonesia 1996 was severely chastized by Indonesia's Minister for Women's Affairs for posing in a bathing suit for photographers at the Miss Universe Pageant where she was an "observer" (see "Minister Blasts Competitor in Miss Universe," *The Nation* (Bangkok), 16 May 1996, A6; "Indonesia back in Miss Universe Pageant after Decades of Ban," *People's Daily* (14 May 2005)).
112 See "Nigeria's journalist on the run," BBC News, 27 November 2002.
113 See Areeya, "The Year that Changed a Life," 34.

## 3 Gender, democracy and revolutionary photo albums

1 See Robert Bartley, Chan Heng Chee, Samuel P. Huntington and Shijuro Ogata, *Democracy & Capitalism: Asian and American Perspectives*, Singapore: Institute of Southeast Asian Studies, 1994; Daniel Arghiros, *Democracy, Development and Decentralization in Provincial Thailand*, Richmond, UK: Curzon, 2001, pp. 16–42.
2 Daniel A. Bell, *East Meets West: Human Rights and Democracy in East Asia*, Princeton, NJ: Princeton University Press, 2000; Bartley *et al.*, *Democracy & Capitalism*.
3 Kurt Schock, *Unarmed Insurrections: People Power Movements in Nondemocracies*, Minneapolis, MN: University of Minnesota Press, 2005.
4 L.H.M. Ling, *Postcolonial International Relations: Conquest and Desire between Asia and the West*, New York: Palgrave, 2002, pp. 145–69.
5 William A. Callahan, "The Discourse of Democracy in Thailand: A Struggle for Meaning," *Asian Review 1993*, vol. 7, pp. 126–70.
6 Kathy E. Ferguson, *The Man Question: Visions of Subjectivity in Feminist Theory*, Berkeley, CA: University of California Press, 1993, pp. 191–2.
7 See Seth Mydans, "Thais with a Different Look, Flaunt Your Genes!," *New York Times*, 29 August 2002.
8 Edward Said, *Orientalism*, New York: Vintage, 1978, p. 207; also see Malek Alloula, *The Colonial Harem*, Minneapolis, MN: University of Minnesota Press, 1986.
9 Jan Nederveen Pieterse and Bhikhu Parekh, "Shifting Imaginaries: Decolonization, Internal Decolonization and Postcoloniality," in Jan Nederveen Pieterse and Bhikhu Parekh (eds) *The Decolonization of the Imagination: Culture, Knowledge and Power*, London: Zed Press, 1995, p. 11.
10 Rey Chow, *Woman and Chinese Modernity: The Politics of Reading between East and West*, Minneapolis, MN: University of Minnesota Press, 1990, p. 53.
11 See Kathy E. Ferguson, *The Feminist Case Against Bureaucracy*, Philadelphia, PA: Temple University Press, 1984.
12 William A. Callahan, *Contingent States: Greater China and Transnational Relations*, Minneapolis, MN: University of Minnesota Press, 2004, pp. 103–49.
13 Mahathir Mohamad and Shintaro Ishihara, *The Voice of Asia: Two Leaders Discuss the Coming Century*, Tokyo: Kodansha International, 1995.

14 Voice of Malaysia radio, 29 May 1993, as quoted in Victor Mallet, "Confucius or Convenience?," *Financial Times* in *Bangkok Post*, 22 March 1994, 4.
15 Cited in Ien Ang, "Desperately Guarding Borders: Media Globalization, 'Cultural Imperialism,' and the Rise of 'Asia'," in Yao Souchou (ed.) *House of Glass: Culture, Modernity, and the State in Southeast Asia*, Singapore and London: Institute for Southeast Asian Studies, 2002, p. 28.
16 Lee Kuan Yew, *Sishinian zhenglun xuan* [Selections from 40 Years of Political Writings], Singapore: Lianhe zaobao, 1993, p. 579; also see Fareed Zakaria, "Culture is Destiny: A Conversation with Lee Kuan Yew," *Foreign Affairs*, 1994, vol. 73: 2, 113.
17 Cited in Zakaria, "Culture is Destiny," p. 119.
18 Mahathir Mohamad, "Corruption of democracy in the world," *The Nation* (Bangkok), 8 October 1993, A6.
19 Garry Rodan and Kevin Hewison, "A 'clash of cultures' or the convergence of political ideology," in Richard Robison (ed.) *Pathways to Asia: The Politics of Engagement*, Sydney: Allen & Unwin, 1996, p. 34.
20 Stephanie Lawson, "Cultural Relativism and Democracy: Political Myths about 'Asia' and the 'West'," in Robison, *Pathways to Asia*, p. 110.
21 Geraldine Heng and Janadas Devan, "State Fatherhood: The Politics of Nationalism, Sexuality, and Race in Singapore," in Andrew Parker, Mary Russo, Doris Sommer and Patricia Yaeger (eds) *Nationalisms & Sexualities*, New York: Routledge, 1992, p. 348; Chua Beng-Huat, *Communitarian Ideology and Democracy in Singapore*, London: Routledge, 1995; Chan Sin Yee, "The Confucian Conception of Gender in the Twenty-First Century," in Daniel A. Bell and Hahm Chaibong (eds) *Confucianism for the Modern World*, Cambridge: Cambridge University Press, 2003, pp. 331–2.
22 Mark R. Thompson, "Pacific Asia after 'Asian values': Authoritarianism, Democracy, and 'Good Governance'," *Third World Quarterly*, 2004, vol. 25: 6, 1079–95; Soek-Fang Sim, *Asian Values, Asian Democracy: The Legitimisation of Authority and De-Legitimisation of Dissent in Everyday Popular Discourse in Singapore in the Late 1990s*, unpublished PhD thesis, University of London, 2002, pp. 299–332.
23 This "Asian values debate" ran from 2001 to 2002 in the *Korea Journal*, including nine articles and two group discussions. For representative articles see Hahm Chaibong, "Why Asian Values?," *Korea Journal*, 2001, vol. 41: 2, 265–74; Lee Seung-Hwan, "'Asian Values' and Confucian Discourse," *Korea Journal*, 2001, vol. 41: 3, 198–212.
24 Xiaoqin Guo, *State and Society in China's Democratic Transition: Confucianism, Leninism, and Economic Development*, London: Routledge, 2003, pp. 12, 232–5; Bell, *East Meets West*, pp. 277–336.
25 See Daniel A. Bell and Hahm Chaibong (eds) *Confucianism for the Modern World*, Cambridge: Cambridge University Press, 2003, pp. 6–13, 31–129.
26 Guo, *State and Society*, pp. 175–216; David C. Lynch, "International 'De-centering' and Democratization: The Case of Thailand," *International Studies Quarterly*, 2004, vol. 48: 2, 339–62; James Gomez, "Alliance of Asian Democracy Groups Needed," *The Nation* (Bangkok), 12 April 2000.
27 Lawson, "Cultural relativism and democracy," pp. 108–9; Rodan and Hewison, "A 'clash of cultures,'" p. 49.
28 Roland Barthes, *Mythologies*, New York: The Noonday Press, 1972, pp. 109–59.
29 Schock, *Unarmed Insurrections*; William A. Callahan, "Challenging the Order: Social Movements," in Richard Maidment, Jeremy Mitchell and David Goldblatt (eds) *Governance in the Asia-Pacific*, London: Routledge, 1998, pp. 150–71.
30 Project 28 Days, *Bayan Ko! Images of the People Power Revolt*, Hong Kong: Project 28 Days, 1986.

31 Alan Clements and Leslie Kean, *Burma's Revolution of the Spirit: The Struggle for Democratic Freedom and Dignity*, Bangkok: White Orchid Press, 1995.
32 *June Four: A Chronicle of the Chinese Democratic Uprising*, London: University of Arkansas Press, 1989; translated from *Bei zhuang de mingyun: zuiheping kaishi, zui xuexing jiehsu*, Hong Kong: Ming Pao Publishing House, 1989.
33 *Catalyst for Change: Uprising in May*, Bangkok: *Bangkok Post*, 1992.
34 See the new journal *Inter-Asia Cultural Studies*, which is edited by a cooperative of Pacific Asian scholars and published in English; also see Sun Ge, "Globalization and Cultural Difference: Thoughts on the Situation of Transcultural Knowledge," *Inter-Asia Cultural Studies*, 2001, vol. 2: 2, 267; Callahan, "Challenging the Order," pp. 165–7.
35 Pieterse and Parekh, "Shifting Imaginaries," p. 11.
36 Clements and Kean, *Burma's Revolution of the Spirit*, p. 9.
37 Ibid., p. 109.
38 Hayden White, *Metahistory: The Historical Imagination in Nineteenth-Century Europe*, Baltimore, MD: Johns Hopkins University Press, 1973, pp. 8–12.
39 Michael J. Shapiro, *The Politics of Representation: Writing Practices in Biography, Photography, and Policy Analysis*, Madison, WI: University of Wisconsin Press, 1988, p. 124.
40 Alan Trachtenberg, *Reading American Photographs: Images as History, Matthew Brady to Walker Evans*, New York: Hill and Wang, 1989, p. xv; also see David Campbell, "Cultural Governance and Pictorial Resistance: Reflections on the Imaging of War," *Review of International Studies*, 2004, vol. 29, 57–73; Roland Barthes, *Camera Lucida: Reflections on Photography*, New York: Hill and Wang, 1981.
41 Trachtenberg, *Reading American Photographs*, p. 89.
42 *Yi shi wei jing, mianxiang weilai: jinian Zhongguo renmin kangri zhanzhengji* [Take history as a mirror, to create the future: Commemorate China's war of resistance against Japan], Beijing: Zhonggong dangxiao chubanshe, 2005, 1.
43 Ibid., pp. 71–118.
44 Ibid., p. 79.
45 White, *Metahistory*, pp. 1–42.
46 Jeffrey N. Wasserstrom, "Afterword: History, Myth and the Tales of Tiananmen," in Jeffrey N. Wasserstrom and Elizabeth J. Perry (eds) *Popular Protest and Popular Culture in Modern China*, 2nd edn, Boulder, CO: Westview Press, 1994, pp. 279–89.
47 Northrop Frye, *Anatomy of Criticism: Four Chapters*, Princeton, NJ: Princeton University Press, 1957, pp. 187–8, 195; Wasserstrom, "Afterword," p. 279.
48 Jean Bethke Elshtain, *Women and War*, Chicago, IL: University of Chicago Press, 1995, pp. 4–9.
49 Shapiro, *The Politics of Representation*, p. 4.
50 Also see Cynthia Enloe, *Banana, Beaches and Bases: Making Feminist Sense of International Politics*, updated edn, Berkeley, CA: University of California Press, 2000, pp. 5–6.
51 Elshtain, *Women and War*, p. 258.
52 Shapiro, *The Politics of Representation*, p. 130.
53 Bertil Lintner, *Outrage: Burma's Struggle for Democracy*, Bangkok: White Lotus, 1990, pp. 140, 153. SLORC dissolved itself in 1997, renaming itself the State Peace and Development Council (SPDC).
54 Ralph Summy also uses a picture of Aung San Suu Kyi to illustrate his article on democracy and non-violence (Ralph Summy, "Democracy and Nonviolence," *Social Alternatives*, 1993, vol. 12, 15–19).
55 Project 28 Days, *Bayan Ko!*, pp. 60, 66, 67, 73.

56 Ibid., pp. 80, 88, 104.
57 Ibid., pp. 61, 64, 65.
58 Ibid., p. 71.
59 Clements and Kean, *Burma's Revolution of the Spirit*, pp. 6, 8, 10, 15, 17, 19, 20, 21, 24, 25, 26–7, 29, 35, 40–1, 107.
60 Ibid., p. 50.
61 Aung San Suu Kyi, "Keynote Address to the NGO Forum Plenary, Fourth World Conference on Women," Bangkok: Asian Forum for Human Rights and Development Videos, 1995.
62 Clements and Kean, *Burma's Revolution of the Spirit*, p. 77.
63 *June Four*, p. iii.
64 The Thai volumes also carry the burden of evidence. "Record" is in the name of the most important Thai language albums (Reporters' Association of Thailand, *Banthuk yiewkhao na samoraphum thanon rajadamnoen phrusaphakom B.E. 2535* [Journalists' Records from the Battleground on Rajadamnoen Road May 1992], Bangkok: Reporters' Association of Thailand, 1992; Manager Special Issue, *Banthuk "paap kham-hetkarn" prawatthhisat phrusaphakorn thamin* [Historical records of "pictures-speeches-events" of Black May], Bangkok: Manager, 1992; The Nation and Krungthep Turakit, *Banthuk phrusaphat maia wiphayok* [Records of Sad May], 2nd edn, Bangkok: The Nation Publishing Group, 1992).
65 Shapiro, *The Politics of Representation*, p. 141.
66 Jiefangjun huabaoshe [People's Liberation Army Pictorial] (ed.) *Beijing pingxi fangeming baoluan – Quelling the Counter-revolutionary Rebellion in Beijing*, Beijing: Changchung chubanshe, 1989; also see Zheng Nianjun, *Zai jieyande rizili* [In the days of enforcing martial law], Beijing: Jiefangjun wenyi chubanshe, 1989.
67 Lee Feigon, "Gender and the Chinese Student Movement," in Wasserstrom and Perry, *Popular Protest and Popular Culture in Modern China*, pp. 132–3.
68 Rey Chow, "Violence in the Other Country," in Chandra Talpade Mohanty, Ann Russo and Lourdes Torres (eds) *Third World Women and the Politics of Feminism*, Bloomington, IN: Indiana University Press, 1991, p. 82.
69 Jiranand Pitpreecha, in "Women Man the Front Lines," *Nation Weekly Briefing*, 23 May 1992, vol. 1: 30, 34.
70 *June Four*, p. 81 (text), p. 76 (photo).
71 See Li Jie in Geremie R. Barmé, *Shades of Mao: The Posthumous Cult of the Great Leader*, Armonk, NY: M.E. Sharpe, 1996, pp. 141, 142.
72 See Bruno Barbey, *mai 68: ou l'imagination au pouvoir*, Paris: L'Difference, 1998.
73 Tulsathit Taptim, "Same Old Rhetoric," *The Nation* (Bangkok), 10 May 1992, A10.
74 Sungsidh Piriyarangsan and Pasuk Phongpaichit, *The Middle Class and Thai Democracy*, Bangkok: Chulalongkorn University and Friedrich Ebert Stiftung, 1993, p. 38.
75 William A. Callahan, *Imagining Democracy: Reading the Events of May in Thailand*, Singapore and London: Institute of Southeast Asian Studies, 1998, pp. 35–84.
76 *June Four*, p. 24 (photo), pp. 26–7 (text).
77 Michael Dutton, *Streetlife China*, Cambridge: Cambridge University Press, 1998, pp. 62–159; Børge Bakken, *The Exemplary Society: Human Improvement, Social Control, and the Dangers of Modernity in China*, Oxford: Oxford University Press, 2000, pp. 317–53, 377–407.
78 *June Four*, p. 24.
79 *People's Daily* in ibid., p. 26.

80 People's Liberation Army Pictorial, *Quelling the Counter-revolutionary Rebellion in Beijing*.
81 *June Four*, pp. xii, 80, 81.
82 Ibid., pp. x–xi.
83 Ibid., p. 57.
84 Vera Schwarcz, "Memory and Commemoration: The Chinese Search for a Livable Past," in Wasserstrom and Perry, *Popular Protest and Popular Culture in Modern China*, p. 171.
85 *June Four*, p. 17.
86 Ibid., pp. 17, 41.
87 Ibid., pp. 65, 44, 69.
88 See Pekka Korhonen, *Japan and Asia Pacific Integration: Pacific Romances 1968–1996*, London: Routledge, 1998, p. 8.
89 See, for example, Roxanne Lynn Doty, *Imperial Encounters: The Politics of Representation in North-South Relations*, Minneapolis, MN: University of Minnesota Press, 1996, pp. 127–44; Alexander Woodside, "The Asia-Pacific Idea as a Mobilization Myth," in Arif Dirlik (ed.) *What is in a Rim? Critical Perspectives on the Pacific Region Idea*, 2nd edn, Lanham, MD: Rowman & Littlefield, 1998, pp. 37–52.
90 Chen Xiaomei, *Occidentalism: A Theory of Counter-Discourse in Post-Mao China*, Lanham, MD: Rowman & Littlefield, 2002, p. 41.
91 Ibid., p. 36.
92 Jinhua Dai, "Foreword," in Chen, *Occidentalism*, p. xxiii.
93 Chen, *Occidentalism*, p. 14.
94 Li Tuo, "Resisting Writing," in Liu Kang and Xiaobing Tang (eds) *Politics, Ideology, and Literary Discourse in Modern China: Theoretical Interventions and Cultural Critique*, Durham, NC: Duke University Press, 1993, p. 274; also see Li Jie in Barmé, *Shades of Mao*, p. 141; Michael Schoenhals, *Doing Things with Words in Chinese Politics: Five Studies*, Berkeley, CA: Institute of East Asian Studies, University of California, 1992, pp. 1–29.
95 Li Tuo, "Resisting Writing," p. 275; also see Richard Gordon and Carma Hinton, "The Gate of Heavenly Peace," Boston, MA: Longbow Productions, 1995.
96 Geremie Barmé and Linda Jaivin (eds) *New Ghosts, Old Dreams: Chinese Rebel Voices*, New York: Times Books, 1992; Wasserstrom and Perry, *Popular Protest*.
97 *June Four*, pp. 17, 138; also see Rey Chow, *Writing Diaspora: Tactics of Intervention in Contemporary Cultural Studies*, Bloomington, IN: Indiana University Press, 1993, p. 82.
98 Elshtain, *Women and War*, p. 258.
99 White, *Metahistories*, p. 9; Korhonen, *Japan and Asia Pacific Integration*, pp. 63, 6–8.
100 Barmé, *Shades of Mao*; Michael Dutton, "Mango Mao: Inflections of the Sacred," *Public Culture*, 2004, vol. 16: 2, 161–87.
101 Jonathan Hay, "Zhang Hongtu/Hongtu Zhang: an Interview," in John Hay (ed.) *Boundaries in China*, London: Reaktion Books, 1994, p. 282.
102 Also see Zhang Hongtu, *Chairmen Mao Series*, www.MoMao.com (accessed on 14 August 2005); also see Barmé and Jaivin, *New Ghosts, Old Dreams*, pp. xxv, 404.
103 *The Nation* (Bangkok), 22 February 1993.
104 Benedict Anderson, "Cacique Democracy in the Philippines: Origins and Dreams," in Vicente L. Rafael (ed.) *Discrepant Histories: Translocal Chapters on Filipino Cultures*, Philadelphia, PA: Temple University Press, 1995, pp. 3–4.
105 Aung San Suu Kyi, *Freedom from Fear*, revised edn, London: Penguin, 1995, pp. 200–1.

## 4 Popular politics, civil society and social movements

1 See Daniel Arghiros, *Democracy, Development and Decentralization in Provincial Thailand*, Richmond, UK: Curzon, 2001.
2 Xiaoqin Guo, *State and Society in China's Democratic Transition: Confucianism, Leninism, and Economic Development*, London: Routledge, 2003, pp. 12, 232–5; Daniel A. Bell, *East Meets West: Human Rights and Democracy in East Asia*, Princeton, NJ: Princeton University Press, 2000, pp. 277–336.
3 Corazon Aquino in Corazon Aquino, Oscar Arias and Kim Dae-jung, *Democracy in Asia*, Seoul: Asia-Pacific Peace Press, 1995, pp. 15–16; Richard Rorty, "Idealizations, Foundations, and Social Practices," in Seyla Benhabib (ed.) *Democracy and Difference: Contesting the Boundaries of the Political*, Princeton, NJ: Princeton University Press, 1996, pp. 333–6.
4 The debate on civil society in South Korea ran from 1997 to 1998 for a total of six articles; an earlier version of this chapter was the fifth article in this series.
5 Richard Robison, Kevin Hewison and Garry Rodan, "Political Power in Industrializing Capitalist Societies: Theoretical Approaches," in Kevin Hewison, Richard Robison and Garry Rodan (eds) *Southeast Asia in the 1990s: Authoritarianism, Democracy & Capitalism*, Sydney: Allen & Unwin, 1993, pp. 21–4.
6 David Steinberg, "Civil Society and Human Rights in Korea: On Contemporary and Classical Orthodoxy and Ideology," *Korea Journal*, 1997, vol. 37: 3, 151, 163.
7 Hahm Chaibong, "The Confucian Political Discourse and the Politics of Reform in Korea," *Korea Journal*, 1997, vol. 37: 4, 66–73.
8 Wang Hui, Leo Ou-fan Lee, with Michael M. J. Fischer, "Is the Public Sphere Unspeakable in Chinese? Can Public Spaces (*gonggong kongjian*) Lead to Public Spheres?," *Public Culture*, 1994, vol. 6, 604.
9 Steinberg, "Civil Society and Human Rights in Korea," p. 163; Gordon White, Jude Howell and Shang Xiaoyuan, *In Search of Civil Society: Market Reform and Social Change in Contemporary China*, Oxford: Clarendon Press, 1996, p. 4; William T. Rowe, "The Problem of 'Civil Society' in Late Imperial China," *Modern China*, 1993, vol. 19: 2, 142; Suzanne Ogden, *Inklings of Democracy in China*, Cambridge, MA: Harvard University Press, 2002, pp. 26–7.
10 Shu-Yun Ma, "The Chinese Discourse of Civil Society," *China Quarterly*, 1994, no. 137, 183; Wang, Lee with Fischer, "Is the Public Sphere Unspeakable in Chinese?"
11 Li Xuejun, "Zhongguo fazhan NGO de biyaoxing yu duice" [The necessity for developing NGOs in China and the way to deal with them], *Zhonggong Sichuan shengwei dangxiao xuebao* [Journal of the Sichuan provincial party school], 2004, no. 4, 93; Zhu Jiangang, "Caogen NGO yu Zhongguo gongmin shehuide zhangda" [Grassroots NGOs and the growth of China's civil society], *Kaifang shidai*, 2004, no. 6, 46; Zhao Yinhong, "Zhongguo NGO fazhande dute lishi beijing fenzi" [An analysis of the unique historical background of the development of NGOs in China], *Qiushi*, 2003, no. 11, 108.
12 Suzanne Ogden, Kathleen Hartford, Lawrence Sullivan and David Zweig (eds) *China's Search for Democracy: The Student and Mass Movement of 1989*, Armonk, NY: M.E. Sharpe, 1992; White *et al.*, *In Search of Civil Society*; Heath B. Chamberlain, "On the Search for Civil Society in China," *Modern China*, 1993, vol. 19: 2, 199–215; Tony Saich, "The Search for Civil Society and Democracy in China," *Current History*, September 1994, 260–4; Adrian Chan, "In Search of Civil Society in China," *Journal of Contemporary Asia*, 1997, vol. 27: 2, 242–51; Edmund S.K. Fung, *In Search of Chinese Democracy: Civil Opposition in Nationalist China, 1929–1949*, Cambridge: Cambridge University

Press, 2000; Ian Johnson, "The Death and Life of Civil Society in China," *Perspectives on Politics*, 2003, vol. 1: 3, pp. 551–4.
13 White *et al.*, *In Search of Civil Society*; Heath, "On the Search for Civil Society in China," p. 202; Fung, *In Search of Chinese Democracy*; Ogden, *Inklings of Democracy in China*, pp. 61–3; Bruce Cumings, *Parallax Visions: Making Sense of American–East Asian Relations at the End of the Century*, Durham, NC: Duke University Press, 1999, pp. 95–120.
14 White *et al.*, *In Search of Civil Society*, p. 10; Fung, *In Search of Chinese Democracy*.
15 Ma, "The Chinese Discourse of Civil Society," p. 182; Ogden, *Inklings of Democracy in China*; Zhao, "An Analysis of the Unique Historical Background," p. 110; Deng Guosheng, "Zhongguo feizhengfu zuzhi fazhande xin huanjing" [The new environment for the development of China's NGOs], *Xuehui*, 2004, no. 10, 12.
16 Liangwen (Wayne) Kuo (ed. and trans.) "Taiwan's Social Movements: A Discussion of the State and Civil Society," *Chinese Sociology and Anthropology*, 1997, vol. 29: 4, 3.
17 Kuo, "Taiwan's Social Movements," p. 4.
18 Cho Hein, "The Historical Origin of Civil Society in Korea," *Korea Journal*, 1997, vol. 37: 2, 31–5.
19 Chan, "In Search of Civil Society in China," pp. 242, 243.
20 Thomas Burger, "Translator's Note," in Jürgen Habermas, *The Structural Transformation of the Public Sphere*, Cambridge, MA: MIT Press, 1989, p. xv.
21 Habermas, *The Structural Transformation of the Public Sphere*, p. 1.
22 Hayden White, *Metahistory: The Historical Imagination in Nineteenth-Century Europe*, Baltimore, MD: Johns Hopkins University Press, 1973.
23 Andre Schmid, "Rediscovering Manchuria: Sin Ch'aeho and the Politics of Territorial History in Korea," *Journal of Asian Studies*, 1997, vol. 56: 1, 29.
24 Ibid., p. 43.
25 Stephen E. Welch, *The Concept of Political Culture*, London: Macmillan, 1993.
26 Lucian W. Pye with Mary Pye, *Asian Power and Politics: The Cultural Dimensions of Authority*, Cambridge, MA: Harvard University Press, 1985.
27 See Li Hongyan, "Developments in the Study of Confucianism on the Mainland of China in Recent Years," *Social Sciences in China*, 1997, vol. 18: 1, 17–30.
28 Richard Madsen, "The Public Sphere, Civil Society and Moral Community: A Research Agenda for Contemporary Chinese Studies," *Modern China*, 1993, vol. 19: 2, 183.
29 Barret L. McCormick, Su Shaozhi and Xiao Xiaoming, "The 1989 Democracy Movement: A Review of the Prospects for Civil Society in China," *Pacific Affairs*, 1992, vol. 62: 2, 182–202; Guo, *State and Society in China*, pp. 70–8.
30 Su Shaozhi, "Problems of Economic Reform in China," in Edward Friedman (ed.) *The Politics of Democratization: Generating from East Asian Experiences*, Boulder, CO: Westview, pp. 225–6.
31 White *et al.*, *In Search of Civil Society*; Madsen, "The Public Sphere," p. 188.
32 Ma, "The Chinese Discourse of Civil Society," pp. 188, 191; Wang, Lee with Fischer, "Is the Public Sphere Unspeakable in Chinese?," p. 601; Ogden, *Inklings of Democracy in China*, p. 287; Guo, *State and Society in China*, 88ff.
33 Welch, *The Concept of Political Culture*, p. 59.
34 Vladimir Tismaneanu (ed.) *In Search of Civil Society: Independence Peace Movements in the Soviet Bloc*, New York: Routledge, 1990; Zbigniew Rau (ed.) *The Reemergence of Civil Society in Eastern Europe and the Soviet Union*, Boulder, CO: Westview Press, 1991.
35 Ma, "The Chinese Discourse of Civil Society," p. 180; Chan, "In Search of Civil Society in China," p. 245.

36 Frederic Wakeman, "The Civil Society and Public Sphere Debate: Western Reflections on Chinese Political Culture," *Modern China*, 1993, vol. 19: 2, 108–38; William T. Rowe, "The Public Sphere in Modern China," *Modern China*, 1990, vol. 16: 3, 309–29; Rowe, "The Problem of 'Civil Society' in Late Imperial China"; Mary Backus Rankin, "Some Observations on a Chinese Public Sphere," *Modern China*, 1993, vol. 19: 2, 158–82; Madsen, "The Public Sphere"; Chamberlain, "On the Search for Civil Society in China"; Philip C.C. Huang, "'Public Sphere'/'Civil Society' in China?: The Third Realm between State and Society," *Modern China*, 1993, vol. 19: 2, 216–40; Chan, "In Search of Civil Society in China"; Wang Miaoyang, Yu Xuanmeng, and Manuel B. Dy (eds) *Civil Society in a Chinese Context*, Washington, DC: The Council for Research in Values and Philosophy, 1997; Zhu, "Grassroots NGOs and the growth of China's civil society," p. 38.
37 Habermas, *The Structural Transformation of the Public Sphere*, pp. 32–3.
38 Strand in Wakeman, "The Civil Society and Public Sphere Debate," p. 132; Wang, Lee with Fischer, "Is the Public Sphere Unspeakable in Chinese?," p. 602; Chan, "In Search of Civil Society in China," p. 246.
39 Rowe, "The Problem of 'Civil Society' in Late Imperial China," p. 146; Rowe, "The Public Sphere in Modern China," p. 314.
40 Madsen, "The Public Sphere," p. 190.
41 Rowe, "The Problem of 'Civil Society' in Late Imperial China," pp. 143–53; Guo, *State and Society in China*.
42 Han Sang-Jin (ed.) *Habermas and the Critical Theory Debate in Korea*, Seoul: Seoul National University Press, 1998.
43 Han Sang-Jin, "The Public Sphere and Democracy in Korea: A Debate on Civil Society," *Korea Journal*, 1997, vol. 37: 4, 78–97.
44 Hahm, "Confucian Political Discourse," p. 65.
45 Ibid., pp. 66–72.
46 R.B.J. Walker, *Inside/Outside: International Relations as Political Theory*, Cambridge: Cambridge University Press, 1993, pp. 149–51.
47 White *et al.*, *In Search of Civil Society*, p. 6; Ogden, *Inklings of Democracy in China*, pp. 26–7; Robert P. Weller, *Alternative Civilities: Democracy and Culture in China and Taiwan*, Boulder, CO: Westview Press, 1999, p. xii.
48 William A. Callahan, "Resisting the Norm: Ironic Images of Marx and Confucius," *Philosophy East and West*, 1994, vol. 44: 2, 279–302.
49 Han, "The Public Sphere and Democracy in Korea," p. 79.
50 Koh Byong-Ik, "Confucianism in Contemporary Korea," in Tu Wei-ming (ed.) *Confucian Traditions in East Asian Modernity: Moral Education and Economic Culture in Japan and the Four Mini-Dragons*, Cambridge, MA: Harvard University Press, 1996, p. 197; Ministry of Culture and Sports, *Religious Culture in Korea*, Seoul: Holly M., 1996, pp. 8–10.
51 Koh, "Confucianism in Contemporary Korea," p. 199.
52 Weller, *Alternative Civilities*, p. 139.
53 See Roger T. Ames, "Continuing the Conversation on Chinese Human Rights," *Ethics and International Affairs*, 1997, no. 11, 198.
54 Lin Tongqi, Henry Rosemont, Jr and Roger T. Ames, "Chinese Philosophy: A Philosophical Chapter on the 'State-of-the-Art'," *Journal of Asian Studies*, 1995, vol. 54: 3, 730.
55 Michel Foucault, "Governmentality," in Graham Burchell, Colin Gordon and Peter Miller (eds) *The Foucault Effect: Studies in Governmentality*, London: Harvester Wheatsheaf, 1991, p. 91.
56 Chen Xiaomei, *Occidentalism: A Theory of Counter-Discourse in Post-Mao China*, 2nd edn, Lanham, MD: Rowman & Littlefield, 2002.
57 See Callahan, "Resisting the Norm."

58 Kim Kwang-Ok, "The Reproduction of Confucian Culture in Contemporary Korea: An Anthropological Study," in Tu, *Confucian Traditions in East Asian Modernity*, pp. 202–27; Steinberg, "Civil Society and Human Rights in Korea."
59 Perry Link, *Evening Chats in Beijing: Probing China's Predicament*, New York: W.W. Norton, 1992, pp. 184, 190.
60 Michel Foucault, *The History of Sexuality*, vol. 1, New York: Vintage, 1980, p. 95.
61 Chulhee Chung, "Social Movement Organizations and the June Uprising," *Korea Journal*, 1997, vol. 37: 2, 24–41.
62 See William A. Callahan, *PollWatching, Elections and Civil Society in Southeast Asia*, Aldershot: Ashgate, 2000.
63 Lim Hy-Sop, "Historical Development of Civil Social Movements in Korea: Trajectories and Issues," *Korea Journal*, 2000, vol. 40: 3, 8.
64 Han, "The Public Sphere and Democracy in Korea," p. 80.
65 Chan, "In Search of Civil Society in China," p. 248.
66 Ma, "The Chinese Discourse of Civil Society," p. 182; Kuo, "Taiwan's Social Movements."
67 Ma, "The Chinese Discourse of Civil Society," p. 185.
68 Ibid.
69 Ibid.
70 Heath, "On the Search for Civil Society in China," p. 203; Michael B. Frolic, "State-led Civil Society," in Timothy Brook and Michael B. Frolic (eds) *Civil Society in China*, Armonk, NY: M.E. Sharpe, 1997, pp. 46–67; Randy Kluver, "Elite-Based Discourse in Chinese Civil Society," in Randy Kluver and John H. Powers (eds) *Civic Discourse, Civil Society, and Chinese Communities*, Stamford, CT: Ablex Publishing, 1999, pp. 11–22; Yijiang Ding, *Chinese Democracy after Tiananmen*, Vancouver: UBC Press, 2001; Ogden, *Inklings of Democracy in China*.
71 White *et al.*, *In Search of Civil Society*, pp. 186–7.
72 Zhu, "Grassroots NGOs," p. 37; Zhao, "An Analysis of the Unique Historical Background," p. 109; Ogden, *Inklings of Democracy in China*, p. 268; Weller, *Alternative Civilities*, p. 126.
73 "500 xianjin renmin zuzhi yinling Zhongguo NGO chaoliu: quanguo sianjin minjian zuzhi biaoyinghui zai jing zhaokai" [500 advanced people's organizations show China's NGO wave: nationwide advanced people's organizations award ceremony opens in Beijing], *Xuehui*, 2005, no. 1, 4–5.
74 Deng, "The New Environment for the Development of China's NGOs," p. 18; Zhao, "An Analysis of the Unique Historical Background," p. 110.
75 Weller, *Alternative Civilities*, p. 126, Ogden; *Inklings of Democracy in China*, p. 285.
76 Zhu, "Grassroots NGOs," p. 46; Guo, *State and Society in China*, pp. 217–36.
77 Li, "The Necessity Developing NGOs in China," p. 95.
78 Steinberg, "Civil Society and Human Rights in Korea," p. 161.
79 Kim, "The Reproduction of Confucian Culture in Contemporary Korea," pp. 202, 204.
80 Kim Cheol-Hyeon, Director of the Religious Affairs Division of the Ministry of Culture and Sports, Interview in Seoul, 13 August 1997; Kim, "The Reproduction of Confucian Culture in Contemporary Korea," p. 213.
81 Kim, "The Reproduction of Confucian Culture in Contemporary Korea," p. 210.
82 Ibid., p. 202.
83 Hong Sun-hee, "Ban on Same-Surname Marriage Lifted: Court's Ruling Puts End to Centuries-Old Taboo," *The Korea Times*, 17 July 1997, p. 3.
84 Hahm Chaibong, "Family versus the Individual: The Politics of Marriage Laws in Korea," in Daniel A. Bell and Hahm Chaibong (eds) *Confucianism for the*

*Modern World*, Cambridge: Cambridge University Press, 2003, p. 337; Lee Seung-Hwan, Interview in Seoul, 30 July 1997.
85 Kim "The Reproduction of Confucian Culture in Contemporary Korea," p. 205.
86 Hahm Chaibong, Interview in Seoul, 3 September 1997.
87 Lew Seok-Choon, "Confucian Capitalism: Possibilities and Limits," *Tradition & Modernity*, 1997, vol. 1: 1, 74–93, translated in *Korea Focus*, 1997, vol. 5: 4, 93.
88 Hahm, "Confucian Political Discourse," p. 66.
89 Bell and Hahm, *Confucianism for the Modern World*.
90 Cited in Asan Foundation, *Asan Foundation Annual Report*, Seoul: Asan Foundation, 1997, p. 246.
91 Ibid., p. 247.
92 Aihwa Ong, *Flexible Citizenship: The Cultural Logics of Transnationality*, Durham, NC: Duke University Press, 1999, p. 127.
93 Kim, "The Reproduction of Confucian Culture in Contemporary Korea," p. 225.
94 Kim Kyong-Dong, "Business and Culture for the Future," *Mécénat*, May–June 1997, translated in *Korea Focus*, 1997, vol. 5: 5, 86–7.
95 Jonathan Tomlinson, *Cultural Imperialism*, Baltimore, MD: Johns Hopkins University Press, 1991, p. 90.
96 Ibid., p. 154.
97 Kim Young Sam, *Korea's Reform and Globalization: President Kim Young Sam Prepares the Nation for the Challenges of the 21st Century*, Seoul: Korea Overseas Information Service, 1997.
98 See Michael Hardt and Antonio Negri, *Empire*, Cambridge, MA: Harvard University Press, 2000.
99 Tomlinson, *Cultural Imperialism*, p. 175.
100 Foucault, "Governmentality," p. 103.
101 Tomlinson, *Cultural Imperialism*, p. 167.
102 R.B.J. Walker, "Social Movements/World Politics," *Millennium: Journal of International Studies*, 1994, vol. 23: 3, 675, 669.
103 Lowell Dittmer, Haruhiro Fukui and Peter N.S. Lee (eds) *Informal Politics in East Asia*, Cambridge: Cambridge University Press, 2000; Ogden, *Inklings of Democracy in China*, p. 266; Weller, *Alternative Civilities*, p. 107; Cao Haidong, "Zhongguo xinsheng dai NGO chiqi," [The rise of China's new generation of NGOs], *Jingji*, 2004, no. 5, 45.
104 White *et al.*, *In Search of Civil Society*, p. 209.
105 Ibid., p. 208.
106 Mau-Kuei Chang, "Civil Society, Resource Mobilization, and New Social Movements: Theoretical Implications for the Study of Social Movements in Taiwan," *Chinese Sociology and Anthropology*, 1997, vol. 29: 4, 12.
107 Ibid., p. 13.
108 Ibid., p. 9.
109 Ibid., pp. 14, 20–33. For a similar theoretical shift in Southeast Asian studies see Vince Boudreau, *Resisting Dictatorship: Repression and Protest in Southeast Asia*, Cambridge: Cambridge University Press, 2004, pp. 22–5, 30–6.
110 William A. Callahan, *Imagining Democracy: Reading the Events of May in Thailand*, Singapore and London: Institute for Southeast Asian Studies, pp. 99–103.
111 Chang, "Civil Society, Resource Mobilization, and New Social Movements," p. 14.
112 Weller, *Alternative Civilities*, pp. 7, xii.
113 Ibid., p. 119.
114 L.H.M. Ling and Chih-yu Shih, "Confucianism with a Liberal Face: Democratic Politics in Postcolonial Taiwan," in Fred Dallmayr (ed.) *Border Crossings:*

## 212  Notes

       *Toward a Comparative Political Theory*, Lanham, MD: Lexington Books, 1999, p. 219.
115 Weller, *Alternative Civilities*; Ling and Shih, "Confucianism with a Liberal Face," p. 229.
116 Odgen, *Inklings of Democracy*, p. 316; Richard Curt Kraus, *The Party and the Arty in China: The New Politics of Culture*, Lanham, MD: Rowman & Littlefield, 2004, pp. vii–viii.
117 Weller, *Alternative Civilities*, p. 126.
118 Odgen, *Inklings of Democracy*, p. 264. The instability of accounting for NGOs shows how some are registered, and others are beyond the gaze. While Ogden counts 200,000 local NGOs in the late 1990s, the Minister of Civil Administration reported that there were 260,000 people's organizations in 2004, and an article in a journal closely monitored by the Propaganda Department said that there were about 870,000 NGOs in China by 1998 ("500 Advanced People's Organizations Show China's NGO Wave," p. 4; Zhao, "An Analysis of the Unique Historical Background," p. 108).
119 Weller, *Alternative Civilities*, p. 129; also see Cao "The Rise of China's New Generation of NGOs," p. 45; Li Zhou, "Public Goods, Environmental Protection and the Development Paradigm in Rural China," *China and World Economy*, 2004, vol. 12: 6, 86–97.
120 Weller, *Alternative Civilities*, pp. 110, 126, 129; White *et al.*, *In Search of Civil Society*, p. 215.
121 Weller, *Alternative Civilities*, pp. 140–2; Ogden, *Inklings of Democracy in China*, p. 267.
122 Ling and Shih, "Confucianism with a Liberal Face," p. 229; Chang, "Civil Society, Resource Mobilization, and New Social Movements."
123 Chang, "Civil Society, Resource Mobilization, and New Social Movements," p. 20.
124 Weller, *Alternative Civilities*, pp. 13, 110; Chang, "Civil Society, Resource Mobilization, and New Social Movements," p. 14.
125 Bronwen Dalton and James Cotton, "New Social Movements and the Changing Nature of Political Opposition in South Korea," in Garry Rodan (ed.) *Political Oppositions in Industrializing Asia*, London: Routledge, 1996, pp. 272–99.
126 Lim, "Historical Development of Civil Social Movements in Korea," p. 17.
127 Chulhee Chung, "Social Movement Organizations and the June Uprising," pp. 91–2.
128 Lim, "Historical Development of Civil Social Movements in Korea," p. 16; also see Callahan, *Imagining Democracy*, pp. 99–102; Kurt Schock, *Unarmed Insurrections: People Power Movements in Nondemocracies*, Minneapolis, MN: University of Minnesota Press, 2005, p. 165.
129 Lim, "Historical Development of Civil Social Movements in Korea," p. 21.
130 Ibid., p. 16.
131 See the CCEJ website www.ccej.or.kr, and the CCEJ's acceptance speech on Right Livelihood Award website, www.rightlivelihood.org/speeches/2003-ccje.htm (accessed on 8 July 2005).
132 Ibid.; Lim, "Historical Development of Civil Social Movements in Korea," p. 17.
133 See the Inaugural Declaration of the CCEJ in 1989, www.ccej.or.kr/english.
134 Han, "The Public Sphere and Democracy in Korea," p. 85.
135 Ibid., pp. 85, 86.
136 Ibid., p. 86; Hagen Koo, "The State, Minjung, and the Working Class in South Korea," in Hagen Koo (ed.) *State and Society in Contemporary Korea*, Ithaca, NY: Cornell University Press, 1993, pp. 131–62.
137 Kim "The Reproduction of Confucian Culture in Contemporary Korea," p. 223; Koo, "The State, Minjung, and the Working Class in South Korea," p. 144.

138 Chen, *Occidentalism*; White *et al.*, *In Search of Civil Society*, pp. 186–7.
139 Kim Kwang-Ok, "The Role of *Madangguk* in Contemporary Korea's Popular Culture Movement," *Korea Journal*, 1997, vol. 37: 3, 5.
140 Ibid., p. 7.
141 Ibid., pp. 10, 13.
142 Ibid., p. 15.
143 Kim Kwang-Ok, Correspondence, 31 March 1998.
144 Kim, "The Reproduction of Confucian Culture in Contemporary Korea," p. 223.
145 Zheng Jiadong, "Jiushiniandai ruxue fazhanzhongde jigawenti" [Issues of the Development of Confucian Studies in the Nineties], Paper presented at the International Conference "The Contemporary Significance of East Asian Philosophy with emphasis on Korean philosophy," Seoul, South Korea, July 1997, p. 1; also see Li, "Developments in the Study of Confucianism."
146 Lee Seung-Hwan, "Who Dares Bring Disgrace on Tradition?," *Tradition & Modernity*, 1997, vol. 1: 1, 176–97.
147 Han Sang-Jin, "Globalization and Postcolonialism: Confucianism and East Asian Development," Paper presented at the Kwangju Biennale International Symposium on "Globalization and Postcolonialism," Kwangju, South Korea, October 1997.
148 Tu Weiming, "Cultural China: The Periphery as the Center," in Tu Weiming (ed.) *The Living Tree: the Changing Meaning of Being Chinese Today*, Stanford, CA: Stanford University Press, 1994, p. 33; Kim Dae-Jung, "Is Culture Destiny? The Myth of Asia's Anti-Democratic Values," *Foreign Affairs*, 1994, vol. 73: 6, 189–94.

## 5 Corruption, political reform and the deferral of democracy

1 See William A. Callahan, "Political Corruption in Southeast Asia," in Robert Williams (ed.) *Party Finance and Political Corruption*, London: Macmillan, 2000, pp. 163–98; Yan Sun, "The Chinese Protests of 1989: The Issue of Corruption," *Asian Survey*, 1991, vol. 31: 8, 762–82; Frederic Charles Schaffer (ed.), *Elections for Sale; The Causes and Consequences of Vote Buying*, Boulders, CO: Lynne Rienner Publishers.
2 Amien Rais cited in Adam Schwarz, "A Sense of Disgust," *Far Eastern Economic Review*, 14 May 1998, 26.
3 There is an ancient Thai phrase for corruption, *charat bangluang*, which means "cheat the people, deceive the government" in the sense of local officials squeezing high taxes from the people, but not transferring all of this revenue to the state. Because corruption has expanded far beyond this pre-modern state-centric practice, the new loan-word was forged (Sumalee Bumroongsook, Thai historian, Interview in Bangkok, 15 December 2003).
4 Chalmers Johnson, "Tanaka Kakuei, Structural Corruption, and the Advent of Machine Politics in Japan," *Journal of Japan Studies*, 1986, vol. 12: 1, 19.
5 Lucian W. Pye, "Money Politics and Transitions to Democracy in East Asia," *Asian Survey*, 1997, vol. 37: 3, 213–28; Johnson, "Tanaka Kakuei," pp. 27–8.
6 Johnson, "Tanaka Kakuei," pp. 19–20.
7 Johnson, "Tanaka Kakuei," pp. 23–8.
8 Chalmers Johnson, *Japan: Who Governs? The Rise of the Developmental State*, New York: WW Norton & Company, 1995, pp. 210–11.
9 Michel Foucault, *Madness and Civilization: A History of Insanity in the Age of Reason*, New York: Vintage, 1973; also see Peter Bratsis, "The Construction of Corruption, or Rules of Separation and Illusions of Purity in Bourgeois Societies," *Social Text* 77, 2003, vol. 21, 19.

10 Bratsis, "The Construction of Corruption," pp. 4, 9.
11 Ibid., p. 14.
12 Michael Johnston, "The Search for Definitions: The Vitality of Politics and the Issue of Corruption," *International Social Science Journal*, 1996, vol. 149, 332.
13 Fred Riggs, *Thailand: The Modernization of a Bureaucratic Polity*, Honolulu, HI: East-West Center Press, 1966; Anek Laothammatas, *Business Associations and the Political Economy of Thailand: From Bureaucratic Polity to Liberal Corporatism*, Boulder, CO: Westview Press, 1992.
14 Pasuk Phongpaichit and Chris Baker, *Thailand: Economy and Politics*, 2nd edn, Oxford: Oxford University Press, 2002, pp. 147–86; Danny Unger, *Building Social Capital in Thailand: Fibers, Finance and Infrastructure*, Cambridge: Cambridge University Press, 1998; Kevin Hewison, "Resisting Globalization: a Study of Localism in Thailand," *Pacific Review*, 2000, vol. 13: 2, 279–96; Pasuk Phongpaichit and Chris Baker, *Thaksin: The Business of Politics in Thailand*, Chiangmai: Silkworm Books, 2004, p. 9.
15 See William A. Callahan, *Imagining Democracy: Reading "the Events of May" in Thailand*, Singapore and London: Institute for Southeast Asian Studies, 1998; Pasuk and Baker, *Thailand: Economy and Politics*, pp. 341–84.
16 Gothom Arya, "Election System and Events in Thailand," Bangkok: Election Commission of Thailand, 2001, p. 1, available online at http://www.ect.go.th, (accessed on 26 July 2003).
17 See Hewison, "Resisting Globalization"; Kevin Hewison, "Thailand's Capitalism Before and After the Economic Crisis," in Richard Robison, Mark Beeson, Kaishka Jayasuriya and Hyuk-Rae Kim (eds) *Politics and Markets in the Wake of the Asian Crisis*, London: Routledge, 2000, pp. 192–211; Pasuk Phongpaichit and Chris Baker, *Thailand's Crisis*, Chiangmai: Silkworm Books, 2000.
18 See Pasuk and Baker, *Thailand: Economy and Politics*, pp. 173–86.
19 Gothom, "Election System and Events in Thailand," p. 7.
20 Sombat Chantornvong, "The 1997 Constitution and the Politics of Electoral Reform," in Duncan McCargo (ed.) *Reforming Thai Politics*, Copenhagen: Nordic Institute of Asian Studies, 2002, p. 203.
21 P-Net in ANFREL (Asian Network for Free Elections), *The Emergence of New Politics in Thailand: ANFREL Election Report, 6 January–18 August 2001*, Bangkok: ANFREL and FORUM-ASIA, 2001, p. 98.
22 International Monetary Fund, *Good Governance: The IMF's Role*, Washington, DC: IMF, 1997. The World Bank started this discussion in 1991. See World Bank, *Governance and Development*, Washington, DC: World Bank, 1992.
23 See Bratsis, "The Construction of Corruption," p. 29.
24 Thirayuth Boonmi, "Good Governance: A Strategy to Restore Thailand," translated by Savitri Gadavanij, in McCargo, *Reforming Thai Politics*, pp. 31, 29–30.
25 See Michael Kelly Connors, *Democracy and National Identity in Thailand*, London: RoutledgeCurzon, 2003, pp. 155–7.
26 Chai-anan Samudavanaija, *The Thai Young Turks*, Singapore and London: Institute for Southeast Asian Studies, 1983.
27 Duncan McCargo, "Alternative Meanings of Political Reform in Contemporary Thailand," *The Copenhagen Journal of Asian Studies*, 1998, vol. 13, 5, 7.
28 William A. Callahan and Duncan McCargo, "Vote-buying in the Thai Northeast: The July 1995 general election," *Asian Survey*, 1996, vol. 36: 4, 376–92.
29 Sombat, "The 1997 Constitution," p. 204.
30 *Constitution of the Kingdom of Thailand*, Bangkok: Council of State, 1997, Sections 126–9, available online at www.krisdika.go.th/home.jsp, (accessed on 22 February 2005).
31 Ibid., Section 118(7).

32 Ibid., Sections 107, 109, 125.
33 Ibid., Section 68.
34 Sombat, "The 1997 Constitution," p. 204.
35 Dominic Faulder, "The Best Government Reformer," *Asiaweek*, 19 August 2000.
36 P-Net in ANFREL, *The Emergence of New Politics in Thailand*, p. 100.
37 Gothom, "Election System," pp. 15–16.
38 See Duncan McCargo, "Thailand's January 2001 General Elections: Vindicating Reform?," in McCargo, *Reforming Thai Politics*, p. 253.
39 Sombat, "The 1997 Constitution," p. 218.
40 *Far Eastern Economic Review*, 11 January 2001, p. 23.
41 Most of the information for the following argument comes from a confidential report. To maintain the anonymity of interviewers and interviewees, I have changed the names of the provinces to Sumaleeburi, Subinburi and Sainsburi. See Centre for Information on Local Politics in the Northeast, *Kan chai nguen ha siang khong phak kanmuang nai kan luektang phuthaen rasadorn, 6 Makkarakhom 2544* [Political Party Campaign Expenditure for the House of Representatives Election 6 January 2001], Mahasarakham: University of Mahasarakham, 3 May 2001. Also see Daniel Arghiros, *Democracy, Development and Decentralization in Provincial Thailand*, Richmond, UK: Curzon, 2001, pp. 256–68.
42 William A. Callahan, *Pollwatching, Elections and Civil Society in Southeast Asia*, Aldershot, Hampshire/Burlington, VT: Ashgate, 2000, p. 27.
43 Duncan McCargo, "Thailand's Political Parties: Real, Authentic and Actual," in Kevin Hewison (ed.) *Political Change in Thailand: Democracy and Participation*, London: Routledge, 1997, p. 115.
44 Cited in McCargo, "Thailand's January 2001 General Elections," p. 250.
45 Ibid., p. 253.
46 Aurel Croissant and Jorn Dosch, "Old Wine in New Bottlenecks? Elections in Thailand under the 1997 Constitution," working paper, Leeds, UK: University of Leeds, 2001, p. 13, available online at http://croissant.uni-hd.de/old_wine_in_new_bottlenecks.htm (accessed on 22 February 2005).
47 Peter Jansen, "Coup de Technocrats," *Asian Business*, April 1991, p. 16.
48 Pasuk and Baker, *Thailand's Crisis*, p. 125; Connors, *Democracy and National Identity*, p. 164.
49 Sombat, "The 1997 Constitution," p. 203.
50 Duncan McCargo, "Introduction: Understanding Political Reform in Thailand," in McCargo, *Reforming Thai Politics*, p. 5.
51 Cited in Michael Kelly Connors, "Political Reform and the State in Thailand," *Journal of Contemporary Asia*, 1999, vol. 29, 202.
52 Prawase Wasi, "An Overview of Political Reform," in McCargo, *Reforming Thai Politics*, p. 23.
53 Cited in Connors, *Democracy and National Identity*, p. 164.
54 For a discussion of *jao pho* and politics see James Ockey, "The Rise of Local Power in Thailand: Provincial Crime, Elections and Bureaucracy," in Ruth McVey (ed.) *Money & Power in Provincial Thailand*, Singapore and London: Institute for Southeast Asian Studies, 2000, pp. 74–96.
55 ANFREL, *The Emergence of New Politics in Thailand*, p. 20; also see Pasuk Phongpaichit and Chris Baker, "Chao Sua, Chao Pho, Chai Thi: Lords of Thailand's Transition," in McVey, *Money & Power in Provincial Thailand*, p. 39.
56 For an analysis of clean/dirty as a guiding distinction in corruption discourse see Bratsis, "The Construction of Corruption," p. 20.
57 Sombat, "The 1997 Constitution," p. 210.

58 McCargo, "Alternative Meanings of Political Reform," p. 17.
59 Ibid., p. 20.
60 Anek Laothammatas, *Song nakhara prachathipatai: Naewthang kanmuang sethakit peua prachathipatai* [A Tale of Two Democracies: The Road to Political Economic Reform for Democracy], Bangkok: Matichon Books, 1995. For a version in English, see Anek Laothammatas, "A Tale of Two Democracies: Conflicting Perceptions of Elections and Democracy in Thailand," in R.H. Taylor (ed.) *The Politics of Elections in Southeast Asia*, Cambridge: Cambridge University Press, 1996, pp. 201–23.See Anek Laothammatas, "A Tale of Two Democracies: Conflicting Perceptions of Elections and Democracy in Thailand," in R.H. Taylor (ed.) *The Politics of Elections in Southeast Asia*, Cambridge: Cambridge University Press, 1996, pp. 201–23.
61 Ibid., p. 202.
62 Viengrat Netipho, "Itthiphon nai kan muang thongthin khong Thai: suksa koranee muang Chiangmai" [Influence in Local Politics in Thailand: Case Study of Chiangmai], *Journal of Social Sciences* (Bangkok), 2000, vol. 31: 2, 209.
63 Ananya Bhuchongkul, "Vote-buying: more than a sale," *Bangkok Post*, 23 February 1992, p. 8; Callahan, *Pollwatching*.
64 Anek Laothammatas, "Sleeping Giant Awakens: The Middle Class in Thai Politics," *Asian Review 1993*, vol. 7, 122.
65 Ananya, "Vote-buying," p. 8.
66 Anek, "Sleeping Giant Awakens," p. 125.
67 See Somchai Phatharathananunth, "Civil Society and Democratization in Thailand: A Critique of Elite Democracy," in McCargo, *Reforming Thai Politics*, pp. 130–1.
68 Raymond Williams, *The Country and the City*, London: Chatto & Windus, 1973, p. 1.
69 Prawase, "An Overview of Political Reform," p. 26; Thirayuth Boonmi, "Good Governance," p. 30.
70 For an analysis of the contradictory construction of the middle class in 1991–92 see Callahan, *Imagining Democracy*, pp. 35–84.
71 See Somchai, "Civil Society and Democratization in Thailand"; Naruemon Thabchumpon, "NGOs and Grassroots Participation in the Political Reform Process," in McCargo, *Reforming Thai Politics*, pp. 183–99.
72 Thawan Masjarat, "Nangsao Sayam" [Miss Siam], in *Mednangrak*, Bangkok: Tonor 1999, Inc., 1998, p. 104. Siam was Thailand's official name before 1939.
73 See Chatthip Nartsupha, *Noekhid setthakit chumchon: khosanue thaeng thrisadi naiparibot taeng sungkhom* [The Concept of Community Economics: A Theoretical Proposal for an Alternative Society], Bangkok: Satabun Withithat, 2001, pp. 167–96; Hewison, "Resisting Globalization."
74 See Duncan McCargo, *Politics and the Press in Thailand: Media Machinations*, London: Routledge, 2000, pp. 1–30.
75 Connors, "Political Reform," p. 204; Benedict Anderson, "Murder and Progress in Siam," *New Left Review*, 1990, no. 181, 33–48.
76 See Ockey, "The Rise of Local Power," pp. 79–80.
77 Ibid., p. 83.
78 Pasuk and Baker, "Chao Sua, Chao Pho, Chai Thi," p. 38.
79 Callahan, *Pollwatching*, pp. 125–41.
80 *Far Eastern Economic Review*, 9 November 2000, 19.
81 Viengrat, "Influence in Local Politics in Thailand," pp. 223–5.
82 Callahan, *Pollwatching*, chapters 4 and 8.
83 Naruemon, "NGOs and Grassroots Participation," pp. 194–5.
84 Cited in ANFREL, *The Emergence of New Politics in Thailand*, p. 65.

*Notes* 217

85 See Duncan McCargo and Ukrist Pathmanand, *The Thaksinization of Thailand*, Copenhagen: Nordic Institute of Asian Studies, 2005; Pasuk and Baker, *Thaksin*.
86 Anderson, "Murder and Progress in Siam"; Bratsis, "The Construction of Corruption." I would like to thank Kevin Hewison for raising this point.
87 Pasuk and Baker, *Thailand's Crisis*, p. 155.

## 6 Cosmopolitanism, nationalism and diasporic politics

1 See Paul J. Bolt, *China and Southeast Asia's Ethnic Chinese: State and Diaspora in Contemporary Asia*, Westport, CT: Praeger, 2000; Tu Weiming (ed.) *Confucian Traditions in East Asian Modernity*, Cambridge, MA: Harvard University Press, 1996.
2 Arjun Appadurai, *Modernity at Large: Cultural Dimensions of Globalization*, Minneapolis, MN: University of Minnesota Press, 1996, pp. 19–21, 165.
3 Wang Gungwu, *China and the Chinese Overseas*, Singapore: Times Academic Press, 1991, pp. 1–10.
4 Benedict Anderson, *Imagined Communities: Reflections on the Origin and Spread of Nationalism*, revised edn, London: Verso, 1991, pp. 122–3.
5 Kasian Tejapira, "Pigtail: A Pre-History of Chineseness in Siam," *Sojourn*, 1992, vol. 7: 1, 108.
6 The more common terms for this group, "overseas Chinese" and "diasporic Chinese", are also problematic. Unless otherwise noted, in this chapter I will use them interchangeably to refer to ethnic Chinese populations who reside outside of the PRC, Taiwan and Hong Kong.
7 Sterling Seagrave, *Lords of the Rim: The Invisible Empire of the Overseas Chinese*, London: Bantam Press, 1995; Andrew Tanzer, "Overseas China: the Giant Economy that Knows No Borders," *Forbes*, 18 July 1994, pp. 138ff.
8 Daniel Chirot and Anthony Reid (eds) *Essential Outsiders: Chinese and Jews in the Modern Transformation of Southeast Asia and Central Europe*, Seattle, WA: University of Washington Press, 1997; also see Yossi Shai and Aharon Barth, "Diasporas and International Relations Theory," *International Organization*, 2003, vol. 57: 3, 449–79.
9 Donald M. Nonini and Aihwa Ong, "Introduction: Chinese Transnationalism as an Alternative Modernity," in Aihwa Ong and Donald M. Nonini (eds) *Ungrounded Empires: The Cultural Politics of Modern Chinese Transnationalism*, London: Routledge, 1997, pp. 11, 26; also see Aihwa Ong, *Flexible Citizenship: The Cultural Logics of Transnationality*, Durham, NC: Duke University Press, 1999, pp. 12–14.
10 See James Clifford, "Diasporas," *Cultural Anthropology*, 1994, vol. 9: 3, 302–38; Pheng Cheah and Bruce Robbins (eds) *Cosmopolitics: Thinking and Feeling Beyond the Nation*, Minneapolis, MN: University of Minnesota Press, 1998; Liu Hong, "Old Linkages, New Networks: The Globalization of Overseas Chinese Voluntary Associations and its Implications," *China Quarterly*, 1998, no. 155, 607; Jiemin Bao, "Same Bed, Different Dreams: Intersections of Ethnicity, Gender, and Sexuality Among Middle- and Upper-Class Chinese Immigrants in Bangkok," *positions: east asia cultures critique*, 1998, vol. 6: 2, 475–502.
11 Wang Gungwu, *The Chinese Overseas: From Earthbound China to the Quest for Autonomy*, Cambridge, MA: Harvard University Press, 2000.
12 See Wayne Arnold, "Chinese Diaspora Using Internet to Aid Plight of Brethren Abroad," *Wall Street Journal*, 23 July 1998; Christopher Rene Hughes, "Nationalism in Chinese Cyberspace," *Cambridge Review of International Affairs*, 2000, vol. 13: 2, 205–6; Liu Hong, "New Migrants and the Revival of

Overseas Chinese Nationalism," *Journal of Contemporary China*, 2005, vol. 14: 43, 310.
13 Ong, *Flexible Citizenship*, pp. 19, 24, 110–36, 175.
14 Prasenjit Duara, "Nationalists Among Transnationals: Overseas Chinese and the Idea of China, 1900–1911," in Ong and Nonini, *Ungrounded Empires*, London: Routledge, 1997, p. 56.
15 See Appadurai, *Modernity at Large*.
16 Peter J. Katzenstein (ed.) *The Culture of National Security: Norms and Identity in World Politics*, New York: Columbia University Press, 1996.
17 See Michael J. Shapiro, *Methods and Nations: Cultural Governance and the Indigenous Subject*, New York: Routledge, 2004.
18 Jutta Weldes, Mark Laffey, Hugh Gusterson and Raymond Duval, "Introduction: Constructing Insecurity," in Jutta Weldes, Mark Laffey, Hugh Gusterson and Raymond Duval (eds) *Cultures of Insecurity: States, Communities and the Production of Danger*, Minneapolis, MN: University of Minnesota Press, 1999, pp. 1–33.
19 Ibid., pp. 17, 20.
20 Richard Robison, Mark Beeson, Kaishka Jayasuriya and Hyuk-Rae Kim (eds) *Politics and Markets in the Wake of the Asian Crisis*, London: Routledge, 2000; Meredith Woo-Cumings (ed.) *The Developmental State*, Ithaca, NY: Cornell University Press, 1999.
21 See, for example, Bruce Cumings, *Parallax Visions: Making Sense of American-East Asian Relations at the End of the Century*, Durham, NC: Duke University Press, 1999; Arif Dirlik (ed.) *What is in a Rim? Critical Perspectives on the Pacific Rim Idea*, 2nd edn, Lanham, MD: Rowman & Littlefield, 1998.
22 Peter L. Berger, "An East Asian Development Model?," in Peter L. Berger and Hsin-Huang Michael Hsiao (eds) *In Search of an East Asian Development Model*, Oxford: Transaction Books, 1988, pp. 7–8.
23 See Gary G. Hamilton, "Overseas Chinese Capitalism," in Tu, *Confucian Traditions in East Asian Modernity*, p. 331.
24 Tu, *Confucian Traditions in East Asian Modernity*; Pasuk Phongpaichit and Chris Baker, *Thailand's Crisis*, Chiangmai: Silkworm Books, 2000, p. 210.
25 Duara, "Nationalists among Transnationals," p. 50; also see Appadurai, *Modernity at Large*, p. 4.
26 Appadurai, *Modernity at Large*, p. 158.
27 Wang, *China and the Chinese Overseas*, pp. 216, 236, 253.
28 See Michael D. Swaine and Ashely J. Tellis, *Interpreting China's Grand Strategy: Past, Present, and Future*, Santa Monica, CA: Rand Corporation, 2000; Yongnian Zheng, *Discovering Chinese Nationalism in China: Modernization, Identity and International Relations*, Cambridge: Cambridge University Press, 1999.
29 See Zheng, *Discovering Chinese Nationalism*, p. 157; Pi Mingyong, "Minzu zhuyi yu rujia wenhua" [Nationalism and Confucian Culture], *Zhanlüe yu guanli*, 1996, no. 15, 51–7.
30 See He Dongchang, "Preface," in National Education Committee, Elementary Education section (ed.) *Wuwang guochi* [Never Forget National Humiliation], Tianjin: Xinlei chubanshe, 1991, p. 1.
31 For an early discussion of the dynamic between *Guoxue* and National Humiliation see Hou Hongjian, "Guoxue, guochi, laoku sanda zhuyi biaolie" [Three Principles: National Studies, National Humiliation and Hard Work], *Jiaoyu zazhi*, 1915, vol. 7: 7, 21–4.
32 Guo Qifu (ed.) *Wuwang guochi: zaichuang huihuang* [Never Forget National Humiliation: Recreating the Glory], Wuhan: Wuhan daxue chubanshe, 1996, p. 126.

33 Ibid.
34 For a more detailed discussion of National Humiliation and international politics, see William A. Callahan, "National Insecurities: Humiliation, Salvation and Chinese Nationalism," *Alternatives*, 2004, vol. 29: 2, 199–218; Peter Hays Gries, *China's New Nationalism: Pride, Politics and Diplomacy*, Berkeley, CA: University of California Press, 2004, pp. 43–53; William A. Callahan, "History, Identity and Security: Producing and Consuming Nationalism in China," *Critical Asian Studies*, 2006, vol. 38: 2 (forthcoming).
35 See Liu, "New Migrants and the Revival of Overseas Chinese Nationalism."
36 See Bolt, *China and Southeast Asia's Ethnic Chinese*, pp. 3, 9, 1; Zhao Wen, "Dui 'Zhongguo jingji quan' gezhong yilunde pingshu" [A Review of "Chinese Economic Sphere" Discourse], *Huaqiao Huaren lishi yanjiu*, 1995, no. 1, 63–70; Callahan, *Contingent States*, pp. 8–12.
37 John Naisbitt, *Megatrends Asia*, London: Nicolas Brealey, 1996, p. 7; Tu Weiming, "Cultural China: the Periphery as the Center," in Tu Weiming (ed.) *The Living Tree: The Changing Meaning of Being Chinese Today*, Stanford, CA: Stanford University Press, 1994, p. 12.
38 Wang, *The Chinese Overseas*, p. 43; Adam McKeown, "Conceptualizing Chinese Diasporas, 1842 to 1949," *Journal of Asian Studies*, 1999, vol. 58: 2, 323.
39 Ren Guixiang and Zhao Hongying, *Huaqiao Huaren yu guogong guanxi* [Overseas Chinese and Nationalist Party-Communist Party Relations], Wuhan: Wuhan daxue chubanshe, 1999, p. 2.
40 Wang, *The Chinese Overseas*, p. 47.
41 Ibid., p. 53.
42 Ibid., p. 46; Duara, "Nationalists Among Transnationals," pp. 42–3.
43 Ren and Zhao, *Overseas Chinese*, pp. 380–1, 1.
44 Shen Jinglin, "Foreword," in Revolutionary History Museum of China (ed.) *Zhongguo: cong quru zouxiang huihuang, 1840–1997*, vol. 1 [China: From Humiliation to Glory, 1840–1997, vol. 1], Beijing: Zhongguo minzu sheying yishu, 1997, p. 7; Callahan, *Contingent States*, pp. 146–57. This museum is one of the key institutions of the discourse of National Humiliation.
45 Shen, "Foreword," p. 5; Yang Wanxiu, "Zhongguo jindaishi kaiduan yu huaqiao" [Overseas Chinese and the Start of Modern History in China], *Bagui qiaoshi*, 1991, no. 9, 47.
46 Ren and Zhao, *Overseas Chinese*, p. 380.
47 Cited in Wang, *The Chinese Overseas*, pp. 68–9.
48 Ibid., p. 67. This is the main topic of Ren and Zhao's *Overseas Chinese and Nationalist Party-Communist Party Relations*.
49 See Liu, "New Migrants and the Revival of Overseas Chinese Nationalism," pp. 301–3.
50 Wang, *The Chinese Overseas*, p. 60.
51 Ren and Zhao, *Overseas Chinese*, pp. 8–9.
52 McKeown, "Conceptualizing Chinese Diasporas," p. 326; Yang, "Overseas Chinese," p. 45.
53 Liang Zhiwen (ed.) *Wuwang guochi* [Never Forget National Humiliation], Jilin: Jilin wenshi, 1999, pp. 25–31; Jiang Gongsheng, *Guochi shi* [History of National Humiliation], Shanghai: Xinhua shuju, 1927, pp. 281–93; Yang, "Overseas Chinese," p. 43.
54 See Clifford, "Diasporas"; Gerard Chaliand and Jean-Pierre Rageau, *The Penguin Atlas of Diasporas*, New York: Penguin, 1997.
55 Ian Buruma, "The Joys and Perils of Victimhood," *New York Review of Books*, 8 April 1999, 4.
56 Chirot and Reid, *Essential Outsiders*.

57 Asavabahu [King Rama VI], "The Jews of the East," in Kenneth Perry Landon, *The Chinese in Thailand*, Oxford: Oxford University Press, 1941, pp. 34–43.
58 Anthony Reid, "Entrepreneurial Minorities, Nationalism and the State," in Chirot and Reid, *Essential Outsiders*, p. 51.
59 Chang Noi (pseud.), "Revisiting Dark Corners of Our Political Past," *The Nation* (Bangkok), 24 September 1997; also see Kasian Tejapira, *Chaosivilai: kanmuang wattanatham Thai tai ngoa IMF* [Civilized People: Thai Political Culture under the Shadow of the IMF], Bangkok: Mulanithi Komol Kheemthong, 1999, pp. 33–7.
60 See Robison, *Politics and Markets*.
61 See Kevin Hewison, "Thailand's Capitalism Before and After the Economic Crisis," in Robison, *Politics and Markets*, pp. 192–211.
62 "Khamprakat haeng yuksamai" [Declaration of the Era], *Setthasart kanmuang*, 2000, no. 15, 13ff; Prapat Panyachatirat, Kitti Limsakun, Patadej Thammacharee and Jiradej Sakunneeya, "Khamprakat chatniyom mai" [Manifesto of Neo-Nationalism], *Setthasart kanmuang*, 2000, no. 15, 225–8.
63 Numerous articles in newspapers and magazines were published on the topic, as well as a special issue of another Thai journal, *Kanmuang mai-New Politics*, which is much more critical of neo-nationalism ("Chatniyom: udomkan, yutthasat, yutthawiti?" [Nationalism: Ideology, Strategy or Tactic?], *Kanmuang mai* (Special issue on Nationalism), 2001, vol. 1: 4, pp. 24–39). It is noteworthy that the neo-nationalist articles appeared in *Setthasart kanmuang*, a journal otherwise known for its critical left-wing perspective.
64 Wittayakorn Chiangkoon, "Chatniyom tang setthakit lae sangkhom prachatthipatai mai khue tang rod khong sangkhom Thai" [Economic Nationalism and New Social Democracy is the Survival of Thai Society], *Setthasart kanmuang*, 2000, no. 15, 199–204; Narong Chokwattana, "Phonkratob thurakit jak wikrit kanmuang pajuban" [The Business Impact of the Current Political Crisis], *Setthasart kanmuang*, 2000, no. 15, 81–113; Kasian, *Civilized People*, p. 41.
65 See Ministry of the Interior, *Setthakit chumchon phungtongeng: naew khwamkit lae yatthasat* [The Self-Sufficient Economy: Thoughts and Strategies], Bangkok: Krasuang mahatthai, 1998.
66 Kevin Hewison, "Resisting Globalization: a Study of Localism in Thailand," *Pacific Review*, 2000, vol. 13: 2, 291; Chang Noi (pseud.), "Nationalism and White Peril," *The Nation* (Bangkok), 13 November 2000.
67 Chang, "Nationalism and White Peril."
68 *The Nation* (Bangkok), 12 February 1998.
69 Narong Phechprasert in Nantiya Tangwisutijit, "Rethinking Nationalism: Is It Always Evil?," *The Nation* (Bangkok), 5 November 2000, p. 5.
70 Amarin Khoman, "Thai mee ekkarat pro rao mee chatniyom" [Thailand Has Independence Because We Have Nationalism], *Setthasart kanmuang*, 2000, no. 15, 177–82; Pasuk and Baker, *Thailand's Crisis*, p. 176.
71 Chaiwat Satha-Anand, Interview in Bangkok, 14 December 2000; Prapat, "Manifesto of Neo-Nationalism," pp. 225–8; Dej Phomkhacha, "Khamprakat lakkan lae jet jamnong kan pattana peua khuampen Thai" [The Manifesto of Principles and Wishes to Develop the State of the Free], *Setthasart kanmuang*, 2000, no. 15, 205–10; Somchai Rattanakomut, "Chatniyom: prarachatdamri nai prabat somdej pramongkut klao kap tangkae wikrit settakit" [Nationalism: King Vajiravudh's Ideas and Solutions for the Economic Crisis], *Setthasart sanmuang*, 2000, no. 15, 45–55; Pasuk and Baker, *Thailand's Crisis*, p. 215; Chang, "Nationalism and White Peril."
72 "Declaration of the Era," pp. 18–22; Narong, "The Business Impact," pp. 94–5; Kasian, *Civilized People*, p. 41; Pasuk and Baker, *Thailand's Crisis*, pp. 161ff.

73 Likhit Dheravekhin, "Prachathai tong ruamjai kan ku chat pracharat tong prakat khuampen Thai" [Thai People Have to Unite to Save the Nation], *Setthasart kanmuang*, 2000, no. 15, 171–6; also see Amarin Khoman, "Unctad Go Home!," *Bangkok Post*, 13 February 2000.
74 Kasian, *Civilized People*, p. 197; also see Chang, "Revisiting Dark Corners of Our Political Past"; "Nationalism: Ideology, Strategy or Tactic?"
75 Narong Chokwattana in "Nationalism: Ideology, Strategy or Tactic?," p. 24; Dej, "The Manifesto of Principles and Wishes to Develop the State of the Free"; Wittiyakorn, "Economic Nationalism"; Kasian, *Civilized People*; Nidhi Aoesriwong in "Nationalism: Ideology, Strategy or Tactic?," p. 9.
76 Kasian Tejapira, "Imagined Uncommunity: The Lookjin Middle Class and Thai Official Nationalism," in Chirot and Reid, *Essential Outsiders*, p. 88; Likhit, "Thai People Have to Unite to Save the Nation"; Amarin, "Thailand Has Independence Because We Have Nationalism"; Nantiya, "Rethinking Nationalism"; Kasian, *Civilized People*.
77 Kasian, *Civilized People*, pp. 40–1; also see Suwanna Satha-Anand, Interview in Bangkok, 27 August 1999; Author's interviews in Phuket, December 2000.
78 Hewison, "Thailand's Capitalism," p. 219; Pasuk and Baker, *Thailand's Crisis*, p. 218.
79 Rajeswary Ampalavanar-Brown, "Overseas Chinese Investments in China – Patterns of Growth, Diversification and Finance: The Case of the Charoen Pokphand," *China Quarterly*, 1998, no. 155, 611.
80 Wichit Srisang, "Khamprakat chatniyom mai" [Manifesto of Neo-nationalism], *Setthasart kanmuang*, 2000, no. 15, 224; also see Chang, "Nationalism and White Peril."
81 Suthachai Yimprasert, "Lathichatniyom kap kan totan jakrawatniyom America 14 tulakom B.E. 2516 lae 6 tulakom B.E. 2519" [New Nationalism and Anti-American Imperialism During 14 October 1973 to 6 October 1976], *Setthasart kanmuan*, 2000, no. 15, 68; Chang, "Nationalism and White Peril"; Narong Phechprasert in Nantiya, "Rethinking Nationalism."
82 "Declaration of the Era," pp. 22–6; Likhit, "Thai People Have to Unite to Save the Nation"; Wichit, "Manifesto of Neo-nationalism, pp. 221ff; Kasian, *Civilized People*, p. 41.
83 McKeown, "Conceptualizing Chinese Diasporas," p. 322; Liu, "Old Linkages, New Networks."
84 Viraphon Sopha, farmers' organizer in Northeast Thailand, in "Nationalism: Ideology, Strategy or Tactic?," p. 26; Pasuk and Baker, *Thailand's Crisis*, pp. 172–4; Chang, "Revisiting Dark Corners of Our Political Past."
85 *Diqijie shijie Huang shizong guanzonghui* [Seventh World Huang Clan Convention (in Thai and Chinese)], Bangkok, 4–5 December 1999; Liu "Old Linkages, New Networks," p. 586.
86 See Callahan, *Contingent States*, pp. 179–217.
87 Huang Youhe in *Diqijie*, p. 16; Huang Song in *Diqijie*, p. 13; Huang Tongqing in *Diqijie*, p. 18. Bolt and McKeown make similar points for other migrant associations (Bolt, *China and Southeast Asia's Ethnic Chinese*, p. 31; McKeown, "Conceptualizing Chinese Diasporas," p. 326).
88 Liu, "Old Linkages, New Networks," p. 586; *Diqijie*, pp. 47–8.
89 Thai Foreign Ministry official, Interview in Bangkok, 15 December 2000.
90 Ah Gok Liang, Manager of the Huang Association of Thailand, Interview in Bangkok, 16 December 2000.
91 *The Penguin Atlas of Diasporas* has a map that traces the Southern route. Curiously, it does not list Phuket as a site on this itinerary (see Chaliand and Rageau, *The Penguin Atlas of Diasporas*, p. 131).

92 Lt. Phummisak Hongsyok, mayor of Phuket Municipality and vice president of the Hokkien Association, Interview in Phuket, 21 December 2000.
93 McKeown, "Conceptualizing Chinese Diasporas," p. 316; Carl A. Trocki, *Opium, Empire and the Global Political Economy*, London: Routledge, 1999.
94 Small businessman, Interview in Phuket, 28 December 2000; Phummisak, Interview.
95 Thai-Hua School alumni, Interview in Phuket, 21 December 2000.
96 Wang Gungwu, *Community and Nation: China, Southeast and Australia*, new edn, Sydney: Allen & Unwin, 1992, p. 40.
97 *Thirakruek phiti poed akhan mai chalong khrup rop 90 pi Phuket Thai-Hua* [Commemoration on the Grand Opening of the New Building for the 90th Anniversary of the Phuket Thai Hua School, 17 February 1999], Phuket: Krongthong, 1999, p. 93; Kasian, "Imagined Uncommunity," p. 95.
98 *Nangsue thi raruk sanchao Kathu shangwat Phuket 1 kanyayon B.E. 2539* [Chinese Temple at Kathu, Phuket], Phuket: Wisetoffset compu, 1996, p. 12; Chaiyooth Pinpradab, vice president of the Kathu Temple, Interview in Phuket, 19 December 2000. In Thai "*sanjao*-Chinese temple" means a Daoist rather than a Buddhist temple.
99 Officers of the Hokkien Association of Phuket, Interview in Phuket, 25 December 2000; Chaiyooth, Interview.
100 Niranam (pseud.), "Kan jat tang samakhom chao changwat Mahasarakham" [How the Mahasarakham Association Was Founded], in Thasaanachan Phumiphan (ed.) *Samakhom chao changwat Mahasarakham B.E. 2536* [Mahasarakham Association 1993], Mahasarakham: Aphichart kanphim, 1993, p. 9; Nareerat Parisuthiwuttiporn, history lecturer at the University of Mahasarakham, Interview in Mahasarakham, 8 August 2001; Thasaanachan Phumiphan, Interview in Mahasarakham, 9 August 2001.
101 See Nareerat Parisuthiwuttiporn, "Role of Chinese in Mahasarakham: Municipal to Local Politics," Working Paper Series, Centre for Thai Studies, University of Leeds, UK, 2000, p. 6; Yoko Ueda, "The Entrepreneurs of Khorat," in Ruth McVey (ed.) *Money & Power in Provincial Thailand*, Singapore and London: Institute for Southeast Asian Studies Press, 2000, p. 181.
102 Niranam, "How the Mahasarakham Association Was Founded," pp. 12, 10.
103 Thasaanachan, Interview.
104 Thavesilp Subwattana, History Professor at the University of Mahasarakham, Interview in Mahasarakham, 10 August 2001.

**Conclusion**

1 See William A. Callahan, "How to Understand China: The Dangers and Opportunities of Being a Rising Power," *Review of International Studies*, 2005, vol. 31: 4, 701–14; Shaun Breslin, "Power and Production: Rethinking China's Global Economic Role," *Review of International Studies*, 2005, vol. 31: 4, 735–53; Arif Dirlik, "Asia Pacific Studies in an Age of Global Modernity," *Inter-Asia Cultural Studies*, 2005, vol. 6: 2.
2 William A. Callahan, *Contingent States: Greater China and Transnational Relations*, Minneapolis, MN: University of Minnesota Press, 2004, pp. 1–24.
3 Jinhua Dai, "Foreword," in Chen Xiaomei, *Occidentalism: A Theory of Counter-Discourse in Post-Mao China*, 2nd edn, Lanham, MD: Rowman & Littlefield Publishers, 2002, p. ix.
4 Zhang Hongtu, "Chairmen Mao," www.MoMao.com (accessed on 14 August 2005); Geremie R. Barmé, *Shades of Mao: The Posthumous Cult of the Great Leader*, Armonk, NY: M.E. Sharpe, 1996, p. 47.
5 Barmé, *Shades of Mao*, p. 12.

## Notes 223

6 Edgar Snow, *The Other Side of the River: Red China Today*, London: Gollancz, 1963, p. 151; Barmé, *Shades of Mao*, p. 14.
7 David E. Apter and Tony Saich, *Revolutionary Discourse in Mao's Republic*, Cambridge, MA: Harvard University Press, 1994, pp. xiv, xi.
8 Ibid., p. x.
9 Ibid., p. 10.
10 See ibid.; Michael Schoenhals, *Doing Things with Words in Chinese Politics: Five Studies*, Berkeley, CA: Institute of East Asian Studies, University of California, 1992.
11 Apter and Saich, *Revolutionary Discourse in Mao's Republic*, p. 306; Xin Yuan in Barmé, *Shades of Mao*, p. 197; Barmé, *Shades of Mao*, p. 40.
12 Chen Yun in Schoenhals, *Doing Things with Words in Chinese Politics*, p. 26.
13 Apter and Saich, *Revolutionary Discourse in Mao's Republic*, pp. 312–18.
14 Edgar Snow in Barmé, *Shades of Mao*, pp. 19–20.
15 Michel Foucault, "Governmentality," in Graham Burchell, Colin Gordon and Peter Miller (eds) *The Foucault Effect: Studies in Governmentality*, London: Harvester Wheatsheaf, 1991, pp. 91–2.
16 See Michael Dutton, "Mango Mao: Inflections of the Sacred," *Public Culture*, 2004, vol. 16: 2, 174; Xin Yuan in Barmé, *Shades of Mao*, p. 196.
17 Schoenhals, *Doing Things with Words in Chinese Politics*, p. 19.
18 Barmé, *Shades of Mao*, p. 9.
19 Schoenhals, *Doing Things with Words in Chinese Politics*, pp. 24–5.
20 Zhou Jihou in Barmé, *Shades of Mao*, p. 203; Barmé, *Shades of Mao*, pp. 19–20.
21 Dutton, "Mango Mao," p. 182.
22 Zhang Hongtu in Barmé, *Shades of Mao*, p. 214.
23 For a Chinese view of this see Hai Feng in Barmé, *Shades of Mao*, p. 238.
24 Dutton, "Mango Mao," p. 183.
25 See Julia Kristeva, *About Chinese Women*, London: Boyars, 1977; Rey Chow, *Woman and Chinese Modernity: The Politics of Reading between East and West*, Minneapolis, MN: University of Minnesota Press, 1991, pp. 7–9.
26 Rey Chow, *Writing Diaspora: Tactics of Intervention in Contemporary Cultural Studies*, Bloomington, IN: University of Indiana Press, 1993, pp. 12–13, 18.
27 Many thanks to Alexander Akin for pointing this out. Revolution Books has stores in key university cities.
28 Central Dept of Propaganda and News and Publishing Administration Circular Concerning Publication Work Related to the Commemoration of the Centenary of Comrade Mao Zedong's Birth (24 March 1992) in Barmé, *Shades of Mao*, p. 235.
29 Barmé, *Shades of Mao*, p. 20.
30 See Xin Yuan in Barmé, *Shades of Mao*, pp. 195–200.
31 Schoenhals, *Doing Things with Words in Chinese Politics*, p. 20.
32 Dutton, "Mango Mao," p. 171.
33 "Central Department of Propaganda Request for Instructions Concerning the Disposal of Extant Objects Related to 'Loyalty' (28 July 1978)," in Barmé, *Shades of Mao*, p. 129; also see Zhou Jihou in Barmé, *Shades of Mao*, pp. 201–10.
34 Zhou Jihou in Barmé, *Shades of Mao*, p. 203.
35 Barmé, *Shades of Mao*, p. 9.
36 Xin Yuan in Barmé, *Shades of Mao*, p. 195.
37 See Gao Jiangbo in Barmé, *Shades of Mao*, pp. 135–7.
38 See, for example, a recent restaurant review of a Beijing branch: Ye Jun, "Mao Family Cuisine," *China Daily*, 12 August 2005.
39 Barmé, *Shades of Mao*, p. 5.
40 Anonymous in Barmé, *Shades of Mao*, p. 283.

41 Barmé, *Shades of Mao*, p. 12.
42 This passage has been adapted from Wang Shuo in Barmé, *Shades of Mao*, pp. 225, 226, and Wang Shuo, *Please Don't Call Me Human*, Howard Goldblatt, trans., London: No Exit Press, 2000, p. 273.
43 See Schoenhals, *Doing Things with Words in Chinese Politics*, p. 21.
44 Zhang Hongtu, "Chairmen Mao"; Barmé, *Shades of Mao*, pp. 43, 101, and the front cover.
45 He Xin in Barmé, *Shades of Mao*, p. 157.
46 See Vera Schwarcz, "Memory and Commemoration: The Chinese Search for a Liveable Past," in Jeffrey N. Wasserstrom and Elizabeth J. Perry (eds) *Popular Protest and Popular Culture in Modern China*, 2nd edn, Boulder, CO: Westview Press, 1994, p. 177.
47 See Jiang Shui and Tie Zhu, *Mao Zedong's Military Philosophy and Modern Business Wars*, in Barmé, *Shades of Mao*, p. 183; Mao is prominent in the advertisement announcing the launch of *Forbes Global* see *Financial Times*, 15 January 1998, p. 7.
48 Barmé, *Shades of Mao*, p. 35.
49 Ibid., p. 22.
50 Robert J.C. Young, *Postcolonialism: A Very Short Introduction*, Oxford: Oxford University Press, 2003, p. 112.

# Bibliography

In this bibliography, Chinese names have been alphabetized by their family names, and Thai names by their given names, which are both conventionally presented first in these countries.

"500 xianjin renmin zuzhi yinling Zhongguo NGO chaoliu: quanguo sianjin minjian zuzhi biaoyinghui zai jing zhaokai" [500 advanced people's organizations show China's NGO wave: nationwide advanced people's organizations award ceremony opens in Beijing], *Xuehui*, 2005, no. 1, 4–5.
Ahluwalia, Pal and Peter Mayer, "Clash of Civilizations – or Balderdash of Scholars?," *Asian Studies Review*, 1994, vol. 18: 1, 21–30.
Allen, Robert C., "Talking About Television," in Robert C. Allen, (ed.) *Channels of Discourse: Television and Contemporary Criticism*, Chapel Hill, NC: University of North Carolina Press, 1987, pp. 1–16.
Alloula, Malek, *The Colonial Harem*, Minneapolis, MN: University of Minnesota Press, 1986.
Amarin Khoman, "Thai mee ekkarat pro rao mee chatniyom" [Thailand Has Independence Because We Have Nationalism], *Setthasart kanmuang*, 2000, no. 15, 177–82.
Ames, Roger T., "Continuing the Conversation on Chinese Human Rights," *Ethics and International Affairs*, 1997, no. 11, 177–205.
Ampalavanar-Brown, Rajeswary, "Overseas Chinese Investments in China – Patterns of Growth, Diversification and Finance: The Case of the Charoen Pokphand," *China Quarterly*, 1998, no. 155, 610–36.
Anderson, Benedict, "Murder and Progress in Siam," *New Left Review*, 1990, no. 181, 33–48.
—— *Imagined Communities: Reflections on the Origin and Spread of Nationalism*, revised edn, London: Verso, 1991.
—— "Cacique Democracy in the Philippines: Origins and Dreams," in Vicente L. Rafael (ed.) *Discrepant Histories: Translocal Chapters on Filipino Cultures*, Philadelphia, PA: Temple University Press, 1995, pp. 3–50.
Anek Laothammatas, *Business Associations and the Political Economy of Thailand: From Bureaucratic Polity to Liberal Corporatism*, Boulder, CO: Westview Press, 1992.
—— "Sleeping Giant Awakens: The Middle Class in Thai Politics," *Asian Review 1993*, vol. 7, 78–125.

## 226  Bibliography

—— *Song nakhara prachathipatai: Naewthang kanmuang sethakit peua prachathipatai* [A Tale of Two Democracies: The Road to Political Economic Reform for Democracy], Bangkok: Matichon Books, 1995.

—— "A Tale of Two Democracies: Conflicting Perceptions of Elections and Democracy in Thailand," in R.H. Taylor (ed.) *The Politics of Elections in Southeast Asia*, Cambridge: Cambridge University Press, 1996, pp. 201–23.

ANFREL (Asian Network for Free Elections), *The Emergence of New Politics in Thailand: ANFREL Election Report, 6 January–18 August 2001*, Bangkok: ANFREL and FORUM-ASIA, 2001.

Ang, Ien, "Desperately Guarding Borders: Media Globalization, 'Cultural Imperialism,' and the Rise of 'Asia'," in Yao Souchou (ed.) *House of Glass: Culture, Modernity, and the State in Southeast Asia*, Singapore and London: Institute of Southeast Asian Studies, 2001, pp. 27–45.

Appadurai, Arjun, *Modernity at Large: Cultural Dimensions of Globalization*, Minneapolis, MN: University of Minnesota Press, 1996.

Appiah, Kwame Anthony, "Is the Post- in Postmodernism the Post- in Postcolonial?," *Critical Inquiry*, 1991, vol. 17: 2, 336–57.

Apter, David E. and Tony Saich, *Revolutionary Discourse in Mao's Republic*, Cambridge, MA: Harvard University Press, 1994.

Aquino, Corazon, Oscar Arias and Kim Dae-jung, *Democracy in Asia*, Seoul: Asia-Pacific Peace Press, 1995.

Areeya Chumsai, *Muat Pop* [Lt. Pop] (English title: *Boot Camp*), Bangkok: Future Publishing, 1998.

Arghiros, Daniel, *Democracy, Development and Decentralization in Provincial Thailand*, Richmond, UK: Curzon, 2001.

Aristotle, *The Politics*, New York: Penguin Classics, 1981.

Asan Foundation, *Asan Foundation Annual Report*, Seoul: Asan Foundation, 1997.

Asavabahu [King Rama VI], "The Jews of the East," in Kenneth Perry Landon, *The Chinese in Thailand*, Oxford: Oxford University Press, 1941, pp. 34–43.

Aung San Suu Kyi, "Keynote Address to the NGO Forum Plenary, Fourth World Conference on Women," Bangkok: Asian Forum for Human Rights and Development Videos, 1995.

—— *Freedom from Fear*, revised edn, London: Penguin, 1995.

Bakken, Børge, *The Exemplary Society: Human Improvement, Social Control, and the Dangers of Modernity in China*, Oxford: Oxford University Press, 2000.

Bamrungsuk, Surachart, *United States Foreign Policy and Thai Military Rule 1947–1977*, Bangkok: Editions Duang Kamol, 1988.

*Banthuk "paap kham-hetkarn" prawatthhisat phrusaphakorn thamin* [Historical Records of "Pictures-speeches-events" of Black May], Bangkok: Manager, 1992.

*Banthuk phrusaphat maia wiphayok* [Records of Sad May], 2nd edn, Bangkok: The Nation Publishing Group, 1992.

*Banthuk yiewkhao na samoraphum thanon rajadamnoen phrusaphakom B.E. 2535* [Journalists' Records from the Battleground on Rajadamnoen Road May 1992], Bangkok: Reporters' Association of Thailand, 1992.

Bao, Jiemin, "Same Bed, Different Dreams: Intersections of Ethnicity, Gender, and Sexuality Among Middle- and Upper-Class Chinese Immigrants in Bangkok," *positions: east asia cultures critique*, 1998, vol. 6: 2, 475–502.

Barbey, Bruno, *mai 68: ou l'imagination au pouvoir*, Paris: L'Difference, 1998.

Barmé, Geremie R., *Shades of Mao: The Posthumous Cult of the Great Leader*, Armonk, NY: M.E. Sharpe, 1996.

—— *In the Red: On Contemporary Chinese Culture*, New York: Columbia University Press, 1999.
—— and Linda Jaivin (eds), *New Ghosts, Old Dreams: Chinese Rebel Voices*, New York: Times Books, 1992.
Barmé, Scot, *Luang Wichit Wathakan and the Creation of a Thai Identity*, Singapore and London: Institute for Southeast Asian Studies, 1993.
Barthes, Roland, *Mythologies*, New York: The Noonday Press, 1972.
—— *Image/Music/Text*, New York: Hill and Wang, 1977.
—— *Camera Lucida: Reflections on Photography*, New York: Hill and Wang, 1981.
Bartley, Robert, Chan Heng Chee, Samuel P. Huntington and Shijuro Ogata, *Democracy & Capitalism: Asian and American Perspectives*, Singapore: Institute of Southeast Asian Studies, 1994.
Bell, Daniel A., *East Meets West: Human Rights and Democracy in East Asia*, Princeton, NJ: Princeton University Press, 2000.
Bell, Daniel A. and Hahm Chaibong (eds), *Confucianism for the Modern World*, Cambridge: Cambridge University Press, 2003.
Berger, John, *Ways of Seeing*, New York: Penguin Press, 1977.
Berger, Peter L., "An East Asian Development Model?," in Peter L. Berger and Hsin-Huang Michael Hsiao (eds) *In Search of an East Asian Development Model*, Oxford: Transaction Books, 1988, pp. 3–11.
Bolt, Paul J., *China and Southeast Asia's Ethnic Chinese: State and Diaspora in Contemporary Asia*, Westport, CT: Praeger, 2000.
Boudreau, Vince, *Resisting Dictatorship: Repression and Protest in Southeast Asia*, Cambridge: Cambridge University Press, 2004.
Bratsis, Peter, "The Construction of Corruption, or Rules of Separation and Illusions of Purity in Bourgeois Societies," *Social Text* 77, 2003, vol. 21, 9–33.
Breslin, Shaun, "Power and Production: Rethinking China's Global Economic Role," *Review of International Studies*, 2005, vol. 31: 4, 735–53.
Buruma, Ian, "The Joys and Perils of Victimhood," *New York Review of Books*, 8 April 1999, 4–9.
—— and Avishai Margalit, *Occidentalism: The West in the Eyes of Its Enemies*, New York: Penguin, 2004.
Bush, George [H.W.], "Text of Remarks by the President at the Conclusion of the United States-Pacific Island Nations Summit," Honolulu: East–West Center, 27 October 1990.
Callahan, William A., "The Discourse of Democracy in Thailand: A Struggle for Meaning," *Asian Review 1993*, vol. 7, 126–70.
—— "Resisting the Norm: Ironic Images of Marx and Confucius," *Philosophy East and West*, 1994, vol. 44: 2, 279–302.
—— *Imagining Democracy: Reading the Events of May in Thailand*, Singapore and London: Institute of Southeast Asian Studies, 1998.
—— "Challenging the Order: Social Movements," in Richard Maidment, Jeremy Mitchell and David Goldblatt (eds) *Governance in the Asia-Pacific*, London: Routledge, 1998, pp. 150–71.
—— *PollWatching, Elections and Civil Society in Southeast Asia*, Aldershot: Ashgate, 2000.
—— "Political Corruption in Southeast Asia," in Robert Williams (ed.) *Party Finance and Political Corruption*, London: Macmillan, 2000, pp. 163–98.
—— *Contingent States: Greater China and Transnational Relations*, Minneapolis, MN: University of Minnesota Press, 2004.

—— "National Insecurities: Humiliation, Salvation and Chinese Nationalism," *Alternatives*, 2004, vol. 29: 2, 199–218.

—— "How to Understand China: The Dangers and Opportunities of Being a Rising Power," *Review of International Studies*, 2005, vol. 31: 4, 701–14.

—— "History, Identity and Security: Producing and Consuming Nationalism in China," *Critical Asian Studies*, 2006, vol. 38: 2 (forthcoming).

—— and Duncan McCargo, "Vote-buying in the Thai Northeast: The July 1995 General Election," *Asian Survey*, 1996, vol. 36: 4, 376–92.

—— and Steve Olive, "Chemical Weapons Disposal in the *South Pacific*," *boundary 2*, 1995, vol. 22: 1, 263–85.

Campbell, David, *Writing Security: United States Foreign Policy and the Politics of Identity*, revised edn, Minneapolis, MN: University of Minnesota Press, 1998.

—— "Cultural Governance and Pictorial Resistance: Reflections on the Imaging of War," *Review of International Studies*, 2003, vol. 29 (Special Issue), 57–73.

Cao Haidong, "Zhongguo xinsheng dai NGO chiqi" [The Rise of China's New Generation of NGOs], *Jingji*, 2004, no. 5, 45.

Castle, Gregory (ed.), *Postcolonial Discourses: An Anthology*, Oxford: Blackwell Publishers, 2001.

*Catalyst for Change: Uprising in May*, Bangkok: Bangkok Post, 1992.

Centre for Information on Local Politics in the Northeast, *Kan chai nguen ha siang khong phak kanmuang nai kan luektang phuthaen rasadorn, 6 Makkarakhom 2544* [Political Party Campaign Expenditure for the House of Representatives Election 6 January 2001], Mahasarakham: University of Mahasarakham, 3 May 2001.

Chai-anan Samudavanaija, *The Thai Young Turks*, Singapore and London: Institute for Southeast Asian Studies, 1983.

Chaliand, Gerard and Jean-Pierre Rageau, *The Penguin Atlas of Diasporas*, New York: Penguin, 1997.

Chamberlain, Heath B., "On the Search for Civil Society in China," *Modern China*, 1993, vol. 19: 2, 199–215.

Chan, Adrian, "In Search of Civil Society in China," *Journal of Contemporary Asia*, 1997, vol. 27: 2, 242–51.

Chan Sin Yee, "The Confucian Conception of Gender in the Twenty-First Century," in Daniel A. Bell and Hahm Chaibong (eds), *Confucianism for the Modern World*, Cambridge: Cambridge University Press, 2003, pp. 312–33.

Chang, Mau-Kuei, "Civil Society, Resource Mobilization, and New Social Movements: Theoretical Implications for the Study of Social Movements in Taiwan," *Chinese Sociology and Anthropology*, 1997, vol. 29: 4, 7–41.

"Chatniyom: udomkan, yutthasat, yutthawiti?" [Nationalism: Ideology, Strategy or Tactic?], *Kanmuang mai* (Special issue on Nationalism), 2001, vol. 1: 4, 24–39.

Chatthip Nartsupha, *Noekhid setthakit chumchon: khosanue thaeng thrisadi naiparibot taeng sungkhom* [The Concept of Community Economics: A Theoretical Proposal for an Alternative Society], Bangkok: Satabun Withithat, 2001.

Cheah, Pheng and Bruce Robbins (eds), *Cosmopolitics: Thinking and Feeling Beyond the Nation*, Minneapolis, MN: University of Minnesota Press, 1998.

Chen Xiaomei, *Occidentalism: A Theory of Counter-Discourse in Post-Mao China*, 2nd edn, Lanham, MD: Rowman & Littlefield Publishers, 2002.

Chirot, Daniel and Anthony Reid (eds), *Essential Outsiders: Chinese and Jews in the Modern Transformation of Southeast Asia and Central Europe*, Seattle, WA: University of Washington Press, 1997.

Cho Hein, "The Historical Origin of Civil Society in Korea," *Korea Journal*, 1997, vol. 37: 2, 24–41.
Chow, Rey, *Woman and Chinese Modernity: The Politics of Reading between East and West*, Minneapolis, MN: University of Minnesota Press, 1991.
—— "Violence in the Other Country," in Chandra Talpade Mohanty, Ann Russo and Lourdes Torres (eds) *Third World Women and the Politics of Feminism*, Bloomington, IN: Indiana University Press, 1991, pp. 81–100.
—— *Writing Diaspora: Tactics of Intervention in Contemporary Cultural Studies*, Bloomington, IN: University of Indiana Press, 1993.
Chua Beng-Huat, *Communitarian Ideology and Democracy in Singapore*, London: Routledge, 1995.
Chun, Allen, "An Oriental Orientalism: The Paradox of Tradition and Modernity in Nationalist Taiwan," *History and Anthropology*, 1995, vol. 9: 1, 27–56.
Chung, Chulhee, "Social Movement Organizations and the June Uprising," *Korea Journal*, 1997, vol. 37: 2, 24–41.
Clements, Alan and Leslie Kean, *Burma's Revolution of the Spirit: The Struggle for Democratic Freedom and Dignity*, Bangkok: White Orchid Press, 1995.
Clifford, James, "Diasporas," *Cultural Anthropology*, 1994, vol. 9: 3, 302–38.
Connors, Michael Kelly, "Political Reform and the State in Thailand," *Journal of Contemporary Asia*, 1999, vol. 29, 202–26.
—— *Democracy and National Identity in Thailand*, London: RoutledgeCurzon, 2003.
—— "Ministering Culture: Hegemony and the Politics of Culture and Identity in Thailand," *Critical Asian Studies*, 2005, vol. 37: 4, 523–51.
*Constitution of the Kingdom of Thailand*, Bangkok: Council of State, 1997, Sections 126–29, available online at www.krisdika.go.th/home.jsp, (accessed on 22 February 2005).
Croissant, Aurel and Jorn Dosch, "Old Wine in New Bottlenecks? Elections in Thailand under the 1997 Constitution," working paper, Leeds, UK: University of Leeds, 2001, p. 13, available online at http://croissant.uni-hd.de/old_wine_in_new_bottlenecks.htm, (accessed on 22 February 2005).
Cumings, Bruce, *Parallax Visions: Making Sense of American-East Asian Relations at the End of the Century*, Durham, NC: Duke University Press, 1999.
Dai Jinhua, "Foreword," in Chen Xiaomei, *Occidentalism: A Theory of Counter-Discourse in Post-Mao China*, 2nd edn, Lanham, MD: Rowman & Littlefield Publishers, 2002, pp. ix–xxiii.
Dalton, Bronwen and James Cotton, "New Social Movements and the Changing Nature of Political Opposition in South Korea," in Garry Rodan (ed.) *Political Oppositions in Industrializing Asia*, London: Routledge, 1996, pp. 272–99.
Dean, Mitchell and Paul Henman (guest eds), "Governing Society Today," a special issue of *Alternatives*, 2004, vol. 29: 5, 483–618.
Dej Phomkhacha, "Khamprakat lakkan lae jet jamnong kan pattana peua khuampen Thai" [The Manifesto of Principles and Wishes to Develop the State of the Free], *Setthasart kanmuang*, 2000, no. 15, 205–10.
Deng Guosheng, "Zhongguo feizhengfu zuzhi fazhande xin huanjing" [The New Environment for the Development of China's NGOs], *Xuehui*, 2004, no. 10, 12–8.
Department of the Army, "Final Second Supplemental Environmental Impact Statement for the Storage and Ultimate Disposal of the European Chemical Munitions Stockpile," Program Manager for Chemical Demilitarization, Aberdeen Proving Ground, Maryland, 1990.

Dillon, Michael, "Sovereignty and Governmentality: From the Problematics of the 'New World Order' to the Ethical Problematic of the World Order," *Alternatives*, 1995, vol. 20: 3, 323–68.
—— "Culture, Governance and Biopolitics," in Francois Debrix and Cynthia Weber (eds) *Rituals of Mediation: International Politics and Social Meaning*, Minneapolis, MN: University of Minnesota Press, 2004, pp. 135–53.
Ding, Yijiang, *Chinese Democracy after Tiananmen*, Vancouver: UBC Press, 2001.
*Diqijie shijie Huang shizong guanzonghui* [Seventh World Huang Clan Convention (in Thai and Chinese)], Bangkok, 4–5 December 1999.
Dirlik, Arif, *The Postcolonial Aura: Third World Criticism in the Age of Global Capitalism*, Boulder, CO: Westview, 1997.
—— (ed.), *What is in a Rim? Critical Perspectives on the Pacific Rim Idea*, 2nd edn, Lanham, MD: Rowman & Littlefield, 1998.
—— "Introduction: Pacific Contradictions," in Arif Dirlik (ed.) *What is in a Rim? Critical Perspectives on the Pacific Rim Idea*, 2nd edn, Lanham, MD: Rowman & Littlefield, 1998, pp. 3–14.
—— "Culture Against History? The Politics of East Asian Identity," *Development and Society*, 1999, vol. 28: 2, 167–90.
—— "Asia Pacific Studies in an Age of Global Modernity," *Inter-Asia Cultural Studies*, 2005, vol. 6: 2.
Dittmer, Lowell, Haruhiro Fukui and Peter N.S. Lee (eds), *Informal Politics in East Asia*, Cambridge: Cambridge University Press, 2000.
Doty, Roxanne Lynn, *Imperial Encounters: The Politics of Representation in North-South Relations*, Minneapolis, MN: University of Minnesota Press, 1996.
Duara, Prasenjit, "Nationalists Among Transnationals: Overseas Chinese and the Idea of China, 1900–1911," in Aihwa Ong and Donald M. Nonini, *Ungrounded Empires: The Cultural Politics of Modern Chinese Transnationalism*, London: Routledge, 1997, pp. 39–60.
Dutton, Michael, *Streetlife China*, Cambridge: Cambridge University Press, 1998.
—— "Mango Mao: Inflections of the Sacred," *Public Culture*, 2004, vol. 16: 2, 161–87.
Eco, Umberto, *A Theory of Semiotics*, Bloomington, IN: Indiana University Press, 1976.
Elshtain, Jean Bethke, *Women and War*, Chicago, IL: University of Chicago Press, 1995.
Emmerson, Donald K., "Singapore and the 'Asian Values' Debate," *Journal of Democracy*, 1995, vol. 6: 4, 95–105.
Enloe, Cynthia, *Bananas, Beaches and Bases: Making Feminist Sense of International Politics* Berkeley, CA: University of California Press, 1989.
—— *The Morning After: Sexual Politics at the End of the Cold War*, Berkeley, CA: University of California Press, 1993.
Feigon, Lee, "Gender and the Chinese Student Movement," in Jeffrey N. Wasserstrom and Elizabeth J. Perry (eds) *Popular Protest and Popular Culture in Modern China*, 2nd edn, Boulder, CO: Westview Press, 1994, pp. 165–76.
Ferguson, Kathy E., *The Feminist Case Against Bureaucracy*, Philadelphia, PA: Temple University Press, 1984.
—— *The Man Question: Visions of Subjectivity in Feminist Theory*, Berkeley, CA: University of California Press, 1993.
—— and Phyllis Turnbull, *Oh, Say, Can You See? The Semiotics of the Military in Hawai'i*, Minneapolis, MN: University of Minnesota Press, 1999.

Flitterman-Lewis, Sandy, "Psychoanalysis, Film, and Television," in Robert C. Allen (ed.) *Channels of Discourse: Television and Contemporary Criticism*, Chapel Hill, NC: University of North Carolina Press, 1987, pp. 172–210.
Foucault, Michel, *The Order of Things: An Archaeology of the Human Sciences*, New York: Pantheon Books, 1970.
—— *Madness and Civilization: A History of Insanity in the Age of Reason*, New York: Vintage, 1973.
—— *The History of Sexuality*, vol. 1, New York: Vintage, 1980.
—— "Afterword: The Subject and Power," in Hubert L. Dreyfus and Paul Rabinow (eds) *Michel Foucault: Beyond Structuralism and Hermeneutics*, New York: The Harvester Press, 1982, pp. 208–26.
—— "Governmentality," in Graham Burchell, Colin Gordon and Peter Miller (eds) *The Foucault Effect: Studies in Governmentality*, London: Harvester Wheatsheaf, 1991, pp. 87–104.
Frolic, Michael B., "State-led Civil Society," in Timothy Brook and Michael B. Frolic (eds) *Civil Society in China*, Armonk, NY: M.E. Sharpe, 1997, pp. 46–67.
Frye, Northrop, *Anatomy of Criticism: Four Chapters*, Princeton, NJ: Princeton University Press, 1957.
Fung, Edmund S.K., *In Search of Chinese Democracy: Civil Opposition in Nationalist China, 1929–1949*, Cambridge: Cambridge University Press, 2000.
Gordon, Richard and Carma Hinton, "The Gate of Heavenly Peace," Boston, MA: Longbow Productions, 1995.
Gothom Arya, "Election System and Events in Thailand," Bangkok: Election Commission of Thailand, 2001, available online at www.ect.go.th, (accessed on 26 July 2003).
Gries, Peter Hays, *China's New Nationalism: Pride, Politics and Diplomacy*, Berkeley, CA: University of California Press, 2004.
Guo Qifu (ed.), *Wuwang guochi: zaichuang huihaung* [Never Forget National Humiliation: Recreating the Glory], Wuhan: Wuhan daxue chubanshe, 1996.
Guo, Xiaoqin, *State and Society in China's Democratic Transition: Confucianism, Leninism, and Economic Development*, London: Routledge, 2003.
Habermas, Jürgen, *The Structural Transformation of the Public Sphere*, Cambridge, MA: MIT Press, 1989.
Hahm Chaibong, "The Confucian Political Discourse and the Politics of Reform in Korea," *Korea Journal*, 1997, vol. 37: 4, 66–73.
—— "Why Asian Values?," *Korea Journal*, 2001, vol. 41: 2, 265–74.
—— "Family Versus the Individual: The Politics of Marriage Laws in Korea," in Daniel A. Bell and Hahm Chaibong (eds) *Confucianism for the Modern World*, Cambridge: Cambridge University Press, 2003, pp. 334–59.
Hall, Rodney Bruce, "The Discursive Demolition of the Asian Development Model," *International Studies Quarterly*, 2003, vol. 47, 71–99.
Hamilton, Annette, "Cinema and Nation: Dilemmas of Representation in Thailand," *East–West Film Journal*, 1993, vol. 7: 1, 81–105.
Hamilton, Gary G. "Overseas Chinese Capitalism," in Tu Wei-ming (ed.) *Confucian Traditions in East Asian Modernity: Moral Education and Economic Culture in Japan and the Four Mini-Dragons*, Cambridge, MA: Harvard University Press, 1996, pp. 328–42.
Han Sang-Jin, "The Public Sphere and Democracy in Korea: A Debate on Civil Society," *Korea Journal*, 1997, vol. 37: 4, 78–97.

—— "Globalization and Postcolonialism: Confucianism and East Asian Development," Paper presented at the Kwangju Biennale International Symposium on "Globalization and Postcolonialism," Kwangju, South Korea, October 1997.

—— (ed.), *Habermas and the Critical Theory Debate in Korea*, Seoul: Seoul National University Press, 1998.

Hardt, Michael and Antonio Negri, *Empire*, Cambridge, MA: Harvard University Press, 2000.

Hauʻofa, Epeli, "Our Sea of Islands," in Rob Wilson and Arif Dirlik (eds) *Asia/Pacific as Space of Cultural Production*, Durham, NC: Duke University Press, 1995, pp. 86–98.

Hay, Jonathan, "Zhang Hongtu/Hongtu Zhang: An Interview," in John Hay (ed.) *Boundaries in China*, London: Reaktion Books, 1994, pp. 280–98.

Hayes, Peter, Lyuba Zarsky and Walden Bello, *American Lake: Nuclear Power in the Pacific*, New York: Penguin, 1986.

Heng, Geraldine and Janadas Devan, "State Fatherhood: The Politics of Nationalism, Sexuality, and Race in Singapore," in Andrew Parker, Mary Russo, Doris Sommer and Patricia Yaeger (eds) *Nationalisms & Sexualities*, New York: Routledge, 1992, pp. 343–64.

Herodotus, *Histories*, New York: Everyman Library, 1964.

Hewison, Kevin, "Thailand's Capitalism Before and After the Economic Crisis," in Richard Robison, Mark Beeson, Kaishka Jayasuriya and Hyuk-Rae Kim (eds) *Politics and Markets in the Wake of the Asian Crisis*, London: Routledge, 2000, pp. 192–211.

—— "Resisting Globalization: a Study of Localism in Thailand," *Pacific Review*, 2000, vol. 13: 2, 279–96.

Hoogvelt, Ankie, *Globalization and the Postcolonial World*, 2nd edn, London: Palgrave, 2001.

Hou Hongjian, "Guoxue, guochi, laoku sanda zhuyi biaolie" [Three Principles: National Studies, National Humiliation and Hard Work], *Jiaoyu zazhi*, 1915, vol. 7: 7, 21–4.

Huang, Philip C.C., "'Public Sphere'/'Civil Society' in China?: The Third Realm between State and Society," *Modern China*, 1993, vol. 19: 2, 216–40.

Hughes, Christopher R., "Globalization and Nationalism: Squaring the Circle in Chinese IR Theory," *Millennium*, 1997, vol. 26: 1, 103–24.

—— "Nationalism in Chinese Cyberspace," *Cambridge Review of International Affairs*, 2000, vol. 13: 2, 195–209.

International Monetary Fund, *Good Governance: The IMF's Role*, Washington, DC: IMF, 1997.

Jiang Gongsheng, *Guochi shi* [History of National Humiliation], Shanghai: Xinhua shuju, 1927.

Jiefangjun huabaoshe [People's Liberation Army Pictorial] (ed.), *Beijing pingxi fangeming baoluan – Quelling the Counter-revolutionary Rebellion in Beijing* [bilingual], Beijing: Changchung chubanshe, 1989.

Johnson, Chalmers, "Tanaka Kakuei, Structural Corruption, and the Advent of Machine Politics in Japan," *Journal of Japan Studies*, 1986, vol. 12: 1, 1–28.

—— *Japan: Who Governs? The Rise of the Developmental State*, New York: WW Norton & Company, 1995.

Johnson, Ian, "The Death and Life of Civil Society in China," *Perspectives on Politics*, 2003, vol. 1: 3, 551–4.

Johnston, Alastair Iain, "Is China a Status Quo Power?," *International Security*, 2003, vol. 27: 4, 5–56.
Johnston, Michael, "The Search for Definitions: the Vitality of Politics and the Issue of Corruption," *International Social Science Journal*, 1996, vol. 149, 321–36.
*June Four: A Chronicle of the Chinese Democratic Uprising*, London: University of Arkansas Press, 1989; translated from *Bei zhuang de mingyun: zuiheping kaishi, zui xuexing jiehsu*, Hong Kong: Ming Pao Publishing House, 1989.
Kanjana Kaewthep, "'East' Meets 'West': The Confrontation of Different Cultures in Thai T.V. Dramas and Films," in Nitaya Masavisut, George Simson and Larry E. Smith (eds) *Gender and Culture in Literature and Film East and West: Issues of Perception and Interpretation*, Honolulu, HI: University of Hawai'i Press, 1994, pp. 180–96.
Kasian Tejapira, "Pigtail: A Pre-History of Chineseness in Siam," *Sojourn*, 1992, vol. 7: 1, 95–122.
—— "Imagined Uncommunity: the Lookjin Middle Class and Thai Official Nationalism," in Daniel Chirot and Anthony Reid (eds) *Essential Outsiders: Chinese and Jews in the Modern Transformation of Southeast Asia and Central Europe*, Seattle, WA: University of Washington Press, 1997, pp. 75–98.
—— *Chaosivilai: kanmuang wattanatham Thai tai ngoa IMF* [Civilized People: Thai Political Culture under the Shadow of the IMF], Bangkok: Mulanithi Komol Kheemthong, 1999.
—— "The Postmodernization of Thainess," in Yao Souchou (ed.) *House of Glass: Culture, Modernity, and the State in Southeast Asia*, Singapore and London: Institute for Southeast Asian Studies, 2001, pp. 150–70.
Katzenstein, Peter J. (ed.), *The Culture of National Security: Norms and Identity in World Politics*, New York: Columbia University Press, 1996.
"Khamprakat haeng yuksamai" [Declaration of the Era], *Setthasart kanmuang*, 2000, no. 15, 13ff.
Kim Dae-Jung, "Is Culture Destiny? The Myth of Asia's Anti-Democratic Values," *Foreign Affairs*, 1994, vol. 73: 6, 189–94.
Kim Kwang-Ok, "The Reproduction of Confucian Culture in Contemporary Korea: An Anthropological Study," in Tu Wei-ming (ed.) *Confucian Traditions in East Asian Modernity: Moral Education and Economic Culture in Japan and the Four Mini-Dragons*, Cambridge, MA: Harvard University Press, 1996, pp. 202–27.
—— "The Role of *Madangguk* in Contemporary Korea's Popular Culture Movement," *Korea Journal*, 1997, vol. 37: 3, 5–21.
Kim Kyong-Dong, "Business and Culture for the Future," *Mécénat*, May–June 1997, translated in *Korea Focus*, 1997, vol. 5: 5, 85–8.
Kim Young Sam, *Korea's Reform and Globalization: President Kim Young Sam Prepares the Nation for the Challenges of the 21st Century*, Seoul: Korea Overseas Information Service, 1997.
Kluver, Randy, "Elite-Based Discourse in Chinese Civil Society," in Randy Kluver and John H. Powers (eds) *Civic Discourse, Civil Society, and Chinese Communities*, Stamford, CT: Ablex Publishing, 1999, pp. 11–22.
Koh Byong-Ik, "Confucianism in Contemporary Korea," in Tu Wei-ming (ed.) *Confucian Traditions in East Asian Modernity: Moral Education and Economic Culture in Japan and the Four Mini-Dragons*, Cambridge, MA: Harvard University Press, 1996, pp. 191–201.

Koo, Hagen, "The State, Minjung, and the Working Class in South Korea," in Hagen Koo (ed.) *State and Society in Contemporary Korea*, Ithaca, NY: Cornell University Press, 1993, pp. 131–62.

Kornhonen, Pekka, "Monopolizing Asia: The Politics of Metaphor," *Pacific Review*, 1997, vol. 10: 3, 347–65.

—— *Japan and Asia Pacific Integration: Pacific Romances 1968–1996*, London: Routledge, 1998.

Kozloff, Sarah Ruth, "Narrative Theory and Television," in Robert C. Allen (ed.) *Channels of Discourse: Television and Contemporary Criticism*, Chapel Hill, NC: University of North Carolina Press, 1987, pp. 42–73.

Kraus, Richard Curt, *The Party and the Arty in China: The New Politics of Culture*, Lanham, MD: Rowman & Littlefield, 2004.

Kristeva, Julia, *About Chinese Women*, London: Boyars, 1977.

Kuo, Liangwen (Wayne) (ed. and trans.), "Taiwan's Social Movements: A Discussion of the State and Civil Society," *Chinese Sociology and Anthropology*, 1997, vol. 29.

de Lauretis, Teresa, *Alice Doesn't: Feminism, Semiotics, Cinema*, Bloomington, IN: University of Indiana Press, 1985.

Lawson, Stephanie, "Cultural Relativism and Democracy: Political Myths about 'Asia' and the 'West'," in Richard Robison (ed.) *Pathways to Asia: The Politics of Engagement*, Sydney: Allen & Unwin, 1996, pp. 108–26.

Lee Kuan Yew, *Sishinian zhenglun xuan* [Selections from 40 Years of Political Writings], Singapore: Lianhe zaobao, 1993.

Lee Seung-Hwan, "Who Dares Bring Disgrace on Tradition?," *Tradition & Modernity*, 1997, vol. 1: 1, 176–97.

—— "'Asian Values' and Confucian Discourse," *Korea Journal*, 2001, vol. 41: 3, 198–212.

Lew Seok-Choon, "Confucian Capitalism: Possibilities and Limits," *Tradition & Modernity*, 1997, vol. 1: 1, 74–93, translated in *Korea Focus*, 1997, vol. 5: 4, 80–93.

Li Hongyan, "Developments in the Study of Confucianism on the Mainland of China in Recent Years," *Social Sciences in China*, 1997, vol. 18: 1, 17–30.

Li Tuo, "Resisting Writing," in Liu Kang and Xiaobing Tang (eds) *Politics, Ideology, and Literary Discourse in Modern China: Theoretical Interventions and Cultural Critique*, Durham, NC: Duke University Press, 1993, pp. 273–7.

Li Xuejun, "Zhongguo fazhan NGO de biyaoxing yu duice" [The necessity developing NGOs in China and the way to deal with them], *Zhonggong Sichuan shengwei dangxiao xuebao* [Journal of the Sichuan provincial party school], 2004, no. 4, 93–5.

Li Zhou, "Public Goods, Environmental Protection and the Development Paradigm in Rural China," *China and World Economy*, 2004, vol. 12: 6, 86–97.

Liang Zhiwen (ed.), *Wuwang guochi* [Never Forget National Humiliation], Jilin: Jilin wenshi, 1999.

Likhit Dheravekhin, "Prachathai tong ruamjai kan ku chat pracharat tong prakat khuampen Thai" [Thai People Have to Unite to Save the Nation], *Setthasart kanmuang*, 2000, no. 15, 171–6.

Lim Hy-Sop, "Historical Development of Civil Social Movements in Korea: Trajectories and Issues," *Korea Journal*, 2000, vol. 40: 3, 5–25.

Lin Tongqi, Henry Rosemont, Jr and Roger T. Ames, "Chinese Philosophy: A Philosophical Chapter on the 'State-of-the-Art'," *Journal of Asian Studies*, 1995, vol. 54: 3, 727–58.

Ling, L.H.M., *Postcolonial International Relations: Conquest and Desire between Asia and the West*, New York: Palgrave, 2002.

—— and Chih-yu Shih, "Confucianism with a Liberal Face: Democratic Politics in Postcolonial Taiwan," in Fred Dallmayr (ed.) *Border Crossings: Toward a Comparative Political Theory*, Lanham, MD: Lexington Books, 1999, pp. 213–35.

Link, Perry, *Evening Chats in Beijing: Probing China's Predicament*, New York: W.W. Norton, 1992.

Lintner, Bertil, *Outrage: Burma's Struggle for Democracy*, Bangkok: White Lotus, 1990.

Liu Hong, "Old Linkages, New Networks: The Globalization of Overseas Chinese Voluntary Associations and its Implications," *China Quarterly*, 1998, no. 155, 582–609.

—— "New Migrants and the Revival of Overseas Chinese Nationalism," *Journal of Contemporary China*, 2005, vol. 14: 43, 291–316.

Logan, Joshua (director) and Buddy Adler (producer), *South Pacific*, South Pacific Enterprises Inc., 1958.

Lok, Joris Janssen, "Erasing agents," *Jane's International Defence Review*, 1 March 2001.

Loomba, Ania, *Colonialism/Postcolonialism*, New York: Routledge, 1998.

Lynch, David C., "International 'Decentering' and Democratization: The Case of Thailand," *International Studies Quarterly*, 2004, vol. 48: 2, 339–62.

Ma, Shu-Yun, "The Chinese Discourse of Civil Society," *China Quarterly*, 1994, no. 137, 180–93.

McCargo, Duncan, "Thailand's Political Parties: Real, Authentic and Actual," in Kevin Hewison (ed.) *Political Change in Thailand: Democracy and Participation*, London: Routledge, 1997, pp. 114–31.

—— "Alternative Meanings of Political Reform in Contemporary Thailand," *The Copenhagen Journal of Asian Studies*, 1998, vol. 13, 5–30.

—— *Politics and the Press in Thailand: Media Machinations*, London: Routledge, 2000.

—— "Introduction: Understanding Political Reform in Thailand," in Duncan McCargo (ed.) *Reforming Thai Politics*, Copenhagen: Nordic Institute of Asian Studies, 2002, pp. 1–18.

—— "Thailand's January 2001 General Elections: Vindicating Reform?," in Duncan McCargo (ed.) *Reforming Thai Politics*, Copenhagen: Nordic Institute of Asian Studies, 2002, pp. 246–59.

—— and Ukrist Pathmanand, *The Thaksinization of Thailand*, Copenhagen: Nordic Institute of Asian Studies, 2005.

McCormick, Barret L., Su Shaozhi and Xiao Xiaoming, "The 1989 Democracy Movement: A Review of the Prospects for Civil Society in China," *Pacific Affairs*, 1992, vol. 62: 2, 182–202.

McKeown, Adam, "Conceptualizing Chinese Diasporas, 1842 to 1949," *Journal of Asian Studies*, 1999, vol. 58: 2, 306–37.

Madsen, Richard, "The Public Sphere, Civil Society and Moral Community: A Research Agenda for Contemporary Chinese Studies," *Modern China*, 1993, vol. 19: 2, 183–98.

Mahathir Mohamad and Shintaro Ishihara, *The Voice of Asia: Two Leaders Discuss the Coming Century*, Tokyo: Kodansha International, 1995.

Michener, James A., *Tales of the South Pacific*, New York: Macmillan Company, 1947.

—— *The World Is My Home: A Memoir*, New York: Random House, 1992.

Ministry of Culture and Sports, *Religious Culture in Korea*, Seoul: Holly M, 1996.

Ministry of the Interior, *Setthakit chumchon phungtongeng: naew khwamkit lae yatthasat* [The Self-Sufficient Economy: Thoughts and Strategies], Bangkok: Krasuang mahatthai, 1998.

Miyoshi, Masao, *Off/Center: Power and Culture Relations Between Japan and the United States*, Cambridge, MA: Harvard University Press, 1991.

Mulvey, Laura, *Visual and Other Pleasures*, Bloomington, IN: Indiana University Press, 1989.

Naisbitt, John, *Megatrends Asia*, London: Nicolas Brealey, 1996.

*Nangsue thi raruk sanchao Kathu shangwat Phuket 1 kanyayon B.E. 2539* [Chinese Temple at Kathu, Phuket], Phuket: Wisetoffset compu, 1996.

Nareerat Parisuthiwuttiporn, "Role of Chinese in Mahasarakham: Municipal to Local Politics," Working Paper Series, Centre for Thai Studies, University of Leeds, UK, 2000.

Narong Chokwattana, "Phonkratob thurakit jak wikrit kanmuang pajuban" [The Business Impact of the Current Political Crisis], *Setthasart kanmuang*, 2000, no. 15, 81–113.

Naruemon Thabchumpon, "NGOs and Grassroots Participation in the Political Reform Process," in Duncan McCargo (ed.) *Reforming Thai Politics*, Copenhagen: Nordic Institute of Asian Studies, pp. 183–99.

National Education Committee, Elementary Education section (ed.), *Wuwang guochi* [Never Forget National Humiliation], Tianjin: Xinlei chubanshe, 1991.

Niranam (pseud.), "Kan jat tang samakhom chao changwat Mahasarakham" [How the Mahasarakham Association Was Founded], in Thasaanachan Phumiphan (ed.) *Samakhom chao changwat Mahasarakham B.E. 2536* [Mahasarakham Association 1993], Mahasarakham: Aphichart kanphim, 1993, pp. 9–12.

Nonini, Donald M. and Aihwa Ong, "Introduction: Chinese Transnationalism as an Alternative Modernity," in Aihwa Ong and Donald M. Nonini (eds) *Ungrounded Empires: The Cultural Politics of Modern Chinese Transnationalism*, London: Routledge, 1997, pp. 3–33.

Ockey, James, "The Rise of Local Power in Thailand: Provincial Crime, Elections and Bureaucracy," in Ruth McVey (ed.) *Money & Power in Provincial Thailand*, Singapore and London: Institute for Southeast Asian Studies, 2000, pp. 74–96.

Ogden, Suzanne, *Inklings of Democracy in China*, Cambridge, MA: Harvard University Press, 2002.

——, Kathleen Hartford, Lawrence Sullivan, and David Zweig (eds), *China's Search for Democracy: The Student and Mass Movement of 1989*, Armonk, NY: M.E. Sharpe, 1992.

Oldfield, Barney, "Miss America and the 301st Bomb Group," *Air Power History*, 1990, vol. 37: 2, 41–4.

Ong, Aihwa, *Flexible Citizenship: The Cultural Logics of Transnationality*, Durham, NC: Duke University Press, 1999.

Paradee Kiatpinyochai, *The Thai Television Broadcasting Industry: Its Economics & Politics*, unpublished Masters Thesis, Bangkok: Thammasat University, 1990.

Pasuk Phongpaichit and Chris Baker, "Chao Sua, Chao Pho, Chai Thi: Lords of Thailand's Transition," in Ruth McVey, *Money & Power in Provincial Thailand*, Singapore: ISEAS Press, 2000, pp. 30–52.
—— *Thailand's Crisis*, Chiangmai: Silkworm Books, 2000.
—— *Thailand: Economy and Politics*, 2nd edn, Oxford: Oxford University Press, 2002.
—— *Thaksin: The Business of Politics in Thailand*, Chiangmai: Silkworm Books, 2004.
Pieterse, Jan Nederveen and Bhikhu Parekh (eds), *The Decolonization of the Imagination: Culture, Knowledge and Power*, London: Zed Press, 1995.
Pi Mingyong, "Minzu zhuyi yu rujia wenhua" [Nationalism and Confucian Culture], *Zhanlüe yu guanli*, 1996, no. 15, 51–7.
Prapat Panyachatirat, Kitti Limsakun, Patadej Thammacharee and Jiradej Sakunneeya, "Khamprakat chatniyom mai" [Manifesto of Neo-Nationalism], *Setthasart kanmuang*, 2000, no. 15, 225–8.
Pratt, Mary Louis, *Imperial Eyes: Travel Writing and Transculturation*, London: Routledge, 1992.
Prawase Wasi, "An Overview of Political Reform," in Duncan McCargo (ed.) *Reforming Thai Politics*, Copenhagen: Nordic Institute of Asian Studies, 2002, pp. 21–7.
Project 28 Days, *Bayan Ko! Images of the People Power Revolt*, Hong Kong: Project 28 Days, 1986.
Propp, Vladimir, *Morphology of a Folktale*, Austin, TX: University of Texas Press, 1970.
Pye, Lucian W., "Money Politics and Transitions to Democracy in East Asia," *Asian Survey*, 1997, vol. 37: 3, 213–28.
—— with Mary Pye, *Asian Power and Politics: The Cultural Dimensions of Authority*, Cambridge, MA: Harvard University Press, 1985.
Rankin, Mary Backus, "Some Observations on a Chinese Public Sphere," *Modern China*, 1993, vol. 19: 2, 158–82.
Rau, Zbigniew (ed.), *The Reemergence of Civil Society in Eastern Europe and the Soviet Union*, Boulder, CO: Westview Press, 1991.
Reid, Anthony, "Entrepreneurial Minorities, Nationalism and the State," in Daniel Chirot and Anthony Reid (eds) *Essential Outsiders: Chinese and Jews in the Modern Transformation of Southeast Asia and Central Europe*, Seattle, WA: University of Washington Press, 1997, pp. 33–71.
Ren Guixiang and Zhao Hongying, *Huaqiao Huaren yu guogong guanxi* [Overseas Chinese and Nationalist Party-Communist Party Relations], Wuhan: Wuhan daxue chubanshe, 1999.
Reynolds, Craig J., "On the Gendering of Nationalist and Postnationalist Selves in Twentieth-Century Thailand," in Peter A. Jackson and Nerida M. Cook (eds) *Genders and Sexualities in Modern Thailand*, Chiangmai: Silkworm Books, 1999, pp. 261–74.
Riggs, Fred, *Thailand: The Modernization of a Bureaucratic Polity*, Honolulu, HI: East-West Center Press, 1966.
Riverol, A.R., *Live from Atlantic City: The History of the Miss America Pageant Before, After and in Spite of Television*, Bowling Green, OH: Bowling Green State University Press, 1992.

Robison, Richard, Kevin Hewison and Garry Rodan, "Political Power in Industrializing Capitalist Societies: Theoretical Approaches," in Kevin Hewison, Richard Robison and Garry Rodan (eds) *Southeast Asia in the 1990s: Authoritarianism, Democracy & Capitalism*, Sydney: Allen & Unwin, 1993, pp. 9–38.

——, Mark Beeson, Kaishka Jayasuriya and Hyuk-Rae Kim (eds) *Politics and Markets in the Wake of the Asian Crisis*, London: Routledge, 2000.

Rodan, Garry and Kevin Hewison, "A 'Clash of Cultures' or the Convergence of Political Ideology," in Richard Robison (ed.) *Pathways to Asia: The Politics of Engagement*, Sydney: Allen & Unwin, 1996, pp. 29–55.

Rorty, Richard, "Idealizations, Foundations, and Social Practices," in Seyla Benhabib (ed.) *Democracy and Difference: Contesting the Boundaries of the Political*, Princeton, NJ: Princeton University Press, 1996, pp. 333–6.

Rowe, William T., "The Public Sphere in Modern China," *Modern China*, 1990, vol. 16: 3, 309–29.

—— "The Problem of 'Civil Society' in Late Imperial China," *Modern China*, 1993, vol. 19: 2, 139–57.

Saich, Tony, "The Search for Civil Society and Democracy in China," *Current History*, September 1994, 260–4.

Said, Edward, *Orientalism*, New York: Vintage, 1978.

—— "Orientalism Reconsidered," in A.L. Macfie (ed.) *Orientalism: A Reader*, Edinburgh: Edinburgh University Press, 2000, pp. 345–61.

Saneh Chamarik, *Democracy and Development: A Cultural Perspective*, Bangkok: Local Development Institute, 1993.

Schaffer, Frederic Charles (ed.), *Elections for Sale: The Causes and Consequences of Vote Buying*, Boulder, CO: Lynne Rienner Publishers.

Schmid, André, "Rediscovering Manchuria: Sin Ch'aeho and the Politics of Territorial History in Korea," *Journal of Asian Studies*, 1997, vol. 56: 1, 26–46.

Schock, Kurt, *Unarmed Insurgencies: People Power Movements in Nondemocracies*, Minneapolis, MN: University of Minnesota Press, 2005.

Schoenhals, Michael, *Doing Things with Words in Chinese Politics: Five Studies*, Berkeley, CA: Institute of East Asian Studies, University of California, 1992.

Schwarcz, Vera, "Memory and Commemoration: The Chinese Search for a Livable Past," in Jeffrey N. Wasserstrom and Elizabeth J. Perry (eds) *Popular Protest and Popular Culture in Modern China*, 2nd edn, Boulder, CO: Westview Press, 1994, pp. 170–83.

Scott, James C., *Weapons of the Weak: Everyday Forms of Peasant Resistance*, New Haven, CT: Yale University Press, 1985.

Seager, Joni, *Earth Follies: Feminism, Politics and the Environment*, London: Earthscan, 1993.

Seagrave, Sterling, *Lords of the Rim: the Invisible Empire of the Overseas Chinese*, London: Bantam Press, 1995.

Shai, Yossi and Aharon Barth, "Diasporas and International Relations Theory," *International Organization*, 2003, vol. 57: 3, 449–79.

Shapiro, Michael J., *The Politics of Representation: Writing Practices in Biography, Photography, and Policy Analysis*, Madison, WI: University of Wisconsin Press, 1988.

—— *Methods and Nations: Cultural Governance and the Indigenous Subject*, New York: Routledge, 2004.

Shen Jinglin, "Foreword," in Revolutionary History Museum of China (ed.) *Zhongguo: cong quru zouxiang huihuang, 1840–1997*, vol. 1 [China: From Humiliation to Glory, 1840–1997, vol. 1], Beijing: Zhongguo minzu sheying yishu, 1997, pp. 5–7.

Sim, Soek-Fang, *Asian Values, Asian Democracy: The Legitimisation of Authority and De-Legitimisation of Dissent in Everyday Popular Discourse in Singapore in the Late 1990s*, unpublished PhD Thesis, University of London, 2002.

Snow, Edgar, *The Other Side of the River: Red China Today*, London: Gollancz, 1963.

Sombat Chantornvong, "The 1997 Constitution and the Politics of Electoral Reform," in Duncan McCargo (ed.) *Reforming Thai Politics*, Copenhagen: Nordic Institute of Asian Studies, 2002, pp. 203–46.

Somchai Phatharathananunth, "Civil Society and Democratization in Thailand: A Critique of Elite Democracy," in Duncan McCargo (ed.) *Reforming Thai Politics*, Copenhagen: Nordic Institute of Asian Studies, 2002, pp. 125–42.

Somchai Rattanakomut, "Chatniyom: prarachatdamri nai prabat somdej pramongkut klao kap tangkae wikrit settakit" [Nationalism: King Vajiravudh's Ideas and Solutions for the Economic Crisis], *Setthasart sanmuang*, 2000, no. 15, 45–55.

Steinberg, David, "Civil Society and Human Rights in Korea: On Contemporary and Classical Orthodoxy and Ideology," *Korea Journal*, 1997, vol. 37: 3, 145–65.

Su Shaozhi, "Problems of Economic Reform in China," in Edward Friedman (ed.) *The Politics of Democratization: Generating from East Asian Experiences*, Boulder, CO: Westview, pp. 221–31.

Summy, Ralph, "Democracy and Nonviolence," *Social Alternatives*, 1993, vol. 12, 15–19.

Sun Ge, "Globalization and Cultural Difference: Thoughts on the Situation of Transcultural Knowledge," *Inter-Asia Cultural Studies*, 2001, vol. 2: 2, 261–75.

Sungsidh Piriyarangsan and Pasuk Phongpaichit, *The Middle Class and Thai Democracy*, Bangkok: Chulalongkorn University and Friedrich Ebert Stiftung, 1993.

Supatra Kopkijsuksakul, *Kan Prakuat Nangsao Thai (B.E. 2477–2530)* [Miss Thailand Contest: 1934–1987], unpublished Masters Thesis, Bangkok: Thammasat University, 1988.

Suthachai Yimprasert, "Lathichatniyom kap kan totan jakrawatniyom America 14 tulakom B.E. 2516 lae 6 tulakom B.E. 2519" [New Nationalism and Anti-American Imperialism During 14 October 1973 to 6 October 1976], *Setthasart kanmuan*, 2000, no. 15, 57–80.

Swaine, Michael D. and Ashely J. Tellis, *Interpreting China's Grand Strategy: Past Present, and Future*, Santa Monica, CA: Rand Corporation, 2000.

Tanaka, Stefan, *Japan's Orient: Rendering Pasts into History*, Berkeley, CA: University of California Press, 1993.

Thak Chaloemtiarana, *Thailand: The Politics of Despotic Paternalism*, Bangkok: Thammasat University Press, 1979.

Thawan Masjarat, "Nangsao Sayam" [Miss Siam], in *Mednangrak*, Bangkok: Tonor 1999, Inc., 1998.

*Thirakruek phiti poed akhan mai chalong khrup rop 90 pi Phuket Thai-Hua* [Commemoration on the grand opening of the new building for the 90th Anniversary of the Phuket Thai Hua School, 17 February 1999], Phuket: Krongthong, 1999.

Thirayuth Boonmi, "Good Governance: A Strategy to Restore Thailand," Savitri Gadavanij (trans.), in Duncan McCargo (ed.) *Reforming Thai Politics*, Copenhagen: Nordic Institute of Asian Studies, 2002, pp. 29–35.

Thompson, Mark R., "Pacific Asia after 'Asian values': Authoritarianism, Democracy, and 'Good Governance'," *Third World Quarterly*, 2004, vol. 25: 6, 1079–95.

Tismaneanu, Vladimir (ed.), *In Search of Civil Society: Independence Peace Movements in the Soviet Bloc*, New York: Routledge, 1990.

Todorov, Tzvetan, *The Conquest of America: The Question of the Other*, New York: Harper & Row Publishers, 1984.

Tomlinson, Jonathan, *Cultural Imperialism*, Baltimore, MD: Johns Hopkins University Press, 1991.

Trachtenberg, Alan, *Reading American Photographs: Images as History, Matthew Brady to Walker Evans*, New York: Hill & Wang, 1989.

Trinh T. Minh-ha, *Woman Native Other*, Bloomington, IN: Indiana University Press, 1989.

Trocki, Carl A., *Opium, Empire and the Global Political Economy*, London: Routledge, 1999.

Tu Weiming, "Cultural China: the Periphery as the Center," in Tu Weiming (ed.) *The Living Tree: The Changing Meaning of Being Chinese Today*, Stanford, CA: Stanford University Press, 1994, pp. 1–34.

Ueda, Yoko, "The Entrepreneurs of Khorat," in Ruth McVey (ed.) *Money & Power in Provincial Thailand*, Singapore and London: Institute for Southeast Asian Studies Press, 2000, pp. 154–94.

Unger, Danny, *Building Social Capital in Thailand: Fibers, Finance and Infrastructure*, Cambridge: Cambridge University Press, 1998.

United States Army, "The United States Chemical Stockpile Disposal Program," Program Manager for Chemical Demilitarization, Office of the Chief of Public Affairs, Aberdeen Proving Ground, Maryland, 1990.

Viengrat Netipho, "Itthiphon nai kan muang thongthin khong Thai: suksa koranee muang Chiangmai" [Influence in Local Politics in Thailand: Case Study of Chiangmai], *Journal of Social Sciences* (Bangkok), 2000, vol. 31: 2, 168–235.

Virilio, Paul, *Speed and Politics: An Essay on Dromology*, New York: Semiotext(e) Foreign Agents Series, 1986.

Wakeman, Frederic, "The Civil Society and Public Sphere Debate: Western Reflections on Chinese Political Culture," *Modern China*, 1993, vol. 19: 2, 108–38.

Walker, R.B.J., *Inside/Outside: International Relations as Political Theory*, Cambridge: Cambridge University Press, 1993.

—— "Social Movements/World Politics," *Millennium: Journal of International Studies*, 1994, vol. 23: 3, 669–700.

Wang Gungwu, *China and the Chinese Overseas*, Singapore: Times Academic Press, 1991.

—— *Community and Nation: China, Southeast and Australia*, new edn, Sydney: Allen & Unwin, 1992.

—— *The Chinese Overseas: From Earthbound China to the Quest for Autonomy*, Cambridge, MA: Harvard University Press, 2000.

Wang Hui, Leo Ou-fan Lee, with Michael M.J. Fischer, "Is the Public Sphere Unspeakable in Chinese? Can Public Spaces (*gonggong kongjian*) Lead to Public Spheres?," *Public Culture*, 1994, vol. 6, 598–605.

Wang Jisi (ed.), *Wenming yu guojizhengzhi: Zhongguo xuezhe ping Huntingdunde wenming chongtulun* [Civilization and International Politics: Chinese Scholars Comment on Huntington's Clash of Civilizations Thesis], Shanghai: Shanghai renmin chubanshe, 1995.

Wang Miaoyang, Yu Xuanmeng and Manuel B. Dy (eds), *Civil Society in a Chinese Context*, Washington, DC: The Council for Research in Values and Philosophy, 1997.

Wang Shuo, *Please Don't Call Me Human*, Howard Goldblatt (trans.), London: No Exit Press, 2000.

Wanlaya Phuphinyo, *Tho so ying* [A Female Adjutant Officer], Bangkok: Air Force News Press, 1998.

Wasserman, Ursula, "Attempts at Control Over Toxic Waste," *Journal of World Trade Law*, 1981, vol. 15.

Wasserstrom, Jeffrey N., "Afterword: History, Myth and the Tales of Tiananmen," in Jeffrey N. Wasserstrom and Elizabeth J. Perry (eds) *Popular Protest and Popular Culture in Modern China*, 2nd edn, Boulder, CO: Westview Press, 1994, pp. 279–89.

Welch, Stephen E., *The Concept of Political Culture*, London: Macmillan, 1993.

Weldes, Jutta, Mark Laffey, Hugh Gusterson and Raymond Duval, "Introduction: Constructing Insecurity," in Jutta Weldes, Mark Laffey, Hugh Gusterson and Raymond Duval (eds) *Cultures of Insecurity: States, Communities and the Production of Danger*, Minneapolis, MN: University of Minnesota Press, 1999, pp. 1–33.

Weller, Robert P., *Alternative Civilities: Democracy and Culture in China and Taiwan*, Boulder, CO: Westview Press, 1999.

White, Gordon, Jude Howell and Shang Xiaoyuan, *In Search of Civil Society: Market Reform and Social Change in Contemporary China*, Oxford: Clarendon Press, 1996.

White, Hayden, *Metahistory: The Historical Imagination in Nineteenth-Century Europe*, Baltimore, MD: Johns Hopkins University Press, 1973.

White, Mimi, "Ideological Analysis and Television," in Robert C. Allen (ed.) *Channels of Discourse: Television and Contemporary Criticism*, Chapel Hill, NC: University of North Carolina Press, 1987, pp. 134–71.

Wichit Srisang, "Khamprakat chatniyom mai" [Manifesto of Neo-nationalism], *Setthasart kanmuang*, 2000, no. 15, 221–4.

Williams, Raymond, *The Country and the City*, London: Chatto & Windus, 1973.

Wittayakorn Chiangkoon, "Chatniyom tang setthakit lae sangkhom prachatthipatai mai khue tang rod khong sangkhom Thai" [Economic Nationalism and New Social Democracy is the Survival of Thai Society], *Setthasart kanmuang*, 2000, no. 15, 199–204.

Woo-Cumings, Meredith (ed.), *The Developmental State*, Ithaca, NY: Cornell University Press, 1999.

Woodside, Alexander, "The Asia-Pacific Idea as a Mobilization Myth," in Arif Dirlik (ed.) *What is in a Rim? Critical Perspectives on the Pacific Region Idea*, 2nd edn, Lanham, MD: Rowman & Littlefield, 1998, pp. 37–52.

World Bank, *Governance and Development*, Washington, DC: World Bank, 1992.

Yan Sun, "The Chinese Protests of 1989: The Issue of Corruption," *Asian Survey*, 1991, vol. 31: 8, 762–82.

Yang Wanxiu, "Zhongguo jindaishi kaiduan yu huaqiao" [Overseas Chinese and the Start of Modern History in China], *Bagui qiaoshi*, 1991, no. 9, 43–9.

*Yi shi wei jing, mianxiang weilai: jinian Zhongguo renmin kangri zhanzhengji* [Take history as a mirror, to create the future: Commemorate China's war of resistance against Japan], Beijing: Zhonggong dangxiao chubanshe, 2005.

Young, Robert J.C., *Postcolonialism: An Historical Introduction*, London: Routledge, 2001.

—— *Postcolonialism: A Very Short Introduction*, Oxford: Oxford University Press, 2003.

Zakaria, Fareed, "Culture is Destiny: A Conversation with Lee Kuan Yew," *Foreign Affairs*, 1994, vol. 73: 2, 109–26.

Zhang Guolong *et al.*, *Wenming yu yeman* [Civilization and Barbarism], Beijing: Shehui kexue wenlian chubanshe, 1998.

Zhang Hongtu, "Chairmen Mao," www.MoMao.com (accessed on 14 August 2005).

Zhao Wen, "Dui 'Zhongguo jingji quan' gezhong yilunde pingshu" [A review of "Chinese economic sphere" discourse], *Huaqiao Huaren lishi yanjiu*, 1995, no. 1, 63–70.

Zhao Yinhong, "Zhongguo NGO fazhande dute lishi beijing fenzi" [An Analysis of the Unique Historical Background of the Development of NGOs in China], *Qiushi*, 2003, no. 11, 108–10.

Zheng Jiadong, "Jiushiniandai ruxue fazhanzhongde jigawenti" [Issues of the Development of Confucian Studies in the Nineties], Paper presented at the International Conference "The Contemporary Significance of East Asian Philosophy with emphasis on Korean philosophy," Seoul, South Korea, July 1997.

Zheng Nianjun, *Zai jieyande rizili* [In the Days of Enforcing Martial Law], Beijing: Jiefangjun wenyi chubanshe, 1989.

Zheng, Yongnian, *Discovering Chinese Nationalism in China: Modernization, Identity and International Relations*, Cambridge: Cambridge University Press, 1999.

Zhu Jiangang, "Caogen NGO yu Zhongguo gongmin shehuide zhangda" [Grassroots NGOs and the Growth of China's Civil Society], *Kaifang shidai*, 2004, no. 6, 36–47.

# Index

Anand Panyarachun 128, 130, 135–6
Anek Laothammatas 137, 139
Areeya Chumsai 43–5, 46, 64, 66–7, 69
Aquino, Cory 84, 93, 97
Asian democracy 5, 69, 71–3, 75–6, 78, 81, 83, 86, 92, 110, 124, 136, 176
Asian values 5, 71, 73, 76, 99, 181
Aung San Suu Kyi 81–2, 84–6, 93, 97

Barthes, Roland 28, 58, 76
*Bayan Ko!* 4, 77, 81, 83–4
beauty pageants 1–2, 49–50, 53; Miss America 1, 45, 47–50; Miss China 1–4, 17, 177, 189; Miss Siam 52, 56, 61, 177; Miss Taiwan 3, 4; Miss Thailand 4, 17–18, 42, 44, 46–53, 56–69, 73, 97, 177, 188–9; Miss Tibet 3–4; Miss Universe 1–4, 46, 49, 59, 61–3, 67–9; Miss World 1–4, 46, 50
Beautiful Soul 70, 72, 80–1, 84, 93–5
borders 146, 148, 150, 163, 165–6, 168, 170–2, 175
bourgeois politics 126, 136–7, 144, 145
*Burma's Revolution of the Spirit* 77–9, 81–7, 93–4

capitalist modernity 4–5, 10–11, 13, 16, 19–20, 53, 57, 69, 72, 87, 98, 100, 108–9, 110, 114–16, 119, 120, 122–3, 126–7, 140, 145, 146, 151, 174, 176, 177, 181, 189, 191
*Catalyst for Change* 77
civil/military relations 46, 174
civil society 6, 14, 17–19, 22, 23, 42, 46, 71, 75, 77, 92, 98, 175, 190; in Northeast Asia 98–110, 113, 116–17, 122–4; in Southeast Asia 126, 130, 140, 143
community culture 140–1
Confucianism 12–14, 18–19, 74, 100, 103, 105–8, 114, 117–18, 121–2; Confucian capitalism 149; Confucian civil society 110–13, 116; Confucian Foundation 110–12, 114
constitutions 19, 53–4, 56, 59, 62; Thai constitutions 125–6, 128–31, 135
continental geography 17, 40
corruption 88, 92, 124–5, 127–30, 134, 142, 144–5, 161, 184
cosmopolitanism 146–9, 151, 164–5, 172–3
cultural governance 4, 6, 15–16, 46, 57, 69, 71–2, 75, 83, 99–100, 109, 126, 146, 149, 151–2, 161, 169, 171, 174, 178
cultural imperialism 7, 17, 47, 67, 69, 114–15
cultural nativism 47, 52, 69, 100
cultural resistance 4, 5, 6, 11–17, 21, 23, 39–41, 69, 71, 107–8, 118, 190–1

decolonization 7–8, 11–2, 74–8, 92, 95, 97
diaspora 19–20, 114, 146–8, 150, 153, 166, 171, 173
diasporic Chinese 19, 142, 146–7, 149–50, 155–8, 162–3, 166, 168–9
Dirlik, Arif 10–11, 16
discourse of technology 32, 34 *see also* science and safety

## Index

East Asian miracle 71, 124
East/West 7, 11–12, 64, 66, 71, 73, 75, 78, 92, 103–6, 109, 112–13; East vs. West 71, 76, 189
Electoral Commission of Thailand (ECT) 131–5
Elshtain, Jean Bethke 30, 95
empty Pacific 36–7, 41
Enloe, Cynthia 45, 64, 171–2
ethnography 19, 150, 164, 171–2; ethnographic approach 148–9

Ferguson, Kathy E. 22, 27
Filial piety award 113–4, 118
Foucault, Michel 13–15, 107–8, 114–15, 126, 179

gangster politicians 126, 130, 136, 141–2, 143, 145 *see also jao pho*
good governance 127, 129–30, 135, 139–40, 143–5, 159, 167
governmentality 13–16, 107, 115, 174

Habermas, Jurgen 102, 104–5
Han Sang-Jin 105, 120–2
Hau'ofa, Epeli 40–1
hybridity 97, 107

JACADs 22–9, 33–42, 82, 174
*jao pho* 136, 141–4
*June Four* 77, 86–7, 90

Lee Kuan Yew 75, 79, 88
*luk kreung* 68

Mahathir Mohamad 75–7, 79, 93, 160, 168
Mao Zedong 2, 4–5, 9, 73, 87, 95–7, 176–88; as a folk god 181–5; as leader 177–9; Mao cult 179–81
maritime geography 17, 40
media 46, 48–9, 53, 57, 65, 69, 92, 142
*Miss Siam* (short story) 43, 45, 47, 57, 63, 67, 140
monarchy 53–4, 59, 73
Mulvey, Laura 49–50, 57
myth 28–9, 32, 76, 182, 188

narrative 1, 13, 15–6, 22–4, 26, 28, 178, 191
nationalism 19, 45, 49, 53, 60, 62, 69, 72, 81, 94, 140, 147–9, 151; Chinese nationalism 151–4, 157, 162–3; neo-nationalism 150–2, 158–60, 162, 164–5, 168; Thai nationalism 157–89, 161–3, 167
naturalization and reassurance 22–3, 26, 27, 28–30, 32, 36, 41
non-governmental organizations (NGOs) 2, 42, 73, 85, 108–10, 119–20, 130, 143, 145; government-oriented NGOs (GONGOs) 2, 109
nonviolent action 71–2, 83–6, 89, 93, 108, 119

Occidentalism 7–12, 73–4, 94, 107, 162, 189
Orientalism 72, 74, 81, 93–4; oriental discourse 5, 7–12, 189; oriental images 72

pastoral politics 13–14
patriarchy 18, 61, 72–6, 88, 92–3, 97 114
Phibul Songkran, Field Marshall 55–6, 58, 161–2, 167
photography 28–32, 77–97, 185, 189, 202
political culture 99, 103–5, 119, 126, 137–41, 174
political parties 100, 131–2, 134
political reform 19, 125–6, 128–9, 134, 136, 143, 159
politics of issues 20, 73, 93–5, 97, 174, 180, 188, 190
politics of multiplicity 106–10
politics of rhetoric 20, 73, 93–5, 97, 174, 176, 180, 188, 190
politics of technology 21–2
popular culture 4, 182, 184–5, 187
postcolonial 6–9, 78, 81, 97; postcolonial theory 7–13, 74, 189
Pye, Lucian 124

resistance 13, 15, 17, 21, 71, 78, 94, 97, 100, 108, 116, 119, 121, 135, 151, 174, 176, 185, 189, 191

sacred memory 79
science and safety 23, 32–4, 41
self/Other relations 20, 72, 74, 127, 152, 162–3, 171–2, 175–6, 189, 191
semiotics 16–18, 29, 46, 190; diachronic analysis 46–7, 52–3, 64, 69; synchronic analysis 46, 47–52, 64–5
Shapiro, Michael J. 13, 15–16, 79–80, 87
social movements 19, 72, 92, 98–9, 108, 116, 123, 178, 190; Chinese social movements 116–9; Korean social movements 119–22; Thai social movements 126, 140, 145
Songgyun'gwan 110–12
South Pacific 17, 21–7, 29–30, 32, 36–8, 42

technocratic polity 136, 144

terrorism 175
Thai Rak Thai (TRT) Party 132, 134–5, 143–4
Tomlinson, John 114–16
*Tradition and Modernity* 110, 112–15, 121–2
transnational 20, 47, 69, 72, 146, 148, 162–6, 168–70
Trinh T. Minh-Ha 42
Turnbull, Phyllis 22, 27

urban/rural distinctions 137, 139–40
US Army 17, 22, 29, 39

vote buying 19, 125–7, 129–34, 136–145, 176

Wang Gungwu 147, 151, 154
war 79, 175

youth 88–93

# eBooks – at www.eBookstore.tandf.co.uk

## A library at your fingertips!

eBooks are electronic versions of printed books. You can store them on your PC/laptop or browse them online.

They have advantages for anyone needing rapid access to a wide variety of published, copyright information.

eBooks can help your research by enabling you to bookmark chapters, annotate text and use instant searches to find specific words or phrases. Several eBook files would fit on even a small laptop or PDA.

**NEW:** Save money by eSubscribing: cheap, online access to any eBook for as long as you need it.

### Annual subscription packages

We now offer special low-cost bulk subscriptions to packages of eBooks in certain subject areas. These are available to libraries or to individuals.

For more information please contact webmaster.ebooks@tandf.co.uk

We're continually developing the eBook concept, so keep up to date by visiting the website.

## www.eBookstore.tandf.co.uk